The Time of My Life

⊐⊏ Bradford Books

Daniel C. Dennett. BRAINSTORMS. 1979.

Fred I. Dretske. KNOWLEDGE AND THE FLOW OF INFORMATION. 1981.

Jerry A. Fodor. REPRESENTATIONS. 1981.

Hubert L. Dreyfus, Editor, with Harrison Hall. HUSSERL, INTENTIONALITY AND COGNITIVE SCIENCE. 1982.

George D. Romanos. QUINE AND ANALYTIC PHILOSOPHY. 1983.

Stephen P. Stich. FROM FOLK PSYCHOLOGY TO COGNITIVE SCIENCE. 1983.

Jerry A. Fodor. MODULARITY OF MIND. 1983.

Jon Barwise and John Perry. SITUATIONS AND ATTITUDES. 1983.

Norbert Hornstein. LOGIC AS GRAMMAR. 1984.

Izchak Miller. HUSSERL, PERCEPTION AND TEMPORAL AWARENESS. 1984.

Ruth Garrett Millikan. LANGUAGE, THOUGHT, AND OTHER BIOLOGICAL CATEGORIES. 1984.

Robert C. Stalnaker. INQUIRY. 1984.

Daniel C. Dennett. ELBOW ROOM. 1984.

William G. Lycan. LOGICAL FORM IN NATURAL LANGUAGE. 1984.

The Time of My Life

An Autobiography

W. V. Quine

A Bradford Book
The MIT Press
Cambridge, Massachusetts
London, England

© 1985 by The Massachusetts Institute of Technology

This book was set in Caslon by DEKR Corporation and printed and bound by Halliday Lithograph in the United States of America

Library of Congress Cataloging in Publication Data

Quine, W. V. (Willard Van Orman)
  The time of my life.

  "A Bradford book."
  1. Quine, W. V. (Willard Van Orman)   2. Philosophers
—United States—Biography.   I. Title.
B945.Q54A35 1985   191 [B]   84-28883
ISBN 0-262-17003-5

To My Grandchildren

Melissa O'Brien
Benjamin Willard Roberts
Alexander Boynton Quine
and a forthcoming McGovern

Contents

Preface

Writing seventy-odd pages of intellectual autobiography for the Library of Living Philosophers triggered this broader chronicle. It is laced still with professional memoirs and I have cribbed scraps from the more austere piece, but I have tried to render them intelligible to lay readers if read in order. Readers who are drawn to the book by friendship or kinship, rather than by philosophy or logic, can easily pass those passages by.

I have undertaken in this book to tell the truth; not the whole truth, which would tax everyone's patience, but to tell nothing but the truth, to the best of my knowledge and belief. It has not been easy. One place where I was put to the test was where Peter Viereck, the poet, entered my story. He is a professor of history at Mount Holyoke College. After one of his classes, which he had favored with several of the verbal conceits and pat figures for which he is known and loved, a student who was not above buttering up a professor came up to his desk and said, "Professor Viereck, you missed your calling. You should have been a poet."

It was a wrench not to include this anecdote, but I was adamant, for it is not true.

I wanted to tell how I regaled my colleagues with riddles during my first weeks at Oxford. "What's lazier than a Mexican?" "I don't know," they answered brightly, all in a mood for curious local color from beyond the sea. "An Englishman." You could hear a pin drop. The silence was broken only by the twitching of a vaguely pained expression, suffused with just the ghost of a pale gray chill. Confused, I leapt into the breach with another riddle: "And what's lazier than an Englishman?" They rallied visibly. "I don't kn--," they began, and then, choking by way of erasure, substituted a receptive look. "Two Englishmen." I was popular.

At Oxford we had an *au pair* girl named Tecla, and I could not get over the feeling that the name was a garble. I kept trying anagrams. I would say, "Set the table, Tacle." "Bring the treacle, Tecal." "Bring the meat, Cleat." "Take my plate, Clate." "What's for *repas*, Eclat?" "All set, Alcet?" My wife was afraid Tecla might leave.

But I have sacrificed both of these Oxford gems in the fair name of truth.

The most abundant source of truth for this history has been an archive of letters that I wrote to my parents over forty years. I retrieved them after my mother's death and found that I had been a remarkably dutiful son. Ed Haskell illuminated a decade or so with his file of my letters, and sporadic copies in my files have shed further light. I kept a journal of some of my travels, and my wife kept a journal of others. In searching these sources and old engagement books, I have been impressed with the fallibility of my memory and with the pitfalls of historical research. My wife has sparked many corrections and other improvements through the critical reading of two drafts. The publisher's editor, Laurie Kahn-Leavitt, has induced several significant insertions and deletions.

Boston
November 25, 1984

The Time of My Life

O wad some Pow'r the giftie gie us
To see oursels as others see us!

—Robert Burns

Some Pow'r did us the giftie grant
To see oursels as others can't.

In the Beginning 1

My birth in a modest frame house on Nash Street in a southeast-central quarter of Akron on Anti-Christmas, June 25, 1908, brought the population of that industrial city to a figure in the neighborhood of sixty thousand. My father, Cloyd Robert Quine, had been born twenty-seven years earlier and six blocks away.

His father, Robert Stanford Quine, was born in a thatched croft in the Isle of Man in 1850. Today Manx is a dead language known only to Celtic specialists and a few zealous young separatists; but Grandpa Quine grew up bilingual in Manx and English, like most Manxmen of his day. At sixteen he went to sea as a merchant seaman and ranged north to the Faeroes and south to the Falklands under sail. Eventually he took a room at John Slip, a dock near the tip of Manhattan, and in the fullness of time he made his way to Akron. It is said that the two biggest Manx colonies outside Britain were in Cape Town and Cleveland, so perhaps it was the presence in Cleveland of friends of his parents that drew him to Ohio. He worked as a machinist at the Buckeye Mower and Reaper works.

My father's mother, Katharine, was born in the village of Fronhofen, in the Palatinate, and came with her parents to Ohio as a child. Her father, Jakob Motz, acquired a farm a few miles north of Akron. By the time of the Civil War he had prospered sufficiently to pay a proxy to fight the war in his behalf. It was legal to buy a draft exemption in this way. Having lately emigrated because presumably of political unrest in Germany, he would understandably have had little heart for the new disputes over here.

Children were born to Jakob Motz on both continents, and they came to occupy respected places in the German-American community that was the strength, in large part, of nineteenth-century Akron. It was a culture that continued well into the twentieth century, with its *Turnverein* and its *Liedertafel*, its *Bier und Gesang*, its weekly German newspaper, and its ethnic ethic of honest business and hard work.

Katharine Motz met Robert Quine somehow and married him. She lived long enough to bear him two sons, my father for one, and a daughter, my Aunt Bess. Never marrying, Bess lived on in the old house on Sumner Street and took care of her father, concomitantly with her job in the county courthouse, until he died at the age of eighty-five.

My father grew up in a largely German neighborhood and acquired a smattering of the language, with which he would playfully regale me in my youth. He attended Akron's old high school and proceeded straightway to work for a living. When I first knew what he was about he had an office job in a machine shop called the Williams Foundry and Machine Company.

My mother, Harriet Ellis Van Orman, was born in 1874 (a dark secret while she lived) in Wadsworth, a village twelve miles southwest of Akron. Her mother's forebears had come out of Britain by way perhaps of Connecticut generations back, and her father's forebears ultimately out of Holland. Perhaps her father's people came by way of the Dutch belt of southern Michigan, for there was mention of cousins there. The area has been a breeding ground of philosophers with Frisian names—Bouwsma, Frankena, Jellima, Plantinga, Yntema.

The name "Van Orman" is puzzling. I find no place-name like "Orman." My mother said that the name had been "Van Norman" and that one branch of the family had dropped the "N." However, I have heard of far-flung Van Ormans and no Van Normans. Moreover "Van Norman" would still be puzzling, since "Van" calls for a place-name.

At any rate my mother plumed herself on the aristocratic connotations of the preposition. Further, she had a legend of the Brewer Millions ("Brewer" for "Brouwer," no doubt) that were being guarded in Holland by the honest Dutch pending the time when the rightful heirs, herself for one, might come forward with their credentials and claim their due.

She was the youngest of four: three girls and a boy. When she was in her teens the family moved to Adams Street in Akron. Her father, John Henry Van Orman, died soon afterward, reputedly from a bullet that had remained lodged in him since the Civil War. Her mother subsequently married another and older Civil War veteran, Captain Thomas Nash. He had been born in 1832 in a log cabin ten miles northwest of the budding village of Akron. I knew him as a grizzled octogenarian, lean and straight as a ramrod. My mother told of his petty penuriousness, but he was a great favorite of mine. He would push me in my go-cart out Market Street past the statue of the Indian and on out Rose Avenue to the poorhouse. He lived almost to a hundred. I visited him in his last years at the Soldiers' Home in Sandusky.

Unlike my father, my mother went to college: Buchtel, the nucleus of the eventual University of Akron. Her brother Willard, for whom I was named, taught mathematics there until moving to Denver for his health in about 1903. My mother revered him: brilliant, musical, handsome, saintly. I never saw him, but I was made to feel complimented by his name and to look upon mathematics as an admirable pursuit.

My mother taught for ten years in the elementary grades at Spicer, one of the Akron public schools, taking pleasure in the children and pride in her way with them. "Never a harsh word." At some point Grandpa Quine left the Mower and Reaper works and became janitor of the school. Evidently his son Cloyd, my father, came to the school to do something for him from time to time, and it was thus that my eventual parents met.

My mother's sister Clara, called Tattie, had married Fayette Vernon, a Presbyterian minister. They lived in a village called Eighty-Four, in southwestern Pennsylvania. My future parents went there in 1905 and Uncle Fay married them. It was a case of the school teacher, college-trained, marrying the janitor's son. There were hints that she thought she had condescended, however thankful to have done so. Actually she had not quite finished college; for monetary reasons she had switched to normal school. My father, on the other hand, took correspondence courses in law, accounting, and engineering.

My only sibling, Robert Cloyd Quine, was born seventeen months before me. My father was just recovering from typhoid. My mother had acquired an electric needle and learned to remove moles with it for added income. It must have taken close figuring when, in the eleventh month of my life, we moved to 38 Hawthorne Avenue. It was on West Hill, at the growing northwest edge of Akron and a modest step up in the world. It was a seven-room frame house in the style that dominated those years: a square façade surmounted by an isosceles right triangle.

Hawthorne Avenue runs uphill, over the top, and down, to a length of a thousand feet. Our part drained eventually into the Gulf of Mexico, and the other part into the Gulf of St. Lawrence. The street was paved in brick and shaded by maples that littered the sidewalk with their wingèd pods. It was shaded further by an occasional buckeye tree that strewed its shadow with false chestnuts, and by amorphous untrimmed catalpas with the long slim pods that we called Indian cigars.

Our yard was fifty feet wide. A small rise in our neighbor's yard adjacent to our driveway was the original "bank" from which I learned the word. I visualized it later when I read of Alice dozing on a bank and slipping into Wonderland.

A barberry hedge bounded our small front yard. A three-passenger swing hung from the ceiling of the broad front porch. At the back of the house, forming a triangle against an enclosed back porch, there was a trellis loaded with Concord grapes. A big and bountiful cherry tree shaded much of the back yard. In a residual sunny patch my father playfully grew a few vegetables, venturing as far as watermelons, eggplant, peanuts, and pieplant—rhubarb to you—from which my mother would make pieplant pie. Hedges of four-o'clocks waist high (a child's waist) flanked a path that led to an opening in the back fence.

I remember the flood of March 1913 that James Thurber commemorated. He saw it in Columbus, but Akron had it too. A bridge that spanned the Little Cuyahoga at what was then the north edge of town, affording the only crossing in an interval of several miles, was swept away and not replaced for a dozen years. My father took me there and we saw furniture, even a bed, borne along on the swollen stream. Such is the visual memory that I retain, but it has the river flowing the wrong way.

An elusive smell of early spring recalls a scene in which I and others are picking our adventurous way along backyard boundaries where the yards abut back to back. It is an obstacle course of back fences, retaining walls, and squeezeways between back-to-back garages. The encumbered way is wet with winter's traces. The smell of really firm spring was another, headier thing. It connoted open windows, clothes lines loaded with rugs and sheets, and all the merry disorder of spring cleaning.

The hot summers of childhood grind on with never a thought of termination, and one can ask no better. Sometimes I filled a lard pail with cool water and kept it by me for refreshment while I worked at my sandpile or some other obscure project in the back yard. The pail imparted a faint metallic taste, somehow a part of the enveloping serenity of my pointless business.

Or I might be on the shady sidewalk with my contemporaries when an ice wagon clattered up. The man would drop his reins, go to the back of the wagon, bisect a hundred-pound block with his pick, swing half of it to his shoulder pad with his tongs, and proceed to someone's back door. We would jump on to the wagon and come away with handfuls of dripping chips.

My mother bought ice from the Klages Ice and Coal Co., not the City Ice and Coal Co. Our ice cream was Tellings, not Furnas. We took the *Akron Beacon Journal*, not the *Akron*

Times. Our telephone was Bell, not People's. In each of these binary oppositions, ours was *ipso facto* the right one. It seemed odd that some people chose otherwise.

The house next below ours was that of an elderly English couple named Childs and their spinster daughter Ethel. Coming from a land where detached villas bore names, they proudly named it Hawthorne Place and put up a big antique-lettered sign. In the house there were big Chinese vases, which my mother thought a queer idea. No doubt they were valuable. Lest we smash them, my mother told my brother and me to keep our hands clasped behind us. Mrs. Childs declared us model children and always welcome.

The short old couple and their tall daughter were associated in my mind with cartoon characters in "Polly and her Pals," though gaunt Ethel compared unfavorably with the Polly of the pictures. Ethel was the quintessential next-door neighbor, in and out our back door several times a day. "Oo-hoo" was her heralding call.

I showed a little contemporary my copy of *A Child's Garden of Verses*. She said it wasn't mine; that it belonged to the people next door. Their name was right there on it. I protested that it meant that the book was for children. No, it doesn't say children, she replied triumphantly.

There was one great house on Hawthorne Avenue, the Wilcoxes', at the top of the rise—well, great in being twice the size of the other houses and on grounds three times as broad. Mrs. Wilcox drove a silent upright electric automobile. An obsolescent row of horse stalls lined the back of their yard.

Casterton Avenue, the next street west, did not yet have its fill of houses. Casterton's quality, as I think back, was a notch above Hawthorne's apart from the Wilcoxes. Wood gave way on Casterton to brick, stone, or stucco. As each further cellar was excavated, a mound of dirt arose whose loftiness, as remembered, refuses to reduce to scale. We would clamber to those summits and slide down on our pants or careen down in a coaster wagon. There was cleaner fun in prowling a new framework of beams, studs, and rafters in the fragrance of fresh pine sawdust, visualizing the eventual rooms and corridors.

Hawthorne Avenue ended on Merriman Road. Beyond were woods, and a short walk through the woods brought one to a little dirt road—today's Aqueduct Street. I conceived that to each woodland there belonged a particular road that ran through it.

When I was a little older, I walked out Merriman Road with one of my peers. We carried a sketchy lunch and proposed to walk beyond the city limits, thus having ourselves a picnic in the country. It was a conservative undertaking, for at that time Merriman Road crossed the boundary just a quarter of a mile beyond Hawthorne Avenue. It was a satisfying crossing. The broad brick pavement narrowed immediately to rural width, roadside mailboxes emerged, and after a few hundred yards there was a one-room country schoolhouse. We exchanged civilities with a little boy whom the city boundary categorized to our satisfaction as a country boy, a farm kid. We savored on our own part an indefinable sense of urbanity and of having been around.

Sometimes my mother would take my brother Bob and me to Silver Lake. We would go downtown by streetcar, a mile and a half, and then seven miles northeastward by interurban trolley. I was given a lemon to suck, for otherwise I would get carsick. Sometimes I got carsick anyway, but I would never have dreamt of giving up a trip to Silver Lake because of the threat of carsickness.

Silver Lake was an amusement park, and I wonder what the appeal was. Roller coasters were not for the likes of us, nor was the Ferris wheel. We enjoyed the merry-go-round and the small zoo. But I suspect that the appeal was mainly conventional; fun was part of the concept, learned in learning "Silver Lake."

Lemon juice figured not only in warding off carsickness but also in making castor oil less offensive, or so my mother thought. Nausea plagued my early youth. Besides carsickness I had frequent so called bilious attacks, which elicited a course of twelve calomel tablets. These inflicted a vague, dull misery.

Next of Kin 2

My father's brother Harry lived on the far side of town and worked as secretary to F. A. Seiberling, rubber baron at Goodyear. By avocation Uncle Harry was a poet. His wife Sarah was a Jahant, of Alsatian stock. They had four sons. Aunt Sarah was Catholic, and so, in consequence, were they all. Catholicism was a grave offense in my mother's eyes, and she maintained over the years a distance incommensurate with the width of the city.

Our two subfamilies converged just once a year, after Christmas, midway at my grandfather's house. With Grandpa and Aunt Bess we made twelve. Aunt Sarah would play the old treadle organ and Uncle Harry and my cousins would sing. I thought it admirable, and still do. There was no singing at our house. My mother played the piano occasionally and my brother and I were given lessons in the violin and mandolin respectively, but somehow it was embarrassing to sing.

Other contacts with the four cousins were rare. Once or twice we converged at Uncle Dan's. That was my father's uncle Daniel Motz, a farmer at Old Portage, a hamlet since absorbed into Akron. I remember an athletic romp in his hayloft with my brother and some of the cousins. Years later, when we had moved to Orchard Road, the redheaded eldest of the cousins came to play with me and showed me how to open a padlock with a bent paper clip. Years later still I saw something of the next to youngest, John, at Harvard while he was studying law. Nowadays, back in Akron, John and my brother and their wives are close friends.

Uncle Dan's was the scene of an early memory. His farm

was only three miles from home as the crow flies, but, unlike crows, my parents and brother and I made a six-mile journey of it by street car and train. While there I amused myself below a grassy bank, pretending to dig a tunnel to Europe. By evening, I am told, I was so homesick as to cause an untimely end to our visit; Uncle Dan hitched up his horse and drove us home.

This early incident illustrates a tension between the lure of the remote and the drive for the familiar. On later occasions this tension has been good for an agreeable thrill: I am in an unfamiliar place and choose an unfamiliar road toward familiar territory, intent on seeing just where it joins up. I have dreamed this of Akron, and I have contrived it in other places. This thrill of the strange way home is a paradigm of the thrill of discovery in theoretical science: the reduction of the unfamiliar to the familiar.

Early in my memory there was an infusion from the Isle of Man. Grandpa Quine's widowed sister Harriet Crellin immigrated and so did her two sons and two daughters. The sons, Joe and Stan, were young men in buttoned shoes. As a child I saw grown-ups as of two kinds, those that were "found of fun" and others. Joe was fond of fun; Stan not. I noticed Joe's Manx brogue; one detail was that he said "tay" for "tea." I am said to have said "Joe can't talk plain." Also a Manx couple named Caine called on us several times, with a pretty daughter of my age named Mona. She and I made drawings on a blackboard attached to our kitchen wall, a slab of slate that Grandpa Quine had salvaged from Spicer School.

Uncle Fay and Aunt Tattie had left Pennsylvania for Illinois. They came visiting with their son Paul. Aunt Tattie was plump and jolly. Uncle Fay was robust and handsome, sandy hair and complexion, and "found of fun." Paul was a big boy of perhaps ten. His mother asked if he would like an orange, and he said "Yes, if you'll peel it for me," which she did. My father held his peace but was scandalized. Paul became concert master of the Chicago Symphony Orchestra.

Up to the age of seven I had a canonical picture-book

grandmother, my mother's mother, living diagonally across the street from us. Gray-haired, benevolent, seated, full-skirted to the ankles. And occasionally unseated, despite infirmities; for I associate cookies. Grandpa Nash, *miles gloriosus*, lived there too, but was not in evidence on weekdays. Though past eighty, he had an office downtown. I remember watching a parade on the Fourth of July from his office window. I also remember my father saying that he had advised the old man not to put all his eggs in one basket. In vain.

Throughout my boyhood I had a picture-book-grandmother surrogate, Aunt Hattie, my mother's mother's sister. She lived with her husband Harry Hatfield and their spinster daughter Lena in a low old house with a sprawling veranda at the central crossroads of the thinly settled township of Charlestown, twenty-two miles east-by-north of Akron. The house was lighted by coal-oil lamps and heated by potbellied stoves. There was a stereopticon with its stack of double photographs. In the kitchen the dominant mechanical appliance was the cream separator. Each bedroom had its heavy patchwork quilt, its big porcelain pitcher and washbowl, and its chamber pot. The well was in the back porch, broad and deep, with a bucket, chain, and windlass. The back porch adjoined a big woodshed, stocked with fuel for the stoves. Beyond were a great tree of strawberry apples, the traditional privy, a modest barn, a hen house, a corn crib, and a pigpen. Uncle Harry farmed only for subsistence, for by trade he was a blacksmith. His shop was seventy yards down the road, next beyond the general store. I would watch his forge blaze up and his irons go red as he plied the bellows, and I would watch him shoe a horse.

Uncle Harry was a weather-beaten type with a heavy crop of black hair. Aunt Hattie was white-haired, affectionate, active in an unhurried way, and an ample and accomplished cook. A great tureen of boiled chicken and dumplings opened the proceedings, along with mashed potato and corn on the cob. It all ended eventually with both pie and cake. Dinner at old Aunt Hattie's was a meal, virtually, in itself.

Uncle Harry was "found of fun," and on the whole this was much to my liking; but not always. At one of those great dinners he plied me with renewals of chicken, dumpling, potato, all in a jocular spirit, and I obediently ate myself sick. Later my mother pointed out to me the legitimate limits of obedience.

"Lena made seafoam frosting," Aunt Hattie would say. Lena would make an excess of it, which she would pinch up into purplish bonbons. Sometimes she made rich ice cream by means of a churnlike apparatus chilled by chopped ice and rock salt. There was home-corned beef in the vegetable cellar.

In early times we went to Aunt Hattie's by train. Uncle Harry met us by buggy or sleigh at Freedom Station, three miles to the north. Later vists were by car. Once we had cleared the hill at Augerburg, a hamlet two miles short of our goal, the high flagpole across the road from Aunt Hattie's became visible. There was a contest, of course, to sight it first.

Once I went alone for a visit of some days at threshing time. Frank Parker, a prosperous neighboring farmer with modern machines, welcomed the other farmers on a cooperative basis: they brought their grain to his machines, and in turn they helped him. Uncle Harry said, "Frank Parker's gonna frash." I went along for a vigorous and rewarding day pitching the bundles onto wagons.

The Life of the Mind   3

I was very young when my mother came to get me from my crib and I volunteered that 64 and 64 were 128. I had been counting up from some intermediate starting point, perhaps fifty and fifty, adding ones on this side and twos on that. I had stopped where I did because I was shaky on the next move, getting out of the one-twenties. Clearly no infant Gauss was I. Clearly, moreover, I had learned early to bank on generous applause for slight achievements. Little ventures in humorous verse, embarrassingly flat and feeble, were praised and recorded by my mother. I even wondered, for all the tenderness of my years, what was so good about one of my touted creations.

My mother baked bread and rolls in my early years and the smell beckoned. She was also good at pies, cakes, and strawberry shortcake. She made jelly from the fruit of our little quince tree, and she made cherry sunshine by the heat of the sun. Mornings I sat up to my Cream of Wheat at the kitchen table, or sometimes to rice and milk. My mother boiled rice almost to a glutinous mass and treated it as porridge; I never knew proper rice until I grew up.

I sat long hours at the kitchen table making lists, for I was a compulsive compiler. I made an ABC book—A for this, B for that. I compiled weights and measures, streets, countries and their capitals. I lettered my lists on the cardboards that came in shirts from the laundry. There was a long pantry with a wealth of cabinets, and it was there that I stored my lists along with selected comics from the Sunday paper and other comparable documents.

My concern for geography began early. Sprawled at my mother's nineteenth-century geography book, I would ponder Servia, the Turkish Empire, Tibesti, Bornu, Ashantee. I would skip the maps of America as dull, and the map of Asia because I did not know the word. Then one luxurious morning I looked at the map of Asia, and a world of myth became real: Jerusalem, Arabia, India, Persia, China, Japan. I had not associated these storied places with actual modern geography. Two realms were integrated into one—an early experience of scientific revolution.

The continuing charm of geography was due not only to the exotic, but to structure. I was interested in boundaries, and in where you get to when you proceed thus and so. I savored the specification of street ends in the city directory. I relished a proposed revision of Akron street names, for it was a revision toward elegance, minimization.

· 1913   At five I had entered kindergarten in one of the city schools, Portage Path, three blocks from home. I remember wooden chairs with arched backs and spindles. We moved among them in a game. I felt awkwardly tall, but one boy, George Hawkins, was taller.

Proceeding up the academic ladder, I was allowed to skip the second half of the first grade. I got on all right with the children and teachers, except that I found Miss Buswell crabby. "I hate Old Lady Buswell."

Wilbur Myers, my frequent playmate on Hawthorne Avenue, sat next to me in school. One day, having a cold, he took to picking up the glass inkwell that was sunk in his desk top and quietly clearing his throat into it. Persisting in this indelicate operation, he had us both covertly hilarious. Wilbur became almost helpless with laughter, as was his way, and at that point he fumbled the inkwell and spilled a mess of ink and mucus across his desk. The hilarity in Wilbur's face gave way in a flash to abject terror.

In the elementary grades we memorized verses by Celia Thaxter and Alice or Phoebe Cary; also a prose paragraph by John Burroughs that began, "The apple is indeed the fruit of youth. As we grow old we crave apples less. It is an ominous sign." Two further passages from those years are deeply graven in my mind: "Me and John ran down the road" and "They ain't no pencils in the box." These were examples of faulty English that we were called upon to correct.

I did my schoolwork and got good marks, but the work seldom aroused my interest. Sitting in school, I would long for a trapdoor under my desk through which I could slip into the cool basement and out to freedom. Such reading as took my fancy was unrelated to school, as was my passion for geography. Schoolwork was duty and dullish *ipso facto*. This was the fault neither of the curriculum nor of the teachers so far as I am aware, and I resented neither the curriculum nor the teachers at the time. It was due rather to an odd and deep-rooted trait of mine: a mild resistance to instruction. Throughout college and beyond, I have listened only restlessly to lectures, and with flagging attention, unless the topic was exceptionally absorbing or the speaker exceptionally skilled. Similarly for a mathematical proof on the printed page: rather than slogging through it I try to prove the thing myself. Failing, as I commonly do, I only then force myself through the published steps.

Besides school there was Sunday school, in a desultory way. My mother, and consequently my father, belonged to the Congregational Church. My mother considered herself deeply religious, but she got to church only irregularly. My father was a silent partner. My brother and I were sent to Sunday school about half the time, and seldom to church. In later life my mother did indeed become a deaconess and engage in good works.

I may have been nine when I began to worry about the absurdity of heaven and eternal life, and about the jeopardy that I was incurring by those evil doubts. Presently I recognized that the jeopardy was illusory if the doubts were right. My somber conclusion was nonetheless disappointing, but I rested with it. I said nothing of this to my parents, but I did harangue one or another of my little friends, and I vaguely remember a parental repercussion. Such, then, was the dim beginning of my philosophical concern. Perhaps the same is true of the majority of philosophers.

Clubs figured in my early years. The first was a secret society called the T.T.T. Club or—now it can be told—the The Twisted Thread Club. It cut across age groups to the extent of including my brother and his friends as well as me and mine. We had a number of meetings in our attic, hammering out the constitution. It struck none of us as odd that the club envisaged no function beyond the fashioning of its own constitution.

It gave me something more to compile, as did its successors, for we had club after club, some even with purposes that transcended self-constitution. There was a bicycle club and later a hiking club. I was a budding organization man. Now and again we had a club whose tangible substance and reason for being was a "bunk." This was our word for a hovel, built by us of salvaged boards or crates and big enough for us to crawl into for secret conclaves.

A less gregarious project was my imaginary cigar store. From my father and neighbors I collected wooden cigar boxes, fragrant and colorfully illustrated. I collected tobacco tins and the empty containers of cigarettes and chewing tobacco. I went so far as to comb a noisome little dump behind the drugstore for empty cigarette cartons. I sought variety. What resulted was an imposing display in the triangular nook between the back porch and the grapevine, but it got rained out. My mother took pity and gave me a dry alcove for my growing collection.

My cigar store was doubly appealing: it combined collecting and make-believe. The latter category loomed large in my young life. I became lastingly devoted to what I called "adventures," concurrently planned and acted. I recruited neighbor children to the roles when I could; more often I proceeded alone. I drew inspiration from the Sunday comics, from the Saturday movie serials of Ruth Roland or Harry Houdini, from *Tom Sawyer*, from films and stories of the Wild West, and from my geographical ruminations. My tale was a continuous one, however erratic, and I held to my own identity. Drawings and plans of my imaginary houses, maps of my imaginary places, and lists of characters swelled my compilations.

A high stool in the kitchen figured in early adventures. I laid it on its side to represent the hood of my automobile. The car was a Pershaw, named for comic-strip characters Perkins and Hawkshaw. But this phonetic spelling seemed humdrum, set over against "Chevrolet" or the exotic "Ri-Chard." So I changed the spelling to "Porchew," pronounced "Pershaw."

At other times I let the prostrate stool represent the forward end of my private airplane. Whether by car or by plane, my imaginary travels were strictly disciplined. I estimated the time required, and forced myself to sit there on the floor behind the stool enacting the drive or flight at some fixed ratio of minutes to hours. It was a way of enhancing the air of reality. I was compulsive from away back.

The Richards family of Casterton Avenue was one of several whose idiom hinted of Pennsylvania. "The potatoes are all," they would say, meaning that there were no more. "I'd just as leave leave it lay." Bread and butter was "butterbread." Their yard adjoined ours back to back; our path that led amid four-o'clocks to the opening in our back fence was our thoroughfare. Randy Richards was one of the children who got drawn into my adventures from time to time. In the course of one of them it devolved upon him to sign a document. He wrote "E. K. Richards," his father's name. "Why 'E. K.'? Why not 'R. F.'?" "Because I'm supposed to be grown up."

Between our back fence and the Richardses' monumental brick garage there were a hundred square yards of barren ground. Here at the age of perhaps six I outlined with stray bricks what I designated as a boat, for use in an adventure. Jack Chamberlin, my junior by a few months, kicked my bricks away. I gave chase and he ran homeward calling "Banny," his grandmother. By the time I overtook him he had picked up a bottle, with which he parted my scalp.

Jack's grandparents were English, with the resounding name of Windsor. Their ample brick house in Casterton Avenue was shared by Jack, his parents and sister, and two black servants. Jack's father was a jeweler.

Our Dr. Weller, whose son will figure in this history, came and sewed up my scalp. During my brief convalescence Jack came contritely with a book: *Old Mother West Wind* by Thornton W. Burgess. The book unaccountably marked an epoch in my young life. Its characters are talking animals that think and act enough like us to emerge as personalities, while persisting sufficiently in their natural wild ways to impart inklings of natural history. The unharrowing drama unfolds in a sparkling setting of unspoiled, uncleared, ungraded, unpolluted wilderness. I had no recognizable predisposition for this genre; I must have been captured by something in Burgess's style. When my taste for Burgess became known, I was regaled with books by others in the same vein: Howard R. Garis, Arthur Scott Bailey. I duly read them and counted myself glad, but the magic was peculiar to Burgess.

It had a major impact on the course of my adventures. I conceived an incorporated village, enclaved in the city of Akron, under Burgess's name of Green Meadows. Its territory comprised the lots on both sides of Hawthorne and Casterton Avenues. I reckoned driveways as further streets, duly named, and garages as further houses, stores, and village hall. The Richardses' brick garage was the jail, and the barren patch between it and our back fence was identified with Burgess's Smiling Pool. I vividly pictured sparkling waters lapping the brick jail wall and spanned by a bridge where the path came through. I appropriated Burgess's beastly characters by name—Peter Rabbit, Johnny Chuck, and the rest—but made them ordinary people. My recollection of threading the backyard boundaries in early spring probably recalls a ceremonial tracing of the village limits of Green Meadows.

The ground that I came to identify with Smiling Pool was the natural place early and late for one and another "bunk." The bunk of one season accordingly took on the role of a secret retreat under the water. Its name, "La Camouflage," recalls that there was a war on. Too bad about the gender.

Joe Weller, our doctor's son, was of my brother's age and came home from school with him now and then. At length it transpired that he had been inventing and enacting a fictitious life for himself much as I had been doing. From then on we spun our adventures in collaboration, and his bookish mind and seventeen months of seniority did much for the quality of the enterprise. Joe alternated two identities, that of a certain Tom Randolph and that of a Count Balsamo who owned a castle on the island of Cedros or Cerros (maps show both forms) in the Gulf of California. Green Meadows was by then embroiled in a contest between the Unionists, who wanted annexation to Akron, and the Separatists. According to law, as we imagined it, one city or village could not be completely surrounded by another, on pain of annexation; so we plotted new boundries, extending Green Meadows nearly a mile westward to the new Akron city limits beyond Storer Avenue. We dutifully walked the new boundary, as nearly as feasible without again broaching the back yards.

Joe and I were still weaving our adventures, ever more coherently, when I turned thirteen and he was fourteen. At last we felt moved to put away childish things and let more respectable interests take over.

Widening Horizons 4

In 1914 my father built a little garage, strewed crushed white limestone in the driveway, and bought a Flivver or Tin Lizzie, a Model-T Ford. It was a touring car with folding top and detachable side curtains with isinglass windows. It started with a crank. A clumsy driver could break his arm in starting, and a forgetful driver could get run over. There was a rumor, echoed by my mother, that Fords were forever turning turtle.

Our Sunday drives, interrupted now and again by a flat tire or by getting stuck in the mud, opened the world to us. Pavements were being rapidly extended. As an interim measure a single lane would be paved, adhering to one side of the road for a few miles and then switching to the other side. Travelers in either direction would use the paved lane, and he for whom it was the left lane would move over onto the dirt in the infrequent event of an oncoming car or wagon. The freedom of access and movement was thus double what a two-lane pavement could have afforded by the same date.

Driving to my mother's native Wadsworth for an ice-cream soda promptly became a tradition. Driving to Grangerburg, a hamlet eleven miles northwest of Akron, became another, because of the big wheel of good cheese at the general store. Also I seem to remember our driving six miles north of Grangerburg to call on Grandma Beckley in Hinkley. She was my maternal great-grandmother, ninety-odd years old. She had buried several husbands, and was living next to a big old public well. But I wonder; my brother has no memory of seeing her.

In our first year of the car, 1914, we drove to Niagara Falls, 240 miles away. We broke the journey at Erie, where we encountered bedbugs. When we crossed to Canada at the Falls, I was told that we were still in America though having left our country. Thus I learned the word "continent."

The following year we visited Uncle Fay and Aunt Tattie in Bloomington, Illinois. We went by train, Pullman, upper and lower berths, luxurious dining car, heavy linen, black waiters, elegance. I had never seen butter in individual pats. "Oh, cheese!" I said, popping mine into my mouth and regretting it. I was out of my class.

It was hot at my uncle's. My father had expected mitigating breezes. "Well," my uncle said, "it's a *warm* breeze." My father had expected flatter country. "It's rolling," said my uncle. It was the first I had heard of rolling country.

In that era vast passenger steamships plied Lake Erie. My father took us along on a business trip to Detroit aboard the palatial *Eastern States*. There was a glass partition through which we could watch the bright brass pistons.

In 1916 and again in 1917 we drove to Jackson County in southern Michigan for a vacation of a week or two at a hotel called Mack Island, at Wolf Lake. My father liked to fish. The distance was a mere 175 miles, but even so we broke the journey each way, spending the night in the trim, square, brick hotel at Fremont.

Thus it was that the Ford gave our family wings. In the same figurative sense I received my individual wings, and what gave me them was my bicycle.

My father taught me to ride it. He would give me a push, and I would pedal a few stokes and fall in the grass. It was discouraging. When at last I mastered it I was, figuratively and literally, transported. Freed of earthly bonds, I flew up Hawthorne Avenue, over and down, and into where the woods had been. Part of the woods had been cleared and laden with a skein of concrete streets that curved and crisscrossed down the slope. The exhilaration of the swift, silent, effortless, descent was both sensual and intellectual, for I was exploring unknown new streets.

16

Day by day I explored more widely. North Valley Street sedately ascended a long slope and, according to the map, came to a dead end. I wondered why. I found that it ascended the gentle side of a ridge whose far side fell away abruptly to the Little Cuyahoga. I went back repeatedly with other cyclists in tow to admire the scene and slide down the sandy bluffs.

Farther east another street, North Maple, ascended the same ridge. Its pavement stopped at the top, but the street continued unpaved down the steep far side. After passing under one railroad and across another, it ended at the abandoned Ohio Canal. The city directory had left me puzzled about that spot, alleging streets where the map was vague. Exploring, I found humble houses strewn about on both sides of the canal and at the river's banks with no observable pattern. Rural country penetrated upsteam to the heart of Akron.

Akron's longest artery is Market Street. Two of the thousand driveways with which it bristled proved to be little hidden streets, one of which was Oakdale Court. Its farther part was steep, narrow, bumpily paved in a cobbled sort of way, and closely flanked by small houses. It smacked of what I expected of old Europe.

Overlooking the center of Akron was the old Conger estate. A tracery of narrow residential streets had been superimposed on the estate, and the map was inconclusive. It was a rewarding quarter to explore, the more so because of the way it dominated and obscurely linked up with the solid old downtown.

That bit of downtown had personality. Streets and buildings were of red brick. Cherry Street was crooked, running south from Market and abruptly east across the old canal. One of its brick buildings was the Williams Foundry, where my father had his office. Canal Street filtered through an arcade under an old warehouse, crossed Cherry, and abruptly terminated conjointly with Mill and Ash Streets against the great Quaker Oats mill. The quarter was bulldozed in the over-subsidized sixties.

My father prospered perceptibly, as witness the garage, the Ford, the trips by train and steamship. The Ford gave way to a used Oldsmobile. In 1917 he boldly left the Williams Foundry and founded the Akron Equipment Co. He had to start big, for his business was the manufacture of heavy machinery by heavier machinery: the manufacture of molds for tires. The resourcefulness that went into the venture impresses me, for he was by nature conservative.

He improved our house, finishing and partitioning the attic. My mother had longed for sunlight through the south wall of the living room, so a broad double window was decreed. When the great square of blank wall that was to go had been cut loose, she had the thrill of pushing it out with a crash into the yard. But in 1919 he sold the house and moved us up another notch, buying a brick house for thirteen thousand dollars two-thirds of a mile farther west at 16 Orchard Road.

In 1918 he bought us a summer cottage. It stood with seven others in a grove on the southeast shore of the East Reservoir, a few miles south of Akron. The lake is one of the Portage Lakes, which were amassed in 1824 from lesser ponds by dams to feed the summit level of the Ohio Canal.

The canal connected Lake Erie at Cleveland with the Ohio River at Portsmouth, and the summit where it linked the St. Lawrence basin with the Mississippi basin was at Akron—whence the name. The portage that is conspicuous in Akron nomenclature is likewise explained by that divide. Indians carried their canoes eight miles over the hills from the Cuyahoga River in the one basin to the Tuscarawas in the other. There was a shorter and flatter route, taken later by the canal, but in a state of nature it had been swampy and obstructed. The eight-mile portage path was a landmark in the early days. The Greenville Treaty of 1795 declared it the boundary of Indian country. Portage County was named for it—an odd irony, for the subsequent excision of Summit County left Portage County eight miles short of the portage.

Grandpa Quine named our cottage "Ellan Vannin," which is Manx for the Isle of Man. The bare studs and siding were stained a cool greenish brown. Upstairs the partitions left off at ceiling level, but there was no ceiling; one looked up to rafters, roof, and ridgepole. This arrangement made for circulation of summer air and voices. Conversation would continue between rooms after we went to bed, until Grandpa Quine said "Goodnight, all."

My father called him the Boss. He was attentive to him, and brought him to the cottage each weekend. Grandpa was short, round-headed, and bald. He had a bushy white moustache and drank from a moustache cup which was kept for him. He chewed Piper Heidsick plug, which came in a slim, flat tin. He would neatly pare off a morsel with a penknife, unlike Uncle Harry Hatfield, who stoked his cheek with ragged wads of Red Man scrap. Grandpa Quine was usually to be seen of a summer weekend in flat straw hat, shirtsleeves, sleeve garters, and suspenders, sitting at the back door on a bench that he had salvaged from Spicer School. He might be whittling, or splicing a rope, or just sitting. Once I walked around the lake with him—four miles. Along the way I offered him a big carrot, one of two that were in my pocket. Somehow this tickled him, and he spoke of it often.

The view across the lake from our porch included a pair of treeless green hills, the higher of which he named Mount McKinley. To him the name had connotations beyond Alaska, for he had known William McKinley and worked for his election.

A walk that I took repeatedly with my brother Bob was to the hamlet of East Liberty. An end point with a village name enhanced a walk. We carried our lunch, ate it in the shade along the way, and added a pop at the village store. In the days before an arm of the lake was bridged, the walk each way was three dusty miles with five right angles. Two of the five were a mere fifty yards apart, where the dirt road jogged because of a discrepancy between two colliding surveys. Up to 1800 this had been the southern boundary of the Western Reserve of Connecticut. In my youth many roads made such a jog as they crossed that line.

Our cottage was lighted by traditional coal oil lamps and

later by a gasoline lamp with an air pump. We carried our water from a communal hand pump thirty yards away, but for a period we got our drinking water from the spring house at the Enlows' farm. The water was heavy and the lane was long.

The Enlows were an Appalachian family of eight from the panhandle of Maryland. The father was an imposing horseback type with a wide hat and moustache. There were a beautiful grown-up daughter, four sons, and a fat, adenoidous little daughter named Mary. The eldest son was Abner, the next was called Honey, and the youngest were twins— Runt (for Law*rence*) and Ernie. Mary asked, "Have you seed de twids?" "Who?" "De twids. Rudt ad Urdie." Their house was a great cube of old brick with a dormered roof, a fine specimen of the prosperous early farmhouses of the region. Sometimes toward evening I helped Runt or Ernie bring the cows in. I luxuriated in this cowboy role, both for its literary or cinematic overtones and for the sense of power in bending the huge beasts to my will.

Our view of the north shore of the lake was dominated by the Warners' barn, two-thirds of a mile away. Besides a house and barn, the Warners had a little square grocery store. In the first weeks of the summer, my mother and Bob and I would go there in our rowboat and bring back groceries and ice. As the summer wore on we switched to a new store, Myers's (no relation), on a wooded shore at half the distance. Asked what kind of pop she had, Mrs. Myers would plumb the watery depths of her ice chest and say, "Well, we have the red, and we have the wite. . . ."

That shore was notable for a swing. It was a cable suspended from a high tree and ending in a bar to hold on to. There was a high bank at the shore, and a high ladder set back above the bank. From the top of the ladder a swimmer would swing far out over the water and dive or jump. A boy who was not going swimming would likewise swing far out over the water from the top of the ladder, but then he would swing back and out again and back, finally dropping off at the top of the bank. That was still worthwhile, but you had to keep your chin up to the bar in order to clear the edge of the bank. One lanky youth swung out and could not stay chinned. "Oh, garnish," he exclaimed, "I haven't got the strength in my arms to hold up the weight of my body." He bumped the bank on the return swing and finally dropped off, dressed, into shallow water. What I found remarkable was his odd way, just quoted, of expressing himself.

Ours was a congenial summer neighborhood. On an occasional evening, neighbors would gather at a bonfire, roast wieners, toast marshmallows, and unleash a chorus of "Till we meet again" and "Long long trail a-winding." Another delight of an evening was hide-and-seek. Less to my liking, Mrs. Hunsicker would appear of a morning in her big straw hat and drag us off "berrying" on Mount McKinley. Elderberries. It was hot, dusty, and tiresome.

Mondays we went back to Hawthorne Avenue for wash day; by then we had a washing machine and "mangle." It gave me a cosmopolitan feeling to meet my stay-at-home Hawthorne friends on my brief visits from out of town.

There were six major lakes in the group. Ours and two others were linked by long, winding channels, and the shores were in large part lined with cottages. The three further lakes were at other levels, but it was easy to carry a canoe across. After the first summer our canoe superseded the rowboat, except for my father's fishing. I relished the quiet effortlessness of the canoe and spent happy hours exploring every cove and passage.

· 1918 Our first summer at Ellan Vannin was unexpectedly extended by the deadly epidemic of Spanish influenza, which prompted our parents to keep Bob and me out of town. Our mother consulted the principal and took charge of our lessons. It was the season for stocking the Enlows' silo with winter feed, and I had a merry time in its pungent depths, stamping down the ensilage that pelted me from high above.

We were still at Ellan Vannin on November 7. It was my father's thirty-seventh birthday, but distant steam whistles began blowing for some other reason. Could the war be over? My mother and Bob and I rowed over to Myers's grocery to find out. Sure enough! Here was the tabloid, the *Akron Press*, with the screaming headline "Huns quit! War over!" It was a near miss. The armistice was signed four days later.

Youthful Enterprise 5

It was not unusual for a child or two to set up shop on a wooden crate at the sidewalk and sell lemonade, five cents a glass, on a hot summer day. It is still not unusual, except perhaps for the price. Wilbur Myers and I had had a profitable afternoon at this business, some summer back before Ellan Vannin, and he then suggested that it would be fitting to buy his mother a present, since she'd supplied us with this and that. My mother was equally deserving, so we bought two boxes of blue letter paper. I would not have thought of it.

Out Ellan Vannin way a cane-like weed grew along the road that showed an occasional bulge on its stalk, containing a substantial worm that was good for fishing. I would harvest worm-laden segments of the stalks, cut to a uniform length, and peddle them in bundles to the fishermen in their rowboats, gliding up to them in my canoe.

A more nearly intellectual enterprise at Ellan Vannin was my weekly *Grove Gazette*, five cents a copy. Volume I, 1920, was produced laboriously with pencil and carbon paper. I had to copy it all out a second time in order to meet the demand of the cottagers in the grove. Each issue was a sheet closely lettered on both sides with neighborhood news and gossip and a few pirated jokes as fillers. Volume II came only in 1922, by which time I had a typewriter. Volume III, 1923, was the last. Several issues in those years ran proudly to two sheets, four pages.

I had bought the typewriter from our next-door neighbor in Orchard Road for five dollars. It was good except that the connecting rod for the letter *x* was gone. I tried substituting *ks*, but found it unattractive. I then devised a rig that enabled me to strike an *x* by treading a pedal.

That final summer of the *Grove Gazette* marked my start in commercial cartography. I drew a map of the East Reservoir that looks rather professional even to my jaded latter-day eye. I prized the contour maps that were drawn by the Geological Survey with gemlike beauty and precision at an inch to the mile and sold for a dime by the government, and it was from one of these that I enlarged my outline, eight to one. I filled it in with place names, newly contrived when necessary. Beneath the scale of miles I dignified the *Grove Gazette* as publisher. I made a transparent tracing and had blueprints made, which I peddled to my indulgent readership.

By then I was in my second year of high school. The next summer I drew a bigger and more elaborate map, covering all the Portage Lakes. Again I made a tracing and had blueprints made, but presently I learned of a more elegant process for further printings. From the tracing a Van Dyke could be made, which has transparent lines and a black background. Blueprinting from this, we got blue lines on white.

I visited all the stores on the lakes by canoe, selling the maps wholesale in modest lots or leaving them on consignment. I replenished my stock and continued the business through the next summer. When I finally had to wind it up in 1926, I again canvassed the stores but also made the rounds of all the cottages on a retail basis. I felt justified in thus saturating the market and undercutting the stores, since thereafter the field was to be wholly theirs. There was an embarrassing moment, however, at what proved to be the cottage of a storekeeper.

Those were summer enterprises. Other times of year, at Orchard Road, I was engrossed in another enterprise: my stamp business.

I was bound to be an ardent stamp collector. My cigar store was evidence of my urge to collect, my lists were evidence of my urge to organize, and above all there was my interest in geography. My stamp collecting began on Hawthorne Avenue. Bob in his seniority was at it more seriously, and there were yet older young people in the neighborhood who were very serious about it indeed.

At Orchard Road I soon grew up to a Scott album that accommodated all and only the stamps from 1901 to 1920. This period of twenty years became my specialty, and it would still be a good one today, excluding as it does both the less accessible earlier stamps and the explosive output of collector-conscious countries in later years. My collection grew to about five thousand. Before college, putting away childish things, I stopped collecting, and in graduate school, being poor, I sold the collection to a dealer for some trivial sum. This I regret.

Stamp collecting was not an enterprise, in the economic sense in which I am using the term, but it led into one. From a mail-order dealer I would buy a so-called mission mixture, a thousand for a quarter, and cull it for what I could add to my collection. The rest I would sort into the stock-in-trade of my budding Orchard Stamp Co. Further stock accreted in other ways, and I soon was nicely established in our enclosed sun porch, operating a stamp store for neighborhood children and a mail-order business for persons less happily situated.

In those days, a small advertisement in a boys' magazine might read: "100 conundrums, 100 jokes, magic tricks, pictures of movie stars, pictures of all the presidents, and a big mail, all for 3¢." The enumerated items would arrive printed on a sheet or two of newsprint, and the big mail would consist of circulars from dozens of petty mail-order businesses. One of these petty businesses was circular-mailing: "We will mail your circulars, 100 for 10¢." One's advertisements, including mine eventually, would be sent by such a circular mailer with a host of others in a big mail like the one my three cents bought. For his dime an advertiser was thus saved a dollar of postage and gained the benefit of a mailing list.

Thus it was that I entered mail-order business. One of the circulars put me onto a good cheap printer in Schenectady, from whom I ordered circulars advertising my stamp business. These were disseminated by one of the circular mailers, 100 for 10¢. Eventually I was selling packets of stamps or sending approval sheets to fifty customers in eighteen states and four countries. I kept eager and elaborate accounts; my early predilection for compiling gained generous fulfillment. My profits went into my stamp collection. By the time I closed out my business at the end of high school, those profits ran to a mere eighty-four dollars. But the operation was its own reward.

The Chamberlins had moved out of the Windsors' house and lived near Orchard Road. Jack sold stamps too, locally. He called Mozambique "Mozam-cue-ee," and he called himself the Canadian-American Stamp Co. because of a summer cottage in Ontario. In his flamboyance he would unrealistically lay in a hundred copies of one stamp, very unlike my frugal self. But I should add in his behalf that one way and another, not in stamps, he made his million in the fullness of time.

As a boy Jack was a printer as well; he had a little press and a font of type. He proposed a monthly house organ for our two stamp companies. We called it the *O.K. Stamp News*. I wrote; Jack printed. The lead item of Vol. I, No. 1, September 1924, was entitled "OUR DEBUT." The capitals would have nicely dismissed the question of an accent if question there had been, but other trouble intruded: Jack set up "OUR DEBUTANTE" and printed the whole edition before I could see it. It had to be done over, and was. It came out "OUR DEBUTE," again without my having a look. So he printed a third round.

The philatelic press sloped off in easy gradations from the sublime to the ridiculous. At the top there was *Mekeel's Weekly Stamp News*, professionally produced by connoisseurs for connoisseurs. At intermediate levels there were *The Green Postage Stamp*, *Sanguinet's Stamp Saver*, and others—combination news sheets and house organs published by small-time dealers. A notch below these, in respect of size and maturity, stood our *O.K. Stamp News*. Farther down still we encounter *Beck's Stamp Gazette* (Chester Beck, Healdsburg, California). "*Exchanges*," we read: "Send us two copies of your publication and we will recropriate."

When the time came to set type for the second number of the *O.K. Stamp News*, Jack withdrew in favor of other enthusiasms. I turned to my Schenectady printer, who printed six further numbers cheaply and well. The biggest ran to eight pages, six by nine inches. There were news notes, some from my own observing and some credited elsewhere. I did a little review of the new Scott catalogue, a piece on the emergence of Lebanon, one on Liechtenstein, and two deploring the spate of new United States stamps—the bare beginning, we now know, of a deluge. There were two short articles by guest authors. Much of the space went to advertisements, mine and those of other dealers. Some of these were paid for, and others were printed in exchange for my advertisements in other petty journals. By June 1925 I was ready to drop the enterprise; after all, it had been Jack's idea. *Sanguinet's Stamp Saver* took over my eighty-odd subscribers and my residual advertising commitments.

Life at Orchard Road   6

· 1919   To oust the former owners of our new house, my father was driven to litigation. Meanwhile we stayed at Ellan Vannin. In Octeober 1919 we gained possession and the former owners moved across the street. I had learned to look upon the man as wicked. It was interesting to see him from day to day behaving like anyone else and to realize that he was wicked. But there was no open hostility. Before long the poor man died of cancer.

Our house had six rooms and a finished attic. My father added an ell and enclosed a side porch. The yard was a bit larger than at Hawthorne Avenue. Behind the house there was an enormous tree that bore handsome big red apples of an unidentified variety and undistinguished flavor. In front of the house, there was a big tree that bore ugly medium-sized brownish apples of an identified variety, namely russets, and a distinguished flavor. The trees were overgrown remnants of an old and eponymous orchard.

The greatest of Akron's rubber barons were Frank Seiberling of Goodyear and Harvey Firestone. Seiberling had a castle and hundreds of acres on the northwestern outskirts of town. But a second-magnitude Seiberling, Charles, had a mansion and three acres on Market Street right opposite our Orchard Road. West of his was a greater holding, Galt's, then three middling ones, and finally the three-hundred-foot half-timbered palace of Harvey Firestone.

Ours was the outermost street of ordinary lots and houses. The three houses in the next street were more sumptuous, and after that the great estates lined both sides of Market Street. Frank Adams's dozen acres enbraced ponds and bridges and a palace. Next west was the Marks estate, similar but even more extensive, drifting off a length into agriculture.

We had moved onto a propitious interface. Our social contacts were limited to the middle-class side of it, but the farther scene was sightly and the air salubrious. With my little friends new and old I had happy times exploring the great holdings, to the annoyance of the gardeners. A fierce swan with a black bulb on its forehead inhabited the Adamses' ponds, and we would get it to chase us. It would rush over the land or water noisily flapping its great wings. It caught up with one little fellow and knocked him down. On the Markses' grounds there were long grassy corridors between high hedges to explore. Hidden away near the Markses' pond there was a little pump house that promptly became a storied hideaway. I think that in a cosmic balance of utilities the vexations of the gardeners were outweighed by the joys of us who vexed them. It was a bright era, be it noted, before the fall of man—before malice, before vandalism.

With the lapsing of our old activity of inventing and enacting adventures, Joe Weller and I diverted our wild imaginings on several occasions to a jocular vein. We elaborately deceived neighbor children into thinking that my house was riddled with secret passages. Joe, half-hidden in a low recess in the vegetable cellar or on the top shelf of a linen closet, would impersonate me moving into the purported passage; afterward I would emerge ostentatiously from the enclosed eaves of the attic. At one point our duplicity, or twoness, was inadvertently revealed, whereupon Joe noisily fled and I pretended to give unsuccessful chase, representing him to be a burglar. Word got around.

There was canonical activity too: basketball, kick-the-can. In a vacant lot we played one-a-cat, which was baseball simplified for a small complement, each man for himself. Sometimes we competed in track events, which gave me something more to compile. My fortes were chinning and the high jump. Winters we went ice-skating at a pond a mile west. I was poor at it and disliked the cold. Nor did I ever master roller skates.

Portage Path School was a short half mile from Orchard Road. I entered the seventh grade in January, three months after moving to Orchard Road; for my skipping of half the first grade had caused all subsequent grades to begin for me in January. In those days the idea of junior high school, grades seven through nine, was just budding. The seventh and eighth grades were still at Portage Path, but were distinguished from the lower grades in that the teachers had their special subjects and the students moved from room to room. Miss Dambach, a red-haired English teacher, taught us to say "Not prepared," or, if we preferred, "I do not know," when occasion demanded. There usually was an edifying saying on her blackboard: "He can who thinks he can, and he can't who thinks he can't"; "I will study and get ready and perhaps some day my chance will come (Abraham Lincoln)." Miss Skaer, a science teacher, had a more laconic admonition on her board: "B²."

School bullies are an American institution. We had a few,

in varying degrees, but I was not badly plagued by them. My brother Bob tells me that he was. It was perhaps for this reason that our father bought us boxing gloves and installed a punching bag and mat in the cellar. The only school fight that I remember getting into was with Vernon Wolfe at the corner of Market Street and Portage Path. Neither of us won. He had forgotten it when I ran into him fifty-five years later.

The air I breathed was mildly anti-Semitic. I think of Bob Goldsmith, Al Green, and Herb Rose, schoolmates of mine and kindred spirits in stamp collecting. Little Herb, indeed, was the Acorn Stamp Co.: "Great oaks from little acorns grow, and so do stamp collections." I liked these boys. What a pity, I thought, that they are Jews. Then I had a flash of philosophical insight, as memorable as the one that had put paid to my religious faith some years before. Why, I asked myself, is it a pity that they are Jews, rather than its being a credit to the Jews? It was my first implicit appreciation of the principle of *extensionality* by which I have set such store down the decades: the universal is no more than the sum of its particulars.

My father joined the City Club, which occupied three top floors of an office building downtown. When we dined out thereafter, that was where. There was a big paneled reading room with deep chairs and sofas and broad windows commanding the urban scene. The big dining room likewise had dark paneling, complemented by the heavy white linen and glinting silver on the tables. The black waiters were deft and attentive, and quiet elegance reigned. We always ended with a parfait in a high glass. By an unperceived transition we had come to speak of supper as dinner by then, and of dinner as lunch.

My father's sport was fishing, but he took it in moderation. At Ellan Vannin he would sit in the rowboat and dangle a worm. I joined him sometimes and was bored, though I enjoyed the consequent shad, perch, bluegills, and sunfish fried in cornmeal. After the move to Orchard Road, the annual two-week vacations in Michigan carried us farther north than Wolf Lake. I recall passing through Alma after a traffic light was installed; the villagers congregated at the intersection and watched it perform. After a couple of summers we settled on Cedar Inn, at Cedarville on the Upper Peninsula, as our regular retreat. My father would take his outboard motor along and rent a rowboat. By then he was fishing with reel and barbed artificial minnow, but he never worked up to trout fishing with flies. Sometimes he would go off with Akron cronies for a couple of days in a cabin cruiser on Lake Erie, in quest of bigger fish and just possibly a bit of the bibulous merriment that was so alien to my strait-laced mother's world.

Socially my parents were reclusive. I think of five couples that they invited or visited over the years, and fewer in any one period. The earliest I recall were the Luthers. Mrs. Luther was a red-haired Russian beauty, née Leda Nemirovskaya, whom Mr. Luther had met in St. Petersburg in the course of a business trip. He had gone back and helped her escape when the czar fell. It was a harrowing flight, out through the Arctic by way of the White Sea. "Do you know where that is?" Mrs. Luther asked me. "Yes, up by the Kola Peninsula," I said, to her admiring amazement. An early triumph.

The new city limits were just four hundred yards beyond Orchard Road. Walking west on a cindered lane called Mull Avenue, one quickly gained open country. After a mile the lane entered a sodden woodland, largely tamarack. It was a remnant of a once extensive Copley Swamp. Other remnants had by then been turned to the cultivation of celery, whose white stalks contrasted strikingly with the jet-black soil.

My father took Bob and me walking out through the tamarack woods and a mile beyond, where we were faced with a sudden high ridge. The ridge was named for its crown of noble chestnut trees, a species now of wistful memory. We climbed the wooded talus slope of the ridge and came to an overarching cliff of sandstone. A slight path led up around one end of the cliff to a cleft, the mouth of what my father had known in his youth as Wolf Cave. It was perhaps fifty feet long, but narrow; we had to sidle. It made two turns; the middle segment was wholly dark, and the last segment was dimly lighted by a rabbit-sized hole at the end. We boys revisited the place many times, armed with a stub of plumber's candle.

Hawkins Avenue was a dirt road that skirted the northwest city limits. In our Ford years, with me aboard, my father had followed it north to where it frayed to an end at someone's hunting lodge in the wooded valley of Sand Run. Remembering that, I marshaled two or three neighbor boys and cycled forth on a mission of rediscovery. Hawkins Avenue skirted the head of a wooded gulley that aroused our curiosity. Abandoning our original objective, we dropped into the gully, named it Brook Valley, and followed its brook, named Valley Brook. It joined another, which we named Pine Tree Brook. The combined outflow, named Pine Valley Brook, emptied in turn into what we mistakenly took to be Sand Run. We had discovered a corner of a rich domain that we came to call the Hiking Grounds and with which, of course, we promptly associated a Hiking Club.

We haunted the area, Saturday after Saturday over the years, pressing our explorations. There was turnover in personnel. Jack Chamberlin was in for a while, and Joe Weller became a regular; also eventually Fred Cassidy, of whom much more anon. When fully explored and defined, the Hiking Grounds measured about two square miles. It consisted mostly of wooded hills and wooded valleys, that of Sand Run among others. It was intersected by just one back road and contained just one remote farmhouse, though fringed by farms, roads, and a railroad.

We named every brook and path, facetiously. I of course made a map. On what we called Monument Ridge we propped a log as a monument, signifying "Onward and Upward," and deposited a glass jar containing paper and pencil to enable members to report their visits. On some of our hikes Joe and I worked on an ill-starred project of damming Wade Brook to make a swimming hole.

For Joe and me the hikes took the place of the old adventures as an outlet for playful imagination, which turned increasingly to whimsy and burlesque. A great sewer had just been built running from Akron to a new sewage disposal plant at the hamlet of Botzum. As we walked along on top of it into Botzum, Joe conjured up the glossary in the back of Caesar's *Gallic Wars*: "Botzum, Botzi, a town of the Suori." What we had called the Western Reserve Hiking Club became the S. E. W. R., that is, the Society for Exploring the Western Reserve. We also contemplated A. B. C. D. E. F. G. H. I. J. K. L. M. N. O. P., q. R. S. T. U. V. W. X. Y. Z., which would have stood for the Association for Bettering Conditions and Directing Exploration of the Features Geographical and Historical of the Indian Jungles of Kentucky, Louisiana, Mississippi, Northern Ohio, and Pennsylvania, *quondam* the Royal Society of Teachers in the Universities of Virginia, Washington, Xenia, Youngstown, and Zanesville. That *quondam* tells something about young Joe.

Akron has grown onto the Hiking Grounds, and residential cul-de-sacs now cover the once wooded ridges between successive wooded gulleys, penetrating to the heart of our old domain. Prosperity and population are the deadly enemies of conservation. Prosperity can, however, occasionally be diverted into conservative channels, and this has also been done: the residue of the Hiking Grounds is now a metropolitan park.

Once when I was admiring one of the Geological Survey's elegant contour maps I was struck by an unusual convergence of contour lines, indicating a notable slope: four hundred feet of relief in a quarter of a mile. The place was in eastern Hinckley township, sixteen miles away by road. I went with two friends, walking and hitch-hiking. It was indeed a noble slope for that part of the world, and it was topped with rocky ledges. "Whipp's Ledges" has proved to be its name. We came to an open cavern in the floor of which, at an inner corner, there was a vertical hole. Hanging by the hands and dropping perhaps six more inches, one hit bottom. From there a narrow passage led back into the dark. On succeeding visits we brought plumber's candles. The passage penetrated perhaps fifty feet, like Wolf Cave, and after a squeeze and a crouch one arrived in a low den where one could not stand, but three could sit. I remember sitting there with Fred Cassidy and his brother Harold. I shudder now to think how slight a settling of rock could have imprisoned us, unknown to all the world.

Forty years later Fred and I found the cave again. The descent to the passage had been mercifully filled.

High School 7

· 1922   In January 1922 I graduated from Portage Path and entered West High School, a mile and a half from Orchard Road. Within the limits of my generally unenthusiastic attitude toward schoolwork, I was comparatively happy with grammar—with the diagramming of English sentences and my introduction to Latin. Also I liked algebra. After a year, the time came to choose among four programs: Classical, Scientific, Technical, and Commercial. It was time, or so I supposed, to think about a career.

There is that which one wants to do for the glory of having done it, and there is that which one wants to do for the joy of doing it. One can want to be a scientist because he wants to see himself as a Darwin or an Einstein, and one can want to be a scientist because he is curious about what makes things tick. The crackpot is motivated in the first way. He extols some shabby idea which he has conceived for the purpose not really of clarifying the world to himself, but of shaking it. Such being his purpose, he is not his idea's severest critic. In normal cases the two kinds of motivation are in time brought to terms. In early youth one aspires to be president and millionaire and cowboy, independently of any interest in state or business or cows. Later, substantive interests contribute increasingly.

In me the glory motive lingered sufficiently to prevent my

contemplating a career as a cartographer or stamp dealer, despite those substantive interests. In school I was doing well in mathematics, a domain with more scope for ambition; so there was the thought of engineering. The insides of machines bored me, but there remained, I was told, civil engineering. No one thought of an academic career.

I chose the Scientific Course. It meant stopping Latin after Caesar. It meant laboratory work, which I disliked. Mathematics went well, but still, in reaction perhaps to the main trend of my course, I began to look to writing. Here I was moved more by the glory motive than by taste or talent. In my stamp paper my style was straightforward, but it turned labored and pretentious when I wrote for writing's sake. However, I wrote for the school paper and became editor of the senior annual.

I even won the school poetry contest. Little was required.

In the limpid lunar light of a sleepy summer night
Down a winding stream we glide in my canoe.
Hoary oaks with branches spread form a lattice overhead
And a mottled mat of moonlight filters through.

To the paddle's drowsy drip, o'er the liquid glass we slip
Down a silhouetted aisle of black and white
While the locusts' distant wheeze 'mid the dank and dripping trees
But intensifies the stillness of the night.

In this last line, so incongruously good on the heels of its outrageous precursor, the teacher sensed a familiar ring. I was offended. She could not place it, but perhaps I did unwittingly plagiarize the line. If so, one of my well-read readers can identify the source. I cannot.

My mother's revered brother Willard had liked Poe, from whose stories she recoiled with a tolerant shudder; so it was commendable and indeed manly to like Poe. I read all of Poe. I was enthralled by some of his poems, but I suspect that my taste for his tales was somewhat self-induced. Anyway, a summer midway in high school found me effortfully writing, trying to evoke a mood of horror in a style yet more pompous than Poe's.

An interest in philosophy, foreshadowed slightly perhaps by two insights already noted, was abetted by Poe's "Eureka." Then, at the end of high school, I acquired two philosophy books from Bob, who was studying at Oberlin. They were Max Otto's *Things and Ideals* and William James's *Pragmatism*. I read them compulsively and believed and forgot all. Also I read Swami Vivekenanda's *Raja Yoga*. It was not a notably philosophical phase; I was also doing other pretentious reading, including Ibsen, Edward Young, and Samuel Butler.

Thus when I finished high school in January 1926 my interest in philosophy was partly spurious and partly real. "Eureka," for all its outrageousness, fostered the real thing: the desire to understand the universe.

But I conceived a new interest at about the end of high school: word origins. It did not issue from school; my enthusiasms seldom did. My source was George H. McKnight, *English Words and their Background*, which I borrowed from the public library, I do not know why. Naturally the subject proved fascinating. An interest in foreign languages, like an interest in stamps, accorded with my taste for geography. Grammar, moreover, appeals to the same sense that is gratified by mathematics, or by the structure of boundaries and road networks. Etymology, more particularly, was a bonanza. Here one can pursue scientific method without a laboratory, and check one's hypotheses in a dictionary. Each etymology is a case, in miniature, of the strange road home.

Besides closing out my enterprises in stamps and maps during high school vacations, I had jobs. One summer I worked in my father's factory, on tire molds—perhaps for Firestone. After the molds had been cast, the tire manufacturer had had second thoughts and decided to indent his tires with suction cups. To adapt the molds to this innovation, little steel bosses were to be riveted along the inner surfaces of the molds, one boss for each suction cup. My job was to drill two little holes in each boss, for rivets. With my left hand I would hold the little chunk of steel firmly in pliers, and with my right I would lower the fierce drill press onto it, while a trickle of wet graphite played on the grim contact. Sometimes the thin drill would snap in two, a resounding response to a moment's clumsiness. It was harsh work, exacting and violent.

The next summer I worked in my father's office, preparing payroll. My father's second-in-command looked at my accounts one day and told me they should be in ink, not pencil. I retorted that they were in ink. He was annoyed; he had to believe his eyes. In fact my ink was old and watery, and looked like pencil. What strikes me in retrospect is my resentful reaction, where I might have pleasantly replied that it was bad ink and that I would change it. It seems that unconsciously I have always resented a boss. My tendency to be impatient with schoolwork, while intellectually active in other lines, was perhaps part of the same syndrome.

In one of those summers I worked for J. Koch, clothier, at the haberdashery counter. I acquired a skill there: how to loop a necktie quickly about the fingers so as to show how it would look knotted.

I worked in the post office for a week or two with Bob and a classmate of his, sorting mail during the Christmas rush. We stood before banks of pigeonholes, busily reversing the entropy that kept billowing in. It was not unpleasant as routine work goes, but it left me subject to hemorrhoids.

Another painful affliction was boils, big and frequent. A third torment has been hay fever, which, like the hemorrhoids, dates from an identifiable occasion. Joe Weller came to Ellan Vannin and we took my mother for a canoe ride. There is a narrow canal called the Raceway that winds gently, despite its name, for a pleasant mile from a dam in the Tuscarawas to supply the East Reservoir. We paddled the length of it serenely from lake to dam, as I had often done. Then we were moved by a spirit of adventure to lift the canoe over into the Tuscarawas at its outflow from the dam and try paddling down that little river. Fallen trees soon barred our way, so we had to carry the canoe over to the Raceway. It meant crossing a broad field of ragweed, breathing heavily as the two of us lugged the canoe, heavy with its layers of paint. The allergy has plagued me intermittently over the subsequent sixty years.

In high school the lump of learning was leavened by nonsense, thanks largely to Charles William Ufford. We were schoolmates of long standing. I called him Charlie Bill, in retaliation for a Billy Van. He was a studious-looking boy and was at or near the top of the class through all the years. He was a wag, taking after his father, whom he would quote appreciatively: "The duck was so tough you couldn't stick a fork in the gravy." "You could float one of those Mississippi steamboats on a heavy dew." Before Charlie could talk plain he is said to have declared something to be *poddidickus*, and his parents at length determined that he meant "positively ridiculous." It was in character.

My brother Bob was exposed to high-school French before I was, and saw fit to teach me to say "Est-ce que je ne trouve pas le livre?" followed by two gurgles which, he lied, expressed interrogation. I passed my gentle accomplishment along to Charlie Bill. He memorialized it as "Ask the cushion of truth when Polly leave," though admittedly uneasy over the subjunctive.

Charlie and I were given thus to farfetched word play. A frequent dish in the high school cafeteria, peas-and-carrots, was for us *zankies* on the strength of its second syllable. Girls who crowded ahead in the cafeteria queue were entomological American Indians, for *bee* plus *redskin*, for *breadskin*, for *crust*. Outrageousness as such seemed somehow amusing. We collaborated twice in nonsense literature, and I venture to reproduce one of the pieces.

The sun beamed patronizingly upon the glowering earth. Much as the lark at twilight, Olaf O'Hara might have been seen that bright September morn doggedly picking his way along the boulevard. The brilliant lights of Broadway flooded the Stygian gloom with beckon-

ing beams of iridescence. Like sirens of Charybdis, they lured the
weary wayfarer to Elysia of rabid revelry. But the stalwart Olaf
heeded them not, for his thoughts were all of little Audrey. Audrey,
pinnacle of dreams! Audrey, fairest flower of a fled youth!

Grim determination cast a migratory shadow over Olaf's finely
chiselled features. Shifting his quid in the interests of enunciation, he
muttered desperately, "Audrey is the sweetest, sunniest little thing.
You've no idea." Liberty, equality, fraternity—was it worth it?
Olaf had decided. One course lay open to him, and he would follow
it or die in the attempt. Groping his way franticly through the gath-
ering gloom, he emerged victorious on the topmost crag.

"More! More!" shouted the rabid rabble in ecstasy as his frenzied
wails of agony glided stealthily over the rapidly receding horizon.
Olaf bowed modestly and continued. "Friends, I repeat: true de-
mocracy should ever be contempered with due regard for the New-
tonian hypothesis of nebular ratiocination. Should we allow our
homes to be devastated, our children led into slavery, our very
beings promulgated, *by the mailed fist of tyranny? I offer you an*
opportunity, the chance of a lifetime. I stammered once myself; now
look at me! All I am or ever hope to be I owe to little Audrey."
Convolving deliriously, the maddened throng united in eleven re-
sounding cheers for Santa Claus and the fatherland and bore Olaf
away triumphant.

Clowning was rife, and not just with Charlie Bill.
Prompted by the "Charlie Bill" and "Billy Van" bit, a group
of us took to calling one another by our middle names or, in
the case of J. Rollin Chenot, by first name. A comic club,
the Greeters, came into being with this usage as one of its
customs. Greeter greeted Greeter boisterously and with a
prolonged and vigorous handshake, which would continue
throughout a joint incantation of a piece of nonsense called
the Greeter Truce. It began, "Books, ties, vests, flies, shoe-
laces, socks, collars, snaps, trips, cards, ink, Eskimo Pies"
and wore on to fifty places. It was a compact not to violate

one another's person or effects in any of the enumerated particulars. If the truce was violated within twenty-four hours,
the victim would cite the offense and the culprit would prof-
fer his upper arm saying "Please hit me five times, Billy
Van"—or Johnnie Rol, or Billy Bellman, or Eddie Art, or
whoever. To my sorrow Charlie Bill was never a Greeter;
someone kept blackballing him.

We had a clubroom over a member's garage. Of an evening we were given to pounding concrete, which was to say,
trooping along the sidewalks. When one of us departed at
last for home, there was effusive and boisterous valediction.
Having gone our respective ways, we would turn and run
back repeatedly, howling, to resume the farewells. It was
happy hilarity, unsupported by alcohol except for a few occasions when we found access to hard cider.

In my case the Greeter custom of favoring the middle
name became entrenched, and I have regretted it. Knowing
me as Van, people reasonably construe my surname as "Van
Quine." I get listed under the wrong letter. Even apart from
this mistake, my middle name is a nuisance. My name in
full is excessive, and the reduced forms "W. Van Orman
Quine," "W. Van O. Quine," "W. van O. Quine," and
"W. V. O. Quine" strike an American ear or eye as affected.
If my first name had remained dominant, then "Willard V.
Quine" or "W. V. Quine" or, best of all, "Willard Quine"
would have prevailed as a matter of course. When at last I
proposed to cut the Gordian knot and publish as Willard
Quine, my wife and friends told me it was too late; I had
published too much.

Civilized Society   8

Greeter nonsense was not all-embracing. Sometimes Johnny
Rol Chenot, Eddie Art Young, and I met and played current
songs badly on banjo, ukelele, and mandolin. Sometimes I

was drawn into a "young people's" program at the church, despite my dissenting views. The thing was primarily social, but once or twice a discussion session was arranged. I was pressed to present something. I prepared a temperate but forthright statement of my position, and it was well received.

Childish enthusiasm for the Saturday movie serials had given way to enjoyment of the legitimate and illegitimate stage. A stock company put on a different melodrama or comedy each week or two, and the actors in their changing roles became familiar personalities. We delighted also in vaudeville. We would seek the dizzy heights of the second balcony, "nigger heaven," and enjoy a succession of song, dance, slapstick, magic, or acrobatic acts followed by a movie. Sometimes we indulged and aggravated our wide-eyed prurience in a burlesque house, any of three—the Grand, the State, the Miles-Royal.

I was attracted to girls and afraid of them. I was afraid of being ridiculous. It was a want of self-assurance that stemmed from early childhood. I may have been six when Wilbur Myers's mother saw me looking down and away, and conjectured that someday I would achieve things that would make me confident. In my high-school days I learned to dance, awkwardly, and ventured timidly into the social whirl, but dared not try to date the prettiest girl. Still, love found its niche. Two or three couples of us would fare forth companionably in one or another's family car and go dancing or to a show or gather in a girl's home. Dates *à deux*, more daring, were soon taken in stride. Necking, as it was called, supervened in the fullness of time as necking will.

A vivid accessory of such social occasions, dances especially, was Lucky Strike cigarettes. Besides the canonical fifteen-cent pack of twenty there was a ten-cent box of twelve, preferable for brief disposability; for my parents had promised Bob and me a hundred dollars if we did not smoke until we were twenty-one. We concealed our smoking not with a view to fraudulently collecting our hundreds, but in order not to hurt feelings or incur criticism. The secrecy had quietly lapsed by the end of high school. My father was a smoker, and there was no moral issue.

Alcohol, rather, was where morality was at stake. My mother was rabid on the point. Any deviations on my father's part, of which I am unaware, were kept firmly from her. Years later, when Bob and I had homes of our own, we still scrupulously cleared the bottles away when our mother was expected.

Liquor did enliven a Greeter dance in high-school days, happily without reverberations. Pints of Old Log Cabin, so labeled, were circumventing the eighteenth amendment, smuggled across Lake Erie by speedboat or over the ice.

· 1924 The Pennsylvania Railroad offered a five-day schoolboy excursion to Our Nation's Capital in 1924. My father staked Bob and me to the trip. I was impressed with the mountains, the first I had seen, and with the site of the famous Johnstown flood, and with the Horseshoe Bend at Altoona. The eastern limit of my youthful travels, hitherto Buffalo, was advanced now to the Susquehanna.

Traveling with us was a contingent from Canton, Ohio, and among them a handsome and ebullient little extrovert who was naturally the center of activity. When the conductor called out "Baltimore," the boy quipped, "Hi, Balty, do you want some more?" Bob told me he admired the boy's quick wit. It seems odd that Bob at seventeen could admire so flat and dismal a reflex, and that I at sixteen saw nothing amiss. Yet the writing in my stamp paper is mature in style. Maturation is spotty.

Between private initiative and our packaged tour, Bob and I did justice to Washington and nearby Virginia. Monumental Washington was everything that the *National Geographic* had given me to expect, as is borne out by a contemporary letter from my own hand: "Washington sure is a swell place." We walked up the Washington Monument, which, I learned, is as high as Orchard Road is long. We fashionably deplored the fussy ornateness of the State, War, and Navy Building. *Eheu fugaces!* We all now admire the building as a Victorian gem. And what of State, War, and Navy? Each of them has outgrown the building a dozen or a hundred times over, and the building now serves as one of several annexes to the White House.

In my high school there was a mental case—over-age, stooped, haggard, and mocked by cruel students in the street. He would perform pitiably at the blackboard in geometry class, bungling his diagrams and mouthing non-sequiturs. "*That's* true, *too*," he would respond to the teacher's corrections. My seat was next behind his, and out of embarrassment or fellow feeling I treated him civilly. One day he told me he had two young friends from Jamaica. To me with my dreams of exotic places, the news was electric. Visions of Contingent Embarking—the outsize penny stamp, green; visions of Arawak Making Cassava—the two-penny carmine. My eccentric friend invited me to his house to meet them, and I was delighted.

They were Fred Gomes Cassidy and Harold Gomes Cassidy. Their father was an Ulsterman from New Brunswick and their mother was of Spanish and Portuguese stock, Gomes y Cáceres, from Curaçao. Harold, born in Cuba, was my senior by two years; Fred, born in Jamaica, was nearer my age. With their parents and little sisters they had just recently moved from Jamaica to Akron, and they spoke with what was to my ear a strong British accent. They were attractively Latin in aspect and had good manners and bright and lively minds. The year was 1924, and we became firm and lifelong friends.

What with native ability and good Jamaican schooling, they had already finished high school in Akron and were working to earn money for college. Our eccentric friend had been their first friend in America, and for a while they had supposed that that was the way Americans were. For some months the four of us convened periodically at one another's homes for an evening at cards. But I came increasingly to join Fred and Harold also by day, especially Fred, to talk and tramp the streets and the wildwood. It must be confessed that at length we sloughed off the poor fellow who had done us the great service of bringing us together. Brutal perhaps, but he had been no small burden.

Our talk was lively and substantial. I learned about their exotic homeland. I attacked their Anglican faith. I must have regaled them with word origins, too, once I had acquired that enthusiasm. There was a light side as well; Fred had a gift for witty verse and deft pen sketches.

I drew him into the Greeter nonsense, abortively. We elected him and imposed an excessive initiation. Part of it took place in an abandoned meat-packing house, where he was required to walk a long course blindfolded and palpating a cord to which various unpleasant things were tied. Another labor was the unrolling of toilet paper along a downtown sidewalk. Another was the making of two circuits of the second balcony of the vaudeville theater, to the exasperation of the cramped audience. Fred went through the whole ordeal to show his spirit and then protested by resigning. It was admirable on his part, inexcusable on ours.

· 1926   The skew induced in 1915 by skipping half of the first grade had the effect in 1926 of my graduating in January instead of June. This was going to be awkward for the high-school annual, of which I was editor. Since I would not be entering college until fall, I continued in high school through the spring in a postgraduate status.

Charlie Bill, Fred Cassidy, and I met at dawn on Decoration Day—Memorial Day—for an expedition by canoe from Ellan Vannin. Three serene miles of paddling and an easy portage brought us to the old Ohio Canal, which we followed west and south into Barberton, an industrial suburb named for Ohio Columbus Barber of the Ohio Match Co. We were stopped after six miles on the canal by an abandoned lock, beyond which a rushing stream, Wolf Creek, flowed into the canal bed. We proposed to proceed up Wolf Creek, and it was in portaging into it that our serene voyage turned into a shambles. Two of us had to be helped out of quicksand, having sunk to our knees.

Wolf Creek in its lower reaches was industrial and disgusting. We ascended it and its tributary Pigeon Run for eight miles, much of it against a current so swift that the three of us put our backs into poling. Ultimately the stream dwindled until we were poling on the banks and lifting the canoe around each bend. It was an absurd sight, canoeing through the fields.

Parched and ravenous after our ten hours' toil, we set out on foot through a wooded swamp to an inn. Glutted, we regained the canoe at 4:35 and turned gratefully downstream. I trotted along the bank to lighten the load and remove obstacles. "Bloated bodies mouldering 'neath the moon" was Charlie Bill's refrain. We passed perhaps seven of them floating on the fetid waters of Wolf Creek and the canal. First a dog, then a headless sheep. Charlie Bill said next day he could still smell bloated bodies under his fingernails.

Much of the trip back meant groping in dark waterways and fighting a stiff wind. Arrived at last at Ellan Vannin, we collapsed on the shore. We had covered perhaps thirty-seven miles, thirty-five of them in the canoe and twelve of them grueling. Yet spirits, for all the sweat, muck, and slime, were undampened. I felt I had never known a day of wittier chatter and higher comedy. Ah, youth!

I got to Orchard Road near midnight, dropped my muddy clothes, and collapsed on my bed, aching and unwashed. My mother woke me at 6:15, for I was to be at school at seven to rehearse a half-hour play that we were to present in the poetry-and-drama class later in the day. I had not even seen to my costume and whiskers or finished learning my lines, for I had not counted on so late and strenuous an expedition. I got up, contemplated the predicament, went back to bed, and slept till ten, defaulting.

From time to time down the years I have had bad dreams about forgetting to prepare my lessons or my lines. In later years they have related to teaching; I suddenly remember in my dream that I have not made an assignment or prepared a lecture for the impending hour, or that I am scheduled to teach an additional course in some unfamiliar subject in which I keep forgetting to prepare myself. Yet curiously the classic little present case of defaulting in waking life seems not to have rocked me unduly. My teacher's reprimand was as gracious as one could wish.

For two months that summer I worked in the Dime Bank, of which my father was a director. I learned to run a posting machine, entering checks on statements and striking balances. Several of us divided the load alphabetically. When the day's figures failed to balance, we all had to stay until we had ferreted the error out. Ray Brownsword, who worked with me, was eventually president of the bank. There was also young Armand Merola, whose name and foreignness aroused my curiosity as those things will. Queried, he would say only that he was from Massachusetts. I suspect that he was coached in this by a minority-conscious mother, perhaps New Bedford Portuguese. A phrase he applied to some formidable woman haunts my memory: "A two-fisted, double-breasted he-mamma."

Johnnie Rol, Eddie Art, and I drove east in August crowded into the seat of an old Ford runabout, Model T. As we were approaching Philadelphia on the second day, the road passed tantalizingly near the Delaware boundary. I grieved inwardly over not being able to interest my callous companions in deviating so as to nick another state. The trip, even so, abounded in fun and Greeter hilarity.

I had first seen row houses two years before in Washington and from the train window in Baltimore, but there was a new quirk in the rows of Philadelphia. Consecutive façades were systematically varied in form and color, usually in alternation.

After taking in Independence Hall and City Hall Square, we continued east through the night; for the Y.M.C.A. was full for the sesquicentennial. We looked into the state house at Trenton, and by seven we were marveling at the New York skyline from the Hoboken ferry. We stayed in Brooklyn, where Eddie Art had relatives, and there we looked in on a carnival. There was a freak called the Bird Girl, and I was delighted that Eddie Art's cousin actually called her the Boid Goil. The famous dialect was real.

We walked to the top of the world's highest building, the

Woolworth, and up into the crown of the Statue of Liberty. We took the boat ride around Manhattan and the trolley to Coney Island and went to art galleries. One day downtown, the next day uptown, we walked tirelessly, treading and threading the Battery, Wall Street, the Bowery, Chinatown, Greenwich Village, Fifth Avenue, Times Square, Riverside Drive.

We drove home by way of Albany, which meant passing within a very few miles of a little bump of Fairfield County, Connecticut. It was New England, no less; but my unfeeling companions were adamant.

Freshman 9

I began college life in a room at 111 Forest Street, Oberlin. My roommate was Clarence Loesch, a freshman from a farm in Parma, Ohio. He proved to be the easiest of companions, abounding in good cheer. Others in the house were an amiable upperclassman named Owen Jones and three freshmen from Canton, Ohio. One of these was Mark Staley, a bright and humorous character who prospered after college and adopted as his enduring avocation the support and celebration of Oberlin College.

Early in the term some good-natured clowning on the stairway dislodged a spindle or two from the banister. Mr. Thomas, the landlord, accused me of the damage. I denied it, for I had not been there. He rashly called me a liar, so I had no choice but to move out, reluctantly leaving my congenial new friends.

Bob was living at Mrs. Holton's house, called the Hock Shop, at 30 East Lorain Street. A small single was found for me there. Our housemates were upperclassmen, notably Ed Trethaway, Dave Hoffman, and Paul Herrmann, or Heimi. Ed was a slim, dapper arrow-collar type. "Well, [hẽ], fellows!" was his byword, if I may invoke International Phonetic Script. He would come cloudborne from a date with his beloved Katharine and intone "Oh Katherrn!" Later life found him not on the stock exchange as expected, but directing athletics for the Los Angeles schools. Heimi was blond, big, and heavy, the son of a jovial fat baker in Cleveland whose wares we appreciated. Dave, somewhat older, was friendly but less in evidence.

Breakfast at Oberlin was a big sweet nut roll and coffee at Bulgarian Pete Tromboff's Varsity Restaurant. One of the places for other meals was the New Purity, "where the best is none too good."

Travel was normally by hitchhiking, for there was little crime in those days to deter hiker or motorist. It was thus that I went home most weekends that first year, keeping close touch with my Akron friends. With Oberlin friends I would hitchhike from Oberlin in other directions too. One day Bill Bennett and I hitchhiked to Norwalk and back for a breath of air. Another time Tom White and I contemplated hitchhiking to Sandusky. "If it lands heads we go." It was tails. "Two out of three," I urged. Tails again. "Let's go anyway." We started at 10:30 in the evening. At midnight we were walking from Norwalk toward Sandusky with no hope, when a man picked us up and took us to Rye Beach. We walked from there to Sandusky, arriving at three in the morning.

Smoking in those days was forbidden on campus. Girls had to be in at 9:30, or somewhat later on weekends. Drinking was forbidden in college and out, on pain of expulsion. I was one of many who secretly broke this rule from time to time, even to foolish excess, in a spirit of bravado. Raw colorless whiskey was available in pints from blacks in the village, and a coarse red wine—"Dago Red"—could be got in quart milk bottles in neighboring Elyria. Infringements precipitated a scare on the occasion of the Junior Hop, in the spring of my freshman year. Students were summoned to the dean, and reports of the interviews passed *sotto voce* through the rooming houses. At length the boy was expelled who had done the bootlegging.

Must youth rebel? Perhaps it is human nature and has had some subtle survival value for the species. Or perhaps it is regional and plays no part in coming of age in Samoa. At any rate it is endemic in the West. In the late sixties it assumed a horrid air of stalwart self-righteousness, in consequence perhaps of an era of parental indulgence of the whims of childhood. Earlier the paradigm of youthful rebellion was sly naughtiness; the culprit when caught was rueful but not resentful. Greater nonsense was itself no doubt rebellious in spirit, though not mischievous. Similarly for the mockery, in my coterie, of school spirit and the Y.M.C.A. Similarly per haps for my antireligious harangues, though these were reasoned; and here I must even confess to a touch of self-righteousness. But the virulent form of youthful rebellion in my college days was drunkenness. It was fostered, paradoxically, by national prohibition, by college prohibition, and by prohibition on the part of mothers such as mine; for these invested it with glamour and bravado.

So much, just now, for vice; what of studies? I met my science requirement with G. D. Hubbard's geology and my Bible requirement with a term on the Bible by the college preacher and a term on the philosophy of religion. My other freshman courses included intermediate French, differential calculus, and literature. At first I pictured creative writing as my likeliest career, with journalism as entering wedge. But when the time came to choose a field of concentration, I found myself torn three ways—and English was not one of them. There were mathematics, philosophy, and what I called philology, which would have meant a classics major. The glory motive intruded a little: I could not invest philology, or linguistics, with the profundity of philosophy or mathematics.

The decision was eased by Bill Bennett, a knowledgeable senior in English. He told me of Russell, who had a "mathematical philosophy." Mathematics was a dry subject, and stopped short of most that mattered, but the link with philosophy promised wider possibilities. So I majored in mathematics with honors reading in mathematical philosophy, mathematical logic.

Bill's father later ran for mayor of New York. Bill became a broker. Evidently his interest in philosophy continued and grew, for he lately gave books to the Stanford philosophy department.

· 1927   My brother Bob dropped out of Oberlin at the end of my first year, his third. He had decided to finish at Akron University to be near his girl, Virginia Hanson. On another count, however, my prospects at Oberlin took an abrupt upturn: I persuaded Fred and Harold Cassidy to enroll there for their remaining three years. They had meanwhile finished a year at Akron University along with their jobs.

Between examinations, Loesch and I hitchhiked to West Virginia, a new state for us. We were impressed that Ohio had hills of the magnitude of those between Cadiz and Wheeling; impressed also by the magnificent river. We passed the night in Wheeling in an upstairs Greek hotel called the Atlas, for seventy-five cents.

We hatched a heroic plan for that summer, 1927. We would canoe from the Portage Lakes down the Tuscarawas to the Muskingum, down the Muskingum to the Ohio, down the Ohio to the Mississippi, and so to New Orleans, where we would sell the canoe and hitchhike back. I arranged with the Akron newspaper to cover our negligible expenses in return for a concurrent account of our adventure in four Sunday installments. But a great flood then hit the Mississippi, devastating towns and spreading typhoid: so my father wisely banned the project. Thus began the summer of my discontent.

Presently my Uncle Willard's beautiful daughters, Norma and Thalia, came east from Denver and visited us at Ellan Vannin. Norma was my age; Thalia three years older. Norma and I fell in love—I desperately. Their brief visit ended, and my discontent was tenfold.

I thought of escaping to a summer job at Cedar Point, the great amusement park and resort eighty miles away on Lake Erie. Loesch was in Canada, but I knew he would take a job with me if I could find two. So I got Joe Weller to hitchhike to Cedar Point with me. We applied for jobs, he posing as Loesch. We took the steamer to Sandusky in the evening and retired to sleep on benches in the park, but were roused at midnight by police. Joe was newly a Phi Beta Kappa, Amherst, junior year, and his key afforded us favorable identification. We were invited to sleep on benches in the courtroom. Next morning we hitchhiked back to Akron, and in a few weeks Loesch and I had the jobs.

It was a good life, with days free to enjoy the abundant amenities of the resort and the good company of the other employees, some of whom were students. One was Norman Burns, a graduate student at Yale. He shared my views on religion and my fondness for Poe's poems, which he could quote at length. He and I hitchhiked to nearby places and had lively talks. The last I heard, he was an instructor at Beirut. Feminine beauty among my associates was ample and generous to a fault, and I confess that neither my painful diffidence of old nor my newly lovelorn condition betrayed themselves unduly.

Loesch worked days at the Grill, I nights washing dishes at the Luncheonette. We thought that after the place closed for the season we might hitchhike through New England and to Quebec. However, the Grill stayed open a week later than the Luncheonette, and too late for such a trip. Nor could one quit early, on pain of forfeiting accumulated pay.

I hitchhiked home. Bob was there, but our parents were in Michigan. In my lingering discontent I decided to hitchhike to Kentucky. No luggage was required; I could turn a dirty shirt inside out, and a pocket comb and a safety razor would suffice me as toilet articles. Safety indeed! I dismantled the razor and stowed the parts compactly in the tight little watch pocket at my waistband, and then forgetfully thrust my thumb into the pocket and cut it cruelly. Bandaged and with my razor more safely stowed, I set out. Night overtook me at Wilmington, Ohio, where I canvassed such cars as had Cincinnati license numbers, and thus made it to the Cincinnati Y.M.C.A.

Next day I explored Kentucky, a new state for me, traveling on foot, on the running board of a truck, and in cars. There were frontier restorations at Harrodsburg and a dam near Shakertown. I was threading back lanes from the dam to the highway when night fell, so I slept on the ground behind a stone wall until awakened by a mouse on my hand. Increasingly aware of the hardness of the ground, I intermittently drowsed and watched the glowworms. The sun rose splendidly over the hills and the bluegrass. Smugly I recalled the opening lines of the *Rubaiyat*. One fancies oneself, when young.

I hitchhiked to Frankfort and gloated over my smallest capital city to date. The map showed a shortcut from there to Cynthiana, and I waited hours for a ride over it. It dwindled, I found, to a track over the fields. By dusk I had hitchhiked back into Ohio as far as Washington Court House, where an amusing character picked me up and took me eighty-five miles to Mt. Vernon. He said he had worked in forty-seven states; all but Maine. He told of carnivals in the Kentucky mountains, of swindlers in the Florida resorts, and of how tough they come in Brownsville, Texas. In Mt. Vernon I sent a reassuring telegram home and slept on a bench inside the entrance to the Y.M.C.A. Next day in I found that I had contracted chiggers when I slept on the ground among the glowworms.

Sophomore and Junior   10

· 1927 Fred and Harold Cassidy got rooms with me at the Hock Shop, September 1927. Three seniors were there from the year before: Ed Trethaway, Dave Hoffman, and Heimi. A fourth senior, my absent brother's close friend Larry Kiddle, moved in with us from another house. Larry was a snappy and good-looking little fellow with a quick wit and a ready laugh. He had a gift for impersonation and foreign accents. His destiny lay in Ann Arbor as a professor of Spanish.

We felt that the name of the Hock Shop could be improved. I proposed Ἄρθρον, "Arthron," "Joint." Fred elegantly painted the Greek word, using the back of the old sign. In later years it has adorned my Boston study, a sacred relic.

One Sunday that fall Heimi and I hitchhiked to Erie, Michigan, and back, sending postcards to Ἄρθρον from that alien state. Later that fall we retraced those miles and extended them to a circuit of Lake Erie, 630 miles. It was a holiday weekend that had been declared for the inauguration of Ernest Hatch Wilkins as president of Oberlin. We spent the first night in the Y.M.C.A. in Windsor, Ontario, after a burlesque show in Detroit. Next we hitchhiked across Ontario to Niagara Falls and on to Buffalo. There we went to the police station with a view to sleeping in the courtroom or jail, but were directed to the DeGink Institute. The kind old policeman in charge there did not make us put our clothes in the fumigator and sleep in the big room with the ordinary tramps. He gave us a little room to ourselves. "You don't need to be afraid," he said. "The place is clean. It's run by the mayor."

· 1928   Fred, I subsequently learned, had never seen Niagara. Between winter examinations we hitchhiked thither, arriving at night. Canadian officials at the bridge made us fill out forms and then ruled that Fred, as a British subject, could not enter Canada without his original passport into the States. They were further put off by my indicating my religion as atheist. "You mean to say you're an agnostic?" Settling finally on a simple ground for exclusion, they found our funds inadequate for support. So we walked back into Niagara Falls, New York, and requested lodging at the jail. We were given a big, well-ventilated cell. Next day we crossed the bridge from Buffalo to Fort Erie, Ontario, without incident. Then we crossed back and hitchhiked as far as Erie, Pennsylvania, where again we applied to the jail. It was full except for the basement, where there were said to be lice, so we found a fifty-cent hotel. Erie retained a certain character: bedbugs in 1914, lice in 1928.

Larry and I hitchhiked to low haunts in Sandusky. He passed for a French Canadian who could not speak English; I interpreted. We slept in the courtroom that Joe Weller and I had initiated a year earlier. On an Oberlin holiday called the Day of Prayer, Larry and I made a similar trip to Detroit and Windsor. Having blown our small resources, we repaired to the MacGregor Institute and slept in a big room filled with dozens of cots. "Youse is lucky not to have to put your clothes in de fumigator." "Do yez tink dey'd get sore if I din't put me collar in de fumigator?" Such from either side of us. The man on duty had a black beard and looked like a steel engraving in *Harper's Weekly*. His deep voice was in keeping: "It's a warm night, men."

I signed up for a dinner a week at Oberlin's French House. Fred Cassidy earned his meals there washing dishes. It was there that he met Hélène Monod, with whom he was destined to spend decades of connubial and collegial felicity on the Wisconsin faculty at Madison. It was also at the French House that Fred met Ed Haskell, a fellow dishwasher.

Ed was born in Bulgaria, son of an American missionary and a Swiss mother. He learned English, Swiss German, and Bulgarian concurrently—a matter, as he then saw it, of talking like a scholar, a woman, and a peasant. When at length he had grown up to be a freshman at Oberlin, he had a lucky hitchhike. A rich old lady, traveling with her daughter and chauffeur in her limousine, picked him up. She had been intrigued by his violin, which he was carrying, and she became further intrigued by his discourse. She settled a modest living on him, a hundred a month, in perpetuity.

Ed was ambitious, opinionated, contentious in the classroom, and rather shunned as an eccentric by conventional students. Fred proposed that he be invited to move into Ἄρθρον. Happily it was done. It marked a turning point in Ed's life and was a boon to the rest of us. Ed has long been my closest friend. It was he, indeed, who taught me to say, in *schwiezer dütsch,* *"Bischt z'kstabet 'm füwafüfzk z'säge"* ("You are too clumsy to say 'fifty-five'").

· 1928   Ed moved into Ἄρθρον in the fall of 1928, my junior year. Fred and Harold Cassidy were there, and also Dave Hoffman, who was staying for a master's degree. Loesch moved in with us and shared my little single, but he failed and left Oberlin after a term. There were other newcomers, notably Jim Sell.

Jim had majored in classics and then switched to zoology. He was from Allentown, and was given to caricaturing the Pennsylvania Dutch. "Who iss making doce noices, pleece?" One of his stories will suffice to set the tone. He said he had been invited to the home of his Greek professor, Lofberg. He put on his new brown suit and tie, his brown shoes and socks, his tan shirt and brown hat, and appeared at the professor's door. "Well, well," the professor said, "you are very *ensemble.*" "Ahnsahmbel?" Jim pretends to have asked. "Vat meence 'ahnsahmbel,' pleece?" "Well, your suit is brown, and your tie, and shoes, and hat . . ." "Oh, I see. 'Ahnsahmbel' meence 'all ofer bhown.'" In later years Jim took a Ph.D., occupied a high post in a pharmaceutical laboratory, and died in his early sixties.

Jim's roommate was Walt Hoy of Napoleon, Ohio. He ended up as a banker in Napoleon. Among other housemates during that year and the next there was Townsend Lodge, psychologist, who for a brief period many years later became Ed Haskell's father-in-law. Another, Merbert to us, was Herbert Morse. But Fred, Harold, Ed, Jim, Walt, and I were the firm nucleus, along with Loesch for his brief term. We had meal tickets at Martin Inn, whither we would regularly troop down Main Street. After a time we were accorded a back room to ourselves in the inn, and thenceforward styled ourselves the Oberlin Junior Business Men's Association. One of our usual waitresses was an unattractive but good-hearted young woman whom we referred to among ourselves as Stucco. "Beneath that rough exterior there beats a heart of gold." Other waitresses were two pretty and merry little girls, matched in size and in the yellow of their waitress uniforms; whom we called the Cat and the Canary. They lived next door to Ἄρθρον at Mrs. Hakes's, a rooming house for business-school girls. That house was a cynosure for Arthric window watchers, despite lack of encouragement.

Hilarity and horseplay at Ἄρθρον gave way occasionally to music of a sort, what with Ed's fiddle and my mandolin and sundry voices. It was mostly popular and ill-rendered, but Ed played well and came through rewardingly with Bulgarian and Swiss folk songs. We often played poker, drawing friends from other houses. There was serious talk on the part of Ed, Fred, Harold, and me. Ed would conjure up scenes and events of his life in distant places, telling of the ways of Swiss mountaineers and Bulgarians, and would hold forth in a more theoretical vein on the ills of society and on things he had been learning in psychology. I would tell of my adventures on freight trains, *q. v. infra*, and would hold forth on word origins and on what I had been reading in Russell.

Already as a sophomore, having decided in my choice of a mathematics major that Russell was going to be important for me, I had turned to him for leisure reading. *Marriage and Morals* disposed me kindly to my new master. I read *Skeptical Essays, Philosophy, Our Knowledge of the External World, A-B-C of Relativity,* and *Introduction to Mathematical Philosophy.* It was these books, and not my two survey courses in philosophy, that further whetted my appetite for cosmic understanding.

Though my linguistic interest had bowed to mathematics and philosophy in my choice of a major, it had not subsided. I once took Fred to task for coining a hybrid word from Greek and Latin. He asked me for guidelines, and the outcome was our collaboration on a compilation of English suffixes, etymological and semantical, for our amusement. Unwittingly I influenced the course of Fred's career. He became an Anglo-Saxon scholar and a great lexicographer, the authority on Jamaican English and the creator of the monumental *Dictionary of American Regional English,* whose first volume will soon be off the press. He might have taken a different turning and have delighted us with more verse and sketches in a *Bab Ballads* vein.

I took a year of Greek and more French. My mathematics courses brought high marks but often imperfect understanding. I got more pleasure from Stetson's course in psychology, where we read Watson on behaviorism, and from Thornton's in Old French. In playful consequence of a mathematics class I compulsively computed e, the base of natural logarithms, to forty-five places and then memorized it for the dubious entertainment of my friends. I can still recite it.

My literary leaning did not lapse altogether. I took literature courses and contributed to the college magazine. With a misguided sense of tongue in cheek I even wrote a horrid thriller for the pulps, not one of which was so undiscriminating as to accept it.

Much contentment with my mathematics major came in my junior year, with my honors reading. Nobody at Oberlin knew modern logic; however, the chairman of the mathematics department, William D. Cairns, made inquiries and got me the books. They were Venn's *Symbolic Logic*, Peano's *Formulaire de mathématiques*, Couturat's *Algebra of Logic*, Whitehead's *Introduction to Mathematics*, Keyser's *Mathematical Philosophy*, Russell's *Principles of Mathematics*, and the crowning glory, Whitehead and Russell's *Principia Mathematica*.

Peano's symbolic notation took Russell by storm in 1900, but Russell's *Principles*, 1901, was still in unrelieved prose. I was inspired by its profundity and baffled by its frequent opacity. In part it was rough going because of the cumbersomeness of ordinary language as compared with the suppleness of a notation especially devised for these intricate themes. Rereading it years later, I discovered that it had been rough going also because matters were unclear in Russell's own mind in those pioneer days.

Keyser came off badly in my eyes because of a chapter on "Korzybski's concept of man" in which Keyser misapplied a logico-philosophical idea of Russell's, the theory of types. When I remarked this to Cairns, he pointed Korzybski out in a group photograph and told of his buttonholing mathematicians at meetings and holding forth on man as a time-binding animal. This was before Korzybski's *Science and Sanity*.

Principia Mathematica, 1910–1912, is devoted to showing in its three formidable volumes how the various concepts of classical mathematics, or concepts to the same purpose, can be expressed in symbols purely of logic and the theory of classes, or set theory, and how the laws of mathematics can then be deduced from laws of logic and set theory. The basic symbols assumed amount to 'not', 'or', 'every', 'is', pronominal cross-reference, and somewhat more. Long derivations, rigorously carried out step by formal step, issue in definitions of numbers and functions, and in proofs of even such obvious laws as that $x + y = y + x$. But Whitehead and Russell's purpose was not to persuade us of obvious truths; it was to show that these truths and their more recondite suite can be generated from such slim beginnings in logic and set theory, and how.

· 1929 At the end of my junior year my mother bought me the three volumes of *Principia* ($16, $14, $8). She had made me an equally inspired gift on Christmas: Skeat's etymological dictionary, which I persistently consulted and explored over the succeeding half century.

Wild West 11

This is the tale of a forty-day trek across the continent and · 1928 back in the summer of 1928, between my sophomore and junior years. Outbound we were three: Loesch and I and a student named Jerry Taylor. We bought a 1923 Model-T Ford for forty-five dollars and set out on June 21 with tent, bed rolls, stove, and kindred gear. Before we were out of Ohio we ran out of gas, which I replenished by hitchhiking fourteen miles. We camped agreeably, but other troubles followed fast: an ailing muffler, a cloudburst, an irreparable tire. Even so, we deviated from our geodesic now and then to touch an additional state—Wisconsin, Nebraska, Minnesota. My new companions were more sensitive to such values than Johnnie Rol and Eddie Art had been.

After Fort Dodge, Iowa, the roads were unpaved. The prairie was monotonous and empty except for an occasional farm and at long intervals a town, detectable from afar by its water tower. Suddenly one day the Middle West left off and the Wild West set in as we rounded a bend near Chamberlain, South Dakota. The plain gave way to hillocks as we dropped to the Missouri River, and four cowboys in chaps, bandannas, and sombreros rode across the road driving a herd of horses. In the next moment a wagon full of Indians rattled by.

The West manifested itself further in the silver dollars. "I don't like them dollar bills," an old man in Plankinton said. "They make you think you got a lot of money when you ain't got nothin."

On the sixth day we marveled at the colorful Bad Lands and camped in Spearfish Canyon in the Black Hills. Next morning I was proud of my increasing skill in loading the car compactly; we were less cramped. Proceeding then over abominable roads and a long detour, we at length passed Devil's Tower and set about to pitch camp at Clearmont, Wyoming. Lo, no tent! I had rolled it and left it propped against the wall of Spearfish Canyon.

It rained hard, and we tried to sleep under the car. Next morning we draped our wet clothes and bed rolls over a barbed-wire fence. Clearmont indeed!

We could not think of retracing those hard 180 miles for the tent. Pressing westward, we soon espied the Bighorn Mountains. They were a snowy streak spanning the world and suspended in blue—for the slopes below the snow line were nearly as blue, at fifty miles, as the sky. We crossed the mountains and descended precipitous Tensleep Canyon. We negotiated the switchbacks at a perilous rate, having weak brakes and wanting to spare the clutch.

Next came the land of sagebrush that we had learned to love in the movies. Sage and prairie dogs. At Cody we dressed up and joined the revels at an open-air dance floor. Sombreros galore. At Yellowstone we admired the wonders of nature and enjoyed the company of some co-eds from Utah. At McCammon, Idaho, we slept tentless on blankets in the public square. After Salt Lake came the white, flat Salt Lake Desert and then the sagebrush and purple mountains of Nevada. Carson City delighted me—a capital village of sixteen hundred with a state house like a minor county courthouse. In the Sierra Nevada we camped happily, for all our tentlessness, by a cold mountain stream in a forest of redwoods near Strawberry.

Jerry Taylor stopped with relatives in Berkeley preparatory to proceeding to his home in Hawaii. Loesch and I went to the San Francisco jail for lodging. Police hospitality took an unexpected turn this time: we were locked in. The floor of our small cell was filled with tramps, five of us, on blankets. The tramp on my left groaned and spat all night. The corridors rang with angry voices and vomiting. Next morning we were given a tin cup of bad coffee, a chunk of dry bread, and freedom.

We took a six-by-eight room in the Standard House, in an alley called Summer Street on the edge of Chinatown, for fifty cents a night. We sold the car for twenty dollars and shipped our gear home, keeping such essentials as we could stuff into two drum-tight overnight bags. We meant to work our way back east on a freighter, if we could, through Panama.

A day of queuing and waiting at the seamen's bureau in Mission Street dashed those hopes; there was a swarm of jobless seamen ahead of us. We boarded ships at the docks and offered to work for passage, but there was still no hope. So we took the ferry to Oakland and started hitchhiking to Ohio.

Our first ride, in a Velie, ended at the Carquinez Bridge; the man said he was turning off to Crockett. I inadvertently left my bag in his car. Aghast, we walked to Crockett in search of the Velie. I asked in two garages, and I asked the sheriff. The sheriff sent us to an insurance agent, who remembered someone whose son-in-law had a Velie. We found my bag.

Then we decided to try riding freight trains. In the railroad yards we boarded moving boxcars, one after another, each of which ended up on a siding. We slept in a static boxcar and resumed the highway the next morning, July 13. Our appearance was against us, and we waited hours between rides. At last we found ourselves at a railway stop called Nevada Street, out of Auburn, and resolved to try a freight train again. One came, and a kind brakeman let us ride on top. We looped our belts around a board of the catwalk to prevent rolling off, and there we slept, intermittently admiring the moonlit panorama of Tahoe and Sierra. Tunnels were the bad part, twenty-six of them, some very long; we were near to strangling and suffocating from the smoke and fumes.

Grimy, we dropped off in Sparks, Nevada, for a late breakfast. Someone told us to catch freight trains only as they left the yards, for two reasons: so as not to end up on a siding, and so as not to be arrested by yard police. Complying, we boarded an oil car and rode it through the desert night, sleeping on the side planks with our belts secured. We stayed on next day, almost crossing Nevada. At six in the evening, ravenous, we ran to a lunchroom in Wells while the train was stopped. We had dined except for our pie when the train started. We ran for it, missed it, and went back for our pie.

Next we rode in the vent of an onion car. The brakeman found us and let us stay for a dollar apiece. At Montello the train stopped and the brakeman lied that it would be there an hour; it left while we ate. Eventually we caught a fast passenger train, which we rode precariously perched between two express cars—a poor idea. We were shooed off at a stop in the Salt Lake Desert in the cold small hours.

The sun was high and hot again when we joined nine other tramps on a lumber car. Eight of them were respectable, looking for work. The ninth was a derelict, shabby, unshaven, and with an ugly boil. He extolled Sterno jellied alcohol, or canned heat—taken internally. Had he ever worked? Once, but he hurt himself and never tried again.

The brakeman who had betrayed us at Montello reappeared and collected fifty cents from everyone. We crossed Salt Lake on the thirty-mile causeway and dropped off in Ogden, where we gorged after our twenty-four-hour fast.

Our next train left the yard at an alarming speed, but we grasped ladders, climbed to the tops with our satchels in our teeth, and dropped unobserved into the vent of an onion car. Our cell was some thirty inches wide, its floor cruelly corrugated. We were twenty-two hours without food or water, and in the course of them I expounded my newly gained lore about number and the nature of things. We climbed out after 484 miles and walked three miles into Laramie for a big meal; then back again to the yard limit. Summoning courage, we mounted a fleeing oil car in another fast freight. Further tramps gathered on the car, and after fifty miles a brakeman forced us all off the moving train, stamping on hands. He was a brave man, though not to our liking.

It was high, cold country. We slept fitfully in wet grass. We had been in our clothes six days and were grimy from the tunnels. We walked to the road with no hope of a ride. A cowboy told us we were fifteen miles from food. Then a tourist with a loaded car picked us up on his running board and took us to the next town. It was Wellington, Colorado, and a full twenty-five miles. After food, haircut, shave, and shampoo, we hitchhiked to Denver and put up at the Illinois Hotel, fifty cents *per caput* this time, in order to bathe and put our meager wardrobe into shape; for we proposed to visit my lovely cousins.

Their mother, Aunt Laura, was frontier-bred; as a girl in Salida she had stood off an Indian from her cabin window with a shotgun. She looked kindly upon me, but not upon cousin marriages. She got Thalia's husband and his brother to whisk Loesch and me off on a fishing trip. From Estes Park we rode horseback up over Trail Ridge and down into Forest Canyon as far as the timber line, where we left our horses with an accompanying cowboy and slithered down through the steep woods to the stream. It was country where not a dozen people passed in a year. We walked a mile in the canyon, caught and ate trout, and slept on blankets on a bed of boughs. When we had struggled back up the wooded canyon wall, we were met by the cowboy and horses. The horseback ride to Estes Park was restful and the scenery was magnificent.

Late in the afternoon of July 23 we began hitchhiking back to Ohio from the end of the Denver streetcar line. At Strasburg we got a ride of 265 miles with a Post-Toasties salesman that landed us in Scott City, Kansas, after three in the morning. We slept three hours in the box of a parked truck and then posted ourselves beside the muddy road in the forlorn hope of a ride. The village was swollen with migrant farmhands who had nothing better to do than drive round and round. At length the mayor objected to our interfering with traffic on Main Street, so we walked out of town. Late in the afternoon our Post-Toasties man reappeared and drove us to Dighton. The distance was twenty-five miles by the straight road, but our route was devious and punctuated with sales stops. The roads were a pasty mass of black mud, but our man was a stunt driver. He wallowed in second gear, spinning his steering wheel and sliding from ditch to ditch and broadside without respite. Healy, Kansas, was flooded, each street a lagoon with a crown of mud along the middle. Natives walked in hip boots. To enter the café with dry ankles we had to climb over our truck. But we did get to Dighton, in the dark of night. The hotel was jammed with travelers stranded by the flood. The dining room was filled with cots, all occupied. Loesch and I were given bedding on the lavatory floor.

At length we got to La Crosse, where, after a good chicken dinner for fifty cents, we spent the rest of the daylight hours trying in vain for a ride out. Again we were reprimanded for interfering with traffic on Main Street. We passed the night still in La Crosse, on cots in a room with four other sleepers, twenty-five cents each. Our poverty was not really quite that abject, but we were making a game of it.

We had cleared only ninety-eight miles in two days. Twice we had tried resuming the freight trains, but in vain. After a truck carried us north to a busier road, we fared better. At Russell, Kansas, we feasted at Mary's Café. Patrons sat around three big tables and passed the tureens and platters, family style, as often as one wished. Dessert and coffee, too; all you could eat for forty cents.

That night as we alighted in Solomon, Kansas, our ears were assailed first by the resonant, agonized sound of distant vomiting and next by the radio returns of the Tunney-Heaney fight. Then a man ran up and asked us if we wanted to work; there was a shortage of fieldhands. We had two more such offers before we left Solomon. We spent the night in the Pacific Hotel, the horrors of which I shall spare the reader's sensibilities.

Next day we covered 250 swift miles and were put down after dark where there was a lunchroom but nowhere to sleep. Two men arrived in an Illinois car and went in to eat. I followed them and asked if we could ride with them to the next town, nine miles away, where we could find a hotel. They mumbled that they were heavily loaded. I said we would stand on the running boards. They gave in and let us inside, where there was plenty of room. When we got acquainted and they learned where we were going, they let us continue with them through the night, across the whole of Missouri—just as we had hoped. We left them at St. Louis at five in the morning. We got breakfast, mail, and a shoeshine, and took the streetcar across the Mississippi, deciding to forgo sleep despite having covered more than four hundred miles in the twenty hours since Solomon.

The road across southern Illinois was infested with hitchhikers. We admired the professional finesse of one of them. Waiting at a strategic hilltop for a ride, we watched him approach from afar. He walked as if preoccupied, and when he sensed that a car was overtaking him he hailed it as if on a sudden impulse to save steps on some brief errand. He was perhaps forty, hatted and neatly dressed. We saw him repeat the identical maneuver a number of times. Luck changed just as he reached us, and we all stood in the back of a pickup truck. His well brushed and decently pressed trousers were threadbare, he wore no socks, and his neat black shoes were worn through at the soles. He propped up a shovel and half sat against its convex side to cushion himself somewhat against the jolting of the truck. He made a small art of his pointless way of life.

Our next ride broke down, and I hitchhiked for a tow truck. When we turned in at Terre Haute for a night's sleep, it was our first in forty hours.

In the morning we were speeded on our way by a ride on the turtleback of a coupé. Out of Columbus next day we took turns standing precariously on a running board and were thus wafted back to Akron and a normal life. In the forty days since leaving Oberlin we had covered some six thousand miles.

I had had enough, one would think, of the vagabond life. In two months, though, my taste for it revived. There was a college holiday, temptingly called Migration Day, that afforded me three free days. I hitchhiked to Chillicothe, visited the earthworks of the ancient Moundbuilders, and then headed for the region where Ohio, Kentucky, and West Virginia meet—thus Ashland, Kentucky, and on through Huntington, West Virginia. A lift was unlikely after dark in that lonely country, so I caught a bus to the capital, Charleston. This nearly exhausted my means, but I got a bed for a quarter in a squalid brothel. Next morning I visited the state house, still under construction, and then hitchhiked to Canton, Ohio. Night fell, but I caught one more ride, almost to the edge of Akron. I spent my penultimate dime for a sandwich and walked a mile to the streetcar.

Europe and After

Dave Hoffman and I were planning at the end of my junior year, June 1929, to go to Baltimore and try to work our way to Europe on a cattle boat. My father came up with a better idea. He staked Bob and me to a trip to Europe.

Jack Chamberlin was by then a travel agent—Chamberlin Travel Management, Inc., no less—though not yet twenty-one. He had organized a tour for schoolmarms, and we arranged to move intermittently with them. My parents' friends the Webergs sent their son Roy with us.

On the *Duchess of York*, out of Montreal, the three of us shared a stateroom with an inconsiderate black doctor from Grenada. It took five days to get moved to a quiet room for three, and on the sixth night we saw the lights of Europe at Inishtrahull. In the light of day we rounded the ancestral Isle of Man and landed at Liverpool. The Middle Ages came alive as we trod Chester's city walls and "rows" or double-decked sidewalks and the hallowed ways of Stratford-on-Avon. At Chester, predictably, we took a tram to the Welsh border. In London a high point was the labyrinth of narrow lanes and ancient tall slums that Dickens celebrated—destined to be demolished in the Blitz.

We sat up on the crowded night ferry to Dunkirk. Jack Chamberlin met us in Paris, and no sooner were we in our hotel than I sallied forth, sleepless, and tramped for hours, seeming to draw energy from the very pavement.

We went on with Jack and his schoolmarms to Avignon and the Riviera. From the dizzy Corniche at La Turbie I gazed down incredulously on the Principality of Monaco. My dream of small countries was beginning to be fulfilled. At Monte Carlo I played and won—ever so little. We explored the narrow old streets of Genoa, admired the stunning triad of tower, cathedral, and baptistery at Pisa, and went on to Rome.

Jack was a dashing and handsome fellow, a leader and a ladies' man. He was accompanied by a meek little country girl from near Akron whom he had married but would not long retain. Knowing no foreign languages and no history, he depended on local agents for whatever guidance his trusting charges were to get. Miss Marsh, an elderly Latin teacher, became indignant over the lack of cultural fare. "Mr. Chamberlin," she protested, "I am in Rome!" She took me to the Forum and engaged a guide.

I delighted in the miniature State of the Vatican City and made the rounds of the other Roman sights, but these pleasures were marred by painful hemorrhoids. A local doctor operated.

With my penchant for small countries I was bent on visiting San Marino, so I left my companions and took a train to Rimini. Next morning a bus carried me across the magic border and on across those few miles of rolling country to the sudden central mountain, Titano. At the foot of its thousand-foot cliff lay the market village of Borgo Maggiore with its medieval streets and arches, its donkeys and two-wheeled carts, its hooded, wasp-waisted peasant women. The capital village was perched at the top of the precipice, and was approachable by motor over a series of switchbacks up the gentler back of the mountain. At the gate of the capital village, motor transport ended. The narrow streets formed a steep network of interlocked zigzags. After a moderate ascent I entered the Albergo Titano and was led up several flights to my room, only to find a further little street at the level of my window. The hotel was a fusion of many little old houses strewn up the slope.

I sat on the roof of one of the three medieval towers on the mountaintop and gazed down on Borgo Maggiore and out at the Adriatic and the Appenines. I sat in an outdoor café with the literal-minded name of Bel Vedere, sipping cool moscato and admiring another breathtaking panorama. I felt like a reporter for the *National Geographic*. There was no evidence of other tourists. Times have since changed.

Bob, Roy, and Jack met my train in Florence and we

talked far into the night. After doing some justice to the treasures of Florence, we all went to Venice.

The unearthly charm of its canals, footways, and seagirt palaces must have made most visitors, like me, remember Venice as their favorite city. Wheels are discouraged by the steps on the bridges. Canals and an occasional open square or promenade are what space the buildings when they are spaced at all; the lesser footways are incidental slits, twisting according to the architectural whim of the houses. They branch, they go under cover, emerging suddenly on a little arched bridge over a canal, where rows of old stone, brick, and plaster houses and marble palaces rise sheer from the water. An implausible gondola glides around the bend and under the bridge, just barely, a great cleaver topping its high bow and a standing gondolier, in red sash and broad straw hat, slanting off the stern.

After Venice there was a threefold parting of ways. Bob was cutting his travels short so as to get back to his girl. I was dropping off at Verona to go north and visit another little country, Liechtenstein. Roy was continuing with Jack and his party.

At the Austrian customs inspection I found I had brought Bob's suitcase instead of mine. I had his dirty clothes. From Innsbruck I telegraphed Bob at Milan, where he was stopping with Jack's party; Jack could bring my bag to Interlaken, where I was to join him. I knew no German as yet, so I had my troubles with the telegraphing and the emergency purchases.

In Vaduz, village capital of Liechtenstein, the bank was closed for the weekend and the Gasthof Adler could not cash my traveler's check. Mine host lent me a modicum of spending money, and eventually, by dint of some telephoning on my behalf, my check was cashed. I communicated verbally with nobody. I had been able to blunder along with Italian in San Marino and elsewhere, but German was opaque. Liechtenstein, however, delighted me with its story-book castles—Schloss Vaduz, Schloss Gutenberg—and its towering, rugged mountains.

Europe and After

I walked the two miles from the capital to the railway village, Schaan, lugging the largely useless suitcase, and traveled by a sequence of five trains from there to Interlaken, skirting the precipitous shore of the Wallensee along the way.

Jack arrived with his ladies and Roy and my suitcase, and shipped Bob's to him in Paris. But my passport was in it. My record of incompetence is appalling. There was the tent left in Spearfish Canyon, the satchel left in the Velie in California, the switched suitcases at Verona, and now the passport. A man at the express office telephoned forty miles ahead and had someone board the train there, recover my passport from the bag, and send it back.

Roy and I walked five miles toward the Jungfrau and part way up the slope, but then he begged off and we hitchhiked back. Next day in Lucerne, Miss Marsh saw that I regretted not ascending an Alp, so at her suggestion I made inquiries in French and the two of us were off by car, funicular, and cable car to Trübsee, at the foot of the snows, looking out upon six glaciers, all of an afternoon.

Roy and I took final leave of Jack and the ladies at Heidelberg and went to Strasbourg. Roy turned in early; I prowled the lanes of the old town, fell in with low company, and was robbed of twenty dollars. Roy continued to Paris next day, and I to Luxemburg. There I checked in at a dingy, dirty, noisome, dilapidated dive called the Hotel Chicago. In the large saloon there was an Apache atmosphere. Couples were dancing to a wheezy orchestra under a pall of blue smoke, the men in caps. I roamed the city with enthusiasm—the picturesque old quarter Grund and the environs of the ducal palace. It was my fifth miniature country, one more Graustark.

The next day I spent two hours walking in Arlon, thus adding Belgium; two hours also in the cathedral and old streets of Rheims; and by midnight I was ensconced in a little hotel in the Rue St.-Roch, Paris. Roy, fonder of nice things, was in the Chateau Frontenac. I prowled Paris eagerly and at random the following day, and at length bethought myself that I had not noticed the name or address of my hotel. Ultimately, by luck, I recognized the place.

After a few more days of Paris, Versailles, and Chartres, I joined Roy on the *Montcalm* and crossed from Cherbourg to Montreal, forging sundry shipboard friendships no less cordial than transitory.

The year 1929 was a preternaturally prosperous one, pending the crash in October. My father sensed an ominous inflation of values, but Bob's adventurous young friends were investing what they could and expecting multiple returns. Bob followed suit, not to be deterred by our stodgy old father's conservatism, and so did I. I put my all into Fisk Rubber. Happily my all was a paltry three hundred dollars, for I lost it. Our father came through the crash unscathed.

He subsequently bought land that included the old farm of his grandfather Motz. His holdings grew to a hundred acres, twenty of which he planted with a thousand fruit trees. He did the bulk of the work himself as a hobby. His profile remained low. He never joined a country club, and he never ventured farther beyond our borders than a fringe of Ontario and Quebec. Bob and I inherited our Manx grandfather's penchant for travel, but it skipped our father.

In September 1929 I returned to Oberlin for my final year and settled down to my overdue course in German, among others. My big preoccupation was my honors thesis—"A bit of original work," Jim Sell mocked. "to be completed by January."

I had been fascinated by a symmetrical little formula in Couturat having to do with ways of combining classes. By trial and error I found the general law of which that formula was a special case. The goal I set myself for my honors thesis was a proof of this law within the system of *Principia*. Because the general law treats of number, its proof depended on most of the first volume and a half of *Principia*. Working backwards in *Principia* from requisites to prerequisites, I gained a functionally structured understanding of that work; such was the value of the exercise. It kept me busier, through the fall term, than I had ever been. The proof took eighteen pages of symbols. Three years later in Vienna I got the eighteen pages down to three for the *Journal of the London Mathematical Society*. Today if I were editor I would reject the paper for want of intrinsic interest. But it is a gem of typography.

In my freshman and sophomore years my evenings with girls had been scheduled mainly in Akron, both because of preestablished harmonies and because of the Oberlin curfew. By my junior year, however, an affair had budded and bloomed with Naomi Clayton, a senior in Latin from Toledo, Ohio. During my senior year she got a job selling washing machines in Akron, having graduated. Soon she was rooming in Orchard Road, next door to my home. So my weekends in Akron became as frequent again as the pressure of my honors work allowed.

On one such weekend Naomi and I were invited to a bridge party at the home of a girl whom Naomi had known in Toledo. She had moved with her parents to Jefferson Avenue in Akron for a while in the course of her father's military duty. He was a major, and his name was destined to go down in history: George Patton.

· 1930 My thesis was submitted in January, to Jim Sell's gratification I trust. Eighteen hours of general examinations for honors lay ahead. Meanwhile I was invited by Cairns to review Jean Nicod's *Foundations of Geometry and Induction* for the *American Mathematical Monthly*. Nicod had made a neat contribution to logic years before that was familiar to me, but I had no proper background in the topics of this book. I wrote a respectful and ignorant review and was so callow as to give back the book. Still it was a proud moment when I saw the review in print, my first professional publication, 1930.

My four-year average at Oberlin was under A−, for, as an attentive reader will have observed, my seriousness had not been unflagging. However, thanks to my thesis and my honors examinations, I was graduated *summa cum laude*.

Whitehead, whom I admired as one of the authors of *Principia*, was in philosophy at Harvard, and I resolved on graduate study in that department. This switch of departments was not due solely to Whitehead's affiliation. Mathematics as a steady diet unrelieved by philosophy had appealed to me less than philosophy all along. The thought of a teaching career occupied largely with staple mathematics courses struck me as bleak. The thought of a career occupied largely with expounding the classical philosophers strikes me as bleak too, but happily I was spared that.

My application for a scholarship in philosophy at Harvard was supported by my Oberlin professors, and my honors thesis was sent along in evidence. I was awarded a University Scholarship of four hundred dollars, covering tuition.

It was settled that Naomi would come to Harvard with me and we would marry. Nothing was said to my parents on the point. This was not from fear of disapproval, but from diffidence over matters of sentiment. Actually I was not eager for the marriage. At one point, sitting with Naomi in a car on Portage Path, I even ventured to voice my doubts, but a stronger will prevailed. I tend to shy away from present emotional stress and not to consider what stresses the future may bring. I was ready to consider myself committed.

I needed to earn all I could that summer. The telephone company was introducing dials in Akron, and temporary employees were needed to make the rounds of shops and offices to demonstrate them. Women schoolteachers did most of it, but a few men were needed for strictly male resorts. There were innocent resorts where men sat with their sweet sedimentary coffee talking Greek and playing dominoes, and there were guilty resorts, from speakeasies on down. Such was my job, and an interesting one.

When it terminated, I still had over a week before our departure for Harvard, and I wanted still to contrive a week's pay. I reverted to cartography. Mogadore, a village of a thousand just east of Akron, suited the purpose. I mapped it, on the basis of my exploration and the plat book in the courthouse, and had a zinc etching made. I visited all the merchants there and sold advertising space. The result was a printed sheet under the title "Meet the Merchants of Mogadore," bearing my map surrounded by the advertisements. I undertook to deliver a copy to every house in the village. The whole operation took just a week and netted me the equivalent of a week's pay on the telephone job.

Transplanted 13

Naomi and I hitchhiked to Boston. I had been in fourteen countries, but it was my first time in New England. I was impressed with the Boston accent of a truck driver with whom we rode, particularly when he said we were in Ayer. Our last ride was on a fish truck, from which we dropped into Scollay Square. I took a room in Allston Street, between the statehouse and the courthouse, and Naomi stayed with a cousin in Brookline. My scholarship would have been voided by marriage, but I applied to the department chairman, James Haughton Woods, and got a waiver. We were married in Marblehead by a justice of the peace.

We moved into a furnished room and kitchen in Mrs. Sheehan's house at 13 Howland Street, Cambridge, close to Somerville. Learning that we were from Ohio, she told us that she had a brother in Idaho and that the lady across the street was from "Montano." It's a small world.

We shared a bath with a geology student, Robert Miller, whose room was separated from ours by a thin partition in what had been an open arch. Now and again we talked with Miller in adequately raised voices through the partition. One time some sort of damage had occurred, and I told him through the partition, "The old bitch expects me to pay for it." Footsteps. I had thought she was out.

My father sent money sporadically, and we needed it. We could have leaned on him more heavily, but we wanted to minimize our dependence. We practiced rigid economies, eating usually at home on a weekly grocery budget of five dollars. Naomi worked in a Boston department store while I studied.

Still, there were intervals away from books and sales slips. I was entranced by old Boston. Appreciable portions that dated from Federalist and colonial times were still intact in those days. Old streets still radiated northward and northwestward from Faneuil Hall, each revealing from its farther end a distinctive and tastefully framed slice of that great colonial structure. Tiny Marshall Street, with its tinier seventeenth-century tributaries, was another favorite of mine, not yet having lost its terminal backdrop. Boston's West End was a maze of narrow streets lined with Federalist row houses, neighborhood shops, and pushcarts. It blended smoothly with the North End, oldest of old Boston, and with Beacon Hill, rosy relic of the Federalist years. Much of the old North End and most of old Beacon Hill are standing today, poignant reminders of what more there had been.

As an American I have suffered from a chronic and acute antiquity deficiency. I soak antiquity up as a rachitic soaks up orange juice. Antiquity is the charm of Europe, and a European air was what charmed me in old Boston. It invested the old streets and the life in those streets, for life in the North End was an Italian transplant. Within the sadly narrowed confines of that lovely quarter it still is. Now and again Naomi and I would wander through the little streets and stop for dinner in a simple Italian restaurant, where illicit wine was camouflaged in coffee cups. We also frequented Chinatown. It was bigger than the one in New York, and second only to the one in San Francisco. I learned how to cross downtown Boston by a succession of narrow footways, minimizing the use of ordinary streets. I developed two walking tours, one long and one short, on which I would take visiting friends and relatives.

We prized the colonial lanes of Marblehead and the seventeenth-century houses of Salem. To get there one took the ferry from Rowe's Wharf to East Boston and then the narrow-gauge railroad to Revere Beach and on to Lynn. We soon familiarized ourselves also with the Concord shrines.

After five weeks in Howland Street, our border-crossing propensity impelled us to hitchhike into Rhode Island and

Connecticut. Subsequent outings of the kind netted New Hampshire, Maine, and Vermont. As a pious observance of our first New England Thanksgiving, we hitchhiked to Plymouth. We were surprised and cheered to find the country so heavily wooded between settlements of such long standing as Boston and Plymouth. It was very unlike Ohio.

· 1931   A longer trip was precipitated by a bargain offer over Washington's birthday, 1931: Boston to New York by night bus, two dollars. Seats were overbooked, so emergency busses were added with inexperienced drivers. Our bus was old and without springs. Our driver got lost. Then he ran out of gas, but coasted to a closed gas station and roused the proprietor. After regaining the right road, we overtook a disabled sister bus of the line and stopped to tinker and commiserate. Later a drunken driver, trying to pass us in the face of an oncoming car, careened into a tree and demolished his car. When we finally reached the Bronx we prudently got off and took the elevated. We explored lower Manhattan, took the ferry to Staten Island, the streetcar across the island, and the ferry to Elizabeth, whereupon we hitchhiked to Wilmington, Delaware, and Elkton, Maryland, netting me one new state and Naomi two. Twice in Elkton we were asked if we wanted a justice of the peace. Elkton was a Gretna Green.

A few weeks later Naomi's mother died. I had no cash for the sudden trip to Toledo, and the bank was closed. A bank officer cashed my check for as much as he could spare from his pocket, and then certified another check for the rest of our needs. The cash sufficed for tickets only as far as Buffalo, so we went there on the night train, planning to cash the certified check out there when the banks opened next morning. We got to Buffalo before banking hours, so we took the streetcar to Lackawanna with a view to hitchhiking until the banks opened. We got to Dunkirk, and there the banker refused to honor the certified check. At last I won the battle by getting him to telephone the Dime Bank in Akron for a character reference. We took the next train to Toledo.

Happier trips supervened. We hitchhiked to mountains and climbed them. We visited Jim Sell at Woods Hole and steamed to Nantucket. In June 1931 we flew; it was a ride in a little open plane at Squantum for a dollar and a half, and the start of my half-million airborne miles.

Naomi's father, a retired fireman with a mop of wavy white hair, came to visit. After showing him Boston we showed him New York, going by steamship as one did in those gracious days. In the summer my parents visited us and took us touring through northern New England. We espied Calvin Coolidge and his wife on their porch in Plymouth, Vermont, and I timidly took a poor snapshot of them from the doorway of a barn across the road.

Ed Haskell was with us over our first and second Christmases and for a week in the summer, and he has been our most faithful visitor over the succeeding half century. In that first year he was doing graduate work at Oberlin and writing poetry and a novel, *Lance*. His writings gained zest and novelty from his unusual background, and vigor from his sense of social mission. He was a Marxist then and is the contrary now, but his zeal has never flagged. His talk has been rewarding early and late. Though he has little sense of rigor, he has an eye for significant connections on a grand scale. He has lived frugally down the years, content to settle for the basic necessities and to strive for glory and the good of man.

Other Oberlinians had moved to Harvard, like us, for graduate work. Several were friends, whose company we continued to enjoy. Two Oberlin professors came on leave: Freddie Artz, historian, and Herman Thornton, to whom I owed my pleasures in Old French. But old friends were quickly outnumbered by new ones.

Chief of these, in respect of celebrity, was Whitehead. He radiated greatness and seemed old as the hills. He was sixtynine. He was short and stooped, with heavy shoulders and a bald round head. Mrs. Whitehead was tall and thin, wore flowing garments, and smoked through a long silver cigarette holder. The walls of their flat in Memorial Drive were painted black. The Whiteheads were at home Sunday evenings to graduate students in philosophy and their wives. His salon was one room and hers another, and at mid-evening he and she would change places. Their talk, largely monologous, ran to history, education, literature, and politics. Their political talk punctiliously avoided American politics and was mostly reminiscent, peopled with personages. The young were awed and fearful of gaffes. Spontaneity would rekindle as we emerged into the little streets behind the building.

Mrs. Whitehead spoke disapprovingly of Russell. In the old days he had more money than was good for him, she said, and he would loll on the Riviera while "Alty" grubbed away at *Principia*. She was no doubt unfair, but an opposite unfairness is more usual. Whitehead was more genial. "Bertie thinks I'm muddleheaded," he said, "but I think Bertie's simpleminded." On another occasion Whitehead told me he believed Russell to be the greatest analytic thinker the world has ever known, not excluding Aristotle.

Mrs. Whitehead gave Naomi and me a copy of a best-selling novel, *February Hill*. It was by Victoria Lincoln, the wife of a graduate student in philosophy named Victor Lowe. Thereafter I looked forward to meeting Lowe and, through him, this good writer. Meanwhile I ran into one of my acquaintances from Whitehead's classroom. "Hello, Halpern," I said, and we talked. As we parted he said, "By the way, my name is Lowe." Victor and Vicky were soon our good friends.

Another acquaintance from Whitehead's classroom was Nelson Smith of Smith-Patterson, jewelers. He had studied under Santayana and graduated in 1913, and was now resuming philosophy after success in business. After class one day he took me to lunch in his elegant house in Francis Avenue. He and his attractive wife Margot entertained me with reminiscences of Morocco and the mountains of Hungary (for Hungary had had mountains before 1918).

They had young Nathan Pusey rooming in their house, and James B. Conant and P. T. Bridgman were their summer neighbors in Randolph. The names of Pusey and Conant meant nothing to me then, but Bridgman's was one to conjure with. Famous scientists and successful novelists awed me; I had been aware of none at Oberlin. Randolph, moreover, was in Coos County; I knew that northern proboscis of New Hampshire from the map and longed to press that far. The Smiths earnestly invited us, but I had my treadmill.

After Whitehead's class one morning, Nelson got me to walk with him to the divinity school to hear the new Frothingham Professor, Arthur Darby Nock. Nock performed brightly, with an obstacular English accent and a crotchety, codgerly manner. Afterward, walking down Francis Avenue, I said Nock was a quaint old codger. Nelson shushed me, for Nock and his bowler hat and walking stick were just ahead. I came to know Arthur in later years, and I'd guess that that remark, if he heard it, made his day. He cultivated oddity and affected age beyond his years. When he gave that lecture he was not yet thirty.

A group of graduate students that gathered occasionally for illicit wine and licit parlor games—charades, Twenty Questions—included Nat Sharfman, rough and fierce in aspect, and his pretty, delicate little wife Sylvia. The two could have inspired a Japanese print. Nat had a metaphysical concern for the really real, and Whitehead thought him gifted. He subsequently drove a taxi and died young. Paul Henle and John Goheen were in the group, and a man named Sandusky. Paul and John ended up on distinguished philosophy faculties. Sandy impressed me with his quick intelligence, his wide learning, and his skill at Twenty Questions. Enviably, he was through with his preliminary exams and had only his dissertation to write—a dissertation on Whitehead. His wife Beth taught school, and Sandy sat in their flat trying to write. Somehow he was hopelessly blocked. Eventually he became custodian of the biology laboratories.

Fritz Safier lived in an attic in Appian Way across from the Radcliffe campus. He spoke with a German accent and wrote bizarre introspective sketches in a strange and mannered idiom. He introduced me to writings of Kafka, T. S.

Eliot, and Christian Morgenstern. In his room one reclined, because of the proximity of the roof. From his window I would see Henry Leonard walk up the driveway to the ell that he and Priscilla occupied, an ell heated by a potbellied stove. "Lucky man," I thought. He had his Ph.D. and was an instructor. Not a care in the world.

Philippe and Cécile Devaux visited Harvard from Brussels for a term. The four of us dined at home from time to time on a cooperative basis. He and I started translating something of his, but pressure of studies compelled me to let someone else take over. Philippe distinguished himself as perhaps Belgium's leading philosopher over the next half century.

Through Sheffer's logic class I came to know Ted Palmer. In his detailed knowledge of geographical trivialities he was perhaps my equal. He was still an avid stamp collector, as I had once been. He had a taste for the quaint and curious and an exhaustive repertoire of Gilbert and Sullivan and Lewis Carroll. He had once tried for West Point and missed out because of a defect in vision. He went to Amherst, where he majored at first in classics but ended up with a combined major in history and mathematics and a lieutenancy in the reserve. At Harvard he studied law and then switched to mathematics. His interest in mathematics was narrowing to logic in my day, but he has not published in the subject. He became a professor at Rose Polytech.

For ten years Naomi and I were destined never to live more than a year in one place. We were single-minded in leaving Howland Street. There were problems of space, hot water, shared bath, and an upstairs radio that favored bad music and baseball. The children in the crowded neighborhood were petulant and quarrelsome. I studied at home, there being no smoking in the library; so I suffered.

We moved to a sixth-floor flat at 888 Massachusetts Avenue. It consisted of two small rooms separated by a bath and the world's smallest kitchenette, and it cost us thirty-five dollars a month. We might have stayed for years, had it not been for a subsequent year abroad. It was quiet and the view was panoramic. Construction of the Harvard houses was nearing completion; Eliot, Lowell, and Dunster had their towers. The tower of Memorial Hall was still unscathed, and there were as yet no high uglies to dispute the supremacy of the towers.

Somehow I got to thinking of Monaco with its 0.59 square miles (slightly more now). I made measurements on a map of Cambridge and staked out a triangle of 0.59 square miles whose vertices were visible towers. It was a visual aid to my reverie.

Graduate Study 14

I studied hard, unsure of my adequacy to Harvard standards. My four midyear grades, ranging from A− to A+, reassured me, but there remained another reason for intense work: if I could pass the preliminary examinations in that first year, I might get my doctorate in the next. I was moved by financial insecurity; there was a depression and jobs were scarce. The two-year Ph.D. is rare, but C. I. Lewis suggested I try. I had to grind hard for an even chance at the prelims, for my previous philosophy was meager. The chore courses for me were the historical ones: Woods on Plato, Prall on Leibniz, and especially Lewis on Kant. Lewis required a written synopsis of a chunk of the *Critique of Pure Reason* each week, with a limit on the number of pages. It made for grotesquely crowded pages.

Whitehead was not teaching logic. Sheffer was. He talked of peripheral papers by Oswald Veblen and E. V. Huntington. He mentioned Hilbert, if only to protest his doctrine that mathematics was the manipulation of meaningless marks. "I am not a marksian," he said, "but only a symbol-minded logician." He talked of the elements of *Principia*, and of a nebulous theory of formal systems about which he was proprietary and conspiratorial.

American philosophers associated Harvard with logic because of Whitehead, Sheffer, Lewis, and the shades of Peirce and Royce. Really the action was in Europe. In 1930 and 1931 Gödel's first papers and Herbrand's were just appearing, but there were already other notables to reckon with: Ackermann, Bernays, Löwenheim, Skolem, Tarski, von Neumann. Their work had reached few Americans. E. L. Post worked alone in New York, little heeded. America's logical awakening was still to come, beginning with Alonzo Church's graduate course in the Princeton mathematics department in the fall of 1931. I was unaware of these lacks. The logic that was offered ran thinner than I had hoped, but I supposed that *Principia* was still substantially the last word.

Whitehead lectured on Science and the Modern World and on Cosmologies Ancient and Modern. I responded little, even after accustoming myself to his accent. What he said had little evident bearing on problems that I recognized. His lecture hours were mercifully short and his speech exasperatingly slow. My notes were crowded with doodles. For a term paper I took refuge in his relatively mathematical material on "extensive abstraction." But I retained a vivid sense of being in the presence of the great.

I was less patient with his Ingersoll Lecture of ten years later. Rod Firth tells me I came away exclaiming, "Alfred North Whitehead. Mary Baker Eddy. Jesus H. Christ!"

The reading in Sheffer's course was mostly familiar to me, so I undertook a research paper instead. It was a study of symmetric functions, inspired by my honors thesis. What I achieved is of little interest, and the labor was disproportionate. The proofs of the two main theorems rest on forty-three lemmas, all formally derived in *Principia* notation from formulas proved in *Principia*. The painstakingly inscribed symbols are an appalling sight. I worked at it for two months along with my other studies, and ended up devoting furious full time to it for fifteen days and evenings and one night. There had been a subtle and hydra-headed fallacy. I learned that I cannot be sure of a result until I have clearly explained each step in its final form. In its final form the paper was a model of competence point by point but wanting in vision overall.

I met the language requirement in French and German, but it took me two tries in German. The big hurdle loomed in April: the preliminary exams for the Ph.D. They ran to twelve hours and the mortality was nearly half. I passed them, and so could aspire to a Ph.D. in another year—a two-year Ph.D.

Passing the prelims excused one from final exams in courses, but good marks in the prelims *and* finals qualified one for a master's degree. I thought it prudent to hedge the prospective Ph.D. with an A.M., so in June 1931 I became a master of arts. For the next year I was awarded the James Walker fellowship of eight hundred dollars, only half of which went to tuition.

Whitehead consented to sponsor my dissertation, which would count as half of my quota of courses for the year. In September I took him a sketch of my project. He chuckled and expressed pleasure at getting back to mathematical logic. "That's ripping, old fellow," he said after our two-hour conference. "Right jolly!"

A month later Russell came and gave a lecture, introduced by Whitehead—a dazzling juxtaposition. Afterward Whitehead introduced me to Russell and I told him what I was up to. He seemed interested, and when I sent him the resulting book three years later he responded with generous praise and detailed discussion.

I went to Whitehead's flat every two weeks to report my progress and problems. He would listen until I reached a point suited to a philosophical tangent on his part. The sessions impressed me but yielded little logic. I did carry away two technical terms. I wanted one for the length of a sequence x (why not "length"?) and one for the class $3x$ of all classes to which x belongs. He suggested the *cardinal* of x and the *essence* of x. I recall also his reminiscence of writing *38 of *Principia*—a section that had tickled him because of how it simplified later sections.

Outwardly my dissertation was mathematical, but it was philosophical in conception; for it aspired, like *Principia*, to comprehend the foundations of logic and mathematics and hence of the abstract structure of all science. One of my concerns then and thereafter was ontological: a concern to know or decide what there is or are. Natural science evidently needs, along with its concrete objects, some abstract ones too—thus numbers, functions, and classes. Classes sufficed; one saw from *Principia* how to reduce numbers, functions, and the rest to classes.

Properties were vaguely assumed in *Principia* as further denizens of the universe, but they serve no good purpose that is not better served by classes, and moreover they lack a clear criterion of identity. Two sentences may be true of just the same objects and still not be viewed as ascribing the same property; they must be alike in *meaning*, and likeness of meaning eludes definition.

The notion of a property is one of various notions, called *intensional*, that depend thus on the nebulous notion of meaning. Other examples are necessity, possibility, and idioms of propositional attitude such as belief, hope, regret. My critique of meaning and intensions became more explicit down the years, but we see its beginnings in my dissertation, where I shunned properties.

This was one bid for clarity, and another was my insistence on the distinction between use and mention of expressions: between saying that Boston has twenty councilmen and saying that 'Boston' has six letters. For all its obviousness, the distinction gets lost in subtle ways in mathematical writings, and in *Principia* the confusion issues in mathematical inelegance and philosophical muddles. It was largely by clearing up this confusion, indeed, that I was enabled to dispense with *Principia*'s intensional objects.

I strove for economy of notation and definition. Many notations in *Principia* could be dispensed with in favor of other notations of *Principia* without loss of brevity, and thereupon a sheaf of theorems could be dropped that had served to relate those notations. I also strove for economy in basic concepts and axioms, but here my gains were unappealingly artificial. While I was writing these up, papers by Tarski and Gödel appeared in which the neoclassical conceptual basis for logic and set theory was neatly laid. It comprises just the truth functions ('and' and 'not' will do), quantification ('everything x is such that . . .', 'something x is such that . . .'), and the copula 'ϵ' of class membership. But I was not to know this for a while.

I proved that my axioms and rules and my sixty definitions sufficed for *Principia*. It took 290 pages, deluged with symbols. I got my typewriter altered and began typing seventeen days before the April deadline. Production was slow because of the symbols, which far exceeded the alterations of the typewriter. Carbon copies were required. Naomi helped fill in symbols, but was called away to Toledo; then our friend Georgia Stillman pitched in. Long sleepless and with a week's beard, I took the dissertation to Whitehead's flat in the evening of April 1, 1932, with three hours to spare.

I was still twenty-three when I received my Ph.D. A two-year Ph.D. is inadvisable, apart from strong financial motives such as I felt in those depression years. It precludes the unclocked reflection that best suits scholarship. But my reprieve was in store: four untrammeled years of postdoctoral fellowships. The first of these was Harvard's Sheldon Traveling Fellowship, which, to my inexpressible delight, I was awarded for the following year.

Sheldon Fellow   15

Two friends advised me to start the year at Vienna. One was Herbert Feigl, who had come from Vienna to Harvard on a postdoctoral fellowship. The other was my fellow graduate student John Cooley, who had discovered Carnap's *Logischer Aufbau der Welt*.

The department shared my exalted evaluation of my dissertation and undertook to subsidize its publication by Harvard University Press. I had ideas for its improvement, which the April deadline had forced aside. In order that C. I. Lewis might start it through the press in my absence, I postponed our steamship reservations—a bitter sacrifice—and worked in Akron until mid-August revising the manuscript. I mailed it eight hours before we left Akron for Europe.

Our ship was the *President Roosevelt*, out of New York. Passage was $112 apiece, round trip. We went from Akron to New York by bus, but this economy was rubbed out by a pickpocket as we boarded the bus.

The logic of truth functions had been encapsulated by Nicod in a single long axiom. His proof of this reduction was confusingly expressed, and in later literature the confusion flowered into fallacy. While writing my dissertation I had sent a little article to *Mind,* "A note on Nicod's postulate," setting matters right. It was due to appear and I was eager to see it, for it was my first article. We managed to admire it in the New York Public Library before boarding. I was to learn that Łukasiewicz had published a paper in Polish to the same effect, and more, a few months before.

There were shipboard friendships as always: a bright musician named Sandor Rudnyanski, all Hungarian ebullience, and a young lean chemist and his fat wife, both ugly, who were expatriating to Moscow.

We paused here and there in Normandy and in Paris and Strasbourg, and then settled for a week in Liechtenstein. We walked to every *Gemeinde* in that steep and unlikely land, and I mailed Ted Palmer an envelope from every post office for the postmark. Thence eventually to Vienna by local trains—slow but cheap.

We got to Vienna on September 11, 1932. A boarding house was best, both for economy and for language practice. We settled into one in Thurngasse, but found ourselves among American medical students, to the detriment of our language practice. So we moved to one in Hörlgasse, nearby.

I find this item in a letter I wrote to my parents:

I have written a note to the great Wittgenstein. He now teaches in Cambridge, England, but . . . probably spends his vacations here in Vienna. I want an audience with the prophet. It remains to be seen whether he . . . will act on my request (for he doesn't know how nice I am).

Of course he did not answer. But I had excused him in advance, without yet knowing his ways. I have never seen Wittgenstein.

The university was not due to open for seven weeks. We eagerly nipped the nearby borders of Hungary and Czechoslovakia at Berg and Bratislava, and on September 30 we embarked on the Danube steamer *Schönbrunn* for Svištov, Bulgaria. It was a smaller vessel than usual, because of drought and low water, and it was crowded with migratory workers going home to Serbia and Bulgaria. We stepped over duffle bags and sprawling bodies. We slept on upholstered benches in the saloon. After two days we reached the water gap known as the Iron Gate, between Rumania and Yugoslavia, and were all transferred by tender through the reefs to another steamer that awaited us beyond the shallows.

We disembarked at Svištov. In a bleak station restaurant in Levski, ten miles southwest, I asked where I could telephone; for we were to join Ed Haskell, who was visiting his parents in Pordim, ten miles further along. The man indicated that it would mean walking into the village. Then I asked if we could leave our bags while we walked in. This was going on in German, of which he knew little, and pantomime. He rocked his head, sideways. So Naomi stayed with the bags and I did the errand alone. Days later we learned that the rocking of the head is affirmative, and that the man's supposed ungraciousness was our mistake.

Ed's grandfather had come from America as a missionary when Bulgaria was still Turkish territory. Ed's father, married to a Swiss woman, had continued the work, and the mission evolved into an agricultural school. It was there that we stayed two nights with Ed and his parents and brother.

We walked in the village and over the plain, carrying stout sticks to discourage fierce dogs. We saw low sod-covered shelters and an occasional massive shepherd in shaggy sheepskin cloak and high sheepskin hat, perhaps playing a primitive wooden pipe. Slovenly, low-browed water buffalo plied the roads and plowed the fields and wallowed where they might.

Ed proceeded with us by train. He showed us Sofia and his native Plovdiv, or Philippopolis, a city of wildly Turkish aspect built on seven hills. At Edirne, or Adrianople, in Turkey, we slept miserably in three narrow beds, two of which soon manifested bugs. We ended up crowded into a single bed. Next morning we washed our faces and brushed our teeth at a fountain in the square, fascinating the natives. It was in Adrianople that I learned about *yoghurt,* now so familiar. A soup plate of it sprinkled with coarse sugar made a good breakfast. For coffee we whistled to a man somewhere along the sidewalk, who came in with his brazier and produced the little cups of Turkish brew.

As a child, Ed had lived briefly in Saloniki under the Turks. At a neighboring bakery it had been customary to toss loaves one by one to an army wagon, while a soldier counted them aloud as he received them; and thus Ed had learned to count in Turkish. He also knew "yes" and "no" and how to ask "How much?" and how to say "Coffee without." He taught me these things, but we still needed to know how to ask where there was a good place to eat. He accosted strangers in Bulgarian and presently found a bilingual, who taught us the Turkish equivalent of "Nice food, where can find?". We put this gentle accomplishment to use repeatedly in Adrianople and Constantinople. We would not understand the answer, but the accompanying gestures would put us on course.

In Constantinople, or Istanbul, we stayed in a minimal Bulgarian hotel called Yeni Meseret, in the old quarter that the Turks call Sirkeci and more westerly people call Stamboul. We visited Agia Sophia and the mosques of Achmet and Suleiman and then descended into the Byzantine cistern, a vast flooded cellar that one explores by rowboat. The lone attendant was occupied with another tourist some way off, so we three helped ourselves to a boat and explored. When at length we had rowed back to the steps and landed, the attendant came hurrying toward us, visibly agitated. Abhorring controversy, we fled up the steps and boarded a moving streetcar, foiling our pursuer. We rode it to Yedi Kule, or the Seven Gates, and then walked the length of the great Byzantine wall.

One day we cruised the Bosporus by zigzag ferry, stopping alternately in Europe and Asia. At several stops we stayed ashore to prowl for an hour and pick up the next ferry. I was beside myself with delight at being in Asia. "Look! an Asiatic goat! Asiatic houses!" In the Asiatic town of Scutari, called *Üsküdar*, they sold Asiatic cognac, called *konyak*, in Coca Cola bottles.

For three dollars apiece we took deck passage to Athens on a Genoese ship, *Campidoglio*. A consignment of goatskins afforded us a passable bed, soft and warm but malodorous. We identified and admired the successive Greek islands and headlands as we passed.

The rewards of Athens culminated on the Acropolis in the marble elegance of the Erectheon with its caryatids. Its worthy neighbor the Parthenon was mimicked in the lowlands by the Theseion, which was inferior to it in refinement and superior in being whole. The intervening slope, which I have since learned to call the Plaka, was a region of little streets, chalky houses, and medieval Middle Eastern charm. Luxurious living, in Greece, was priced within our exiguous means. We could drink bottled wine and stay in a hotel that had liveried bellhops.

Mount Parnassus was cloudswept and mysterious as we passed it on the train bound for what had by then resumed the name of Thessalonike. We always tried to capture a whole compartment, so that we could all lie down—two on the wooden benches and one on the floor between. From Thessalonike we proceeded up the Vardar to Skoplje, in the young kingdom of Yugoslavia. Skoplje lies in the southern part of the province and former kingdom of Serbia. It is within the ancient land of Macedonia, which is divided among Greece, Yugoslavia, and Bulgaria. Our hotel in Skoplje overlooked a fresh bomb ruin, the work of Macedonian separatists, Komitaji.

We were bent on indulging my passion for crossing borders by going to Albania. At Prizren we engaged a Turk, in fez and cart, to drive us to the border. South Serbia was more colorfully Turkish than Turkey, for Mustapha Kemal had banned the veil, the red pantaloons, the turban, and the fez, but the Turks in Yugoslavia continued in their old ways.

Soldiers stopped us on our way out of Prizren. Why our interest in the border? They were suspicious because of the Komitaji violence, and doubly so because our medium of communication was Ed's Bulgarian. Macedonian is a dialect of Bulgarian, and the Komitaji were based in Bulgaria. We were allowed to pass on the understanding that our Turk would get us back to Prizren by nightfall if he knew what was good for him. In the miles from there to Albania we were stopped repeatedly by soldiers and sent each time to a commandant for questioning. At the border the Yugoslav commandant allowed us to proceed only on the condition that we deposit our money with him pending our return.

Penniless, accordingly, we faced the Albanian guards. Though we had got visas in Istanbul, they would let us proceed only on the condition that we continue to Kukës and register with the police. This was impossible, even apart from our Turk's concern to get back to Prizren by nightfall, for we had no money for food and lodging at Kukës. We succeeded only in persuading the guard to let us penetrate about fifty yards, accompanied, into Albania.

It was a hostile border. Yugoslavian and Albanian guards eyed each other's boots in hopes of a border violation. Regarding a fortification that ranged up the slope along the border, an Albanian guard said that it was Serbian, not Albanian; the Serbs are plainsmen and need forts, but the Albanians are mountaineers and can do without. Still, for all the tension, barefoot Albanians in their eponymous white skullcaps strode the slopes heedless of any border.

Night had long since fallen when we got back to the gates of Prizren. A soldier took our horse by the bridle and conducted us all to his commandant, who consigned the three of us to a hotel of his choosing. We were taken to Urosevac next morning and put on the train with orders not to leave the railway until we were out of Yugoslavia.

Ed left us at Niš, Constantine's birthplace, and headed back to Bulgaria. Naomi and I recovered our spirits in Budapest, admiring the riverfront palaces and enjoying *palacsinka* and Gipsy music in the Café Emke in Karoly Kiraly Ut. Budapest contrasted markedly with Vienna. The Viennese were despondent and economically depressed and there were many beggars. Budapest was cheerful, vital. There was the difference in what had been left to the two countries by the Treaty of Versailles; residual Austria was mostly mountains while residual Hungary was fertile plains. But also there was the irrepressible Hungarian temperament.

Vienna   16

Our boarding house in Hörlgasse, Vienna, was the Pension Wagner-Szamvald, owned by Hungarians. We became good friends with Rudi Stern, an Austrian in the boarding house, and his Irish wife Vera, who believed in ghosts and had photographic evidence of them somewhere or other among her effects. I looked on with ill-concealed revulsion when Rudi unwrapped a block of hog fat, pared off a wedge with his penknife, and ingested it with relish. He called it *Speck*, but I saw no trace of red bacon. A fat deficiency is an effective appetizer. I learned further, when Christmas came, that a can of sliced pineapple was a respected present in the Vienna of that day. At the Christmas festivities I also learned, from the Hungarian proprietor, what I took to be a useful

Hungarian toast: [godəlu:k]. At some point it dawned on me that he was saying "Good luck."

We moved from Hörlgasse to a cheaper and larger room, sumptuously furnished, in Schwarzspanierstrasse. I had a vast desk. The rent, equivalent to thirty-five dollars a month, included breakfast and dinner, served in our room, and such maid service as cleaning, bringing water, and maintaining the tiled Swedish stove. It also included one bath apiece a week; elsewhere a bath could cost extra. We were given a key to the building, saving the forty groschen that one would pay the janitor to be let in after ten. Fuel was extra, about six cents a day. We were the only roomers. Frau von Flesch, the landlady, lived mainly by translating. Manuscripts from past translations provided the toilet paper. Her son, she said proudly, was a *Schriftsteller*. To me the word wryly represented the sheer setting down of sentences as the essential business, with any content as a by-product. We forget that our word "writer" does the same.

Elevators in Viennese department stores were perpetually moving belts bearing a continuous succession of open cubicles to step into. They were admirable. Elevators in apartment houses were like American elevators, but required five groschen in the slot, a groschen being an eighth of a cent. Whether a house had an elevator or not, therefore, the lower floors represented a saving—whether of effort or of groschen. This preference was reflected in a euphemistic nomenclature. What in America would be called the first, second, third, and fourth floors, and in England the ground, first, second, and third, were marked *Parterre, Hochparterre, Mezzanin*, and, at long last, *Erster Stock*.

I attended Moritz Schlick's lectures at the university that fall, less for philosophy than for language practice, and read various things in German, at first painfully with a dictionary. We found two intensive courses in German for foreigners, introductory for Naomi and intermediate for me, and plunged into them for a month. I also plugged away at research in logic, with little to show for it. I kept hoping to hear from Harvard of progress on my book; nearly five months passed without word, despite my letters.

There were no lecture courses in logic. I tried philosophy courses in addition to Schlick's, but was soon discouraged. Swoboda's course, though listed, was not meeting. Other courses were unpredictable; professors would fail to appear. Rudolf Carnap, Vienna's main attraction, had moved to Prague. Inquiry revealed a philosophical society, which I tried, but its concern proved to be the history of metaphysics, and I drifted off. I concluded that command of German was the most I could hope for from Vienna, and I wrote to Berlin, Göttingen, Warsaw, and Prague to explore possibilities there. Berlin had nothing to offer in logic, nor even did Göttingen just then. My response from Prague was a hearty welcome from Carnap, who was to visit Vienna and would talk with me. I had an equally hearty welcome from Łukasiewicz in Warsaw, assuring me that he, Leśniewski, and Tarski would make my visit worthwhile, despite my lack of Polish, by abundant private discussion in an intelligible language.

After an overdue interview with Schlick, the philosophical complexion of Vienna improved. He told me of a little circle of his—known to history as the Vienna Circle, no less—and invited me to come regularly. I attended the next day; they met weekly. Those present included four mathematicians. One was young Gödel, whose slowly but surely world-shaking proof of the incompletability of number theory had appeared the year before. The other three were Karl Menger, Hans Hahn, and Hahn's sister Olga. She was married to Otto Neurath, who was off visiting in Moscow; I did not meet him until seven years later. She was blind and smoked long, thin, crooked stogies, called Virginien, with straw mouthpieces. Of the philosophers present I recall only Schlick and Waismann. Friedrich Waismann was a *Privatdozent*, which meant that his income depended on his enrollment, a low figure. He conducted Schlick's proseminar, and rumor had it that Schlick supplemented Waismann's pay from his own packet. That first evening's paper was a report by Waismann on Bridgman's *Logic of Modern Physics*.

Carnap contracted a fever on arriving in Vienna. I met him in the hospital and we settled on March 1 for the move to Prague. Meanwhile I continued to attend lectures, and by January was understanding every word; early in November, I had not been catching half.

I was to speak to the Vienna Circle on January 20. I prepared a résumé in German of my dissertation. What with blackboard work it went on for an hour and a half, followed by lively discussion. I had been miserably apprehensive, and was much relieved. At that meeting I met Freddie Ayer, now Sir Alfred. He was a newly graduated pupil of Gilbert Ryle's at Oxford and had come to Vienna for a few months with his wife Renée, who later became Lady Hampshire. Freddie's French was fluent, but his German was still inadequate, so he borrowed my dissertation to eke out my lecture.

The Ayers, Naomi, and I were together frequently in the next five weeks. Renée had recently gone around the world, and had crossed North America by motorcycle, weaving in and out of Mexico. She and Freddie were resourceful in matters of shopping and cooking. Two years later, with his influential *Language, Truth, and Logic*, Freddie became the Vienna Circle's best-known spokesman for English readers.

Word about my book came at last from Harvard, and it was bleak. The available funds had shrunk. I hit upon a simplification of notation that would save expense. It meant preparing some fifty pages anew, and incidental improvements ran the revision up another twenty-five.

The old imperial palace, the Hofburg, is embedded among the little streets of old Vienna. Our oft-trodden geodesic to the American Express Co. cut through the midst of all this and never turned monotonous. Occasional long walks, up to eighteen miles, took us through the Vienna Woods or to the high outlook at Kobenzl or the baroque monastery Kloster Neuburg. It was in crossing outer Vienna by successive trams preparatory to one such walk that I became aware of the outlandishness of the Viennese dialect. I had supposed that the accent of cosmopolitan Vienna and a few distinctive words were all there was to it. The real thing proved impenetrable.

The Liechtenstein family were powerful in Vienna long before the founding in 1719 of their little principality on the Rhine. Their twelfth-century castle stands high on a precipitous rock south of Vienna, its sheer walls bristling with turrets and sculptured balconies. In its slimness it would look precarious if the viewer could believe in its solid reality.

Schlick told me that Hans Reichenbach might be visiting from Berlin in a few days—on February 28—and that my wife and I might drop in around eight if we wanted to meet him. We were to take the train for Prague the same evening, so as to dodge an Austrian rail strike that was set for midnight. Eight was an odd hour for a casual call in Europe, but, we reflected, Schlick had lived in America and married an American. We moved our year's luggage to the station, ate hurriedly, and got to Schlick's flat at eight. Despite the casualness of the invitation, it was a state dinner for some twenty guests. We choked down a second dinner and were consoled in our attire by the fact that Reichenbach also was in street clothes.

Thence to the night train and across the border. We waited two of the small hours for our next train and then missed it, failing to understand the Czechish announcer. It was late afternoon when we dropped off in Prague.

Prague and After   17

It's longitude's very uncertain,
Its latitude's equally vague,
*   But there ne'er was a city*
*   So wise or so witty*
As the beautiful city of Prague.

I quote it not for any intrinsic merit, but because I had it from Whitehead. Prague was indeed a beautiful old city, but we began miserably in it. Exhausted on arrival, we set out on a four-day quest for a cheap and acceptable place to stay. We roamed the streets, inquiring in every house that bore the placard "Pokoj," and finally collapsed into some cheap hotel, to renew the quest the next morning. Late in the third day we settled on a tiny room, transferred our luggage from the station, and stowed and arranged our belongings before retiring, just for the joy of being settled. When at last we got to bed, the bugs began to bite; we we were out hunting for a room again the next morning. We ended up in a clean but sparsely furnished room six stories up in the Pension Fišer, Na Petrska 3, in the picturesque Stare Město. There was no elevator, but the ceilings, unlike those in Vienna, were mercifully low.

The next day was an infamous one across the border: Hitler came into power. Luckily we had not been drawn to Göttingen. The full horrors of Nazism were still unimagined, but we had seen something in Vienna of the Nazi spirit. Demonstrators had strewn streets with swastika confetti and painted *"Juda dein Ende"* and *"Kauft nicht bei Juden"* on the walls.

We were overwhelmed by the kindness of the Carnaps. He had written me twice with information and sent a map. I attended his lecture the day after our arrival, and he invited us to their house. Meanwhile his Viennese wife Ina, hearing from him of our lodging problem, tramped the streets with us for three hours, talking broken Czechish with the landladies.

Carnap's lecture room was in the physics institute, Na Venecna. It had been Einstein's. Carnap shared it and Einstein's old office with Philipp Frank, who had succeeded to Einstein's chair. I attended one lecture of Frank's on hydrodynamics. Naomi and I dined with Frank and his pretty Ukrainian wife Hanya at their flat in Srbska Ulic, in a new upland quarter of Prague called Bubeneč. Frank told me I was the first American he had met, never guessing that in six years he would be one himself.

I eagerly attended Carnap's lectures. He was expounding his *Logische Syntax der Sprache,* which Ina was typing. Carnap lent me the typescript sheaf by sheaf. Days when he was not lecturing, Naomi and I would go to their flat at Pod Homolkou, just beyond the tram line at the west edge of Prague. He and I would discuss his work while Naomi and Ina chattered in their fashion. Naomi would protest when Ina invited us to stay for supper, but Ina would ask "What would happen?" and, having no reply to make, we would stay. But it was made clear that after supper there could be only small talk, no "science," or Carnap would have a sleepless night. He was a big man, mild and genial, with a stern regimen. No alcohol, no tobacco, no coffee.

My study of German in Vienna yielded lavish dividends in Prague, for my dealings with Carnap were in German. It was my first experience of sustained intellectual engagement with anyone of an older generation, let alone a great man. It was my most notable experience of being intellectually fired by a living teacher rather than by a book. One goes on listening respectfully to one's elders, learning things, hearing things with varying degrees of approval, and expecting, as a matter of course, to have to fall back on one's own resources and those of the library for the main motive power. One recognizes that the professor has his own work to do, and that the problems and approaches that appeal to him need not coincide in any very fruitful way with those that are exercising oneself. I could see myself in the professor's place, and I sought nothing different. I suppose most of us go through life with no brighter view than this of the groves of Academe. So might I have done, but for the graciousness of Carnap.[1]

Carnap gave me buckram-bound copies of his great *Logischer Aufbau der Welt* and his little *Abriss der Logistik* and a full

---

1. I have borrowed a half page from my *Ways of Paradox,* second edition.

array of articles. At his seminar I repeated my Vienna talk. One day at his wry suggestion I dropped in at the Clementinum to hear Oskar Kraus, an opponent of the Vienna Circle and of Einstein. On another day Naomi and I were startled to find Ed Haskell at our door, resplendent in a new red beard. He engaged an adjacent room for a few days and provided the occasion for some overdue sight-seeing, to the accompaniment of his burgeoning theories.

There was bleak news again from Harvard about my book. I took it hard. And what about a job? The new chairman, Ralph Barton Perry, would only be vaguely optimistic. Then came a cablegram from Whitehead that dispelled all gloom and fulfilled my fondest dreams. I had been elected to Harvard's new Society of Fellows, which was to begin operations in the fall. It meant three years with a comfortable stipend, attractive perquisites, and complete freedom to pursue my researches as I pleased.

It was accordingly with light hearts that we boarded a train on April 6, 1933, for a southern vacation. My Italian was sketchy, and with a view to firming it up I had bought a manual in Prague. I had had to settle for Langenscheidt's *Sprachführer*, and I studied this on the train. It was a perverse way into Italian. Picture the soft Italian *c* and *g* explained phonetically as *tsch* and *dsch* in the thorny traditional German print.

We reveled again in the delights of Venice. I was tickled by a succinct snatch of dialogue with a native of whom I was asking directions in my new language. *"So." "Sa?" "Sì."* ("I know." "You know?" "Yes.") Padua, Ferrara, Ravenna, and Rimini passed our inspection, with highest marks to Ravenna for the cool, naive serenity of the Early Christian mosaics. On then to San Marino, whose charm after four years was undiminished. Having renewed my good memories of Borgo beneath and the capital above, we struck out to the village of Faetano in the southeast corner of the tiny republic. The way consisted of paths, stony lanes, fields, and a creek bed. We reached the mountaintop hamlet at dusk. The villagers stood listening to a German broadcast and asked me what it was. It was a children's story. There was no inn, so we walked back to the capital in the night.

We hit Rome disgracefully: hit and run, for it was Holy Week and indeed the nineteenth centenary of the crucifixion. By nine in the evening we were in Naples, seeking in vain a hotel that was neither full, dear, nor dirty. At midnight we entrained for Sicily and slept well on the wooden benches, having rented cushions for a dime at the station. Dawn revealed the mountainous and castled coast of Calabria, from which we ferried to Sicily and settled into Taormina. Ever since Assisi it had been headlong flight.

On the slopes of Etna we fell in with a young German anthropologist vacationing from Trier. He traveled light and knowledgeably with a knapsack. We had haggled in the Balkans, but he disclosed a new level of sophistication in the art of haggling. When you have offered your maximum, he said, hold the amount out in the palm of your hand and withdraw it coin by coin, rending the poor merchant's heart. It works. Also he reported that the most economical fare in that place-time was artichokes and eggs, in a *trattoria*. We happily complied. We left him at the waterfront in Catania, where he bargained with Greek skippers for a crossing of the Ionian Sea.

At Syracuse we took steerage passage on the *Città di Palermo* to Libya, on our fourth and darkest continent. There was a men's dormitory and a women's, and on each bunk a burlap pad. Everyone was issued an aluminum dish with which to queue at a window for *pasta*.

Tripoli: narrow passages, Arabs, Berbers, black Sudanese, fezzes, turbans, burnooses, veils. There were veiled men, Tuaregs perhaps; a long band of linen served as hood, veil, and wrap. The white Arab city extended from the Italian waterfront inland a half mile to open desert and camels. I drank palm wine in the shop of a formidable red-sashed Berber who strained the stuff into a tumbler from a big urn whose neck was stuffed with coconut fibre. In the market we ate eggs and potato cooked in delicate pastry envelopes that were dropped into a vat of hot oil. Seven hours of this and we were aboard ship again, bound for Malta.

Maltese women wore broad hoods, canopies on wire frames. The language, written with an abundance of q's and x's in unlikely places, was said to be an Anglo-Italian corruption of Arabic; I learned later that experts trace it to Punic. I also learned later, from George Hanfmann, that sensational neolithic remains were being uncovered just about then. Our own most rewarding sight was the dry old walled town of Medina, or Città Vecchia, across the island.

Then we were off again to Sicily, to the timeless serenity of the Greek temples by the sea at Acragas, the rugged and jumbled interior of the island, the ordered magnificence of Monreale. The great palace in Palermo and the little cloister of San Giovanni degli Eremiti were fascinating in their Arabo-Norman incongruity, but a fascist soldier marred my day by threatening us with his bayonet when we approached the cloister.

We sailed to Naples, visited Pompeii, and made our amends to Rome, compulsively visiting everything in three days. Maintaining the same pace, we did Florence in a day and a half—and not unappreciatively. We had a technique. We would stop walking only while looking at something, rather than stopping between sights. We would lunch on bread, salami, cheese, and pastry while walking, and would sit to a meal only after dark.

Finally Bologna, Verona, and off to Vienna for an evening with Rudi and Vera Stern in Hörlgasse.

Warsaw and After   18

The train from Vienna to Warsaw, May 5, 1933, was fast and made few stops. Our year's luggage was stowed under the wooden seats and on the racks. We were joined by two pleasant young men and talked with them in German. A vendor came through and we bought tea, in glasses. When the train subsequently slowed to a stop, our companions said hurriedly that we must change trains. One man proceeded to help me get our trunk-suitcase from under the seat. It seemed odd that we had to change trains, but it was no time for questions. To our further bewilderment, the men then left, telling us to stay aboard. Our train moved on with us to Warsaw.

I discovered only in Warsaw that the men had got off with my wallet. They had seen when I paid for the tea that I put the wallet in my side pants pocket. The trunk-suitcase maneuver had served to gape the pocket so that one of the men could pluck out the wallet. It was a marvel of engineering. My reconstruction of the crime was confirmed when my wallet arrived at the office of the American Express correspondent in Warsaw, bereft of its few złoty but retaining its travelers' checks. It had been dropped in a mailbox at the junction point for Łódż.

It was midnight when we got off in Warsaw after our fourteen-hour ride, and three in the morning when we settled on a makeshift hotel room.

Łukasiewicz was solicitous to the point of creativity. He guessed that I would call at the agency Orbis for mail, and he arranged with them to phone him when I did so. Thus it was that he, his wife, Naomi, and I were together in a café at noon directly after that rigorous first night. We went home with them and I talked logic for hours with him while his wife worked on our lodging problem by telephone. They had us stay for lunch—four o'clock in Poland—and we were joined afterward by Leśniewski. The two professors were neighbors in the seventeenth-century Stare Miasto, the one picturesque quarter of Warsaw. Talk continued for another two hours while Naomi and Mrs. Łukasiewicz, unsuccessful at the telephone, went out and searched the city for lodgings. They found only dirty rooms at high prices. At length Łukasiewicz phoned a hotel and got a quotation for the night. We planned to contiunue the search with their help the next day.

We had been with them eight hours. When we got to the hotel we learned that the rate quoted to Łukasiewicz had been for a single occupant; so we set out into the night, searching further. We settled into the Hotel Victoria, Ulic Jasna 26, and this became our home throughout our stay in Warsaw. It was a small room with a narrow bed, and, as I wrote to my parents, the rate was "very high in comparison with the rest of Europe when figured for a three-week period." How high? Seventy cents a night. *Eheu*, once more, *fugaces*.

Naomi contracted blood poisoning in her leg, and it spread alarmingly. I got a doctor through the American consul, but he understood none of my few languages adequately. When Łukasiewicz heard of the case, he rushed Naomi to the hospital and invoked the best treatment.

While she was in the hospital I took many meals in the Jewish quarter, because of the degree of mutual intelligibility of Yiddish and standard German. I also dined with Tarski and his wife Marja in their flat downstream at Żoliborz (Jolis Bords). Once also the Leśniewskies invited me to dinner, *Sonnabend*. A sensible word, I reflected; why say Sun*day evening?* But on Sunday morning I had an alarming thought: what if it means Sunday *eve*, hence Saturday? The dictionary bore me out, and I rushed to the Stare Miasto to apologize for having missed the party. I had known Saturday only as *Samstag*.

Łukasiewicz's kindness to us would have been extraordinary in anyone, and was the more so in the dean of Polish logicians and former Minister of Education under Paderewski. Leśniewski and Tarski likewise were unstinting of their time and hospitality. One day, after attending lectures for four hours, I spent several hours in random discussion with Tarski, Lindenbaum, and others in the logic seminar. Next day I was at Leśniewski's house discussing with him from ten until two, and then Naomi and I were with the Łukasiewiczes from five until eleven; there was tea and talk in their home followed by music and talk in a fancy café. The day after that we were with the Łukasiewiczes for nine hours;

first a concert (my treat for once), then dinner at their house, and finally a walk across the Vistula into Praga, where we wandered into a Russian wedding.

I went regularly to Tarski's vigorous, high-level seminar, in which for my sake he banned Polish in favor of German and French. I went to Leśniewski's lectures, which consisted in filling the blackboard with formulas; no language problem there. I went to Łukasiewicz's lectures, which were two hours long with a recess. Formulas helped; for the rest, he would brief me in German before and after the lecture and during the recess.

So much time went into discussion with these three generous men, and into studying the articles in French and German with which they plied me, that I had no time to study Polish. With Leśniewski I would argue far into the night, trying to convince him that his system of logic did not avoid, as he supposed, the assuming of abstract objects. Ontology was much on my mind.

I met Kotarbiński, Ajdukiewicz, Kuratowski, Sobociński, and Jaśkowski. Sobociński, thin and frail, spoke only Polish and Russian; Leśniewski interpreted him for me into German. But he lived to be a robust American professor. Jaśkowski chose to write his pioneer paper on natural deduction in English, and I helped him.

I presented a paper in Tarski's seminar that was substantially what I had presented in Vienna and Prague. My ideas, however, were getting healthily dislodged; I was catching up with latter-day logic. I had bitterly suppressed all thoughts of my book, for the duration of the *impasse* at Harvard; but in Warsaw's bright light I was suddenly grateful for the delay. Thoughts flooded in, some of them newly conceived and others perhaps resuscitated from unconscious levels to which I had meanwhile suppressed them. On the midnight train out of Warsaw, as May turned to June, I happily began outlining drastic revisions.

It was a northbound train. We went to Königsberg, as Kaliningrad was called in Kant's day and mine. Nazi Germany was already bristling with militarism. We soon continued to

Tilsit, crossed the Niemen into peace-loving, ill-starred Lithuania, and subsided into Klaipeda, *quondam* Memel.

A Soviet freighter was anchored in the harbor. Beyond our reach there was a rowboat. Boys were playing on a rope that was strung across the water, and I got one of them to cross over and fetch me the rowboat. I rowed out and boarded the Russian ship. Sailors were smoking cigarettes rolled in newspaper. The skipper knew German, and I came to terms with him for passage to Helsinki and Leningrad. The figure seemed very low even then, even to me; so it must have been a great bargain. The hitch was that we would need visas. We tried to get them but were told that it would take a month.

Lowering our sights, we took a train to Latvia. Just barely; just to the village of Priekule, slightly over the border. There was a simple little wooden hotel and, down the road, a restaurant. We took a room in the one and a leisurely dinner in the other. When we returned to the hotel, it was locked; we had to be let in. We were amazed to find that it was nearly midnight, though just dark. The season had advanced one day since Klaipeda, our latitude had advanced a hundred miles, and the effect was as if we had rounded a shoulder of the earth. It was my farthest north, and remained so for twenty-six years.

Our next new country was an addition to my prized collection of miniature states: Danzig. It was bigger than Andorra, which was still a remote agendum, but smaller than Luxemburg. We looked into Marienwerder in Danzig's hinterland and Neufahrwasser and Zoppot on the coast, and we admired the ornate Hanseatic houses in the mellow center of the rich old capital. These glories were smashed, years later, and the state receded into history. Today new history is in the making, in the name of Solidarność.

At Stettin, as we used to call it, we boarded a ship for Copenhagen. As she slipped down the estuary a group of young Germans aboard raised harmonious voices in the "Lorelei."

In spick and span Copenhagen we took a room in a little hotel on the wharf of Nyhavn and were devoured by bedbugs. The manager blamed them, not implausibly, on a foreign sailor. When we had done summary justice to the corkscrew steeples and the Tivoli gardens, we rode the ferry to Malmö. It yielded us another country, Sweden. It was my thirtieth, with two more in the immediate offing. Not bad for a youth of twenty-four, though as a man of seventy-five I boast 113. In other respects Malmö was unrewarding. If we had known more we would have walked on a few miles and had a look at Lund.

From Copenhagen we took the night steamer to Lübeck, in steerage as usual, and were issued hammocks. The sea was choppy. As we sat in our hammocks in the evening, swinging gently and idly conversing, we found ourselves on the verge of seasickness. We went to the deck and I proceeded to expound Cantor's proof that there are more irrational numbers than ratios. Naomi had to concentrate to follow the proof, and I in those days had to concentrate to get it straight; and thus the threat passed. It was mind over matter.

As we were walking across Lübeck, a healthy-looking idler asked me for money. I refused, and he responded with an arrogant remark about the new Germany and grim days in store for America. Here in person, I sensed, was the new Germany indeed.

We added another country by taking a train slightly into the Netherlands. At Winschoten, a town of trim little brick houses, we applied at a trim brick hotel. The clerk was unfriendly and denied having a room. It came to me later that it was because he thought we were Germans; I was using German.

We took the next train back to Germany. It stopped at Nieuwe Schans, the Dutch border town. I ran into the station to buy postcards and encountered a group of hostile young Dutchmen. Instead of responding hostilely to hostility as one instictively does, I flashed my passport; for after all I shared their hostility to the new regime across the border. Affability supervened.

At nearby Leer, in the German part of Frisia, our reception was again unfriendly. The Dutch had thought we were German because I spoke German; the Germans thought we were Dutch because I spoke German imperfectly. But we got a room, and the next day we went on to Hamburg. The central quarter along the Alster was picturesque then. There were narrow streets and massive old warehouses with tackle dangling from their beetling lofts.

We had kept a green memory of the alluring green scene at Cobh in Ireland from ten months before, when our ship had anchored and a tender had taken a dozen enviable passengers ashore. We learned that on our return voyage from Hamburg to America we could get off at Cobh and continue on the next ship of the line a week later. Thus it was that on June 14, 1933, we sailed on the *President Roosevelt* again, but only to Ireland.

Fifteen hundred dollars went a long way in those days, and we had gone a long way on ours. It would have been a deplorable waste of opportunity not to go as far as we could. We had done so, and with all our frugality we were about at the end of our resources. Ireland was a free ride, thanks to the steamship arrangement, except for the week ashore. In the course of the year I had learned my haggling in sterner schools than Ireland, and I brought it to bear on the landlady of a boarding house in Cobh. We struck a deal for the week. On maturer reflection later, she regretted the figure and asked if we would mind leaving. But the ship had sailed, our poverty was dire, and I had to hold her to our bargain.

Irish railways offered cheap tickets, good for unlimited travel within a specified area for a week. Ours was County Cork. We went to Ballydehoy and Ballineen, to Schull and Skibbereen, to Baltimore and Cork. We looked out on Fastnet from the peat bogs on Mount Gabriel, and we kissed the Blarney Stone. We exceeded County Cork only at one point, when we walked across the bridge from Youghal, Sir Walter Raleigh's home, into County Waterford.

In Cork we quarreled like fishwives. I have forgotten what it was about. I may have been at fault, for I am impatient; but it emerged over the years that Naomi was given to unreasonable manic phases, alternating with phases of depression.

The bus ride from New York to Akron on June 29 left us with seven dollars. We spent the summer with my parents at Ellan Vannin, except for visits to relatives in Toledo and to old Arthrites—Ἄρθρον hands of Oberlin days—in Ann Arbor, Napoleon, and Cleveland. I reviewed a volume of Peirce's papers and worked on my book.

Et in Arcadia Ego 19

The founding fathers of the Society of Fellows were Lawrence J. Henderson, A. Lawrence Lowell, and, in a secondary way, Whitehead and John Livingston Lowes. Henderson was a blood physiologist turned sociologist. Lowell was the retiring president of Harvard. Lowes was the author of the celebrated *Road to Xanadu*. The million that launched the enterprise was Lowell's gift, anonymous at the time. About eight college graduates from anywhere, aged under twenty-eight, were to be elected each year to a three-year Junior Fellowship, thus maintaining a quota of about twenty-four. The annual stipend was $1250 if the man was under twenty-five when elected, and otherwise $1500, plus room and board in one or another of the palatial new Houses. If the man was married he received an additional $750 in lieu of room and board, but he was still given a study and non-resident membership in one of the Houses and all the meals he cared to take. Fellows had the privileges of library, laboratory, and classroom, but could not take courses for credit. They could use their time as they pleased.

The governing board, called Senior Fellows, comprised the four founding fathers and, *ex officio*, the new president of Harvard and the Dean of the Faculty of Arts and Sciences. These were James Bryant Conant and Kenneth Murdock. A seventh was Charles Pelham Curtis, a lawyer and member of the Harvard Corporation. We Junior Fellows were alarmingly privileged that first year, for the distinguished Senior Fellows outnumbered us at table seven to six.

A richly paneled lounge and dining room had been built for the Society within Eliot House. Each Monday during term the Senior and Junior Fellows and a few guests met in these rooms for sherry and dinner. We dined well. Henderson, the chairman, was a Francophile, an oenophile, and a gourmet. Prohibition had been repealed in the nick of time, and Henderson had enlisted the aid of his friend Blanchard, a geographer at Grenoble, in stocking the Society's cellar with Vosne-Romanée and Gevrey-Chambertin.

At each place there was a candlestick, two troy pounds of silver, engraved with a fellow's name. At the end of his incumbency the fellow was to be presented with it, and permitted to buy another at cost. For years the cost was sixteen dollars; now it runs into hundreds. What with one occasion and another—Junior Fellowship, Senior Fellowship, second marriage, retirement—I now have five.

The dinners were for conversation. Speeches and papers were banned. There was late lingering over port and madeira, which moved along the table in a silver cart presented by President Lowell. The table was said to have been the very breakfast table of Oliver Wendell Holmes, and it was presided over in an ornate highbacked chair by our own autocrat, L. J. Henderson. He was bald and had an ample, reddish beard and a penetrating cold, pale eye. Vilfredo Pareto was his guiding light. He was quick to detect or to suspect rationalization and self-deception, and to bear down on the young offender. He was a force for good.

Lowes was a little man in his late sixties, with a heavy head of black hair, a deep voice, and a prematurely failing memory. Lowell was seventy-seven, rubicund, with white hair and flowing white moustache, an ideal image of statesmanly eminence. Charlie Curtis, like Lowell a Boston Brahmin, was still in his forties. He had been partly cured of a stammer, and the remedial cliché that he kept interjecting was "what's 'er name." He had wide interests in an unscientific way and enjoyed working at Homer.

One of the Junior Fellows that first year was the psychologist B. F. Skinner. Fred exceeded the age limit by well over a year. The Senior Fellows had established their flexibility by thus breaking their own rule in their first election, to everyone's benefit. Fred and I were congenial, sharing an interest in language and a behavioristic bias in psychology. It has been wrongly assumed that I imbibed my behaviorism from Fred; I lately learned from his autobiography that in fact my exposure to John B. Watson slightly antedated his. It was particularly in language theory, rather, that Fred opened doors for me. My linguistic interest had run to etymological detail; he put me onto Bloomfield and Jespersen and gave me a first American edition of John Horne Tooke.

Another Junior Fellow that year was Garrett Birkhoff, like his father a mathematician and now, like Fred and me, a Harvard professor emeritus. The others were John Chester Miller, a second-generation Swede from Seattle working on Samuel Adams; Tom Chambers, a pupil of our subsequent friend and neighbor George Kistiakowsky in chemistry; and Fred Watkins, in government.

Before the Harvard Houses were established, a segment of Mount Auburn and Bow Streets had been occupied by private buildings in which rich students had their lodgings along, in extreme cases, with their valets. Two of the buildings that came to constitute Adams House had been a sumptuous part of this Gold Coast. Adams was the House to which I was assigned for non-resident privileges. A more commonplace relic of the Gold Coast was Ridgely Hall, at 65 Mt. Auburn Street; there Naomi and I succeeded in engaging a three-room flat for under thirty-nine dollars a month on the condition of a two-year lease.

My study in Adams House was excessive on two counts. It consisted of two big rooms, though sketchily furnished, and it was absurdly near our flat, where I had a study. But I made a point of working in Adams House part of the time, to show my appreciation. I looked out on what I called the Piazzetta di San Paolo, at the junction of Bow and Arrow Streets. It is flanked by the Italian-style church of St. Paul, complete with campanile, and Longfellow Courts, which could also fit plausibly into an Italian scene.

The high and spacious rooms that were my study in Adams House were a heritage of the Gold Coast. So were the unusally lavish common rooms and a big swimming pool, the only one in the Harvard Houses. Hating to waste an asset, I swam regularly, though not very fond of swimming.

The tutors' table at Adams House was frequented by the young sociologist Talcott Parsons, the young historian Charles Taylor, the rising economist Ed Mason, the philosopher Raphael Demos, and a bushy-browed instructor in government from the wilds of Craig, Colorado, named Overton H. Taylor and known as Nat because of his preoccupation with natural law.

Naomi started a project of teaching art appreciation and German to children in our flat while I worked in Adams House. Also we took to holding open house on Thursday evenings for German conversation. Friends converged in increasing numbers. We would practice German for a dutiful period, and then English would break through with an access of pent-up wit and spirit.

Though we had been outraged by Nazism from the start, our attachment to the language continued. We had learned it in Austria, not Germany, and it had been the medium of my intellectual *Wiedergeburt* in Prague and Warsaw. I was continuing a voluminous correspondence with Carnap, and this was bilingual: I wrote in German and he in English, and we enclosed carbon copies and sent back corrections of each other's language. Carnap was preparing in this way for a possible move to America, and I was continuing to improve my German. Years later, however, with the mounting of Nazi horrors, I had scruples about using German in victimized lands. In Holland I would lean on my pocket Dutch dictionary rather than resort to German. Even in unvictimized Zurich, not being up to *schwiezer dütsch*, I shunned standard German in favor of French.

Ed Haskell moved to Cambridge and took a room near us. Many were our walks and talks. He was pivotal in our German evenings, for his German was virtually native. Frank Manuel, a young doctor in history, also did well; but others were halting. At length the German component withered and Thursday evenings became just a jolly open house.

Ted Palmer turned up after six months on geographical detail for Webster-Merriam, and his store of geographical curiosities was inexhaustible. Java and the adjacent island of Madura, he told me, constituted a province of the Dutch East Indies known as Java and Madura. The eastern half of this province, comprising the eastern part of Java and the whole of Madura, constituted a subprovince known merely as East Java. He delighted in these illogical bits, and I with him.

Ted and I resolved upon some serious walking. The first day we walked thirty miles, hitchhiked twenty-eight, and spent the night in Putnam, Connecticut. Next day we walked fourteen more into bad weather and hitchhiked home. It was in these days that Ted put me onto P. G. Wodehouse. I had frequent pleasure from Wodehouse thereafter, strangely commingled with a guilty feeling that I was wasting my time.

One Jim Loder, who lived above us, drew us into poker. At Ἄρθρον, poker had been a social vehicle with insignificant stakes. High stakes were ugly; one then dreaded to lose, and also disliked hurting one's good friends by winning. However, Jim edged the stakes up, and Naomi and I lost more than we could afford. For a couple of days we spent long and suspenseful hours at the game, not for pleasure or excitement, but to get out of a jam. Happily we recouped most of our loss and quit, well inoculated.

Through Jim we met Peter Pezzati. He was a gifted young painter in an academic vein, mainly of portraits, and a protégé of Charles Hopkinson. He was born and raised in Boston's North End and spoke Italian fluently. Though not college-bred, he was widely read and had broad interests, notably in word origins. He spoke with contagious enthusiasm, and indefatigably.

Friends multiplied that year, through a merging of four circles: town, Society of Fellows, ex-Ohio, and philosophy. Looking back, I am bewildered by the social whirl—so different from later years. I begrudged some of the time thus spent, preferring to get on with my work. I wish all that varied and effortless socializing, all that casual dropping in on one another, could have been thinned and spread over the decades.

Sparked perhaps by our sessions on my dissertation two years before, Whitehead conducted a logic seminar in the fall of 1933. He even presented a paper on logic before the Mathematical Association of America, which met at Harvard that December. I suppose my old teacher Cairns of Oberlin was behind the invitation. At Cairns's request I summarized it for the *American Mathematical Monthly*. The paper appeared in *Mind*: "Indication, classes, number, validation." I thought ill of it.

At that meeting I met Haskell Curry. It was my first experience in America of spirited shop talk with an active research logician. He was working at Schönfinkel's combinatory logic, something I had tinkered with in Warsaw and to which I shall recur. For Curry it became a lifelong specialty.

The first year of my Junior Fellowship went largely to the revision of my book. I got the basic concepts down to the ordered pair, the inclusion of one class in another, and class abstraction. This last is the idiom 'the class of all objects x such that ...'. On this threefold basis I defined the truth functions, quantification, and membership. The book improved on my dissertation in economy of axioms and succinctness of proof notation. Sheffer got me to expound the ideas twice in his seminar, and Whitehead took them up in his.

· 1934   Type was set by Harvard Press in Randall Hall, a low brick building that adorned the corner that now cringes beneath William James Hall. It was luxurious to carry galley proofs straight to the compositor and consult with him on spacing of symbols, breaking of formulas, styles of alpha. But what to name the book? Whitehead liked *Structure and Sequence*. Huntington liked *A Generalized System of Logic*. Pottinger of Harvard Press liked *Mathematical Logic* or *A System of Logic*. Some liked *Sequential Logic*. Sheffer proposed *Quinine Logic: A Bitter Pill*. The upshot was uninspired: *A System of Logistic*. Whitehead introduced it with a preface.

It came out in November 1934, and I proudly opened it, as one will, to two misprints. "What is particularly annoying," I wrote my parents, "is that I had corrected both of them in the proofs, but the corrections had been overlooked by a careless typesetter. One must treat a printer as an enemy whose every move must be watched."

Editors could be trying, too. I sent a nine-page article, "A method of generating part of arithmetic without use of intuitive logic," to the *Bulletin of the American Mathematical Society*. There was no argument about acceptance or content, but still the editorial correspondence ran far longer than the article. One of my letters alone ran to two thousand dreary words, devoted mainly to explaining, case by case, that a symbol was being referred to rather than used, and that my quotation marks were consequently needed, in contrast to other places where I scrupulously withheld them. The editor was intent on dropping them all, in conformity with his "style."

The little paper that occasioned this tiresome turmoil had been sparked by a discussion with Huntington. It is appealingly simple, and perhaps interesting for its kinship to the algorithm of recursive functions that was about to emerge and dominate the logical scene.

I wrote two book reviews: one grudgingly, of the fourth Peirce volume, and one gladly, of Carnap's *Logische Syntax der Sprache*.

Pillar to Post

At first Naomi and I had been delighted with our flat in Ridgely Hall, but by spring our joy had ebbed. There were loud radios, loud parties, and loud students carousing in the street. I persuaded the manager to waive the second year of our lease on the condition of my paying the summer rent but vacating the flat. So Naomi and I spent another summer, 1934, with my parents. We returned to Boston by way of the Baltimore and Ohio Railroad, stopping overnight out of curiosity at Cumberland, Maryland. On the way out of Akron my pocket was picked, for the third time.

Our new flat was at 52 Garden Street in Cambridge, looking out on lawns. We had living room, bedroom, kitchen, and bath, and a Murphy bed could be let down from a closet in the hall. A narrow little room paved with tile just accommodated my desk and its swivel chair, which, on its casters, rolled gratefully over the tile floor. I took the door off the adjoining closet, filled the opening with removable bookshelves, and settled contentedly into my cozy study.

The new academic year added seven Junior Fellows. Harry Levin, George Homans, and Bright Wilson all are now Harvard emeriti. George Hass was in medicine and Conrad Arensberg was in social anthropology, fresh from a year's fieldwork in Ireland. Benedict Einarson, a Greek scholar, was an unfailing source of curious and recondite lore. He was fat, jolly, and the best of company. We learned only later that he was desperately unhappy. Finally there was Dave Griggs, geologist. He was a motor cyclist and a demon at the wheel of a car. In the Nevada desert he taught himself to fly a plane and flew it to the east coast to apply for a license. While a Junior Fellow he went to Europe, as Fellows are enabled to do if their work calls for it. Driving across Hungary he crashed into a cyclist. The cyclist died and Dave spent six months in a Hungarian hospital. During the Second

World War he had responsible duty with the Air Force, piloting generals around strategic points. He suffered painful publicity later in the Robert Oppenheimer case. He met an untimely but not a violent death.

Most of us thirteen Junior Fellows were soon close friends, dropping in on one another. We took to anagrams, and the level of play, what with Benedict, Harry, and Fred Skinner, was exhilaratingly high.

I had offers or overtures from Ann Arbor, Princeton, and Oberlin. They were not to be taken lightly, for the depression was continuing and academic openings were scarce. Fritz Safier had won his Ph.D. in philosophy with flying colors and promptly gone into training for government work, not even hoping for a job in philosophy. To have prudently given up my third year as Junior Fellow, however, would have been a bitter sacrifice. I dismissed such thoughts with relief when Ralph Barton Perry told me that I could count on something, however modest, a year later at Harvard.

I had been expounding Carnap to Henderson and Curtis. This led to Carnap's honorary degree at the Harvard tercentenary two years later, and meanwhile it led to my being asked to give a series of three lectures on him. I complied in November 1934. There I was, as Charlie Curtis put it, standing under a bas-relief of the metaphysician George Herbert Palmer, telling a gathering of professional philosophers that philosophy is nothing but syntax and that metaphysics is meaningless. And, Charlie added, not only telling them so, but proving it to them. But perhaps a lawyer's idea of proof is not a logician's.

I had dreaded my lectures. When I addressed the Vienna Circle in German, with my written paper in hand, I had been nervous, but this home occasion was far worse. I no longer felt shielded by the allowances that are extended to a foreigner. I felt it would no longer be fitting to read my lectures, yet I had to write them out, or I should be speechless; so I tried memorizing, pacing, memorizing. The typescript went with me to the podium even so, a vital precaution. On the podium my panic promptly subsided, for a lifetime.

Anxiety, in moderation, did persist. I was up all night before my third lecture, making improvements. To this day I have written out my lectures in advance, except for classroom teaching, and even for the classroom my lecture notes have always been full. But I am reporting this, not recommending it. Once at the beginning of class a student's question set me off on a spirited tangent and I extemporized through the hour, with my notes untouched. The class applauded.

At any rate, there was a stir about Carnap after my three lectures. Professors Prall, Sheffer, and Lewis were curious and met with me repeatedly to pose questions. Prall even volunteered to translate the *Logische Syntax*, and I urged the idea, but the Countess Zeppelin got there first.

· 1935   I returned gratefully to more technical ventures in logic when I could, and my thoughts turned to the variable. The 'x' that we have been seeing in quantifiers and class abstraction is a *bound variable*. Unlike the free variables or unknowns of algebra, it is merely a pronoun of internal cross-reference linking up positions within a formula. What Schönfinkel showed, in 1918, was how to translate logic and set theory into a blocklike algebraic style devoid of bound variables. Convenience is lost, but a deep understanding is gained of the work done by bound variables—and indeed by relative pronouns and by variables and pronouns generally. Set theory and elementary logic were inextricably interlocked, however, in Schönfinkel's scheme. I became interested in accomplishing the same thing for the elementary level independently of set theory, so as to isolate more narrowly the business of the variable. An outcome was an essay in algebraic logic entitled "Toward a calculus of concepts," which appeared a year later as the opening article of the new *Journal of Symbolic Logic*. Another was the fanciful "Concepts of negative degree."

In June 1935, I set forth on a jaunt with Ted Palmer and a biology student named Fish. We traveled in Fish's little Ford and slept under his umbrella tent. On Cape Breton Island we rounded rugged North Cape on Cabot Trail, two hundred rough miles of it. We heard Gaelic at Inverness and saw signs in that language. Tucked into the side of this Scotch country were two parishes, Chéticamp and Margarée, where everyone spoke French. At North Sydney we left the car and boarded ships, separate ones. Ted and Fish sailed to Corner Brook, near Cape Ray, and crossed Newfoundland to St. John's by the narrow-gauge railroad, with a view to visiting the French colony of St. Pierre and Miquelon on the return voyage. But I was impatient to see St. Pierre and fearful of bypassing it on the way back; so I sailed from North Sydney to St. Pierre, joining Ted and Fish afterward in St. John's.

It was foggy as we approached St. Pierre. *"Il est tout le timps brumeux à St.-Biaille,"* a Canadian sailor from Trois-Rivières *("Trois-Riviailles")* told me in his remarkable accent. The capital village was a compact, weather-beaten French seaport of 3500 inhabitants. The men wore berets. Outside was desolation; hardly a path. There was short grass, moss, and occasionally a patch of knee-high spruce that produced a strange illusion in the fog. In the reduced visibility, the miniature forest looked full size and seemed to extend down a vast valley as far as the eye could reach. Striding into it, giantlike, I towered over the forest and was across the valley in a moment.

It is a round island three to four miles across, and I walked about six miles in it. The interior, rising to eight hundred feet, disappears upward in the fog like a high mountain. At one shore there are cliffs, dropping perhaps two hundred feet into the sea. The fog made a surprise package of everything, unwrapping each object only as one came to it. The wet air was cold for June, and penetrating; I wore everything I had, including two pairs of trousers.

St. Pierre and Miquelon were my thirty-third country, and Newfoundland my thirty-fourth, for it had not yet joined Canada. Ted and Fish met my ship at St. John's, the easternmost city of North America. Its harbor is nicely closed in by hills, but the city was bleak, its dwellings boxlike. Beyond, there were meager fenced fields straggling up the hill-sides, and here and there a scrawny woodland.

The ship did indeed put in at St. Pierre on the way back. In the bunkroom with us there was a French fisherman from Brittany who spoke no English. He told us of the rigors of the Grand Banks, where he would stay a month at a time. *Pecheur d'Islande*, nearly enough.

New friends emerged in Cambridge: Mr. and Mrs. Thomas A. Thomas. He was about fifty, distinguished in appearance, with a pointed white beard. He was a historian, but not attached to a university. Someone said he had written a great work on Florentine art, lost the manuscript, and lost heart. They were friends of the Whiteheads. The only time the Whiteheads went calling in three years, they went to the Thomases, and so did we. Another time, we met the anthropologist E. A. Hooton at the Thomases.

By July 1935, Naomi was seven months pregnant. Mrs. Thomas was solicitous, lending baby equipment and having us to meals. By then, moreover, the annual question of moving had arisen again, over noise: radios and dogs. I had got by with earplugs until the people in the flat below us locked their howling dog into their flat and went away. The janitor's passkey did not fit their door. The police and the Animal Rescue League arrived, still to no avail. Our dog-fancying neighbors came home that night, but repeated the routine the next day. So we bespoke a flat in Bowdoin Street.

Elizabeth was born with difficulty: forceps and incisions. Moving day was two days later. With Naomi's sister Marguerite, who came from Toledo to help, I put in a vigorous intervening day alternating between the hospital and the dismantling and packing. Mr. Thomas took us home with him to dinner. Early next morning the movers came. We saw some things into the van, and walked ahead carrying the Havilland. Two hours later the movers arrived and found that the desk and piano could not be got into the flat. I had counted on hoisting them through a window, but I had not reckoned with a tortuous passage or a rickety porch roof. We could not take the flat.

We sat, unbreakfasted, with the movers in the van in the rain. The Havilland was loose in a basket. Armloads of clothes that we had transported earlier were loose on the freight. We were tired and dirty, I was bearded, our relevant clothes were deep in trunks, and I was due that evening, after hospital hours, to call on the Whiteheads.

I telephoned James Angell McLaughlin, later Mac-Lachlan, a red-haired professor at Harvard Law School, whose top floor we had considered weeks before. We had been steered to it by Mrs. Thomas and had liked it, except for the price. McLaughlin now shaded the price a bit, and we moved in. It was in a big square house with a mansard roof at 91 Washington Avenue, perhaps the highest point in Cambridge. Years later the house burned to the ground.

The Whiteheads, hearing my account of our ordeal, predictably asked Marguerite and me to dine with them next evening. They shared with the Thomases and other kind people the misconception that it is a saving of time and labor to be guests on busy days.

Terminal Fellow   21

The third crop of Junior Fellows, September 1935, yielded five. George Hanfmann, from Siauliai, Lithuania, has since had a distinguished career excavating Sardis and is a Harvard emeritus. Ivan Getting, born in America of Slovak parents and fluent in Slovak, subsequently founded Raytheon and made untold millions. Paul Ward, a historian, became president of Amherst. John Bardeen, a friendly but silent man, came to be the only man ever to win two Nobel prizes in physics. Finally there was Henry Guerlac, who came in as a chemist but turned historian of science; he has distinguished himself at Cornell. I called him Henri Guerlac de Sabrevois, after Kenneth Roberts's villain in *Arundel*. Henry told me that Roberts had failed Henry's father's French course and had named his villain after his teacher in revenge.

Charlie Curtis divorced his wife and married a writer, Frances Prentiss. It was said that he settled most of his fortune on his first wife, but in any event there was disapproval in Boston society. He was called upon to resign from the Harvard Corporation and from the Society of Fellows. Several of us Junior Fellows went to L. J. Henderson in protest. He said the case of the Corporation was pragmatic: Charlie had lost his usefulness as a link between the university and Boston society. He said further, what is not true today, that one could not be a Senior Fellow without some other Harvard office. We Junior Fellows all chipped in and bought Charlie a first edition of Hobbes's *Leviathan* as a farewell gift. Benedict found it in Cornhill, I think for seventy-five dollars. It is now worth thousands. Charlie's widow gave it to me after his tragic death in a fire years later, on condition that I leave it to the Society of Fellows. I lately jumped the gun, presenting the book at the Society's fiftieth anniversary.

Ed Haskell returned from a year in New York in the fall of 1935 and shared a flat with Norman Mattis in Linnaean Street, near us. On spring days I was in and out their window, short-cutting the vestibule. It was in Ed's communist phase, and I remember a spirited harangue in which he hoped to have brought me around. He did well, but not well enough. Certainly I was more sympathetic then than since. But I also had good things to say of Pareto.

We had known Norm at Oberlin, where he had been precociously an instructor. He was now at Harvard as an instructor in public speaking. He was bespectacled, slight, slightly bald, slightly hesitant and deferential. He was amiable, urbane, erudite, and not visibly ambitious. He was a close and valued friend—much missed when he moved some years later to North Carolina.

I wrote "Truth by convention" in the fall of 1935 for a Whitehead *Festschrift*, drawing upon my 1934 lectures on Carnap. The lectures had been uncritical, but "Truth by convention" already bore the seeds of my apostasy. I also held an informal seminar in my study that fall and winter, mainly on Carnap's *Logische Syntax*. The participants were a professor, Prall, an instructor, Henry Leonard, and some graduate students, including Nelson Goodman, Charles Stevenson, and John Cooley. The high point was the advent of Carnap himself, from Prague. He was to spend the winter quarter lecturing at Chicago. He and Ina stayed with us from December 23 to 28. He was to address the annual philosophy convention, so on December 28 five of us drove in someone's car to Baltimore: Carnap, Prall, Goodman, Leonard, and I. We moved with Carnap as henchmen through the metaphysicians' camp. We beamed with partisan pride when he countered a diatribe of Arthur Lovejoy's in his characteristically reasonable way, explaining that if Lovejoy means A then p, and if he means B then q. I had yet to learn how unsatisfying this way of Carnap's could sometimes be.[1]

Goodman, Leonard, and I drove back to Cambridge, stopping in New York at the Lafayette, a French hotel off Washington Square. On the way they told of a project of theirs. They broached it diffidently, for I had seemed unsympathetic when Henry spoke of it on an earlier occasion. I became interested as I heard more, and I was able to help them on a technical problem. We talked in our hotel room until four in the morning. They were concerned with constructing a systematic theory of sense qualities, and their effort had much in common with Carnap's *Logischer Aufbau der Welt*. As an auxiliary they had developed a logic of the part-whole relation, which I recognized as Leśniewski's so-called mereology. They had been meeting fortnightly on their project, and I happily joined them in subsequent meetings. Leonard was called away, but Goodman and I continued to meet. Their project flowered in Nelson's dissertation, which he revised and published as *The Structure of Appearance*.

My own thoughts tended rather to the notorious paradoxes

1. I have lifted a few more lines from my *Ways of Paradox*, 2d ed.

of set theory. The best known is Russell's, in which it is observed that the class of all those classes that are not members of themselves must be a member of itself if and only if not. Russell blocked the paradoxes by his "theory of types." His types are levels—thus individuals, classes of individuals, classes of such classes, and so on. He banned as meaningless any sentence that affirmed or denied membership other than from one type to the next. The ban seemed *ad hoc.* I sought a scheme of contextual definition that would account for this ban and at the same time reduce classes themselves to a mere eliminable manner of speaking. My venture, sketched in "A theory of classes presupposing no canons of type" and expounded at length in my informal seminar, did not work. But it brought a fringe benefit, a little mathematical theory of the concatenation of sequences. This stood me in good stead in three subsequent writings, enabling me to dispense with classes in some of the constructions that had seemed to need them.

Coeval with Russell's theory of types there was Zermelo's system, which I was late in encountering. Russell had begun with the common-sense view that every membership condition determines a class, and then invoked his types to excise the troublesome membership conditions as meaningless. Zermelo dropped that common-sense view and devised axioms providing for the existence of such classes as he needed. After the debacle last noted, I moved to the Zermelo tradition and undertook to improve upon it. By now my basic notations, in terms of which the rest were defined, were the neoclassical ones as of Tarski and Gödel: just quantification, the copula 'ϵ' of membership, and the truth functions—say 'and' and 'not'. The outcome, "Set-theoretic foundations for logic," is a more elegant system than Zermelo's, but it departs from classical lines in not recognizing an empty class.

• 1936   The Association for Symbolic Logic was founded in 1935, and the *Journal of Symbolic Logic* appeared in March 1936. There had been debate over the name. It was felt that "symbolic" was a characterization *per accidens.* But Huntington's judgment prevailed. His argument was that the subject *is* symbolic logic. The journal, under Church's untiring and judicious direction, raised the subject to new heights of prominence and activity.

I had reviewed six books before the *Journal of Symbolic Logic* began. My reviewing of books and articles for the *Journal* then became a steady background activity. It was burdensome, but it kept me posted.

The Carnaps came back to Harvard for the summer and he gave a course. After each lecture some of us sat in the Yard and discussed for an hour or so. Occasionally some of us went to the beach at Ipswich with the Carnaps. There might be the MacLanes, the Goheens, Herbert Feigl, Nelson Goodman, or Albert Wohlstetter and his fiancée Roberta Morgan.

We changed dwelling as usual. Perhaps the reason had to do with heat or hot water. Jim McLaughlin was a thorny type, though perhaps no less tractable than I. At any rate we found splendid quarters, comprising one floor and part of another in a little old brick row house at 61 Frost Street in Cambridge. White wooden shutters unfolded from recesses beside the windows, and a back lawn spanned the row of four houses. Ted Palmer recognized our new home by spotting the bookshelves from the sidewalk; there was a characteristic Gestalt of close-fitting and tight-packed shelves that he remembered from our successive previous dwellings.

Loesch drove from Cleveland to Cambridge and the two of us made the trip to Quebec that had been denied us nine years before. We would have hitchhiked then; we now drove. We stopped to climb Katahdin, New England's sightliest mountain. It meant an eight-hour hike, what with the long approaches. From the top we admired the woods of northern Maine, uncut and uninhabited for a hundred miles beyond. After Quebec and lesser French towns, we diverged at Burlington. He headed west and I waited five hours for a train to Boston. It was a Sunday; no beer, no movies, just a grassy slope and the view over Lake Champlain.

My big brother and
I in Akron, 1910.

My parents and
grandfather Quine at
"Ellan Vannin"
about 1917.

38 Hawthorne
Avenue, my home
until 1919.

16 Orchard Road,
my home from 1919
to 1930.

My map of one of
the Portage Lakes,
blueprinted for sale
to summer neighbors,
1923.

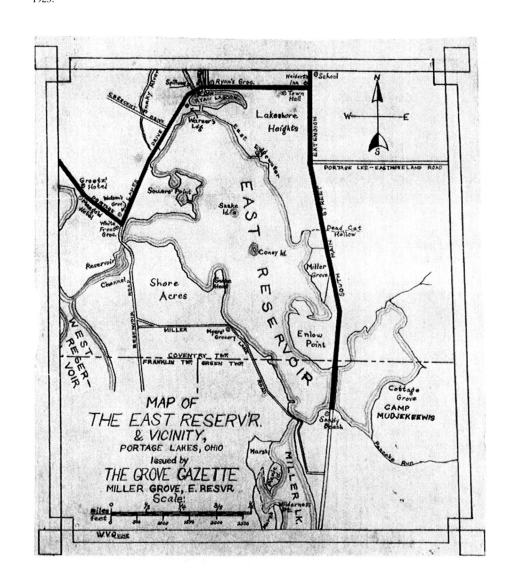

O.K. STAMP NEWS

VOL.2 NO.1   AKRON, OHIO   JANUARY, 1925

PRECANCEL NUMBER

AKRON HARDING PRECANCELS

We have at last obtained authorita
tive and fairly accurate informatio
concerning Akron Harding P
through Mr. A. S. M
1909 of

PHILATELIC DISSERTATION

By "LR" Saunders

To All the Readers of This Growing
Philatelic Paper:

One result of growing that cannot be
voided is the getting larger part of it
d that is what the editor has finally
n forced to do—give this paper a
ger dress and here it is with a hope
the readers will like it and send in
rial that will make the inside pages
se in numbers at the same propor-
s the cover has.

Hardings and Walloons I am
ng are issues that have done more
d to some extent against) the
l game than any other single
he bad has to be taken with
in all lines and philately is no
though many people think so.

o t nued on Page 2

COLLECT ECONOMICALLY

t discussing the above sub-
t of stamps, an attractive
a fine perforation gauge.
pplicants for OSCO BAR
VALS.

approvals contain a fine
s at from 50% to 80%
The prices range from
s. Reference required.
STAMP CO.
AKRON, OHIO

O.K. STAMP NEWS

VOL.1   AKRON, OHIO   OCTOBER, 1924   NO.1

OUR DEBUT

Yes, here's another addition to the already over-
crowded philatelic press.

However, we will endeavor to proceed with tac-
tics equally beneficial to the subscriber and the advertiser. It is our opinion that the best news to the
philatelist is ... dvertisement of the stamps he
needs ... he is willing to pay, and this we
... in our columns. In each issue
... ews and philatelic notes which
... nd of value to our readers.
... elic attempt across the con-
... ible, we are only charging
... twelve issues. This does
... penses, so we hope you
... and trouble we have had.

OINS RANKS

the ranks of stamp
officially known as
governed under a
government is at
d the stamps of
part.

as issued over

answering ads

O.K. Stamp News

Vol. 1. Akron, Ohio, December, 1924, No. 3.

MERRY CHRISTMAS

We wish all of our readers the proverbial
"MERRY CHRISTMAS" and the best of
prosperity and happiness during the New
Year.

Liechtenstein Leaves Philately

The little principality of Liechtenstein,
high up in the Tyrol Alps, the third smallest
independent state in the world but a highly
efficient producer of postage stamps, has decided to use Swiss stamps. Although the
country is self-governing, its post office has
been in the management of Switzerland
since 1921. However, the little state continued to issue its own stamps up to the present time. It is reported that the remaining
supply of Liechtenstein stamps, numbering
about nine million, has been destroyed. This
should make these 1921-24 issues well worth
having as the common Liechtenstein
stamps today flooding the market were issued in 1920, and straightway sold to a syn-
dicate at less than face value. These labels,
of course, will not be affected by the super-
sedure of Liechtenstein's postal issues.

SUBSCRIBE NOW. We're growing rapidly

Another of my early
enterprises, 1924
and 1925.

Myself, left, and
John Rollin Chenot,
1926.

With my brother,
right, in front of
"Arthron," Oberlin,
1927.

At age nineteen.

With Jerry Taylor in
the Model T, 1928.

Fellow tramps on a
lumber car, Salt
Lake Desert, 1928.

With Clarence
Loesch on Trail
Ridge, Colorado,
1928.

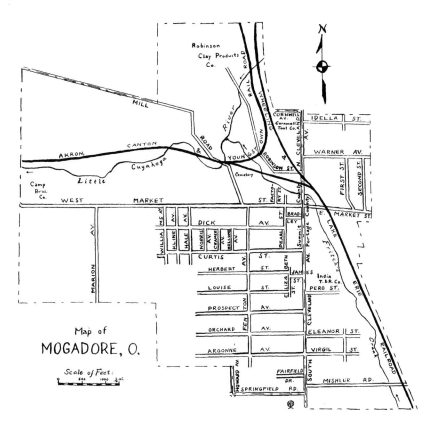

My map of Mogadore, 1930. It was printed with ads of local merchants. I put a copy at each house.

With my first wife,
Naomi, at "Ellan
Vannin," 1932.

Ina and Rudolf
Carnap, Prague,
1933.

Society of Fellows, 1933.
Top row:
B. F. Skinner,
myself,
Kenneth Murdock,
Garrett Birkhoff,
Fred Watkins,
Charles P. Curtis.
Bottom row:
Tom Chambers,
James Bryant Conant,
A. Lawrence Lowell,
John Livingston Lowes,
Alfred North Whitehead,
John Chester Miller,
Lawrence J. Henderson.

At age twenty-
seven.

From left:
Raphael Demos,
Cornelius Benjamin,
Ernest Nagel,
Paul Weiss,
Haskell Curry,
Morris Cohen,
Harvard, 1939.

Otto Neurath,
J. H. Woodger,
Alfred Tarski,
E. C. Berkeley,
myself,
Haskell Curry, and
Stephen Kleene, on
steps of Emerson
Hall, Harvard, 1939.

Nelson Goodman at
Rockport, 1941.

A stroll on the
Viaduto do Cha, São
Paulo, 1942.

As lieutenant
commander in
Washington, 1945.

At age thirty-eight.

TENNANT'S
HARBOR
1947

Willard

My ink sketch of
Tenants Harbor,
Maine, 1947.

With my bride
Marjorie and her
father, Augustus S.
Boynton, Meriden,
Connecticut, 1948.

Faculty Instructor

My accession to the Harvard faculty launched the university on its fourth century. The launching was further expedited by tercentenary celebrations, lectures, and conferences. Carnap received his honorary degree and gave a lecture; likewise Einstein. Whitehead spoke at a mathematics luncheon. The social whirl was vertiginous. Fred Cassidy was visiting us, and we invited Harry Levin over to meet him. Unexpectedly we were joined by Haskell Curry, who was up from Penn State, and Harold Langford from Ann Arbor. The next evening Oberlin Professors Cairns and Yeaton and their wives came to dinner. On three successive evenings we dined with the Carnaps—at home, at the Whiteheads, and as guests of Charlie Curtis.

My faculty instructorship was a three-year appointment. In the first term I gave a graduate lecture course in mathematical logic in the mathematics department and a seminar in the philosophy of mathematics in the philosophy department. Five students enrolled in the lecture course, just three of whom stayed to the end; but there were numerous auditors. Nobody enrolled in the seminar, but again there were many auditors, one of whom volunteered to enroll so as to keep it going.

I was assigned five undergraduates for individual weekly tutorial sessions. The tutorial system at Harvard was at its height. Every undergraduate got the full treatment from a full-fledged faculty member. It required me to turn to classical texts and traditional issues in philosophy—a burden, however salutary. I was made a tutor at Eliot House, with meals in hall, the companionship of the senior common room, and a pleasant office off the great lawn.

Tuesdays the philosophy faculty met for lunch and business in the Faculty Club. I was the youngest, for assistants and annual instructors did not count as faculty. Others present were Demos, Hocking, Lewis, Perry, Prall, Sheffer, and Whitehead. Demos, John Wild, and Donald Williams were added in the next years.

Preparation for teaching left me painfully little time for the research that had been my way of life. But research was needed even for my teaching; for in my graduate course in the spring I would be presenting set theory, and I needed to settle on a system.

I conjectured that if I followed Zermelo in dropping the presumption that every membership condition determines a class, then I could enjoy Russell's safeguards against the paradoxes without declaring formulas to be meaningless, as he did, when they violated the theory of types; I needed only refrain from assuming the corresponding classes. I called these formulas *unstratified* and easily defined stratification without appealing to types. A welcome normalization of ontology ensued; each of Russell's types had had its own empty class, its own universe class, its own number 1, its own 2 and so on, but now these reduplications collapsed. A further fault of the theory of types was that an infinitude of individuals had to be postulated to make the construction of arithmetic come out right; and this assumption seemed to encroach on questions of fact beyond logic and mathematics. It now ceased to be needed.

My old teacher Cairns, pillar of the Mathematical Association of America, was a continuing force acting at a distance. He had solicited my first book review, back in 1930. He had been behind Whitehead's lecture to the Association and my résumé of it in 1933. Now came an invitation to address the Association, expenses paid, in North Carolina at the end of 1936. What I have set forth above was the burden of my paper on that occasion, under the title "New foundations for mathematical logic."

"New foundations" is stronger than the theory of types, and therefore more in danger of dissolving into paradox. The likeliest place for trouble was in connection with Cantor's theorem, the one that had been my defense against seasickness on the Baltic. I sent off an analysis of that connection:

"On Cantor's theorem." A proof of consistency, however, is another matter. The question arises of the consistency of the method of proving the consistency. One hopes only to prove that one's system is consistent if some more trusted system is consistent. A remarkable lot of relative consistency proofs for "New foundations" has been produced, but the system has still not been shown consistent relative to Zermelo's or *Principia*. The literature on "New foundations" has run to some fifty articles and monographs by twenty mathematicians, and symposia on the subject continue in Belgium to this day.

I made a jaunt of my trip to North Carolina. I slept in New York and then took a train to Cape Charles so as to see the Delmarva Peninsula. It was a flat patchwork of pine forests, truck farms, scrubby woodlots, and sleepy southern villages with picturesque shanties and stately old mansions. My ship from Cape Charles put in at Old Point Comfort and then proceeded in the night to Norfolk, where I slept in a hotel. Next morning a ship and a train got me to Norline, North Carolina, where I boarded another train, two hours later, that was to take me sixteen miles to Henderson. An axle of its locomotive broke, and three mail cars tipped into the muck. Steel shavings two inches thick curled from the wheels of the locomotive. After an hour the train moved again. At Henderson I waited an hour for a bus that took me the remaining forty miles to Durham. It was a nostalgic way to travel, even that long ago. I could have gone directly by overnight train, as I knew, and thus it was that I went home after the meeting.

My paper was too long; I had to talk fast and skip. But it was well received, as I discovered by overhearing comments that were not intended for me.

My graduate course in mathematical logic in the spring · 1937   term of 1937 was a pleasure, thanks to "New foundations." I had a number of auditors and two enrolled students. One of these, a graduate student in philosophy, failed abysmally. The other, an undergraduate in mathematics named George

Brown, made A+. George went on to Princeton, and it was he who compiled Gödel's 1940 monograph from his lectures.

I also gave the basic logic course, required for concentrators in philosophy. No text was available along modern lines. I coped with Eaton's pedestrian *General Logic* and Jevons's nineteenth-century *Elementary Lessons in Logic,* and filled in. I tried to tame the logic of quantification so that it could be mastered by the general student in a short course. The project endured down the years.

In those days undergraduate courses had to be repeated at Radcliffe. It meant preparing additional material, because the girls did not take up time with questions and discussion as Harvard boys did.

On Clarence Lewis's advice I joined the American Philosophical Association. At David Prall's urging I joined the teachers' union, but soon dropped out, unsympathetic with the strident politics.

In May 1937 our daughter Norma was born. Marguerite again stood by. A few weeks later we took the train to Toledo, deposited both babies with Naomi's aunt, and lit out southwest with Marguerite and her friend Fred in a new car. They were driving it from the factory in Detroit to a dealer in California in order to get there, and we went along as far as El Paso in order to glimpse Mexico.

Mexico had appealed to me from childhood, in a romantic way. There were the sinister, swarthy *hombres* with sweeping mustachios and broad sombreros, well known from the Western melodramas. My impressions of Mexico had had even earlier beginnings, when my mother told me of her childhood visit to her honorary Uncle Ellis, who had a ranch and general store at Encinal, Texas, near Laredo. She had wandered off and got lost, as one so quickly can in the undifferentiated orchard-like wilderness of mesquite. Uncle Ellis was desperately worried. There were Mexicans out there! "Never turn your back on a Mexican", Uncle Ellis used to say, if my mother was to be believed, and believed indeed she was, implicitly.

The buildup was thus formidable. When at last we were

well past Van Horn, Texas, and could be quite sure that the barren mountains off younder were in Mexico, the thrill far exceeded what might have been expected in one who, like me, had already trodden Asiatic and African soil. But there was the buildup hitherto adumbrated, and there was the foil: the incongruous contiguity with humdrum U.S. America. It was like Dorothy's translation from dull, gray Kansas to the Land of Oz.

Somewhat by chance, we had prepared ourselves with the language. One of my selections from James Haughton Woods's books after his death had been a Spanish grammar, and it had prompted Naomi and me to work at Spanish for a while.

We took a room in an El Paso hotel and went to Mexico by streetcar, of all things, over the international bridge. There were big, strange men aboard with big, dark, rectangular Indian faces. This, I told myself, is what Aztecs were like. Immediately across the little Rio Grande, everything was as Mexico should be: the old mission-style church, the town square with its bandstand, the colorful market, the men in broad sombreros, the women in rebozos, the Indian faces, the language. Surely it was the suddenest border on earth.

A map in the telephone book in our room showed a place where the border deviated briefly from the river, giving Mexico a tract of perhaps a hundred acres north of the river. It was marked as Cordoba Island, though not an island. The streets of El Paso were shown as stopping abruptly at that border, but perhaps only because the map was not concerned with streets in Mexico. We walked over to investigate. The deviant border followed a former bed of the river, and the streets, unpaved in that part of town, all stopped at the border. Cordoba Island was open country with an adobe farmhouse here and there. One of them faced the dry river bed, which served as a dirt road, and had a mailbox across the way; this Mexican farmer was getting his mail in Texas.

When we repatriated, two customs officers pulled up in a car. "What were you doing in Mexico?" They expected us to be surprised to hear that we had been in Mexico, but we disappointed them. Some years later, Cordoba Island was ceded to Texas in return for compensatory adjustments of other anomalies down the river.

We traveled homeward by a succession of busses, the first of which carried us through southeastern New Mexico. We saw an extraordinary mirage, for all the world like a lake close at hand. "It's a *my*ridge," a local passager explained.

The summer brought our annual change of dwelling—this time a reluctant change, due to a raise in rent. We moved to a semi-detached frame house that Henry and Priscilla Leonard had occupied, at 21 Waverly Avenue in hither Newton. The distance was a nuisance—four miles, by bicycle or by streetcar and bus—and there was a furnace to stoke. But the rent was low.

My courses in the fall of 1937 included one on logical positivism, primarily on Carnap. It was generous of my senior colleagues to let me go so nearly my own way. Nevertheless the new course was less satisfying and harder to prepare than the ones in logic that had gone before. The teaching of logic is primarily expository, with an occasional touch of the inspirational. The research that precedes it has yielded something precise and subtle to explain and something elegant, perhaps, to glory in. The other kind of teaching is shakily speculative. The mood oscillates between the defensive and the conjectural. Exposition on the teacher's part, and effort to grasp on the student's part, cease to be pure and singleminded. I hoped that in time I would take as much satisfaction in characteristically philosophical courses as in logical ones, but this did not come about in forty years. Still I have never regretted the combination. Mathematics alone would not have served.

I had retrospective thoughts on *A System of Logistic* and what might have been. That system was based on class inclusion, class abstraction, and the ordered pair. I now discovered that I could define membership in terms of inclusion and abstraction, and then define ordered pair by an expedient due to Wiener. Hence my "Logic based on inclusion and abstraction." Though charmed by this economy, I continued to prefer Tarski's and Gödel's classical basis because of the neat pedagogy of treating first the truth functions, then quantification, and finally classes.

· 1938 In January 1938 I became vice-president of the Association for Symbolic Logic for three years under Curry. He found much to be busy about as president. Relatively little of it spilled over onto me, but more than I liked. I took warning never to accept the presidency, and declined it the next time around.

A paper on the theory of types that I gave at New York University in February made for a lively visit. I met Carl (called Peter) G. Hempel, who had just come to America to be Carnap's assistant. He had left Nazi Germany with his Jewish wife and had been living in Belgium, befriended by his fellow exile Paul Oppenheim. I had known Peter through his writings, and we soon became close friends. Others present included Ernest Nagel and J. C. C. (called Chen) McKinsey. Then began also my association with the multidirected Edmund C. Berkeley, who was enthusiastic about applying elementary logic to insurance policies.

Miller Chapman and Paul Henle published a logic text, which I adopted desperately and to little advantage in my logic course that spring. In Sheffer's phrase, I used it less as a text than as a pretext. Miller, like Paul, had been in our circle in graduate school. Since then he had been divorced by his attractive wife Rosamond and had got a teaching job with the U.S. Department of Agriculture in a short-lived program in which farmers were being taught philosophy—a program that Sheffer criticized as "putting Descartes before the horse." Rosamond worked as secretary for Ralph Barton Perry, her Grandperry, and gave parties for philosophers in her peaked studio flat in Kirkland Street.

Naomi had been in and out of hospitals during our marriage and had had four minor to middling operations. In April 1938 she was back in the hospital with bronchitis and pneumonia, and I lived in Eliot House while a nursemaid attended the babies in Newton. In July she went back to the hospital with a uterine infection and was operated upon again. Meanwhile we had moved, as usual—this time to a half house at 76 Grozier Road, near Fresh Pond in Cambridge.

It was about then that I became aware of Naomi's college debts, of nine to twelve years' standing. So I signed on for summer school. My outline for that course was a tentative outline of my next book, *Mathematical Logic*.

I was awarded the fall term off with pay, a junior sabbatical, to continue with the book. Taking climate into consideration, and cheap living, and foreign language, preferably Romance, and supposedly salubrious conditions for babies, and sufficient isolation to withstand the lure of ever farther places, we decided on the Azores. We sublet our flat to Morris Cohen, who was to visit Harvard for the term.

On an Azore   23

On August 14, 1938, John Goheen drove us to East Boston to board the *Saturnia* for Ponta Delgada on the island of São Miguel. The crew, monoglot, spoke Italian. The passengers, diglot, used English by preference if juvenile and Italian or Portuguese if adult. My Italian was adequate to simple needs and I was happy to practice it. But I devoted the five-day crossing to the study of Portuguese, which I had not had time to look into until then. Over the next five months I would be packing it in. My Italian, for all its faultiness, had got to flowing fairly freely on the way over, but proved to be utterly blocked on the homeward voyage; blocked by Portuguese.

Portuguese was rich in surprises. There was the declined infinitive—first, second, and third person—as if to say "for me to go," "for thee to go," "for him to go." There were compound but yet monosyllabic pronouns, equivalent to "it to him," "them to me," and the like. There was tmesis, to put a name to it: a verb stem would be split from its ending for the insertion of an object pronoun.

The phonetics were challenging. I quote from my letter to Einarson:

Greetings from amid the once regrettedly trans- but now god-thankedly cisatlantic quaintni. Along with the cobblestones, balconies, panniers, ewers, etc., one of the most conspicuous quaintni is the language. The vowels are a secret; half of them are inaudible and the other half are pronounced in a way which one repudiates and supplants whenever explaining pronounciation.

In Spanish there are five vowel sounds, clean as can be. In the island Portuguese I found nine, counting "silent but professed" as one and "silent and unprofessed" as another.

Chegamos means "we arrive," *chegámos* means "we arrived." An ox is called a boy and a rabbit is called a quail.

The grammar book I had brought was poor; I did not know about Ford, Hill, and Coutinho. We had to abstract supplementary laws from observation. For phonetics we were almost wholly dependent on observation and interrogation. So much the more fun.

A tender brought us from the ship to the landing, where the central plaza or *praça* of the little city of Ponta Delgada was dominated by an old stone church in the traditional Portuguese baroque. The streets were narrow and solidly lined with plastered façades, white or delicately tinted and topped with the traditional hemicylindrical red tiles. The sidewalks were paved in three-inch stone blocks, black and white, painstakingly arranged in fanciful mosaic.

We settled temporarily into a little hotel called the Pensão Central. It boasted a Portuguese judge, a Brussels-trained Portuguese engineer, and a police commissioner among its regular diners, and we became friends. But it was unsanitary and no place for babies. Our ten days there were marred by ill health and fear of worse, while we sought better quarters. With the help of our new friends we ended up at Rua da

Misericordia 29 as the sole boarders, save one, of the well-born but impoverished spinsters Olívia and Leonôr Pontes. They and their niece Maria da Luz and their tireless servant Maria do Carmo gave us a good home for nearly five months. We had two big rooms, laundry, and abundant board for a million *réis* a months, or forty-four dollars. Naomi and I had the freedom of the town and the countryside, leaving the babies in good hands.

We were awakened before dawn by an unearthly groaning of axles and clatter of wheels on the cobblestones. The narrow street was filled far and near by heavy two-wheeled carts loaded with sugar beets. Each cart carried a lantern and was drawn by an ox with a barefoot driver walking beside him goad in hand. We were awakened thus morning after morning, and liked it.

The city fathers maintained the continuity of the street fronts by statute. If a house was gone, its façade was preserved so as to hide the vacant lot and keep the street scene intact. The streets were chasms, and continued thus into the countryside, where high walls of stone or turf closed off the fields. Networks of these walls could be seen even on the green slopes of distant volcanoes.

Dignified old ladies wore broad, stiff black hoods—canopies, like those we had seen in Malta. Barefoot women in shawls bore loads on their heads—a bundle, a basket, an urn. One woman had a bundle of faggots on her head fully five feet long and three feet through. Men carried loads suspended from the ends of a bar resting on one shoulder. The draft animals, in order of frequency, were donkeys, mules, oxen, horses, ponies, men, goats, and sheep. The carts usually had two wheels. We saw a fat man squeezed into a tiny one drawn by a sheep. Cars were rare then, except for a dozen taxies and some long-range busses.

Three quarters of the people were said to be unlettered and perhaps nine tenths were unshod. Country people were in large part so poor that they raised their own tobacco and rolled their own cigarettes in cornhusks rather than spend just over two cents for a pack of twenty-four. Perhaps they could have afforded three fifths of a cent, which is what the pack could have sold for without tax.

Commonly a family would have a one-room stone house in a village and a little patch of land a mile away, and would transport the fertilizer and the produce on their heads and shoulders. A poor villager would cook his pumpkin and turnip tops on a tripod once a day. If less poor, he might have a black sausage smoking in the flue above, but many subsisted for long periods on just peppers and corn bread. Cripples were numerous.

Even in town, in homes with intermittent electricity and rudimentary plumbing, cooking facilities were meager. Where we lived, the meals for the day were cooked over an open fire in the morning and kept warm under blankets. Supplies were fresh daily, there being no refrigeration. The management thus suffered inconveniences, but we fared well.

We ate *garoupa*, which was perhaps grouper; *sardinhas*, fresh and full grown; squid *em sua tinta*, and limpets. A stew of dried cod was unkind to the gums, and a stew of corned beef and cabbage recalled Ireland and Dinty Moore. There were exotic strong sausages. Good bananas abounded, good figs, gooseberries, medlars, *maracujá*. The flavor of one strange fruit was like the smell of geraniums. A fresh, soft, white goat cheese, round like a pancake, was purveyed plopped on a banana leaf. Pleasant bottled wine from the Portuguese mainland was available cheap in both colors, and there was a coarse island wine called *vinho de cheiro*. A good brandy bore the confusing name *Macieira*, "apple tree"; it was a family name.

Discomforts were minor: straight chairs without arms, plank-bottomed beds, cornhusk mattresses, flies, and microbes that kept tab on our observance of reasonable precautions. There was an outlying hotel that surely had armchairs, bedsprings, and running water in the rooms, and perhaps screens in the windows, but it was expensive by our standards and unthinkable for an extended stay.

Apart from a few walks and bus rides through the interior,

our days ran to type. I would read Portuguese for an hour after breakfast and then work at logic for three. After lunch, while the babies slept, Naomi and I would walk for an hour and perhaps stop at a sidewalk café to drink coffee and read the Portuguese newspaper. Then four more hours of logic. Evenings were of three sorts: more logic, conversation with Portuguese friends, or the weekly movie. French and American movies were overprinted with Portuguese translations, which were doubly welcome because of the poor sound track; Portuguese movies were hopeless, what with poor sound and no overprints.

Most of the town came to the movie. Gentlefolk sat in the pit, usually in seats reserved for the season. There were bleachers for the poor, and standing room for the poorest. Impoverished gentlefolk, who could not afford the sixteen cents for the pit and would be embarrassed in the bleachers, stayed away.

The press was controlled. The civil war in Spain was reported as the Hispano-Soviet war. Sympathy with Hitler was less pronounced, there being long-standing friendship with England to consider. Natives were chary of political talk in public places. In the café we sometimes got onto politics with the rabbi, but always in German, and with care to paraphrase any pertinent proper names.

· 1939   We came to know Dr. Alfredo Bensaúde, patriarch of a rich old Ponta Delgada family. He owned the tobacco factory and the tea factory, had founded a technical school in Lisbon, and had been professor of mineralogy at Coimbra. He was informed on history, philosophy, archaeology, anthropology, and natural science, and was writing on the history of the Jews. He said he thought it not unlikely that all his ancestors for two thousand years had been Jews living in what is now Portugal. We had lively talks in his house. A frequent guest there was the principal of the island's *liceu*.

A son-in-law of Bensaúde's from Latvia, Wulf Gotz, showed us through the tobacco factory and loaded me down with pipe tobacco and cigarettes. He had conceived an unbounded admiration for Husserl's philosophy, and made me a present of the *Logische Untersuchungen* in three volumes. The subjectivity of its technical terms and the unbridled use of introspection leave me at a loss. I have not grasped the rules of the game.

I became a topic of speculation. I probably was of Portuguese extraction—otherwise why my interest in São Miguel and in learning the language? Another theory was that I was to be the new United States consul there. The incumbent consul was not liked and was said not to have tried to learn the language.

It was a rough January 13, 1939, when we boarded the *Vulcania* for New York. The tender soared and plunged in the great waves and troughs, and a sailor lifted each passenger deftly to the rope ladder at the crest of a wave. We steamed westward in our great ship, and I watched the receding of the by now familiar island with a gray, liverish boredom that I came little by little to interpret as an unconscious and compulsive repression of seasickness. I went below and took to my bunk for a dozen or twenty hours. Naomi and the babies were likewise prostrated. When at length I summoned my spirits and faculties and stood forth, the decks and public rooms were virtually deserted. Fiddles had been raised around the dining tables, but the decanters had tumbled over them and the floor ran red with wine. Hand ropes were strung to implement one's way along the decks, and thus at length one gained the bow, where the spectacle of an angry sea beggared description. Having been sick for a day and risen above it, I was immune and could luxuriate in the cosmic upheaval day in and day out. Naomi emerged after a few days, but not the babies. Elizabeth, aged three, would jump from her berth saying "I feel fine!" and be sick. The storm did not abate. Windows high above porthole levels were smashed by waves. The *New York Times* rated our arrival as news fit to print on page one.

We spent frequent evenings with Norman Mattis and his friends. Nat Griffin was a retired Smith College professor who went on from year to year on Rockefeller grants in support of a project on Guido. His much younger wife, Ann Mary, was husky, irrepressible, and quick with German expletives from her years with a Nazi officer. Eugene McCarthy, unemployed, was in the physiology and psychology of vision. Mac was a gifted raconteur, and incredulity was no bar to the enjoyment of his tales. Occasionally there was Ted Packard, Norman's senior colleague in public speaking, and Ted's wife Alice. They were a bright and congenial crowd, and our bibulous evenings were lively and long.

My first nephew, Kit, was Christopher Morley Quine, named for an illustrious friend of Bob and Virginia's. Kit's parents came visiting without him, and our three-year-old Elizabeth was disappointed. "Why you didn't bring Aunt Kit?"

That spring Naomi and Howard Mumford Jones's wife Bessie started a project to help refugees from the Nazis. It took the form of a shop and restaurant, featuring wares and dishes of central Europe and manned by women who had fled those unhappy regions. It came to be called the Window Shop and to occupy the old house that was said to have housed Longfellow's village blacksmith. It throve for decades.

My three-year appointment as faculty instructor was to have expired that June, 1939, and the philosophy department recommended my promotion to assistant professor. Presently, however, Harvard's newly created Committee of Eight abolished the assistant professorship and extended the three-year faculty instructorship to five years. The department, up in arms, then recommended me for immediate promotion to associate professor with tenure, but the administration refused. At the same time I had money problems. I had finally contrived to pay off, as I supposed, the last of Naomi's college debts, only to be confronted with an unsuspected accumulation of debts that she had subsequently contracted. Actually there were heavy further college debts too, still undiscovered.

Behind me were a well-reviewed book, a well-reviewed essay "Truth by convention," and eighteen articles in periodicals. Another book was on the way and had already been inquired after by three publishers. I was vice-president of the Association for Symbolic Logic and seven years a doctor. I felt woefully miscast as instructor and would have welcomed an offer. I wrote to eight acquaintances in outlying places indicating as much, but nothing came of it.

Count Korzybski had become eminent. My reservations with regard to him had dated from my reading of Keyser's laudatory chapter, ten years back. Meanwhile Korzybski's *Science and Sanity* was published. It was a vast volume, bristling with names of scientists and terms of science, but dedicated to the promotion of sanity by the extirpation of semantic confusions. There was the principle of non-identity: $cow_1 \neq cow_2$, and indeed even $1 \neq 1$, since the two numerical inscriptions are spatially distinct. There was non-Aristotelian logic; it is wrong to suppose, e.g., that everything is either black or white. There were the levels of abstraction, all well and good except that several hierarchies got conflated. The book dwelt at length on the ills of the world, with little risk of contradiction, and then touted "general semantics" as the way out.

Cornelius Crane, scion of flush-toilet millions, was grateful for psychological help that he credited to Korzybski. He endowed the count with an Institute for General Semantics, which presently came into being at the easily remembered address 1234 East 56 Street, Chicago, adjacent to the university campus. One was apt to suppose, however wrongly, that it was an institute of the university.

Ed Haskell had moved to Chicago for graduate study, and he took up somehow with Korzybski. When he learned of my discontent at Harvard, he wondered if there might be an interesting place for me on Korzybski's program. Meanwhile *Science and Sanity* had been gaining an uncritical following among our students. Naturally I could rate it low on the strength of samples, and naturally the enthusiasts could protest the smallness of my samples. Partly because of this challenge and partly out of restlessness and curiosity, I accepted Korzybski's invitation to spend a week of August 1939 in his intensive seminar.

The Wayward Waywode, as I called him, held forth seven hours a day. His harangue was embellished with contrived citations of colloid chemistry, set theory, and other recondite branches of science, which served to impress if not to contribute. As we filed out to lunch, an English teacher said he regretted not knowing chemistry, so as to get the full thrust of Korzybski's ideas. A psychiatrist said that for his own part he needed no knowledge of philosophy or mathematics or engineering or the rest in order to appreciate Korzybski's "general semantics"; it had helped his patients, and he was a pragmatist. That his patients were helped I can believe. Folk wisdom and sympathy can help troubled spirits.

A bright young follower of Korzybski's who was in regular attendance that summer was S. I. Hayakawa, affectionately known to the Wayward Waywode as the Heathen. Arguing with me, Hayakawa defended the canon with creative imagination beyond its deserts. His subsequent book *Language in Action* was widely taken up in English courses. In the troubled 1960s he distinguished himself as one of the few responsible and courageous college presidents. He later became a senator.

In September, 1939, Harvard was the scene of a Conference for the Unity of Science. Basically this was the Vienna Circle, with some accretions, in international exile. J. H. Woodger, Ernest Nagel, Charles Morris, and I pressed Tarski to accept an invitation, and funds were found to bring him. We hoped that once here he might find a better post than the one he had in somewhat anti-Semitic Warsaw. Reluctantly he came, and his life was saved; for the Germans then invaded Poland. Their massacre of the Jews included Tarski's parents.

Their name was Tajtelbaum. Tarski had signed his earliest publications thus, but had then changed his name to shield his children from discrimination; his wife Marja was a Gentile. The change, made so long ago, proved providential; it saved the lives of Marja and the children. They were in Warsaw through all the horrors of the Nazi invasion, occupation, and massacres, the Uprising, and the Russian occupation, despite Tarski's unflagging efforts to bring them out. He contacted Justice Stone of the Supreme Court through his son Marshall the mathematician; he contacted Lane, our ambassador to Poland, through the chancellor of the university at Berkeley; but our State Department was flaccid in the face of the Nazis in the early years and in the face of the Communists afterward.

It was at this conference in September 1939 that I at last met Neurath. He was editing the quarterly of the Vienna Circle, *Erkenntnis*, renamed the *Journal of Unified Science* and relocated in Holland. He was fat, and signed his letters to intimates with a sketch of an elephant. The sixteen papers of the conference were preprinted from an intended volume of Neurath's quarterly and distributed at the conference, but the volume itself was stopped at press by the German invasion of Holland.

My contribution was "A logistical approach to the ontological problem." Some philosophers repudiated abstract objects; others, I among them, repudiated properties but settled for classes, and repudiated unactualized possibles. But which of these philosophers, for all their repudiation, were still making unacknowledged references to those very objects? What counts as reference? I argued that the objects assumed, or referred to, are the values of the bound variables. The point seemed obvious, but it needed to be made to clarify issues.

Numerous logicians and wives who had attended the conference struck out for an outing on Mount Monadnock. There were Church, Curry, Kleene, Rosser, Tarski, and perhaps Carnap. When we were on the rocky summit, Tarski slipped and opened his scalp. Two of us made a cradle of our fists and wrists and carried him down the mountain. A doctor in Jaffrey sewed him up.

Goodman and I continued to meet. A by-product was our somewhat playful "Elimination of extra-logical postulates." Decades later I tightened and modernized our result, in the sardonically entitled paper "Implicit definition sustained." In this form the result is that any true statement can be reduced to a purely arithmetical truism by defining its component terms in certain ways that still preserve coextensiveness with their original interpretations.

My brother Bob was suffering marital anguish that reached the limit of his endurance in October 1939, when he disappeared to Bermuda. I alone knew where. After a time he surfaced, and was cajoled into coming home by his wife's representations that our mother was ailing. Ultimately they divorced. During these troubled times and Bob's subsequent romance with Rosalie, my beloved sister-in-law now these forty years, Bob came to know our home in Cambridge as Sanctuary Much.

· 1940   In March 1940 we moved to an old brick town house at 65 Sparks Street in a row of four. It had high ceilings and was spacious beyond our needs, but the rent was moderate out of proportion. Intermittently we sublet two to four of our superfluous rooms. Notable among our roomers were the philosophers Roderick Chisholm and Roderick Firth, who were graduate students.

Mathematical Logic   25

The logic of truth functions and quantification is usually couched in *schemata* in which letters stand as dummies for terms and clauses. This medium is vivid and efficient, but it fostered ontological and semantic confusions and condoned foggy philosophical notions about the application of logic and mathematics. In *Mathematical Logic*, bent on clarifying these muddles, I shunned schemata in favor of a more explicit idiom. Today the separation of use and mention is better heeded and related issues are less beclouded. We can now enjoy the convenience of schemata with little risk of misinterpretation. I think I helped.

In the chapters of *Mathematical Logic* on set theory I at first meant to follow "New foundations," but was deterred by a shortcoming. "New foundations" grew out of the theory of types, we saw, but it grew askew. It is more liberal than the theory of types both in its grammar (that is, as to what formulas are meaningful) and in its ontology (that is, as to what classes exist), but the grammatical liberation exceeded the ontological one. This asymmetry is found to impede certain arguments by mathematical induction.

How might I strengthen the ontology, then, without reviving the paradoxes? Taking a leaf from von Neumann, I threw in ultimate classes (as I now call them): classes that are not members of any classes. The old classes, capable of membership, are then spoken of more particularly as *sets*.

Von Neumann had assumed classes corresponding to all *predicative* membership conditions, that is, conditions in which the variables range only over sets. I took the more liberal line that has been taken again more recently by Kelley and Morse: I assumed classes corresponding to *all* membership conditions, the only restriction being that ultimate classes are never members. Stratification ceased to be a condition for class existence, and became rather a condition for being a set. Mathematical induction then proceeded swimmingly, and so did much else. Too much, as I learned two years later.

I developed an algebra of the concatenation of signs and reworked in it the proof of Gödel's celebrated incompleteness theorem, to the effect that there can be no sound and complete proof procedure for number theory. I worked for a while also at Gödel's completeness theorem, to the effect that we do have complete proof procedures for the logic of quantification. When I had done what I could with this in an expository way, I felt that it would still be disproportionately hard reading. It was not as hard as my treatment of his incompleteness theorem, but then the one theorem is world-shaking and the other is not. So I omitted it, never dreaming how easy a presentation of it would appear one day in my *Methods of Logic*.

The need to acknowledge sources, in *Mathematical Logic*, issued in historical paragraphs throughout the text. My search for sources led me to examine Frege, whose slim *Begriffsschrift* of 1879 I soon recognized as the real beginning of mathematical logic. There was no discoverable copy of it in America; I recovered its content rather from an old review by P. E. B. Jourdain.

My celebration of Frege in *Mathematical Logic* and in the classroom must have helped to bring people to see Frege as the father of modern logic. Russell had introduced him to us long ago, but we remained unaware of how much had been done first by Frege. I think Church first learned from my book that his functional abstraction was in Frege. At any rate he returned the favor three years later, pointing out that my notion of referential position and even my example of the Morning Star and the Evening Star were in Frege. I may have got the example through Russell.

In April 1939 the publisher W. W. Norton called on me to persuade me to write a book for him. When I told him I was working on one, he proposed a contract. For wide circulation I wanted to keep the price under four dollars. He said I could do so by waiving royalties on the first thousand in favor of a higher rate on succeeding thousands. My financial straits notwithstanding, I agreed.

Northeastern Press, in Maine, was to print it. Men from there came and conferred with me on typography. There was much to settle—spacing, styles of Greek letters, breaking of formulas. The printer experimented and sent samples, but began typesetting, over my protest, before all was settled. Costly rectifications were entailed.

The book appeared in September 1940. It was priced at

four dollars after all, because it had grown; so I had waived royalties on the first thousand in vain. Nor was the balance soon to be redressed; for the publisher reckoned all my collaboration with the printer as author's corrections, mortgaging my royalties on the second thousand.

What is called a cardinal number in set theory is the size of a class. An ordinal number is the length of a series. A number of either sort may be finite or infinite. Now Burali-Forti's paradox, dating from 1897 and affectionately known to Barkley Rosser as B40, consists in proving on the one hand that there is a greatest infinite ordinal number, and on the other hand that for every ordinal number there is a greater. The reason for its intrusion into this true history is that in October 1941 Rosser succeeded in deriving it from the set theory of my *Mathematical Logic*.

Cantor's paradox is parallel but treats of cardinal numbers. I knew how the argument that naturally led to it was obstructed in *Mathematical Logic*, and I had published the essential considerations as early as 1937. I was more surprised than pleased to learn now from Rosser's result that in some lethal respect Cantor's paradox and B40 were not parallel enough.

I devised a repair that entailed minimal disruption of the book, and prepared a correction slip for insertion in the unsold copies. I like to think it was inserted in some. I also published a less superficial alternative in a quick paper, "Element and number." These were slipshod repairs.

By November 1946 the second thousand copies of the book were exhausted and I had begun to get royalties. At that point the publisher discontinued the book. I had made $80.64.

Harvard University Press took it on. The correction slip was firmly imprinted, and I revelled in further spot corrections, which I made in the reproduction proof by cannibalizing one copy into another. For instance Paul Weiss had pointed out to me that Paul was not one of the twelve apostles, contrary to one of my examples; so I cut a 'Jo' from a

'Jones' and an 'h' and an 'n' from elsewhere and covered my 'Paul' with a 'John'.

In the fall of 1949, Hao Wang showed what should have been done after the B40 disaster. If the sets of *Mathematical Logic* were really not to exceed the classes of "New foundations," the bound variables in their membership conditions should be limited to sets for their values. Such was Wang's neat repair of *Mathematical Logic*, occasioning the revised edition, 1951.

"New foundations" retained interest, for Wang proved that *Mathematical Logic* as revised is consistent if and only if "New foundations" is consistent. This being the case, the strategic place in which to tackle the consistency problem is still "New foundations." Its ontology is sparser, lacking the ultimate classes, and furthermore a finite set of axioms suffices, as Hailperin showed.

Though superior to "New foundations," the system of *Mathematical Logic* is not ideal. Rosser has shown that the class of natural numbers cannot be proved in that system to be a set, unless the system is inconsistent. One must postulate that it is a set in order to found the theory of real numbers, and the postulate is an unwelcome artificiality.

The vicissitudes of *Mathematical Logic* have carried us eleven years ahead of my main story, which I now resume.

Tenure 26

In April 1940 I received a curiously deferred promotion. I was to become associate professor with tenure in September 1941. An official promise of tenure is already tenure, so my tenure began in April 1940, but without the title and the raise in pay. Publicity was to be deferred for a year, but I was permitted to anticipate it to the extent of emblazoning the title page of *Mathematical Logic* with my new rank. I cautioned the publisher against leaking it in his advertisements, but he went his way. Apologetic letters to President Conant from the publisher and me were graciously received.

Tarski, the Hempels, Feigl, and the Wohlstetters were all near in the summer of 1940. We had lively outings, joined by some or all of Nelson Goodman, Henry Leonard, Charles Stevenson, John Cooley, John Goheen, and Mason Gross. We gathered on the beach at Ipswich, at Goodman's newly built summer house on the rocks at Rockport, and on Edmund Morgan's broad lawn on the slope of Arlington. He was Roberta Wohlstetter's father and a law professor at Harvard.

My brother Bob came visiting, and with him Naomi and I ranged as far afield as the Isles of Shoals. I had first known of this obscure archipelago in elementary school, as the childhood home of Celia Thaxter. The islands are rocky, desolate, and ten miles off shore. Politically they are curious: a state line passes among them, crossing a breakwater. Part of the little cluster of islands lies in the town of Rye, New Hampshire, and part in Kittery, Maine. On the mainland the two towns are not even contiguous; they are separated by the city of Portsmouth.

I sailed for a week with John Cooley on the *Linnet*, his sleek thirty-eight-foot sloop, which I had seen abuilding in Boston Harbor. We boarded her in Salem along with two of John's Hartford friends, Phil Hewes and Hilliard Barbour, whom I came to know as Hilliard of the Halyards. A whale, spouting and diving, welcomed us to the open sea. After Cape Elizabeth we were befogged. Occasionally a ship loomed dimly at a hundred yards, heralded by foghorn. We listened for bell buoys to check our position from time to time. They tolled a melancholy knell as they rose and fell in the waves, all unseen and far from shore. More desolate still was the groaning and wailing of another kind of buoy, the growler. In due course—literally—we discerned high above us the dim outline of the lighthouse at Portland Head. We put in and found an anchorage for our third night.

Ensuing days were clear. On awakening we would look out on wooded and rocky islands and go over the side for a dip. Once under way, there was satisfaction in taking bearings on the charts with parallel rules and then identifying buoys and beacons as they passed. Geographical detail began to matter; a mistake could engender a sickening crunch. There was exhilaration in the rush of letting out sheets and backstays for a quick change of tack in a strong wind and heavy sea. John was an accomplished seaman and skipper. Sailing one morning from the picturesque port of Friendship to the open sea, we had to reckon with reefs and narrow channels, and the wind was dead ahead; so it was an occasion for sharp and skillful tacking.

We luxuriated in lobster. Off Port Clyde we bought them from a lobsterman as he was taking them into his boat. John was a good cook and an earnest judge of wine. He was lean and looked ascetic and hard-bitten, and he was serious and reflective about his pleasures. In his devotion to sailing, he would spend whole summers aboard *Linnet;* eventually he sailed her to Scotland. Winters he skied. He was a graduate student, between Yale and Harvard, for quite some years, pursuing philosophy with a sober and enduring interest. On the Columbia faculty in later years, he did his job cheerfully and conscientiously but cared nothing for academic advancement. He retired early and lived alone in a practical little house of his own design in rural Connecticut. A neighbor who came into the house to help with something is quoted by John as saying, "Why, it don't look at all like a hen coop from the inside."

On August 23, 1940—to get back to that—we lay at anchor in Penobscot Bay at Camden. I shouldered my duffle bag and took a bus to Rockland to meet a train that would be bearing Naomi and our small daughters; for we were to spend the ensuing week with the logician Steve Kleene and his parents in their ancestral farmhouse in the Camden Hills.

Steve had been one of Alonzo Church's brilliant graduate students in logic at Princeton in the earliest days, the other being Barkley Rosser. By the time of our visit he had already done much of the work in proof theory for which he is justly celebrated, creating recursive number theory and hierarchy theory. Steve was rugged, like John Cooley. In his youth he had spent a winter alone in that house, coming and going on snowshoes over snow so deep that he had to climb through a window.

We gathered blueberries. Steve had built a long canvas incline that he could shake as the berries rolled down it, thus shucking the stems. He wore clogs that he had made himself—a bit of plank, cut to shape, with a broad piece of leather over the instep. He outlined my feet on a board and sawed me a pair.

That fall my introductory course in logic resumed, and with it the textbook problem. Things are different today; complimentary copies of some sixty introductory American logic texts adorn the picture molding in my office, and most of them cover the elements of modern logic. My *Mathematical Logic* was just out, but it was too austere for a course aimed at undergraduates in all fields. John Cooley was my teaching assistant, and we got by that fall with some mimeograms of his that were to develop two years later into a text of his own. Meanwhile, between July and December, I wrote *Elementary Logic*. Relaxing the austerity of *Mathematical Logic*, I ventured full use of schemata, scrupulously hedged about with expository precautions. I called them *frames*. Schemata were not yet generally recognized for what they are, and usage was not yet cut and dried. I was cutting and drying.

The fall term of 1940 is graven in my memory for more than just the writing of *Elementary Logic*. Russell, Carnap, and Tarski were all at hand. Tarski had a makeshift research appointment at Harvard and was in need of a job. Carnap had a visiting professorship with us. Russell was giving the William James Lectures, backed by a seminar. The lectures became *An Inquiry into Meaning and Truth*. There was an effort, issuing from Brown University, to promote periodic gatherings for discussion. Huntington, Lewis, Sheffer, Prall, and Ivor Richards were among the Harvard participants, and the Brown contingent included Baylis, A. A. Bennett, and Ducasse. Our three-star cast managed to bow out after two of these unwieldy sessions, and to meet in the seclusion rather of Ivor's study or Carnap's flat along with a few of us younger devotees. Carnap, Tarski, and I continued to meet more persistently, along with Goodman or John Cooley. By way of providing structure for our discussions, Carnap proposed reading the manuscript of his *Introduction to Semantics* for criticism.

My misgivings over meaning had by this time issued in explicit doubts about the notion, crucial to Carnap's philosophy, of an *analytic* sentence: a sentence true purely by virtue of the meanings of its words. I voiced these doubts, joined by Tarski, before Carnap had finished reading us his first page. The controversy continued through subsequent sessions, without resolution and without progress in the reading of Carnap's manuscript.

Hempel was teaching at Queens College in Flushing, along with Goheen, and by December Tarski was established at City College. The convention of philosophers and logicians in December 1940 was at Penn. Goodman and I drove down in his car, picking Tarski up in New York on the way. I was impressed with the parklike character of the new Merritt Parkway, devoid of billboards; billboards had been thought inseparable from capitalism. I was further impressed by the swift transit on the new expressways, culminating in the Pulaski Skyway. After the convention we all went to the Hempels' house in Flushing, where Nelson and I stayed the night. There was more of that nice blend of merriment and high-grade discussion.

Naomi's sanguine and energetic phases had seen, in previous years, the inception of her nursery classes and the Window Shop. In the winter of 1940–1941, she was furiously at work on a book whose good title I appropriated three chapters back: *On an Azore*. She wrote an article on the same subject, which she hoped to sell to *Harper's*. She worked through an agent and went to New York in connection with the project. Nothing had come of it when her depressed phase supervened.

· 1941   My own writing that spring, apart from the usual spate of reviews for the *Journal of Symbolic Logic,* was the essay that I was asked to contribute to the Whitehead volume in Schilpp's Library of Living Philosophers. I wrote "Whitehead and the rise of modern logic." Meanwhile the free world was collapsing before the onslaught of the Nazis. I found myself on the mailing list of a periodical leaflet called *Poland Fights,* and read in it of the horrors of Oświecim. To toy with logical abstractions and philosophical speculations in the face of these things seemed disproportionate. I wondered if I might make myself useful in cryptanalysis. Inquiries led in June 1941 to my enrollment in a correspondence course in elementary cryptanalysis, administered by the Navy. By then I had also heard of a government program of cultural relations with Latin America and had written to the State Department asking about that.

Mexico in Depth 27

Aztecs dream of blood and battle.
Aztec babies coo and prattle.
Baby dawdles with his rattle,
Papa with his atl-atl.

Two young people, my student Donald Davidson for one, were bent on a motor trip through Mexico. Sensitive to the proprieties, they proposed that I make a third. From a rendezvous in Defiance, Ohio, on Independence Day, 1941, we drove southwest. At Cairo we gazed for a while at the mighty confluence of the Ohio and the Mississippi. At my urging we next set our course for New Madrid, Missouri, where there was a boundary anomaly that had taken my fancy. The westernmost bit of Kentucky is five miles away from the rest of that state, cut off by a meander of the Mississippi that lets a promontory of Missouri intervene. Inhabitants of those twenty far-flung square miles can consort with their fellow

Kentuckians only by detouring through Tennessee. We looked across at this twice-trans-Mississippian bit of Kentucky farmland from New Madrid.

In sweltering Texas we stopped now and again at a roadside ice house, bought a great watermelon from off the ice, and divided it roughly by dropping it on the pavement. We savored the Spanish quality of San Antonio and plunged on through the boundless dry parklands of dusty green mesquite trees. There was the magic of the Wild West again, enhanced by the tale of my mother's childhood visit; for we came to Encinal itself. The general store was the same one, surely, that had belonged to Uncle Ellis.

It was Laredo for the night, but naturally we crossed the Rio Grande forthwith to sleep in Nuevo Laredo, Mexico, in a little hotel on the canonical plaza. Continuing southward in the succeeding days, we watched the vegetation change with the latitude. At first, along with the mesquite, there was sagebrush, stunted yucca, and prickly pear. The flat, leaf-like, but succulent bodies that grow end to end to form the prickly-pear plant suggest bare human feet, despite their greenness, and the four or five fruits along the outer rim suggest so many green toes. As they ripen, the toes turn purple and one's thoughts turn to gangrene.

As the miles slipped by, the prickly pear became a tree, while the mesquite trees shrank to shrubs and the sagebrush disappeared. The organ-pipe type of cactus (cereus) emerged, and it in turn became higher and more ramified as we proceeded. Yucca grew higher as well, and, when not branched, looked increasingly like palms. After another hundred miles, we were driving through a forest of palmlike yucca—or *were* they now palms? The one does not become the other; yuccas are in the lily family, palms in the palm family. Functional parallelism works wonders.

There ensued a hundred miles and more of tropical jungle, inhabited by Huasteca Indians whose huts were woven of withes and thatched with palm fronds. Some huts were rectangular, others cylindrical with conical roofs. After Tamazunchale (pronounced Thos. & Charlie), we began our tortuous ascent to the vertiginous brinks of the high plateau. Here the walls of the huts were palisades of cereus, planted as hedges.

Towns on the plateau were in the Mediterranean tradition, with tight rows of white plastered houses tight to the street. The roofs were of the traditional half-round red tiles or, occasionally, of thatch. Most streets were narrow and either unpaved or paved with cobblestone with a slight gutter down the middle. Facing the plaza there might be a big square sixteenth-century church that once doubled as a fortress. It would typically have a baroque partial façade of dark stone in bas-relief, set against the broader surface, pale and blank, of the square front of the church.

The average townsman was an Indian with a dash of Spanish. He wore a sarape, either impaled as a poncho or shawl-wise, and a big sombrero. If elegant he might wear a holster and pearl-handled pistol. (Echoes of Uncle Ellis: "Never turn your back on a Mexican.") The women wore their hair in two long braids and wore a rebozo over the head or around the shoulders.

We stood in a moonlit cobblestone square in Zimapán. Silhouetted against a backdrop of plastered houses, six sombreroed figures harmonized with strong, mellow voices to the staccato accompaniment of two guitars, for no apparent audience.

On Sundays, in a big town, the young ladies would promenade counterclockwise around the plaza in their finery, and the swains clockwise. In the fullness of time the two concentric circles would dissolve into pairs.

Several times a day, in the street or market, I would pay a cent for a luscious, thick slice of ripe pineapple. I might vary it with a banana or, for an exotic taste sensation, a mango.

Mexicans named streets for political abstractions. There is the Calle del 16 de Septiembre, and an Avenida del 5 de Mayo; nor did they limit themselves to dates. We also saw a Calle del Artículo 123, a Calle Sufragio Efectivo, and a Calle No Reelección.

Our farthest south was south indeed: Acapulco, on the

south coast of North America, south of 17°. The sun was fiercely vertical at noon. There were big iguanas and many flamingoes. The sea was room temperature, body temperature; it differed only in texture from the air. Rain-forested mountains were an immediate backdrop, rising from the beaches. One bit of beach had a little lagoon behind it, into which an abundance of fish would be swept at high tide, even an occasional shark, and be trapped as the tide receded. Fishing there was a gathering operation. Acapulco was a sleepy town in those days, a minor port and a modest resort visited by a few Mexican families on vacation.

Turning back northward, we crossed again a great wild region of steaming jungle and the brown Río Balsas. At the pottery town of Iguala we loaded up on their wares. Then we continued to Taxco.

We stayed a week, delighted with the narrow, steep cobblestone streets, the plaza shaded with Indian laurels, and the beautiful chirrurgueresque Parroquía de Santa Prisca in brown sandstone with its ornate façade, twin towers, and brightly tiled dome. There was an arched street alongside the church, and from it a steep stairway down to a colorful open market. Great wooded mountains rose behind the town, which straggled painfully up their lower slopes. The town was dominated at one end by a cliff, the *Cantera*, that rose to a dizzy height and culminated in a green brow of gently rounded pasture grazed by placid cows who knew better, one hoped, than to graze backward.

A long drink of tequila, fresh limes, and soda was locally known as a *berta* after the proprietress of a cantina facing the plaza. We would sit in Berta's of an evening, sipping bertas and listening to Don Vicente and the boy Tito play their guitars and sing Mexican songs. A favorite, which I heard there for the first time, was "María Elena" ("Tuyo es mi corazón . . .").

We stayed in an obscure hotel that had its own filter for purifying the drinking water. The filter looked crude, but we trusted it all week without ill effect. When we left, the others waited in the car while I slipped down to the market to buy us a stack of slabs of pineapple for breakfast. Since I was buying nearly the equivalent of a whole pineapple, I took the opportunity to have the woman pare a new one, not yet subject to the swarming of flies. Sensing that I had sanitation in mind, she doused her machete in her pail of poisonous water before hacking off the husk of the pineapple. Then she dunked the pared pineapple in the poisonous water, sloshed water over her chopping block, and proceeded to the slicing. I was touched by her misguided solicitude and did not interfere; what could those few drops of water do? I delivered the goods and said nothing of the affair, but we all three had cramps and diarrhea by nightfall. Evidently the tacky filter in the hotel had been doing a valiant job.

My inquiry about the program of cultural relations with Latin America had meanwhile been forwarded by the State Department to Henry Allen Moe. In a letter that awaited me in Mexico City, he wrote that Brazil was a possibility. This thought was thenceforward much in my mind.

From the great Toltec pyramids at Teotihuacán we drove through the little state of Tlaxcala and on to Cholula, town of a hundred churches. It had bristled with heathen shrines and Cortés supplanted each with a church, as was his wont. One of them crowns a hill that had just been found to conceal a pyramid, the biggest in the world. Tunnels were being dug.

We sought out the little church of Santa María de Tonanzintla, at an offbeat edge of Cholula. The white plaster walls of the interior were ornamented with bright little vignettes of colorful fresco—of fruit, flowers, and angels with feathers in their hair. They were the work of Indian converts just after the Conquest.

On, then, a few miles to Puebla, notable for its blue-tiled colonial palaces and its secret convent that defied the ban of convents. We put in a bad night with bedbugs.

We went west again over the mountains next day to Amecameca, with the idea of climbing Popocatépetl. The climb begins at midnight, so we planned to get a proper sleep, free of bedbugs, and to arrange next day for a guide and gear. But when we looked into the only hotel we found it shabby, dirty, and overpriced; so we decided to try the climb that very night. It was already ten at night, and people said we could not get a guide or gear till the next day. A book mentioned two guides, however, so I inquired for the house of Felipe Pérez. It was a hut of adobe, the floor was of dirt, and the walls were hung with wooden figures of saints. We settled on six dollars for guide, crampons, and alpenstocks. It was raining hard and the electricity was off. In a roadside shelter a noisome meal was served us by an Indian hag, fingering with black fingernails in steaming pots and vats by candlelight.

At midnight, with a guide roused by Pérez and a boy to guard the car, we started driving up a back road to the Paso de Cortés, the saddle between the snowy heights of Ixtaccíhuatl and Popocatépetl, where a highway has since been put through. We set off on foot at 2:15. Dawn brought warmth when our toes and fingers felt about to freeze; Don did get frostbite. It was perhaps at about fifteen thousand feet that the thinness of the air had reduced our progress to spurts of fifteen short steps on all fours up the steepening grade; for we had had no time to acclimatize. The surface by then was loose volcanic ash covered with light snow, and with each step we sank back part way. At perhaps sixteen and a half thousand feet, collapsing and gasping with pounding heart after each short step, I told Don to signal me from the next visible horizon. I would continue to that point if it was the crater's rim; if it was not—and it was not—I would stay and save myself for Brazil. He, fool or hero, got to the rim and looked down into the steaming sulphur from well over seventeen thousand feet.

Vigor renewed disproportionately with each stride of our fast descent. We got to the car at four in the afternoon. We had tried in vain to rouse the gasoline man the night before, and now we found that too little remained to start the car. By pushing, coasting, and briefly starting the engine by momentum where necessary, we made the eighteen-mile descent to Amecameca.

As we drove from there to Cuernavaca in the night, we passed low cliffs that seemed vaguely to be carved in bas-relief, perhaps of battle scenes. My two companions had the same impression, though we were too exhausted to speak of it till the next day. There was no mention of it in the books, and we put it down to illusion. Forty years later I learned otherwise. In the new museum of anthropology in Mexico City there is a cast of part of a pre-Columbian bas-relief from that vicinity.

On another day we drove to Tepoztlán, having read the book about it by the ethnographer Robert Redfield. It nestles under precipitous heights and pinnacles. As we walked about the town with open book, we were joined by a native who recognized people in the pictures. "He died," the man said in Spanish. "He sang well." The man invited us to lunch in his adobe abode, with his wife and her mother. With them he talked Náhuatl, the language of the Aztecs. The old woman ground corn on a *metate*, slapped the wet meal into tortillas, and toasted them on a *comal*, or clay disk, over a wood fire. We all sat around a great pot and reached into the stew of meat and beans with our tortillas.

Often the simple traditional hotels were clean and pleasant. The one at Zitácuaro, on the road into western Mexico, was such a one. Its cobblestone patio was surrounded by a rough wooden gallery off which the rooms opened, each with a tiled floor and whitewashed walls. Daylight entered only through the patio, while blank walls faced the world.

On the Lake of Pátzcuaro, Tarascan Indians in little boats wielded nets that look like big butterflies. We visited their island village, Janitzio.

Continuing west the next day, with the lake on our left, I was puzzled to see it suddenly on our right; our road was making a loop of some miles, crossing itself with an overpass. There was no such necessity in the terrain. The planners had evidently wanted to impose a proper view of the lake upon passing travelers. Returning eight years later, I found that impatient motorists had made a rude track by-passing the overpass.

At Zacapu I left my young friends and took a train north. Naomi and the girls had been with Marguerite in California, and I had arranged to meet them for a week in the desert capital of Chihuahua on the way back. I stopped one night in Aguascalientes, a garden spot, and one in Zacatecas, a high mining town. In Chihuahua we settled into a boarding house, where the landlady saw to the girls while Naomi and I prowled the dry city or rented horses and rode out through the limitless chaparral. Occasionally a Tarahumara walked into town from the distant Sierra, dressed in a sort of shirt and loincloth. The men wear their hair long, bound with a red headband. They make violins.

Naomi and the girls took a train north over the desert to El Paso and continued to Boston by train, while I took trains south and east over the desert to Monterrey and continued to Boston with my friends. They obligingly deviated from the geodesic to touch Florida and South Carolina at their northwest corners.

I was in discomfort along the way, owing to an indiscretion. I had acquired in Mexico a taste for chili peppers, and at Vivian, Louisiana, I ingested with some bravado a formidable infusion of them, searing my intestines. Relief came at last at Fancy Gap, Virginia, thanks to Chamberlain's Colic Remedy, "for windy colic."

Flying Down to Rio   28

In the fall of 1941 I was teaching as usual and had become an associate professor. I was coping with the B40 crisis (see Chapter 25) and was engrossed in the correspondence course in cryptanalysis. Concurrently I corresponded with Moe about my possible mission to Brazil: about place, time, money, sponsorship, wartime transportation, and arrangements at Harvard. We exchanged thirty-three letters and telegrams, and there were more to and from related persons. The negotiations fell into three phases, with delay and uncertainty between them. I pictured it in the form of a trilogy: (1) Meet Mr. Moe, (2) How Now, Mr. Moe?, (3) Mr. Moe Comes Through.

Young Henry Aiken and his lovely wife Jean were spending the evening with us in our house in Sparks Street on December 7 when news came over the radio of the attack on Pearl Harbor. For me the shock was combined with relief; at last we would get into the war. In February 1942, with the correspondence course still in progress, the Boston commandant was instructed to request my application for a commission in the Naval Reserve—such are the channels. I complied. Also, playing the alternative, I was listening to shortwave broadcasts in Portuguese and attending Nykl's second Portuguese course; for Moe was still arranging the mission to Brazil, and I was resolved to do my lecturing in Portuguese if I went.

· 1942

The commission came through in April, but not the full lieutenancy that I had been given to expect. Further correspondence ensued, and steps were taken. By then I had put four hundred hours into the cryptanalysis course.

Research in logic had seemed, for a year, like fiddling while Rome burned. I had been repressing my sporadic thoughts on the subject, except as required in my teaching. With the stalling of my commission, thought of logic promptly surfaced and within two days I got off a short article, "On existence conditions for elements and classes." It points out that my impredicative extension (chapter 25 again) of von Neumann's predicative existence condition for classes, in which I was followed years later by Kelley and Morse, is equivalent to Zermelo's basic existence condition plus the existence of a class of all sets.

By May I was still faced with three possible immediate futures: Brazil, Navy, and Harvard. Moe had not completed all the arrangements for Brazil, and he understood that I would cancel Brazil anyway if my proper commission came through.

Third, I was booked for summer courses at Harvard; the university was on a wartime schedule of three regular terms a year, each teacher serving in two. I had been pressed to offer a historical course for once, and had settled on Leibniz.

I was glad to be rescued from Leibniz, for rescued I was. Arrangements for Brazil were concluded by the middle of May, and I went a week later. Commander Hayes wrote me that the confusion over my commission would probably be resolved meanwhile, and that I could be sworn in when I got back in September.

Examinations had to be administered and final grades computed in my two courses. This I left to my graduate assistant, George Berry. George had been indifferent to mathematics and indifferent at it, so he told me, until he took up mathematical logic in my courses, where his work was excellent. As the war went on he was even drawn into the crash program of teaching basic mathematics to naval recruits. He contributed a notable improvement to my *Mathematical Logic,* and he taught logic at Princeton and Boston University down the decades.

Norman Mattis threw a farewell party. Ringling Brothers' circus was in town, and some of its headliners were Norman's guests. There was Truzzi, half Italian and half Russian, "the greatest juggler of all time." He had twelve minutes of the circus to himself alone. There was Miss Ardelty, Russian, of the high bar, equally touted, Miss Maito, Russo-Chinese, of the highwire, and others. They were colorful people, animated talkers, and impressive as people who have had exciting experiences, worked hard, and acquired incredible skills. We went to the circus the next evening and watched our new friends in amazed admiration.

I wrote to Ed Haskell that

the singularly unsordid fact is that this coming Sat. a.m. I am going to board a plane in N.Y. and set about winging my way to a hemisphere yet more southerly than our own. I am to undertake to infuse some knowledge of mathematical logic and mathematical phi-

losophy and logic of mathematics and philosophy of mathematics and logic of philosophy and philosophy of logic, and withal a modicum of gen. semantics ("gen." for "genuine"), into the Brazilian mind (or minds, as the case may be).

Except for my five minutes in the air out of Squantum eleven years earlier, this was my first flight. Shades were drawn at takeoffs and landings, for wartime security. When they were raised, out of New York, we were looking down on the silver lining of a gray day. Soon the clouds broke. I watched the Delaware River slip away, and Wilmington, the Chesapeake Bay, and Baltimore. For a map fancier it was dreamlike, finding each major feature of the seaboard unerringly in place. As we came down at Washington the shades were pulled, but only after we had passed over the front steps of the Capitol. After we took off again, the shades went up to reveal the bends of the Potomac estuary, then the Rappahannock, and eventually the Carolina coast. I identified Savannah, and watched the coast from there to Miami except when the shades were drawn for a stop at Jacksonville. We flew low enough to recognize palms and orange trees and the old mission at St. Augustine. I identified Daytona Beach, where Tommy Milton had made ephemeral history, I recalled, by driving a Duesenburg Twin Eight over the hard sands 156-1/2 miles an hour. After Cape Canaveral and Palm Beach the Everglades were visible inland, like a vast plain dotted with puddles, and Lake Okeechobee shone far away. We flew over uninhabited real-estate developments, relics of the notorious land boom. There were boulevards, squares, and roundabouts, but not a house. We finished the flight in steaming Miami, where a room had been reserved for me in the Columbus. Night flying was only for army pilots and intrepid letter carriers like Antoine de St.-Exupéry.

We took off at dawn and helped the sun to rise from a tropical sea. Cottony clouds stacked up to vast heights, as clouds will in a tropical updraft. I had tried the day before to induce an acrophobic twinge by getting up against the windowpane and suddenly looking steeply down. I could get only a slight twinge. Flying through the top of a towering stack of clouds, however, and looking steeply down two miles to a rippling sea through a cleft whose wispy sides were visible all the way, was as breathtaking as the Grand Canyon twice over. What matters is a visible vertical measure.

We flew over coral flats, dull gray or red-brown. These gave way to a green film of low, tangled mangrove—the coast of Cuba. Then came jungle, palm forest, savanna, palm-thatched huts, a village. Every feature emerged in gemlike miniature, and in vivid relation to what lay far before and far behind. It was a sight that bridged the gap between reality and map.

Presently we were looking at a city of plastered adobe, and its details were taking on natural size. We were completing the transition from map to reality, putting down at Camagüey. With a bump I found myself out of my trance. I ran down a lane from our earthen runway to a roadside stand where I bought Cuban cigarettes and talked with natives, who dropped their postvocalic esses as they had been said to do.

With windows no longer screened against military secrets, I could savor the takeoff. First there is the deliberate business of taxiing downwind and turning around. It is a good buildup. Then you go roaring along the runway, developing more speed than the earth will tolerate. You do not quite know when the earth has let go until you see that you have cleared a curb without disaster, and a hedge, and you are pulling up over the houses. You have entered again that luminous trance in which the world passes before you in miniature, hundreds of miles of it every hour.

We flew up the Golfe des Gonaïves in Haiti, with mountains to port and la Gonave to starboard, the island that gained such an air of mystery from the writings of William Seabrook and the white king Faustin Wirkus. We flew the length of la Gonave, no higher than its highest hill. Any house that I missed, or any path even, was on the south slope.

We flew low over the capital of Haiti, Port-au-Prince, with its wooden baroque cathedral and its jumble of tin-roofed shacks, and landed again. We were confined to the airport, but I talked with a black official about the beauties of Haiti and the terrors of Christophe. His was a strangely gasping French, but intelligible, unlike what is reported of the peasant Creole.

Eastward from Port-au-Prince to the Dominican Republic there extends the Plaine du Cul de Sac. A map of Haiti had hung over my desk for years, and that little plain had been the object of frequent fleeting speculation. Once Naomi and I had had tickets for a freighter cruise around Haiti, only to turn them back when we saw we could not afford it; and in those days, I had pondered our chances of getting across that plain to the Etang Saumâtre and the Lago de Enriquillo and back while the boat was in port or between ports. Now I was flying across the plain, glimpsing virtually every house, road, and field between the gulf behind and the lakes before, and flying on through the desert crags of the Dominican Republic.

We put down at the capital, called Santo Domingo first and last but Ciudad Trujillo at the time. The oldest European settlement in America, it seemed a shabby town of bare boards, plaster, and tin roofs. Off, then, over the rice and sugar fields of the east end of the island. Screens of frosted glass were put into the windows as we flew the length of Puerto Rico and put down at San Juan. From there on the elegant, lush little uptossed islands of the Lesser Antilles had me spellbound. Hours of the preceding quarter-century had gone into poring over maps of them. A score of them were familiar by name and relative position, and now I was seeing them in their radiant green, rugged reality. There was Saba, green volcano in the sea, with the town of Bottom in the crater on top, and Orange Town at the bottom by the beach. This was once the main outlet of gold that had crossed Panama from Peru; now it was an English-speaking

Dutch island. No less comical, all in all, than conical. This much I had known from Ted Palmer. What my delight, then, at skimming over its shoulder! And at flying, low, squarely over the little Dutch island of St. Eustatius, seemingly a one-street island of a dozen houses, but surely more. St. Martin, with its absurd little international boundary across its middle, was visible off to port.

We put down at Antigua for the night of May 24, 1941, and were all whisked by bus halfway around the island to a seaside hotel. Off again at dawn, we flew down the Windward Islands. Green Guadeloupe sprawled maplike under our port beam. On then past Dominica, to find Martinique shrouded in clouds amid an unclouded sea. St. Lucia and St. Vincent were partly hidden, but Grenada shone. It was rugged, a patchwork of forest and tight little farms, with St. George's tucked into a corner pocket.

Screens went up as we approached Trinidad. We put down for an hour in a dull plain under the northern hills. A local soldier of Chinese race talked to me of Port of Spain, which I would not see, a kaleidoscope of the five cardinal hues of humankind.

Then we took off for British Guiana. After a stretch of hilly jungle, the screens were installed again and we landed on a clearing of white sand in the wilds of a savanna. From there we flew into Surinam. Heavy equatorial forest gave way to canefields and rice paddies as we approached Paramaribo, a little semicircular white city in the bend of an estuary. Houses were low, sprawling, roofed with metal, and standing on stilts. We flew upstream twenty miles and put down. There were some alert, intelligent-looking natives who appeared decidedly Oriental, but a local Dutchman told me they were Guiana Indians.

The clouds opened to a violent cloudburst. When the worst was over, we took off and flew along the coast into French Guiana. We had a close view of Devil's Island— three sinister islands really, several miles from the jungles of the coast. The Vichy government had abandoned the prisoners, I gathered, allowing them to get to civilization if they could. Several were said to have reached the mainland in a makeshift boat. Others—we saw them—were still trying to scrape a living on the islands.

We flew past Cayenne, a forbidding tin-roofed village cramped between the jungle and the sea at the mouth of a quiet black river, and continued over heavy jungle, unbroken except by an occasional broad black river. Because of the delay in Surinam, we had a bit of night flying. We crossed the Amazon delta, visible as black masses of forest and wide stretches of dim water, and put down for the night at Belém, a hundred miles beyond the equator. The limousine threaded miles of streets lined with little plastered houses of one or two rooms. Hammocks were visible through lighted doorways. Finally there was downtown Belém, its streets lined with mango trees and decaying palaces from the days of the rubber boom.

We were off again at daybreak, to fly for hours over the closed rain forest, flat, trackless, undifferentiated. Eventually the terrain turned irregular and I could see an occasional trail, or a few native huts. The land rose to a plateau of grasslands and scrub, flat except for an occasional ramified system of gulleys crammed with jungle growth. Evidently the plateau surface was alkaline and the subsoil fertile. The country continued thus for hundreds of miles, seemingly uninhabited. At length the valleys cutting through the crust of the plateau became predominant, with the remnants of plateau isolated as mesas.

I became acquainted with two young men. One of them was an Argentine whose name, which I have forgotten, was as English as Robert Hamilton Stevens. He looked as English as his name, yet his language was Spanish, and his English negligible. The other was an American ensign, a courier with a briefcase that was to be in his possession at all times. He was a son of N. C. Wyeth, whom I knew as the illustrator of books of my boyhood. I knew nothing then of the ensign's brother Andrew, who was to outshine their father in the fullness of time.

After a fuel stop at Barreiras, cattle were visible, and occasionally a road. The state of Minas Gerais, or General Mines, was a pinched and puckered terrain, cultivated in part. We enjoyed bird's-eye views of Pirapora, the head of navigation on the broad river São Francisco, and Belo Horizonte, the landscaped state capital. Then came the implausible vertical contours of the Organ Mountains, and finally Rio de Janeiro.

We repeatedly circled the breathtaking scene. Shifting clouds revealed startling slices of the city at random. There were the Pão de Açucar and the Corcovado—the Sugar Loaf and the Hunchback—and the sundry lesser mountains, each rimmed by solid urban streets of red-roofed white houses and topped by a *favella*—a rustic hamlet of huts or simple houses amid banana trees. There were sparkling curved beaches separated by abrupt high headlands and rimmed always with dense white and red city. At the edge of the almost landlocked Guanabara Bay, the Santos Dumont airport nestled challengingly in the very shadow of these assorted heights. To it we at length descended, having flown four days from New York.

Metropolitan Brazil   29

The Coordinator of Inter-American affairs, Nelson Rockefeller, was paying me what I would otherwise have been getting from Harvard, thus keeping the home fires burning, and in addition he was paying my expenses abroad, in a refreshingly relaxed fashion. He gave me my round trip ticket and a generous wad of cash to use as needed. I would give back what was left. Hotels *en route* were the airline's affair in those days, but the choice was mine in Rio and São Paulo, and I adopted the policy of taking the second-best. The best would be an extravagance, needed for the prestige of a diplomat or high executive but pointless for such an one as I.

The second-best meant gracious living at under two dollars a night. At the end I gave back $258.68.

I was scarcely ensconced in the Hotel Pax, in Rio, when the phone rang. I answered it and understood nothing. Tiring at length of apologizing and hearing more of the same, I hung up. If he was to communicate with me, he would have to face me; my tenuous Portuguese needed visual and situational aids. He rang again, I answered and listened listlessly, and I understood everything. I found that he was speaking slowly. When I had been trying, I had supposed he was talking rapidly and I had tried to interpolate syllables. Thenceforward I was competent at the Brazilian telephone; my panic was gone. I have forgotten which kind Brazilian that caller was.

Through Tarski, I had met Pontes de Miranda, the Brazilian ambassador to Colombia. He lived abundantly at the Hotel Plaza in New York, evidently letting Colombia go its way. He would have interested Ludwig Bemelmans. He wrote *O Problema do conhecimento* and a book of aphorisms, *O Sábio e o artista*, and he nursed a fancied interest in logic. My efforts with him had gone into trying to make him see that the connective 'or' can retain the inclusive interpretation even when it joins contrary clauses. He had a Tudor-style palace in Rio, a wife presiding over it, and a secretary named Laura Austregésilo. They entertained me, and Laura continued to look to my needs and interests. She helped me prepare my first lecture in Portuguese. Through her arranging I met the journalist Rubem Braga, whose witty volume *O Conde e o passarinho* I had enjoyed in Nykl's Portuguese course. She believed to the end that I had been sent by my government to observe and make a *reportagem*. My protestations to the contrary were simply to be expected.

I was welcomed by Ozório de Almeida, a distinguished biologist with a distinguished black beard. He and his wife lived graciously in a handsome house with the inevitable magnificent view. He told me that in the States, when he identified himself on the telephone, he would get the apologetic response: "Oh, I didn't recognize your voice." It interested him that in North America people apparently expect to be recognized by their voices.

Also I was entertained by the Philadelphia painter George Biddle and his Belgian wife in their flat at Copacabana. He and I swam in the tepid sea and talked as we walked the vast arc of white beach backed by the vast arc of luxurious white apartment houses. He was a pioneer jogger, jogging miles each morning on the beach. He was the author of *An American Artist's Story* and a brother of the attorney general.

Strolling idly in a little residential street one day, I yawned cavernously. A man standing in front of his house said with a startled expression, "Feche a boca! Que é isso?" ("Close the mouth! What *is* this?") It was an unaccountable, surrealist moment that has tickled me for years.

Once on a mapless prowl I became aware that whereas the row of house fronts on my left was broken by a side street from time to time, the row on my right was never interrupted. My course, moreover, kept tending to the right. Eventually I verified that I had come full circle. Moving away on a side street to get a perspective over the housetops, I saw that I had circumambulated an abrupt hill, a peak of tropical countryside sticking up through the hard fabric of the city. A cluster of rude rural dwellings was visible toward the top, but no road. As I was wondering how to get through the solid ring of houses that girdled the base of the hill, I saw a black woman with laden head go through a doorway that proved to lead between houses rather than into a house. The path meandered up the hill and I followed it to the top. There I talked with a mulatto who was raking the arid little fenced yard in front of his humble house. He invited me in and we had a tot of *cachaça*, the colorless cane spirit that is the common man's tipple in Brazil. He was in the navy and proudly showed me his identification card. Along with his photograph and other data, it indicated his color. There were *preto* (black), *mulato*, *pardo*, and *branco* (white). His was ticked off as *pardo*.

Lunch in Brazil could be instantaneous and excellent. One stood at a counter off a busy sidewalk and ate *pasteis*.

There were two categories, *doce* and *salgado*: sweet and salty. Each was a pouch of pastry, wet and luscious within. A sweet one might harbor a fresh fig or a plum. The salty ones, kept warm by a light bulb in a little showcase, contained perhaps a bit of fish or a segment of heart of palm. There were chicken legs, built out with mashed potato and crisply browned, with the bone projecting as a handle. Lengths of sugar cane were fed into a mill and the faintly green juice gushed out, two cents for a tumbler. Other mills did the same for oranges, one of them *com cascas*—with the skins— and the other *sem cascas*. The one was gratefully bitter, like strong marmalade.

A meal in a simple Brazilian restaurant might comprise soup, rice, wet red beans, beef, a bowl of lettuce, a piece of cheese with a slab of guava jelly, and a superb demi-tasse, all for thirteen cents. Another staple was manioc, either sauté in strips like parsnips or purveyed by the handful as loose coarse meal, called *farofa*. A traditional repast for Saturday afternoon is the *feijoada*, a heavy, hearty casserole of beans, sausage, and fish. It calls for a good deal of cutting through and washing down, and the need is met with generous libations of *cachaça*. This time-honored custom required more leisure, however, than I could regularly spare, for the rest of such a Saturday was apt to be unproductive.

There was notable dining too, especially in some Italian restaurants in São Paulo that stressed lobster mayonnaise and other delicate renderings of *frutti del mare*.

Brazilian friends took me to a circus. One of them bought *pipoca*, a native novelty that I was meant to find strange and exotic. It proved to be popcorn.

Trams were called *bondes* (pronounced "bondjish" in Rio, "bondis" in São Paulo) because they were financed by a bond issue. They were like the summer streetcars of my early youth. There was a boarding step or catwalk along the side, running the length of the car, and no wall; you moved directly from street to seat. They were as effortless as the stand-up lunch; you walked in your chosen direction, and if overtaken by a car you hopped on. You could get on and off between stops, velocity permitting. Money was no object: a *tostão*, or half a cent, for a short haul. Often the seats were full and the catwalk was crowded with hangers-on, two deep. The collector of fares, a young acrobat, would pick his way along the catwalk outside this double file, reaching over and between intervening shoulders to secure himself with one hand while taking *tostões* with the other. Once when I was hanging on, in the second or outer file, my hat struck the awning of a store front, sparing me a bump on the head.

There was a desperate shortage of gasoline. At length it was restricted to taxies, busses, and essential trucks. Cars emerged with *gasogénios*—grotesque superstructures that burned charcoal to produce gas.

My main responsibility in Brazil was a logic course in the Escola Livre de Sociologia e Política of the Universidade de São Paulo. Ideas in logic and adjacent fringes of philosophy had been striking my mind for a year past and getting suppressed, but now the lid was off and the ideas came welling forth and flowing into place. The course organized itself, with new angles and shortcuts that pleased me as I surveyed them. Content was ready and waiting; language was the task outstanding. It was expected that I would lecture in English, but I would not.

Happily I had already progressed in that task when Cyro Berlinck, the director of the Escola Livre, came to Rio and told me that I could start a month earlier than expected. On June 17 I flew to São Paulo. I gave the first two lectures that day and the next.

A cold wave set in. Headlines screamed *Geou em São Paulo*—"It froze in São Paulo." The temperature dropped well into the twenties and persisted there. It was unheard of: São Paulo is ten miles from the Tropic of Capricorn, at a moderate altitude of three thousand feet. Canvas blinds were drawn on the open trams. I managed to buy a comparatively heavy raincoat. I moved from my shady room to another hotel where I could get a room on the sunny side; there were no heating facilities anywhere. I sat in my raincoat and wrote with numb fingers. After some days, exhausted by shivering, I contrived a weekend of respite by taking the train down the escarpment to Santos, by the sea.

São Paulo had sprouted some middling skyscrapers. Cocks crew in their shadow. In the middle of the city there was an inconsiderable depression that was the valley of the rivulet Anhangabaú. Planners evidently felt that a city needs a river, if not a harbor, as a focus; so they honored the modest depression with a handsome viaduct, the Viaducto do Chá (of the Tea). It was the proud promenade into the heart of the great city.

A sparkling underground art museum of ultramodern design next to the viaduct displayed paintings that were mostly modern to match and reflected the spirit of my new circle of friends. A pivotal couple were Luis Martins and Tarsila do Amaral, he a music critic and she a painter. Her work fell into three phases, ranging from the surrealistic *Antropófago* movement to a studied naïveté, a delicate angelic spirituality, tongue palpably in cheek. A bronze Brancusi head reposed on a sofa cushion in their flat. Other members of the group were the writer Sergio Milliet and the Russian painter Lasar Segall, a realist partial to grim refugee themes. The evident leader was the mulatto Mário de Andrade, a music critic, poet, and novelist.

An eccentric painter, writer, and architect, Flávio de Carvalho, wrote a book, *Experimento No. 2*, reporting his bold experiment of not removing his hat when a religious procession was passing. The crowd chased him; he took refuge in a building and was besieged for hours. One of his paintings, "Man smoking in the dark," is a red dot on a black canvas. He built one house in the shape of an airplane; another in the shape of a boat. I was one of three guests at his house in the coffee country near Campinas, for a weekend of riding and lively talk.

The communist novelist Oswaldo de Andrade called me [kɑːɪn]. He knew enough about English for my '-ine' but not enough for my 'qu-'. When I departed from a gathering at his house, he said "Apareça, Kain." I admired the succinctness of Brazilian exclamations. *Apareça*, literally "appear" in the polite imperative, meant "Drop around any time." *Pode,* literally "He can," meant "And well he might." *Custou,* "It cost," meant "That sure took a while."

One of my students in the Escola was the young philosopher Vicente Ferreira da Silva, who served as my assistant. I had known of him a year earlier, having reviewed his slight *Elementos da lógica matemática* for the *Journal of Symbolic Logic.* Conversation was an art much cultivated and admired in the cafés, and Vicente was adept at it. In subsequent years he gained recognition in Brazil, writing in an existentialist vein. A volume of his collected works appeared after his untimely death.

I had a solicitous and informative colleague in Donald Pierson of Chicago, the only professor in Brazil whose chair accounted for his full time and income. He had established Brazil's first graduate work in the social sciences, and was training his students by supervised field work. He wrote volumes on Brazilian society along a thousand miles of the Rio São Francisco.

I gave a well-attended lecture at the União Cultural Brasil-Estado-Unidos on "Os Estados Unidos e o ressurgimento da lógica." They published it in their annual volume.

Mail came from Princeton in August that had been sent by air ten weeks before. It was my little paper of April, "Existence conditions for elements and classes," with the referee's helpful criticism. I suppose the censors had been worrying over it, what with the logical symbols and some references in German.

O Sentido and the Bureaucrats 30

I was writing out my lectures for my logic course in full, in my faulty Portuguese, and delivering them without benefit of a native editor. I probably committed howlers, but people were kind and kept straight faces. I departed from my text and extemporized a good deal, as indeed I had to in responding to questions, but I kept on writing the lectures. I was getting portions mimeographed so that the students could study them, and furthermore I wanted to leave my lectures in Brazil as a book so as to have more impact than could be hoped for through a small group in the classroom. So I was embarked on my fourth book, *O Sentido da nova lógica*.

I explained how to extract the logical forms of sentences and test them for validity or deduce them one from another. I handled set theory as in "Element and number" and added what I called the virtual theory of classes and relations, which was a partial simulation of set theory within the innocent logic of truth functions and quantification. I went on to distinguish between referential positions, where terms of like reference are interchangeable, and positions where they are not. Frege had anticipated me here, but I went beyond him in challenging quantification into non-referential positions. I thus questioned, in particular, the coherence of admitting bound variables into contexts governed by modal operators of necessity and possibility. Eager to put these latter bits of *O Sentido* before English readers, I dictated a translation of my Portuguese to an English stenographer in São Paulo under the title "Notes on existence and necessity."

Vicente collaborated with me in converting the faulty Portuguese of my lectures into what we would like to see in print. Whenever he improved the language to the detriment of the thought, I intervened and we forged a third phrasing that was acceptable on both counts.

I was determined to have the whole thing off my hands on leaving Brazil, so as to turn single-mindedly to my war work. I accomplished what my Brazilian friends thought impossible: I finished the book even to preface, bibliography, corrections of typescript, and printer's instructions, before flying on September 11. In those last weeks it meant working until three in the morning and resuming at around eight. Besides the burden of writing a serious book and the burden of a foreign language, there was secretarial trouble. A typist at the Escola Livre was charged with typing the book, but was so taken up with holidays and other matters that I had to recruit scattered supplementary help. Most of the typing was careless. Words were misspelled. Words, lines, and paragraphs were skipped. Formulas were scrambled. I had to hew out a correct and legible printer's copy with eraser, knife, and pen. I was thankful for Brazil's quick stand-up snacks.

I saw *O Sentido da nova lógica* not only as a way of planting something in Brazil that might grow, but also as my farewell to philosophy and abstract science for the foreseeable future in any language. I would have dropped it if I could have foreseen the toil and frustration in Brazil and the frustration afterward. My mad determination to have no residual loose ends proved to have been in vain. The bickering and stalling went on and on. Let me sketch how the affair continued over the next two and a half years, and thus have done with the grim tale.

The publisher, Livraria Martins, required a subsidy. This was to be provided by the Coordinator of Inter-American Affairs in an advance purchase of five hundred copies for free distribution to Brazilian libraries—an excellent solution. But the Coordinator's office, in the person not of Nelson Rockefeller but of one Robert Spiers Benjamin, demanded expert testimony as to the competence of the book. Whom could I cite? Donald Pierson, the editor of the series for which the book was intended? Cyro Berlinck, director of the Escola? What would they know? Vicente and my other students? Some recognized northern logician who reads Portuguese? Find one! I put the absurd matter to Moe and he enlightened Benjamin. By then it was October and I was a naval lieutenant of some weeks' standing. Benjamin thereupon undertook negotiations with the American Council of Learned Societies for a grant to cover the five hundred copies—a mere three hundred dollars. A letter of a certain pattern was purportedly needed for this purpose from the publisher, Martins, and it took three months. Unaccountable further delays ensued. It was late in January 1944 that I at last saw proofs. The book came out on September 29, 1944, so Pierson reported, but on the title page there was an error so ghastly that he forbore to describe it. It was corrected, and in 1945 I at last laid eyes on the book, years after my desperate race with the calendar in São Paulo.

It had been a bad idea, quixotic, tilting with a bureaucratic windmill, where I in my simplicity had expected only eagerness and gratitude. I should have undertaken in Brazil only what was expected of me, and let my exciting new ideas lie fallow in my lecture notes until such time, after the war, as it might be convenient to develop and transmit them through accustomed scholarly channels.

Conferences over subsidy and typography were only part of my burden in those last days before my departure from São Paulo on September 11, 1942. I reworked my plane reservations, for I wanted to fly home by way of the Andes and the west coast of South America. Chile was said to require a visa, though I would be on the ground in that country for only a few minutes and in Chilean air, mostly pretty thin air at that, for only a few minutes more. The requirements were three photographs, a medical examination by a designated doctor, and a letter in duplicate from the airline testifying that my transportation was paid all the way to the States. My airplane ticket was insufficient evidence.

Peru required for a visa that I first get an Ecuadorian visa, as evidence that I could get out of Peru. I would just be flying through Ecuador, with a touchdown at Guayaquil; but I needed an Ecuadorian visa. One requirement for the Ecuadorian visa, unaccountably, was a Peruvian visa to prove that I could get to Ecuador. I pointed out this Mexican standoff between Ecuador and Peru, and somehow I prevailed, but not without legwork, for the Ecuadorian consulate tended to be unattended. My errands for visas ran to thirty-five; nineteen for the Chilean one alone.

I had to ship some excess baggage. In the end it meant lugging the heavy valise a mile to the shipping office on my shoulder, taxis being immobilized by the gasoline shortage. I had a double-length lecture to deliver on the last day, and an ill-timed dinner party. Memories of my last day in Vienna!

Noting my admiration for Frege, Vicente had given me a little halftone portrait of the great man, torn from the frontispiece of a book. It was in the valise that I shipped. The valise got lost in transit, and I especially regretted the loss of the picture. Behmann's little *Mathematik und Logik* bore on its cover an inch-square reproduction of a line drawing of Frege, so I copied it large with pen and ink to redeem my loss. I was so pleased with the result that I tried drawing faces from life—surreptitiously for the most part, at jazz concerts and philosophy meetings. The uneven results encouraged me just often enough so that I continued the practice intermittently down the years. The valise was later discovered in a customhouse, where it had lain for a year.

Up the Other Side   31

The first leg of my homeward journey was short: six hours, three hops, to Corumbá. We flew for a while over a total, static cloud cover that gave the illusion of a polar scene, with its firm, fixed relief of snowy plains and hills. At length the cloud terminated with an abrupt edge and we flew alongside it, commanding two contrasting views: above was the polar snowscape, seen as if from ground level, and below was a bird's-eye view of tropical forest.

Corumbá was a steaming, mosquito-plagued port on the Paraguay River in Mato Grosso, a few miles from Bolivia. It was built on a bluff above the broad river. I photographed some dugout canoes at the river's edge, but Brazilian soldiers stopped me and destroyed my film.

The country east of the river was flat swamp. Jungle alternated with what looked like great bright green fields—scum really, on dead water. The region was said to be suited to grazing in the dry season and to be flooded in the wet season except for occasional heights on which men and cattle settle for the duration of the rains.

One of the passengers, a Peruvian, used English in communicating with the manager of the little hotel instead of venturing Portuguese. Certainly Spanish and Portuguese are not mutually intelligible—not very. Spanish is more intelligible to the Portuguese speaker than vice versa, because of the difference in phonetic complexity (see chapter 25). But it is significant that an innkeeper at the edge of Bolivia did not speak Spanish. It was wild country, infrequently traversed except up and down stream.

Next day we progressed erratically over the jungles of eastern Bolivia, putting down at outposts: Puerto Suárez, Roboré, San José, San Ignacio, Concepción. The first was simply a frontier airport. The second was a village of huts of bamboo, mud, and grass, together with a garrison one purpose of which was to discourage the Indians from cutting the telegraph wires into lengths for use as bowstrings. The three further places had tile roofs and Spanish colonial churches.

We put down for the night at Santa Cruz de la Sierra, where the flat rain forest begins to buckle up into foothills. It was a colonial city, whittled out of the jungle four hundred years before. The central sidewalks were colonnaded and the houses had generous eaves and heavy old tile roofs. Indian women walked with big earthen jars on their heads. The hotel, the Continental, was built like the old ones of Mexico—with windowless rooms opening onto a central patio. It is a burglar-resistant plan, its blank exterior pierced only by a door. Burglary has been a natural force to build against in those latitudes, like wind and rain. Now that North American culture has overtaken that of our southern neighbors in this melancholy particular, the architectural style is one that we might do well to adopt.

There was no water in the rooms. There were taps in the washroom, but they were dry. A tap on a little pipe in the patio emitted a trickle and promptly stopped. A boy brought me a pail of water from an unknown source.

The hotel being crowded, I shared a room with a Bolivian

airplane mechanic named Sánchez, one quarter Indian. We prowled the town and talked. It was an interesting exercise, for I was steeped in Portuguese, and his language was Spanish. I kept drawing on Portuguese vocabulary and converting to Spanish cognates according to familiar phonetic correlations. Often the method yielded a non-word or a semantically wrong one, and then I delved into my rusty Spanish.

In the hotel restaurant there was a good band. I talked with a black Cuban clarinetist; the other musicians were Peruvian, Argentinian, Chilean, and Bolivian. I talked with two children and shared their funny paper. A prehistoric monster figured in one of the cartoons, and they called it a German. I felt that I was among allies.

The Santa Cruz newspaper was a crude little affair. The advertisements ran to palmistry, horoscopes, numerology, and spiritualism.

We flew up across a forested region broken by rugged ascarpments, a succession of faults. Occasionally there was a plateau of forest isolated by cliffs. A Bolivian colonel who sat next to me said that the region was uninhabited. Monkeys and jaguars, yes, but no Indians. As we approached Cochabamba there were rich valleys and prosperous colonial villages, backed by majestic mountains. Cochabamba, altitude 8,400 feet, was a handsome city dominating a tumble of vertiginous green declivities and dominated by a backdrop of snowy summits. At twelve thousand feet we put down at Oruro, a mining town nestled against a barren round mountain amid a limitless barren plain. Llamas and alpacas nibbled at sparse olive-drab shrubs, perhaps creosote bushes. Indians wore white straw hats shaped like high-crowned bowlers, set squarely on the head. They had bright blankets around their shoulders and wore their hair in pigtails.

We flew to the La Paz airport, altitude thirteen thousand. The city was tucked into a canyon a thousand feet below; I was not to see it for another fourteen years. But the snowy peaks of Illimani and Illampu were overwhelmingly in evidence, rising to twenty-one thousand feet. We saw Lake Titicaca stretching far away to the north, but we took a southwesterly course for the tip of Chile. We crossed the divide flying as high as we could, at eighteen thousand feet, through a valley with bare brown slopes rising perilously close on either side of us. At each seat there was a tube through which to breathe oxygen. The turbulence made me too queasy for lunch, which they were so thoughtless or sly as to offer just at that time. In my hundreds of thousands of miles in the air to date, this was my only touch of airsickness. It was ill-timed, for I was ravenous when we landed on the beach at Arica, Chile, soon afterward, but could get nothing to eat until night in Lima.

I was at Arica for a few minutes between planes. Naturally nobody looked at my passport, with the visa that had cost me nineteen errands, a seven-dollar fee, a two-dollar medical examination, and three photographs. It was sheer harassment, and there was more to come.

The coast of Peru is twelve hundred miles long, from Chile to Ecuador, not counting curves. I saw it all. It consists almost entirely of desert, devoid even of cactus and shrubs. At rare points this brown expanse is broken by an intensely cultivated ribbon of green, winding down the middle of an otherwise brown valley. The village and cemetery are put alongside the green on the bare dirt. In a few places there is a moderately green plain of greater extent, dotted with towns and poplars. Arequipa lies in such a plain at the foot of the towering volcano Misti, and Lima with its port Callao lies in another.

When I got out in Lima the airline representative told me I would need a Panamanian visa in order to change planes in the Canal Zone. I had been told the contrary in São Paulo at both the U.S. consulate and the airline. The visa called for depositing $150, recoverable in Panama. It was Sunday and I was to leave Lima the next day at dawn. The Panamanian consul was a friend of the airline representative, who arranged by phone for me to see him immediately. The $150 had to be paid by certified check on a specified Lima bank, but the airline man solved this by taking my travelers' checks and signing a letter to the consul to the effect that the canonical check would be delivered the next morning. But did I have a vaccination certificate? Yes, two. But did I have a certificate of good behavior from the police? Thinking more quickly than is my wont, I said yes, here it is stamped right in the passport. It was a so-called exit visa from Brazil, which had been signed by a São Paulo police officer. The consul said he had never heard of printing the good-behavior certificate in a passport, but the airline man chimed in saying yes, they do it that way in Brazil.

Further pitiless harassment, thus, of a hungry man, a hated gringo.

Lima is overcast for half the year and misty much of that time. In the mist I formed a quick impression of the marble government palaces in Spanish colonial style and the colonial houses with their heavy screened wooden balconies. The steward from the plane lured me out for an expensive night on the town, and I was not at my best when we took off northward at dawn.

We put down at Chiclayo and Talara. The latter, at the northwest corner of Peru, overlooks the westernmost point of South America—as far west as Jacksonville Beach, Florida. Jacksonville, be it noted, was the westernmost point in my whole trip of thirteen thousand miles.

Talara, its brown plain dotted with oil derricks, was the last of the barren country. Soon we were over the equatorial jungles of Ecuador and putting down at Guayaquil. I hardly need say that at this brief stop, our only stop in Ecuador, nobody checked the visa that had cost me ten trips and five dollars.

We slept at Cali, Colombia, and took off, as always, at dawn. In the Canal Zone a U.S. censor went through my papers in fifteen minutes and sealed my portfolio, explaining that if I kept it sealed I could pass the Miami censor without further inspection. Then a man from the airline took me and others to a ministry in Panama City to recover our $150 deposits. It took an hour, after which he joined me in a taxi for a quick look at Miraflores Lock. The airline fed us at the Tivoli in Ancón, and we were off for Miami. Blinds were fitted into the starboard windows momentarily for military security as we passed the western tip of Jamaica. We touched at Camagüey, closing my big loop.

At inspection in Miami, someone broke the seal on my portfolio. The censors thereupon confiscated my films, the carbon copy of *O Sentido,* and the typescript of "Notes on existence and necessity," which I wanted to deliver to the editor in New York the next day. They shipped it all to me when they had come to terms with their suspicions a week later.

Lieutenant 32

I got back to Boston on September 18, 1942, and within an hour I was into the Navy as a full lieutenant. On October 7, in uniform, I reported in Washington for duty. The uniform conferred benefits: it eliminated the problem of choosing a combination of suit, shirt, tie, and socks every day; it invited civil, helpful treatment on the part of strangers; and it carried with it the friendly custom of saluting in the streets. The pattern of work was an abrupt departure, consisting as it did of imposed tasks in a clean-cut eight-hour day. It was a restful change.

Thus it was that our tenancy in Sparks Street came to an end, the longest tenancy in our married life: more than two and a half years. We found a house in Washington at 843 Fifty-first Street, S.E.; Maryland was a block away. The street was two short rows of new brick fronts in the wilderness. Shantied lanes, wooded lanes, paths, and trackless woods all were near at hand. You could get pleasantly lost in twenty minutes. Presently a handful of cabins would begin to take form, and you would come upon a clearing and a little band of blacks.

Elizabeth and Norma, aged seven and five, entered public school in Maryland, a fifteen-minute walk over the country roads. My trip to my office in one of the temporary buildings on the Mall—temporary since the First World War—I described thus to Fred Cassidy:

Here it is 5:55 of a black morning and I have little time to spare before taking my lamp in hand and slogging through the slough that I am learning to call home and so betimes to the office. It's only a few minutes' walk to the edge of the bush, and from there there is an unbroken system of hard-surfaced roads leading all the way to civilization. The resistant surface quickens my pace, and I bound along at a great rate, ever upward and southwestward along the state line, to a point about nine minutes from my sodden dooryard. Here I brood. At length a bus bounds across the state line and scoops me up. First thing I know, I have had my twenty or thirty minutes of reading and have been spewed out on a curbstone in the heart of the capital. A mere twenty minutes' brisk walk thence to the Navy building.

· 1943   Early in 1943 my section of the Navy was moved into what had been a girls' school in Nebraska Avenue, on the far side of Washington. Commuting then became prohibitive. We bought an old Chevrolet for $225. We had been married nearly thirteen years, and it was our first car. We moved to a bungalow at 1006 Elm Avenue in Takoma Park, Maryland, having lived in Fifty-first Street for a period that was unusually short even by our standards: four months. Our new place adjoined the wooded valley of the Sligo Branch of the Anacostia River.

Naomi got an office job in May 1943 in a Washington department store. This enabled us to hire a maid and thus gain more freedom of movement. We turned that freedom to advantage, or to what we meant to be such, by taking a holiday during the interval of forty-eight hours between my swing watches. We took a bus to the Luray Caverns and walked twelve miles down the Shenandoah Valley to Overall Inn, rates $3.50 with rough cabin, plain food, canoes, swimming, and tennis. Next morning we walked ten miles through dull woodland and up the Blue Ridge, skipping the Sunday dinner. For water we counted on a camp at the top, but it was abandoned and dry. We took a new route down, vaguely marked on the map, but it faded out. We bushwhacked and followed rocky stream beds for perhaps five miles. Our mouths so woolen as to impede speech, we came at last to a farm and a pail of water. We hired the farmer to drive us to Overall Inn for a late supper. Back then by bus to Washington, and straight to work.

A breathtaking crater or precipice or a vast panorama or a strange foreign village might have warranted some such mortification of the flesh, but this had been a humdrum mountain at best, closed in by woods all the way. We could have stayed below and swum, played tennis, canoed on the Shenandoah, had our dinner, and gone home in time to sleep before the night watch, if we had had a modicum of the cool judgement that is to be expected of a naval officer.

My duty was in Atlantic radio intelligence. They started me in direction-finding, along with some briefing on the ionosphere. Satisfied at length about security, they inducted me into top secrets. For thirty years afterward I regarded the secrecy as binding, and responded evasively when asked what I had done in the Navy. Then books for popular consumption began to appear in England that told all: we had been reading the German submarine cipher. It would have been better to keep the secret. That cipher had had its day, but there is harm in proclaiming our prowess in the art. It has been brought home to me more than once that security was tighter in America than in Britain.

The cat being out of the bag, it would be affectation to continue to make a mystery of my war work. My group worked closely with the cryptanalysts. They would pass us the deciphered intercepts for translation and analysis. We would pass the digested information to the high command, and also back to the cryptanalysts to afford them hints for breaking into the next day's traffic; for each day's cipher setting presented a new problem, despite our understanding of the general system. There would be days on end when the cryptanalysts would labor in vain. George Girton and I would sit through the lonely midwatch hoping for news from them. Lounging back meanwhile with our feet on our desks and a Mercator projection of the world on the wall at one side, we would try each other on latitudes and longtitudes. "55 N, 63 W: wet or dry?"

Some of us stood swing watches in short cycles; others came only by day, when the office was full and abustle. It was a bright and congenial group, thirty four all told. There were two professors of philosophy, one of English, one of German, and one of Greek, along with half a dozen young college graduates whose careers had not crystallized. The cipher people downstairs were largely mathematicians, two of whom divided their time with us.

My three years and more of duty were limited to Washington except for one brief mission to Ottawa. There was, however, a rewarding mode of domestic travel outside the line of duty. An officer could hitch rides on Army and Navy planes, if there was room, and the view from the plane was unobstructed by frosted window screens. My first such lark began with a ride to Norfolk in a little torpedo plane. I sat on a metal shelf up under the greenhouse, riding backwards and listening in on the communications through earphones. At Norfolk I boarded a seaplane, a Catalina. Inside it was like a freighter, with tanks, tackle, portholes, and heavy iron companionways. I walked upstairs and down and from room to room as we flew to Rhode Island, and every now and then I saw some more men that I had not known were aboard. Surely it was the biggest, heaviest thing that had ever flown. We approached the surface of Narragansett Bay and suddenly there was a wild rush of water along the keel. We skimmed the surface at a dizzy speed and slowed to a stop at the ramp. Wheels were brought out by dinghy and the plane taxied ashore. There I caught a bomber to Brooklyn and went to see Albert and Roberta Wohlstetter in upper Manhattan. We ended up eating rice and beans in a Puerto-Rican place, and I took a train for Washington in the small hours.

· 1944   My years 1944 and 1945 were a tangle of five strands: war, domestic upheaval, sociality, aerial hitchhiking, and logic. I shall let them surface in their original disorder.

Naomi went to the hospital in March 1944 for another operation—tumors again. By April she had recovered to the point of lining up a transcontinental ride and visiting Marguerite in Los Angeles. I encouraged her to extend her trip into Mexico. I had thoughts of joining her during a two-week leave in May, but that was spiked by my being put in command of the office.

She wrote euphorically from the West with stange tidings: first, that she had bought land in Arizona; next, that she was in western Sonora and not coming back. I filed for divorce on grounds of desertion. Ironically, demands from Oberlin resumed about then for payment of her college debts. I thought I had finished paying them in 1939. I resumed payments.

My friend Fritz Safier of 1931 was now in the State Department and lived with his diminutive bright wife Fraenzchen in an old house in Georgetown. I vacated the Takoma Park bungalow, put Elizabeth and Norma in a camp, and moved into the Safiers' basement flat.

Panicked by Marguerite, Naomi came back east in July, a month before a decree of divorce would have taken effect. She insisted on an experimental reconciliation. I was tired, and quailed at the threat of an all-night harangue. I acceded, and thus blew my grounds of desertion. As a naval officer would I have better withstood grilling by enemy captors? Would I have jettisoned my country's interests as readily as I jettisoned my private ones? Not to have been put to that test is something, still, to be thankful for.

A week's leave gave me respite in August. I hitched a ride in a Navy plane and flew low over old haunts. I sighted the

Portage Lakes of my childhood, and I looked down on the very corner in Wellington where I had stood so many Saturdays hitchhiking from Oberlin to Akron. Here I was again, on a hitchhike of a higher type. At Detroit I took up with a pilot and his wife for a swim, dinner at the officers' club, and a movie. Next day I flew over the meanders of the Mississippi to Blytheville, Arkansas. Further hitched flights, eked out with trains and busses, enabled me to visit the home folks in Akron.

Back, then, to naval duty and wedlock. We took the upper half of an ugly wooden duplex in North Danville Street, across the Potomac in hither Arlington, Virginia, upstream from the Key Bridge. Home life was a grim, gray, spiritless depression.

Old friends were accreting in Washington. Barkley Rosser, memorable as the mind behind the B40, had left his post in mathematics at Cornell to join in the effort. Ed Haskell came visiting. Connie Arensberg, social anthropologist from Society-of-Fellows days, was an Army captain on duty evidently rather like mine, and lived nearby. Kazuko Higuchi, a Hawaiian Japanese girl in fine arts whom we had known at Oberlin and Harvard, was serving in naval intelligence after five years in Japan. Among our new friends was Albert Goldsmith, a young civilian with a war job and a sprightly mind. For the sake of exercise, supplementary income, and the gross national product, Albert was hiring out as a farmhand on weekends. He worked for a Polish farmer, and the farmer's wife called him Wojciech. Why? Because it was Polish for Albert! This was hilarious. Albert was Wojciech Złotnik to me thenceforward. Years later I learned that Wojciech really can be said to be Polish for Albert, however devious the explanation.

· 1945   Copies of *O Sentido da nova lógica* reached me in January 1945. I beheld in disbelief this exotic product in a wild language from the ends of the earth, and I the author. It set me to thinking again about logic, and I wrote "On the logic of quantification." What I had called "frames" in *Elementary Logic* came in this paper to be called *schemata*, and what I had called "stencils," containing circled numerals, came here to be called *predicates*. The style of *Methods of Logic* was thus established. I presented a steamlined algorithm for checking validity in the logic of one-place predicates and a concise way of deriving the general logic of quantification.

My note "On ordered pairs" was elicited by Goodman's interest in diminishing the difference in type between a pair and its components. I devised a definition of pairs that equalizes these types, and incidentally simplifies the theory of relations by making every class a relation and vice versa. The definition abets "New foundations," so Rosser adopted it in his *Logic for Mathematicians*, which is based on "New foundations."

By May 1945 we in the office were exulting in the reports of American advances in Germany and were marking them with pins. Consternation set in when the pins began to retreat. Eisenhower was having to accommodate himself to Roosevelt's openhandedness at Yalta. On May 7 the Germans surrendered. From then on our job would be one of putting our records in order, unless we were transferred to the Pacific theatre.

The State Department offered me the post of cultural attaché to Brazil. I was content by then to withdraw from the war effort, knowing the outcome. I was not free to return to my proper profession at Harvard, but it seemed that I might be released from the Navy for the post in Brazil, and I welcomed this as a second best. Accordingly I put it to the State Department to extract me from the Navy. Bureaucratic operations eventuated, predictably, in a standstill. Meanwhile I was promoted to Lieutenant Commander.

My acquiescence in the home scene touched bottom, and I insisted on a final separation. We arrived at a provisional figure for the support of Naomi and the children, and when school closed in June 1945 they moved to Boston. She had won; a divorce and a settlement would now have to be painfully negotiated, since I had given up my original grounds.

I moved to a flat in A Street, S.E., near the Library of Congress, and was plagued with bedbugs. The housing shortage left the landlord unmotivated and me immobilized. There was a resurgence of bugs each Saturday as the people below me cleaned their flat. After some time, D.D.T. became available and brought relief.

My brother Bob and his wife Rosalie rallied around with a will. They had come to visit me promptly at the first break, May 1944. Early in July 1945, with the final separation achieved and hostilities mounting, they promoted a rendezvous with me midway between Akron and Washington. We had an irresponsible and hilarious weekend in and about Uniontown and Ohiopyle.

In Boston, hostility and turmoil. Naomi was telephoning my father in Akron and Commander Hayes in Washington and talking to philosophers at Harvard. Trouble brewed in her new place of employment and in her successive lodging places. Strange characters wove in and out of the loose-knit drama, which I shall not try to unravel. Little Elizabeth and Norma had their problems.

Having three weeks of leave, I hitchhiked to Dayton in a torpedo plane and thence to Roswell, New Mexico, in a Flying Fortress. It took fire as it was landing, but was put to rights. I made my way to Taos. The great adobe house of the Indian *pueblo* there, with its variously offset levels and roof ladders, is the picture-book epitome of the genre. The town of Taos, with its arcaded plaza and its traditional air, is picture-book Mexico. The plaza was thronged and the throng was aflutter, for the news had just come through of Hiroshima. The idea of an atomic bomb was as new to me as to anyone, despite my top-secret clearance; for each secret was wisely restricted to those who needed to share it. People I talked with in the plaza had had more of an inkling than I. They had first been set awondering by the test explosion at White Sands, Alamogordo, away down state. Subsequently they had noticed a local brain drain, of chemists apparently, to Los Alamos in midstate.

At Dallas I caught a ride in a little Army two-seater, a Steerman. There were dual controls, and the pilot let me take over. It was like learning again to drive a car, but with an added dimension. Trying to rectify a tilt, I would tilt further. The controls were perverse: to slow down you would steer upward, and to rise you would step on the gas. I flew the plane through the panhandle of Oklahoma and into Colorado. An apocalyptic storm brewed, darkling and whirling over the plain. The pilot resumed the controls and we skirted the spectacle, fluttering in the gusts. Then the foothills began to crinkle up from the plain, and the Rockies shimmered dimly beyond. It was operatic, heroic, this return through a tempestuous sky to the wild mountains and the cousin of whom I had so often dreamed.

I had a few days with her. She had divorced her husband some years before, but had given no sign. She was a lovely lady, and marrying her was something I could think about. Yes, think about. We had been together so little, ever, and apart so long.

I flew from Denver to Chicago in a bomber. I lay prone in it, gazing straight down at the fugitive planet earth through the glass bottom of the bomb bay. The great plains are divided into mile-square sections by visible boundaries running north-south and east-west. By counting and clocking the boundaries as we passed them, I could compute, if I pleased, our course and speed. Thus if we crossed one east-west line for every four north-south ones, our course was the arc-tangent of 1/4 north of east; and if on that course we crossed eighty north-south lines in fifteen minutes, our speed in miles an hour was eighty times the square root of seventeen. Well, I could if I had the tables.

I visited Fred and Hélène Cassidy in Wisconsin, the family in Akron, and divorce lawyers in Boston, and then sought solace with a fair friend on Cape Cod before going back to my naval duty and bedbugs. I terminated the bumbling proceedings in the State Department regarding my mission to Brazil, for the war was suddenly over and I could soon go back to Harvard.

Tarski, by then a mathematics professor at Berkeley, came to Washington for a week in September, vainly pressing the bureaucrats to help bring his family out of Soviet Poland. We had good discussions of logic and philosophy and some jolly evenings with Waves from my office. We got away to a logic conference in New Jersey, a welcome return to my chosen profession. We talked of writing a book together, but nothing came of it. Late in October he came back for further vain efforts with the bureaucrats. Ultimately it was with the help of the philosopher Anders Wedberg in Stockholm, after the war, that Tarski's family was brought out through Copenhagen.

By November 17, 1945, the paper work involved in getting detached from naval duty subsided. I was cited by Admiral King for "outstanding performance of duty in Naval Communications." My winter in Cambridge went into preparing my spring and summer courses and talking with lawyers. Litigation was destined to go on for another year, with poisonous confrontations. I labored under a chronic, vague anxiety. My former student Babbie Samelson got her friend Lucie Jessner, a psychoanalyst, to take me on at a generously reduced rate. I was grateful and went into it with a will and a lively curiosity, but there was no evident turning point or revelation.

Babbie got me a flat at 9 Ware Street, despite acute shortages, by representing me as Jewish to the Jewish Manager. It pleased me to see Jewishness as an asset rather than a handicap in the competition for flats, and it pleased me doubly to benefit by it, however fraudulently.

The flat was minimal, but I made room for an old piano and applied myself to it with the help of a book on how to learn quickly to play the piano by ear: the LeRoy Method. It was all in the key of G flat: mostly black keys. After progressing to where I was handling four chords, I took off on an easy tangent and simply memorized, from LeRoy's annotated airs, the associations between these chords and notes of the melody. I found myself pounding out heartfelt renderings of anything that I could whistle. It was a dreamlike fulfillment—so much so that I have left it at that and continue to perform at the same impoverished level.

Eugene McCarthy, Norman Mattis's silver-tongued Mac

with the heart of gold, wrote me urgently to get in touch. I
shied off, fearful that he would meddle with my conjugal
nightmare. I dropped Norm's circle, except for Norm, much
though I had enjoyed them all. And I dropped Frae and Ju-
lie Fassett, lovely people, for I had known them through
Naomi.

A new circle was accreting, around Eli Robins. He was a
medical student who had got onto my *Mathematical Logic*
through Babbie and had corresponded with me while I was
in the Navy. He ultimately became head psychiatry professor at Washington University. He and his wife Lee had
bright friends: a girl called U. T. for the University of
Texas; the physicist Leonard Eisenbud and his wife Ruth
Jean; the psychologist Sylvan Tomkins and his beautiful
wife V. J.; and a young man in English who lived with another beautiful wife, his own, in a delightfully sagging flat on
the long-lamented T Wharf, which was the most romantic
and picturesque spot or structure in the once romantic and
picturesque city of Boston.

Through the Eisenbuds I met the communist actor Howard da Silva, who played the bartender in Ray Milland's
"Lost Weekend." I nearly killed the three of them and
Howard's girl and myself. We were crowded into my decrepit Chevrolet and driving out the Concord Turnpike. At
Spy Pond I swerved onto the ramp to point out two new
brick houses that appealed to me. How, then, to get across
the turnpike and head back to Cambridge without working
our way up onto the overpass? I made a quick U-turn and received, on my left side and that of my decrepit Chevrolet,
the impact of a fast car that I had failed to see. We were
luckier than I deserved. Some of us sustained minor injuries,
and my car a major one. Claims were filed and a good lawyer
named Weinstein collected some damages for us, though it
was all my fault. I came away with a phobia that lasted for
months, a fear of impact from the left. I had been in a bad
enough way already, but then perhaps one neurosis offsets
another.

On the way back from an Akron Christmas in 1945 I had a

long session with Ed Haskell and Harold Cassidy in New York. Harold was by then a chemistry professor at Yale. Ed's communist fervor had been reversed by his intimate acquaintance with the party and the system. He was now taken up with broad ideas about cooperation and predation. There were some statistical findings regarding fish populations in which he saw implications for human societies. He was well informed on social and political matters and much concerned about them. Within this compass his ideas were good and capable of bettering society. He was now venturing to generalize them on a cosmic scale, however, into something that he called unified science; and I tried to apply the brakes of rigor to his runaway ambition. Our meeting was followed up by an eighteen-page letter from him and a twenty-page response from me.

Teaching and Writing Again   34

· 1946   I resumed my Harvard duties in February 1946. A notable company of graduate students in logic began to gather: John Myhill from England, Henry Hiż from Poland, William Craig from Germany via California, and Hugues Leblanc from Canada. Hao Wang, still in China, would join us in the fall. Also I had my tutorial responsibilities; one was a sophomore of Zionist proclivities named Burton Dreben, interested in philosophy and politics. Presently he was moving with the graduate students, chopping logic with the best of them.

My resumed teaching from *Mathematical Logic* led to "Concatenation as a basis for arithmetic." The concatenate of two numbers goes with their digits; that of 19 and 23 is 1923. I defined concatenation in terms of elementary number theory and showed that it suffices as the sole operation of elementary number theory.

I was also pondering the philosophy of language. Misgivings over quantified modal logic that I had expressed in Brazil in 1942, and in "Notes on existence and necessity," gained in relevance as the challenge was taken up. Ruth Barcan (Marcus)'s pioneer venture in quantified modal logic appeared in the *Journal of Symbolic Logic* in 1946. Presently so did Carnap's, and also an abstract by Church. I was arguing by mail with Carnap, whose *Meaning and Necessity* I had in manuscript, and he included one of my letters in that book. "The problem of interpreting modal logic" was a further expression of my misgivings.

Robert Lee Durham, retired president of a junior college in Virginia, sent me a hundred dollars and asked me to make it clear to him why an angle cannot in general be trisected by ruler and compass. It was in instructive exercise for me in unfamiliar parts of mathematics. It took me forty-odd hours to ferret out the literature and digest it in twenty pages that I could regard as clear. He expressed satisfaction and proposed paying for publishing it as a pamphlet. I preferred submitting it to the *Mathematics Teacher,* and he acceded. I got no answer from that journal for a long time, and ended up writing them to send it back and forget it.

Another hack job obtruded in April, when A. A. Fraenkel visited Harvard from Jerusalem. He had acquired a manuscript by Leopold Löwenheim, a logician who had made an important contribution in 1915 and was now presumed dead. Fraenkel hoped I would get some graduate student to translate it for *Scripta Mathematica.* I said it would be easier to translate it myself, and did so, under the title "On making indirect proofs direct." It was an annoying task, for the article was inelegant and I kept wanting to reorganize it and thus exceed my prerogative.

I had four refreshing days of sailing with John Cooley on the *Linnet.* At East Boothbay we boarded MacMillan's schooner *Bowdoin,* which was fitting out for a second Arctic expedition. We spent our last night at anchor in Pulpit Harbor, in North Haven Island. It is bordered by low bluffs of gray and white limestone topped with heavy dark forest of fir interspersed with crooked white birch. There were seals, porpoises, wild duck, a nest of ospreys, and an abundance of shag, or cormorants. A shag will take off from a spar or low rock, flutter clumsily, and fly across the water, almost touching it, beating his long crooked wings. The crook of his scrawny neck is eloquent of effort and strain. Then he sits on the water and suddenly somersaults under. Minutes later and far away he surfaces with a fish in his beak. Evidently his weight, a burden in flight, is a help under water.

Harvard was still on the wartime schedule of three equal terms a year. I was booked for summer, with the fall term off. My senior colleagues had caught up with me again in the demand for a historical course, but I was spared Leibniz. I chose Hume. This and introductory logic were my summer courses.

I tried to make a virtue of the necessity. The critical knowledge of Hume that I would need for my course would mesh with my own philosophical thinking, providing enrichment and perspective. The course, moreover, once given, could be readily given again. Rationalize as I might, however, preparation dragged. I dawdled. It was a struggle to keep ahead. By the end of the course my lecture notes were full and ready for a repeat performance in another year, but I could not bear to offer the course again. Determining what Hume thought and imparting it to students was less appealing than determining the truth and imparting that.

Science and the history of science appeal to very different tempers. An advance in science resolves an obscurity, a tangle, a complexity, an inelegance, that the scientist then gratefully dismisses and forgets. The historian of science tries to recapture the very tangles, confusions, and obscurities from which the scientist is so eager to free himself.

After the summer term, with the ordeal of Hume forever behind me, I took a room in Rockport on Cape Ann to facilitate my collaboration with Goodman. He had sold his interest in the Goodman-Walker art gallery in Copley Square and had taken his Ph.D. at Harvard and a job at the University of Pennsylvania. Hempel joined us in Rockport, sensibly brightening the week.

In July 1946 Charlie Curtis took over my divorce case. When at last he felt that my case might not succeed, he arranged that Naomi sue me for divorce on contrived grounds of cruel and abusive treatment. The settlement provided for alimony and the purchase for her of a house she had found in Easton, Massachusetts.

Ensign Marjorie Boynton, ultimately Lieutenant, had been a Wave in my office in Washington and had waxed in my esteem. When I left, she was put in charge of the office in its continuing project of organizing the files for posterity. Now she was out of the Navy and counseling in Ruth Jean Eisenbud's summer camp for children in Wayne County, Pennsylvania. I drove there to see her in August. I visited her on subsequent occasions in New York, where she had taken a job, and we went to Greenwich Village for dancing, Mexican music, or Dixieland. It became clear that we would marry when circumstances permitted.

I began working toward *Methods of Logic* and mimeographed a draft of it for my spring course under the title *A Short Course in Logic*. I handled the logic of quantification in somewhat the style that Gentzen had called *natural deduction*, a formal method of deducing consequences from the premises along lines attractively akin to ordinary informal reasoning. I had got the idea not from Gentzen but from Jaśkowski, when in Warsaw in 1933. Cooley had used a form of natural deduction in his *Primer of Formal Logic*, 1942, and Rosser, unbeknownst, had used variants of it in mimeographed teaching aids. Gentzen's rules had been uncomfortably asymmetrical; Cooley brought more symmetry, and this required increased delicacy in framing the rules lest they conflict. I worked on it.

One of the events at the Princeton bicentennial in December 1946 was a session on Problems of Mathematics in which I was invited to participate along with Gödel, Kleene, Rosser, and others. Gödel's way of lecturing was revealing. He paced back and forth, reading aloud. Someone had coached him in looking up occasionally as he read. Accordingly, when he paced with the blackboard on his left, he glanced up to his left, at a pair of symbols that Rosser had happened to leave on the blackboard; and when he paced with the blackboard to his right, he glanced up to his right at those same symbols. He glanced only once at the audience—at me, as it happened, just as I was glancing at my watch.

From Princeton I went on to Penn for a lecture, to Akron for Christmas, and then on to Mexico. My balcony in Monterrey commanded a canonical plaza and cathedral and, beyond, a profile of barren mountains. I walked in the town, relishing the smells, tamales, tacos, mariachi music, serapes, big hats, and Indian faces. I walked up and along the mountains and admired the yucca, the cactus, and the view. I went on to San Luís Potosí by train, haltingly, hours late. San Luís is on the high plateau, the same plateau to which the highway ascents so dizzily from Tamazunchale; yet I was unaware of an ascent. The railroad had taken the easy way and the highway could have done likewise, if the purpose had merely been a highway to Mexico City. A back road accompanied the railroad, and probably had all along. It dawned on me that the developers had taken the hard way in order to open up regions like that of Tamazunchale.

· 1947   I came to prefer busses to trains. They were more frequent and not so late. They went through the front of a town, not the back, and they stopped for a while at the plaza, where you could stroll and look and ingest the local confection—*dulce de biznaga*, perhaps, or *cajete*. Busses came in two classes: one comfortable and the other bumpy and crowded but cheap and colorful. You took whichever came first. Both kinds raced perilously close to the recurrent vertiginous brink.

From my window in Guadalajara I tried my hand at watercolor. Of an evening I frequented cafés, mostly the Café Amigos. A musician would stroll in, strumming chords on his guitar. I might ask him how many he was—whether solo or with a colleague or two waiting outside—and what he charged for a song. Successive customers in the café would commission songs of their choosing. I developed a repertoire of Mexican songs and an acquaintance among the musicians. I knew one as *el Abrigo* because of his mackintosh; another as *la Tortuga* because of his turtleneck sweater.

Guanajuato was a mountain town with baroque churches and palaces from the silver-mining days. I threaded its *vecindades*—long, narrow foot passages, sinuous, branching, and tightly lined with plastered adobe dwellings.

Ciudad del Maíz was a grubby, primitive outpost near the eastern escarpment of the plateau. After the chastening experience of its noisome hotel, I dropped down to Tampico for a few days. Thence back to Boston in time for February classes.

The G. I. Bill of Rights allowed me a subsidy of tuition, which I spent at Berlitz. I had begun with a view to practicing Spanish, but the Berlitz methods were meant for beginners and proved unrewarding. After my trip to Mexico I switched to Italian, in which I was weaker—but still, I found, not weak enough. So I switched to Chinese, turning the last of my tuition subsidy to twenty hours of private instruction. My teacher opened the proceedings with sounds that I was at first at a loss to sort out even as sounds. Presently I caught onto something like [dzɸ:ʃəʃɸ:mə]. The accompanying gesture of holding out a pencil suggested that she was asking me what it was; so when she went on to say [dzɸ:ʃətjɛn:pi], I appreciated that she was answering her question. The lesson proceeded in this vein for an hour, and was followed by an hour of character recognition. So it went for ten weekly two-hour sessions. I was surprised at how many characters I learned without mnemonic aids, but not surprised at how quickly I forgot them. The twenty hours were worthwhile in giving me some sense of what Chinese is like, which is all I was looking for.

The direct method, as of Berlitz, may be more efficient than the traditional inculcation of explicit rules in the case of students who have not acquired a background of systematic linguistic concepts from studying other languages. For those who have, however, explanations would cut corners and speed things up even in Chinese.

The divorce was granted on May 24, 1947, *nisi*. This meant that it would not take effect for six months. I was forbidden by Massachusetts law to marry for yet another year after that.

The ensuring summer was rich in self-indulgence. I visited Akron and lolled with Bob and Rosalie in the Bass Islands of Lake Erie drinking the local wines. I drove with my new junior colleague Henry Aiken to join John Cooley and Hilliard of the Halyards for six rollicking days on the *Linnet*, glorying in lobster and notable *Abendsuppen*—so-called after Lewis Carroll's "Soup of the evening, beautiful soup." Driving back from Mount Desert, Henry and I stopped at a carnival and got fleeced at games of purported chance. There were days on Cape Cod with Morty White, the Wohlstetters, and the Chisholms. Marge moved to Boston for a training course in nursery-school teaching. She took a basement flat near Saint Cecilia's Church, in a nook of Back Bay that had a touch of personality before the encroachment of the Prudential Center. We frequented summer theaters, listened to music on the Esplanade, and canoed on the Charles, renting a canoe at a different level each time and canoeing from dam to dam.

I also worked. Goodman was back on home ground for the summer, and our collaboration issued in "Steps toward a constructive nominalism." It was an effort to get mathematics into an ontology strictly of physical objects. We settled for a formalist account of mathematics as a meaningless heuristic device, but we still had the problem of meaningful metamathematics, or proof theory, and this encountered an obstacle that I had pointed out in "On universals"; namely, proof theory assumes strings of aigns without limit of length, whereas our program could countenance them only insofar as physically realized. We devised ways of coping with the predicament to some degree.

Our paper created a stubborn misconception that I am an ongoing nominalist. Readers try in the friendliest ways to reconcile my writings with nominalism. They try to read nominalism into "On what there is" and find, or should find, incoherence. Nominalism was our position in "Steps toward a constructive nominalism"; it was the statement of our problem. It would be my actual position if I could make a go of it. But when I quantify irreducibly over classes, I am not playing the nominalist. Quite the contrary.

In September 1947 I had a note from Naomi from California. Marge and I promptly drove to Easton to determine whether Elizabeth and Norma were left behind. Neighbors told us they had all gone to California and might stay the winter. The house and its contents looked ready to come back to, but that was not indicative.

Year of Fulfillment   35

· 1948   I was to speak at Princeton on March 15, 1948. I took the midnight sleeper to New York and met Ed Haskell on a corner at 7:15. We talked for three hours, eating breakfast and walking to the far end of Central Park. Paul Oppenheim, my host, met my train at Princeton and drove me to his house.

Paul's father had been high in the councils of I. G. Farben, rich and philanthropic. By endowment he had founded the University of Frankfurt. He had had a fabulous collection of impressionist masterpieces. As a child, Paul knew Brahms and Clara Schumann; they came to his home. After Hitler took over, Paul's parents committed suicide. Paul escaped to Brussels with the paintings and stored them in two banks. He married Gabrielle Errera, daughter of the chemist.

A gifted logician or scientific philosopher who fled to Brussels from the Nazis would become Paul's protégé, or, as Paul viewed it, his tutor. Paul would help support him, would study and discuss with him, and perhaps collaborate in some small work. Peter Hempel was one such, and the ill-starred Kurt Grelling was another. Grelling was later killed by French Nazis while trying to escape over the Pyrenees.

When the Nazis invaded Belgium, Paul and Gabrielle escaped to America with the paintings from one of the banks. They took a modest house in Princeton and hung it with these priceless works of art. Paul continued to help promising young philosophers of logical bent—among them Kemeny and Putnam. He had no pretentions, but unbounded admiration of genius. He was a friend of Einstein, Bohr, and Gödel.

Bohr and his wife were guests at the elegant luncheon that the Oppenheims gave an hour after my arrival. I talked long with Bohr, but had trouble understanding him because of his Danish indifference to consonants. He was explaining his complementarity, which was unfamiliar to me, and I kept assimilating it to Bridgman's operationalism, which Bohr, of course, said was another thing.

We proceeded then to my lecture, "On what there is." It has been anthologized and translated so many times—close to thirty—that I shall not belabor it. Afterward the philosophers took me to dinner at the Nassau Club. I spent the rest of the evening with my old student George Berry and his new wife at their flat; he was teaching at Princeton. I let myself into the Oppenheims' house at midnight and went to sleep over an article by the linguist Bonfante, whom I was to meet the next day. All this was the selfsame Monday on which I had walked with Ed in New York between trains.

Next day Paul took me to Gödel's house for a talk. Afterward Paul, Bonfante, and I walked and talked for an hour in the country lanes.

In May I presented "On what there is" again at Yale, and Paul Weiss requested it for his *Review of Metaphysics*. At a dinner party at Bernard Cohen's a few days later, I was shown a news release announcing my promotion to full professor. "So now I'm a Harvard professor in the full sense," I wrote my parents. "There is no higher status, I suppose, in the academic world—a sobering thought, considering some of the dopes there are among us."

My logic seminar that spring brought together a spray of budding logicians—Wang, Myhill, Dreben, Hiż, Leblanc,

Craig, and Dunham. At the end of it they gave me Hilbert and Bernays's two-volume *Grundlagen der Mathematik*, inscribed "in appreciation of your teaching and guidance within and outside of this seminar." It was indeed a year of fulfillment, and it was not half over.

The next great news was the birthday gift from my father of a Chevrolet coupé. I flew to Ohio and drove the car to Cambridge. My big job that summer was a mimeographed text entitled *Theory of Deduction*, a second draft of what would come to be *Methods of Logic*.

The sequence of fulfillments peaked on September 2, when with unaccountably streaming eyes I married Marge in her parents' house in Meriden, Connecticut. Her father came for the occasion from Panama, where he was stationed on a government education job.

Jane Thornton was a bright Maryland girl and our fellow officer in Navy days. Marge's middle name having been entered as "none" on Navy papers, Jane hailed our marriage with these lines:

Joyous tidings now proclaim!
Margie has a middle name.

The marriage would not be legal in Massachusetts for another twelve weeks, but we had solved that by renting a house in New Hampshire for the fall semester. I was to have sabbatical leave in the spring, when we would travel.

Pending that, a miniature honeymoon was called for. We settled for a few days at Central Valley, New York, near Bear Mountain, and then went on to Akron. We worked, finishing *Theory of Deduction* and cutting mimeograph stencils; for my fall course was looming. We commandeered a typing bureau in Akron and raced the calendar with our voluminous corrections.

Our new home was a little turquoise bungalow on North Main Street, Nashua, used hitherto only for display. The distance to Cambridge was thirty miles. We commuted together, for Marge was also teaching.

The university calendar had imposed a deadline on *Theory of Deduction* as a mimeogram, but there was much more that I wanted to do to it before going into print. Marge typed the emerging version and raised questions when puzzled, prompting me to improve the exposition.

It occurred to me to start truth-function logic with a technique for turning a formula into a simplest equivalent. It would serve outright as a test of validity or inconsistency, since a simplest equivalent would be valid or inconsistent visibly if at all. It would go far as a test also of implication or equivalence. For every purpose it would render the formulas as perspicuous as they could be. So I proceeded to marshal the familiar little simplificatory transformations, with a view to proving that they sufficed to reduce a truth-functional formula to a simplest equivalent. They did not. I came to see that a complete algorithm for simplification was bound to be too cumbersome to serve pedagogically as the entering wedge in elementary logic, so I dropped the idea.

I was aware that the problem had a bearing apart from pedagogy. When Claude Shannon was studying at M.I.T., in 1937 or 1938, he observed an analogy between electric hookups and, in effect, truth-function logic. His professor sent him to my office in Eliot House, logicians being few and far between. Hookups in series correspond to 'and', hookups in parallel correspond to 'or', and throwing the switch corresponds to 'not'. A truth-functional schema can accordingly be read as a wiring diagram, and an algorithm for simplifying the schemata becomes a technique for economizing on hookups. Shannon's paper appeared in 1939. I remembered all this but had not seen a burning industrial problem in it, since simplificatory transformations of truth-functional formulas are so simple and familiar. What was surprising me at the end of 1948 was the difficulty of getting a *guaranteed simplest* equivalent, but that was a theoretical and pedagogical refinement. I was drawn back into the problem by odd chance in 1951, and by then the complexity of hookups was such that there was indeed an economic premium on a guaranteed simplest.

Meanwhile my year of fulfillment still had a parting salvo in store. On November 22, 1948, I was made a Senior Fellow of the Society of Fellows. My years as a Junior fellow had been its first three years, and they had been golden. Afterward I had frequented the lunches of the Junior Fellows and gone occasionally to the Monday dinners. Now I was to be a fixture. I would be helping to examine and elect the young candidates and sharing the Monday feasts of wisdom and high living for the foreseeable future.

Mexico at Length   36

· 1949   Marge and I vacated Nashua and set out in our Chevrolet coupé for Mexico by easy and gregarious stages. We visited several friends in Princeton, Nelson and Kay Goodman at their old stone house in Schwenksville, Pennsylvania, Clarence and Margaret Loesch in Youngstown, and family in Akron. By February 6, 1949, we were on our own and southwest-bound.

Before Tamazunchale we deviated into back roads to probe two remote hill towns, Tancanhuitz and Xilitla. After the dizzy ascent from Tamazunchale to Jacala, we settled down for two nights at Zimapán. This and the next notable town, Ixmiquilpán (East McGilpin), bore a very different aspect from my memory of 1941. They had been bathed in a misty light and a magic air. Now they were dun, dusty desert outposts. It had been the rainy season in July 1941, and it was the dry season in February 1949. We stayed a night in Pachuca, a city of sixty thousand at an altitude of 8300 feet, a center for silver mining. It is disposed in a bowl rimmed by smooth, barren mountains. The bulk of the city is always visible rising around one in the distance, thanks to its concavity. Its steepness makes for zigzag streets and interesting irregularity of architecture.

At Xochimilco a native poled us in a flat boat through a maze of canals between floating gardens. Xochimilco is a southeastern outlier of the medieval city of Aztec lake dwellers that was Tenochtitlán and came to be Mexico City. West of sodden Xochimilco is the Pedregal, a rough crust of hard lava, six feet thick. It is pierced at one point by a *contradictio in adjecto,* the cylindrical pyramid of Copilco. Antedating the eruption as it must, the pyramid boasts an age of three or nine thousand years, depending on whom one believes.

A mathematics student named Gonzalo Zubieta had written me from Mexico requesting suggestions for a master's thesis in mathematical logic. In reply I told him of our imminent visit and set up a rendezvous, so in Mexico City we discussed logic over *enchiladas a la suiza.* While in Mexico City, I bought a drawing by Diego Rivera for twenty dollars, a profile of an Indian woman, graceful in its economy of line.

After Teotihuacán, Cholula, and Puebla, which I knew from 1941, we pressed southeastward into a mountainous desert bristling with candelabra and pipe-organ cactus forty feet and more in height. This went on for a hundred miles. It was succeeded by a bewildering country of colored earth, pale green, yellow, and bright red, rolling away in barren hills to all horizons. Then we zigzagged up and over a mountain range, while the sun set in garish pinks and purples in amid the peaks. In the dusk we dropped into the Valley of Oaxaca.

We settled for two weeks in a room in the Hotel Marqués del Valle with a balcony overlooking a busy corner of Oaxaca's arcaded plaza. I resumed my writing of *Methods of Logic,* and Marge the reading and typing of it. Looking up from my work, I would see Indians hurrying by with loads on their backs, or trays of fruit or pastries balanced on their heads. Evenings and Sundays a band or a marimba quintet played on the plaza.

Once in the small hours we were awakened by two mellow voices and a guitar below our balcony, serenading some fair neighbor. Another time, lured by a guitar and voice in the dead of night, we got up and unobtrusively followed the song through the dark streets. It was a strange and haunting song. I caught enough of it to be able to buy the sheet music the next day: "La Llorona."

When we were not traveling, our main meal in Mexico came at about two, for it was then that one could get an economical *comida corrida*, which was *table d'hôte* at *prix fixe*. Supper would be peripatetic: *tacos, tamales,* and *enchiladas,* in which we reveled, were to be had from pushcarts along the streets. A variant, in Oaxaca, was the *lonche:* a sandwich in a circular roll. The *lonchero* at a counter under the arcade of the plaza would ask what kind we wanted—cheese, chicken, sausage, or ground meat—but it never mattered; the *lonche* would come through thick with a little of everything. The man would press refried beans into one face of the bun and then add chili peppers, tomato, cheese, chicken, and chopped veal, to perfection. The only really operative option was between strong and mild in respect of pepper: *suave* for Marge, *picante* for me.

A memorable sight in Oaxaca, then as now, was the great sixteenth-century baroque church of Santo Domingo with its rich but tasteful interior. A populous Tree of Life in gilt relief ascends a white wall and spreads its tracery over the white ceiling of the church. The glorious ex-convent of Santa Catalina de Sena was not then to be seen, for it was being used as a prison. There were tenth-century Mixtec pyramids on Monte Albán, overlooking Oaxaca, and much still to be excavated.

The Mixtec culture was succeeded by the Zapotec, which we overtook at Mitla on resuming our southeastward journey. Temples there are trimmed with friezes of narrow stone blocks set at different depths to produce intricate patterns in mosaic relief. We crossed the eastern rim of the Valley of Oaxaca and dropped into the low Isthmus of Tehuantepec. Hotels looked bad, so we pressed eastward through the night. Ascending into the state of Chiapas, we despaired of being able to buy gasoline before Tuxtla Gutiérrez, and the map showed clearly that we could not get there on what we had. I coasted whenever possible as we drove through the moonlit night, determined to minimize the eventual hitch-hike. At five in the morning we rolled into the Hotel Bonampak at Tuxtla Gutiérrez. There had been a thirty-mile error in the map.

The hotel was a meticulously landscaped motor court. Its semi-detached cottages, set among rustling banana trees, were stuccoed, harmoniously tinted, and roofed with red tiles. There was a big blue-tiled swimming pool, rimmed with a concrete walk on which there were concrete blue-tiled tables, each impaled with a huge umbrella. Adjacent there was a roofed bar. The dominant building in the colony was octagonal, of two stories. Upstairs was a ballroom and down-stairs the restaurant, with casement windows all around.

In the cottages the draperies, bedspreads, hand-loomed rugs, and lampshades harmonized nicely with one another and with the tinted inner walls. One regretted the ugly, rag-ged gash in the delicately tinted plaster, through which, as an afterthought, the wire had been drawn to power the table lamp. Yes, and another one over there. A towel rack dropped its bar, a chair fell apart, and the lock on the door was not working.

Night falls fast in the tropics, and the lights in all the oc-cupied rooms and buildings of the motel would consequently go on nearly simultaneously. On and out, blowing a central fuse. Don Roberto Calderón, the proprietor, could then be seen, visibly concerned, walking with an employee to the lit-tle utility building to see what could be done. The lights came on again, but the water stopped. Matters were brought under control in due course, and such was the routine, eve-ning after evening. We made a routine of repairing to the bar by the pool when Don Roberto's routine of repairing began.

Our drink was the excellent long drink of tequila, tree-rip-ened limes, and soda that I had learned to call by the name of *berta*, local to Taxco, eight years before. "Ah, Dongola," the big mestizo bartender said when I described what was wanted. I thought at last I had learned the generic name, and proceeded to use it for the purpose on subsequent evenings, until I detected from the bartender's somewhat clearer enunciation on a later occasion that he had been trying to say "Tom Collins."

We were sitting by the pool, enjoying these drinks by whatever name, when a strong wind caught the great umbrella of one of the heavy concrete tables and sent the whole structure crashing on the pavement. The big bartender righted the heavy table, with some of its little blue tiles dangling piteously from threads of cement, and put its umbrella back into its initial position, ready for another gust. When we proceeded into the restaurant, we found the wind making its mark there, as well. The casement windows stood open outward and unpropped. The wind would slam one of them shut, and shattered glass would scatter across the floor. A servant would sweep up the glass and restore the window to its initial open position. Management and staff were patient to a fault.

It was said that Don Roberto's brother had won millions in the national lottery and had put Don Roberto in the way of building himself a ruin. It was still abuilding at one end even as it decrepitated at the other.

A touring party arrived from Utah in a big vehicle with a built-in larder. The tour leader knew better than to take chances with Mexican food. He provided the hotel cook with makings and instructions; tact to the winds. One morning he brought some fried Spam over to our table, intending a treat. He was a kind man, however tactless, so I said nothing of our preference for Mexican dishes. The poor fellow disappeared next day, sick, despite his precautions. The rest of us were fine.

A woman in that party was an anthropology professor. She had Mormon preconceptions about Indians, and her preconceptions cried out for a confirmatory visit to the Mayan ruins at Palenque. The way had not then been opened to tourists; she had to charter a two-seater and fly in. She came back radiant with confirmation: there it was with the concentric plan around the holy of holies, Mormon style, just as required. My admiration was uneven.

Eastbound from sweltering Tuxtla, we scaled vast mountains and then settled into chilly San Cristóbal las Casas at 7400 feet. It was a town of cobbled streets, faintly lighted. We took a dim room in the rudimentary Hotel España and ate a dim little supper. Next morning we visited the ornate old church of Santo Domingo. A vague sound as of distant organ pipes proved to be the local Indians chanting prayers. A family would stop on the steps and do a long droning chant in an Indian language before entering the church. Then they would enter and stand chanting some more. The women uncovered their heads on entering.

The market drew a startling assortment of these child-sized people. There were barefoot bushy-headed men carrying spears, really pointed planting sticks, and wearing a coarse black cloth draped from one shoulder like a leopard skin. There were men in white tunics, loin cloths, small-brimmed sombreros, and crew cuts; others in cross-stitched togas. There were men in flat sombreros reminiscent of Chinese coolies, and with a pair of red tassels hanging to the shoulders from a kerchief under the hat. These men wore ponchos, their heads through the slit. The ponchos were belted at the waist and fringed at the bottom edge. They wore trim white shorts and sandals with a great flange behind the ankle, as if for protection in walking backward. Similar sandals are shown on Mayan reliefs. Such were the varied tribesmen; and the tribeswomen were scarcely less exotic. It was market day, and they had converged from mountain valleys on all sides. They communicated with the town merchants mostly by gestures. The Indian languages were as varied, presumably, as the costumes.

We were privileged to have come into this remote country so soon after the arrival of the Pan-American Highway. Natives were still unaccustomed to cars, and they scattered in embarrassed laughter to make way for us. We drove on eastward to Comitán, meaning to touch Guatemala if highway construction permitted. It did not. On the far side of Comitán we tried in vain to drive across a little unbridged *barranca* and got trapped in the vee, bridging it. A kind crowd of stalwarts pulled us out with a rope and we drove back to Tuxtla Gutiérrez.

We decided to deposit the car there and probe Central America by plane and bus. Permission to leave Mexico without the car was required, because of import laws. I got the governor of Chiapas to testify in writing to custody of the car in our absence, but I still needed a federal document. This prolonged our happy stay at Hotel Bonampak. While there, I settled at last the details of natural deduction for *Methods of Logic*. By a trick involving alphabetical order and the flagging of variables, I devised a system that was symmetrical, convenient, consistent, and complete, and wrote it up for the *Journal of Symbolic Logic*. On March 23, 1949, we flew to Tapachula, a steaming banana town in the southernmost corner of Mexico, and took a taxi to the border of Guatemala.

Central America and Back 37

Border formalities took four hours. I sensed that the Guatemalan official wanted a bribe, but my parsimony, my stubbornness, and my capacity for moral indignation carried the dreary day. From there we bumped along in a bus through lush vegetation to Malacatán, a cobblestoned village with a primitive tropical hotel. Next morning we rode the same bus to Quezaltenango. The eighty steep, rough miles took five and a half hours, largely in low gear. We climbed from sea level to 9000 feet and then dropped to 7800. Costumes, again, were exotic.

Alarmed by hotel rates, we resolved to take a bus to Guatemala City that same afternoon—another nine grueling hours over mountain ranges—and then fly back to Mexico. Travel hinged, for us, on cheap foreign living.

The bus stopped briefly at Solalá, and we could look

steeply down on Lake Atitlán far below in the moonlight. A resident and his little daughter, of Spanish stock, boarded the bus to talk with the passengers during the stop. Yes, we were from near New York. The girl thought how jolly it must be in New York. "¡Sería muy alegre!" An incongruous thought, I felt, in this strange and colorful culture, this ideal climate, this fantastic landscape.

We got into a Guatemala City hotel at three in the morning and were up at eight. We got our Mexican re-entry permits and plane tickets for the day after and then explored the city. The best sight was a relief map of the republic, as big as a small city lot, with water running in the rivers and standing in the lakes and the two oceans.

In bed that night, seven hours before our scheduled take-off for Mexico, we began to take stock. Panicked by prices, we had already bypassed Chichicastenango and Lake Atitlán. Now we were turning our backs on the rest of Central America. So I counted money, computed, estimated, and arranged to be awakened an hour earlier. This allowed me time before takeoff to investigate air fares in the opposite direction. The result was that we spent that very afternoon not in Tapachula but in San Salvador, having meanwhile changed our tickets and got visas.

San Salvador was an attractive capital with little white palaces and a string of plazas almost corner to corner down the slope. We took a bus to a village and tramped for an hour at the foot of a volcano. It was a region of soft loess, in which roads and paths were cut eight feet deep. We threaded narrow passages between sheer walls.

The geographer Hill of Michigan had told me in Brazil that Honduras was the one country in his experience that seemed devoid of jingoism or national pride. In Tegucigalpa, its capital, I could see his point. Stores were stocked with canned fruit and other canned goods from the States, at high prices, in what could be a paradise of pineapple, mango, and papaya. Bananas were grown in northern Honduras and shipped north, green. Clothes, even mantillas, were imported from the States. The *lempira*, which was the local monetary unit, was represented mostly by U.S. quarters, and the forty-centavo pieces in evidence were exclusively U.S. dimes. Entertainment and music, as far as we saw, were canned in movies and juke boxes or conveyed by radio. The only products clearly domestic in origin were the children.

It was exciting to see these remote capitals, however dull, that I had wondered about since childhood The next one was torrid, squalid Managua, Nicaragua. Then came San José, a Spanish city bustling and prosperous in aspect, the capital of Costa Rica. During our two-day visit there, we were treated to an abortive revolution. An open truck rattled through the street with rebels standing in it, rifles raised. As evening wore on there was the sound of mortar fire. The rebel colonel had occupied the armory, but by morning he was routed and apprehended and President Figueres was still in charge.

Marge's mother had joined Mr. Boynton in the Canal Zone, and so did we. They lodged us in their Hotel Washington, Cristobal, and showed us the sights in their car. Our flight back to Guatemala City was scenic, especially as we crossed the Gulf of Fonseca; the pilot treated us to a close-range circuit of the vast cone of Consigüina, at the western point of Nicaragua, and a glimpse into the crater. Over Guatemala we had another kind of thrill, an abrupt drop of a couple of thousand feet in a downdraft.

We had two nights in Guaetmala City before flying on to Mexico. One reward was a visit to Antigua, the imposing old Spanish capital that was given up after a destructive eruption of the volcano Agua. Another reward was the acquaintance of a traveler from Brooklyn. He had made his way to Chick Chick—*you* know. Chick Chick? *Did* I know? Oh yes, Chichicastenango. There had been complications—something to do with a goil cloik, some goil cloik or other. Well, you see, there was this goil cloik. Further intelligence transpired of his travels and efforts at travel, and I conceived an admiration of his uninformed curiosity about the world and his determination in indulging it.

The last leg of the Pan-American Highway, from the Isthmus of Tehuantepec to our terminal *barranca* after Comitán, had been gravel, some of which approached the coarseness of loose cobblestones. Our tires took a beating. By the time we had driven from Tuxtla Gutiérrez back to the isthmus, they began to blow out. I changed one and stopped at a service station to get it repaired. The repairman, a Salvadoran immigrant, sent a little boy back up the road somewhere with a peso with which to buy a patch. Soon he sent him back again with another peso for another patch, and the tire held air; but after a few hundred yards another tire blew. Our Salvadoran and his runner resumed their activity, but our lifeline was attenuating, and the nearest place where tires could be bought was Juchitán, a hundred miles farther west. We had progressed but little when both of the patched tires had blown again. A Packard with California plates providentially pulled up with two young women and an old couple aboard, and they lent us their spare tire and wheel. Juchitán was their destination, and we could return their tire and wheel when we had bought new tires.

We must stay the night in their house, they said; there was no alternative. On our arrival, long after dark, a gate was opened to a courtyard where we would leave our cars. It was lighted, and big, hearty Indian women were there hanging out clothes amid laughter and animated talk. Women dominate Tehuantepec society; the men seem smaller, when seen at all. They are apt to be off toiling in the fields.

The two young women of the California Packard joined into the lively banter with effortless fluency, and what was remarkable was that it was not Spanish. It proved to be Zapotec. The two were missionaries, former pupils of the Ann Arbor linguist Kenneth Pike, and were putting hymns and Bible stories into a Zapotec orthography of their own scientific devising. One of them, Velma Pickett, had also studied under Zellig Harris at Penn, and knew my work; Harris, she told me, had required his students to study my *Mathematical Logic*. The old couple were the visiting parents of Velma's colleague, Virginia something. We talked linguistics through the evening and agreed to meet again at the headquarters in Mexico City of the nation-wide language project. We learned that all of Juchitán's ten thousand people spoke Zapotec.

Next morning we bought two tires, returned the borrowed wheel, and set out. At Cuernavaca, four hundred miles northwest, I pondered whether it would be worthwhile for Marge's sake to drop south to Taxco. I had liked it in 1941, but it had probably become tourist-ridden, and would be pale after the exotic scenes in Chiapas. Well, it wasn't far; we decided to go and stay overnight. We stayed a month.

We took a room in the Hotel de los Arcos, a hundred yards below the *zócalo* or central plaza. It was a colonial building and a modest, traditional hotel. We had a big private porch. A little unpaved street passed alongside it a dozen feet below. *Peones* and *burros* were its silent traffic. We worked on the porch, I writing *Methods of Logic* and Marge typing and studying it. We would work from breakfast until about two and then walk a quarter of a mile to a little restaurant, Las Palomas, for the *comida corrida*. Back then to our porch, to work until dark. After that we would work in the room for a while and then go up to the *zócalo*. An Indian women would be sitting at the edge of the cobblestone square, a dark *rebozo* over her head and shoulders, and a pail of *tamales* beside her, covered with a towel to keep them warm. We would stand and eat *tamales* for a while: some were laced with plums, others with bits of meat. Then we would walk up a short passage to a smaller square, a *plazuela*, where another Indian woman had established herself for the evening with a makeshift counter and a stock of *tacos*. They were very good, as were the *tamales*. When we were satisfied, we would repair to a gallery overlooking the *zócalo* and drink a long *berta* or two to the strains of *mariachi* music. The leader of the little voice-and-guitar trio was Tito, who as a boy had been the junior member of the duet eight years before at Berta's. We delighted in their exotic staccato songs and close harmony, and were insatiable. Then we might do a little more work, and so to bed. Such was the pattern of most of our thirty days in Taxco, and monotonous they were not.

A Mexican with a truck is apt to give it a name and paint the name on the bumper. One was named "El Jumilito," and I could not find *jumil* in the dictionary. I asked the waitress at Las Palomas. It proved to be an article of diet, more particularly a bug. There is a day each year, she said, when the Indians range over the slopes gathering *jumiles* from the leaves of bushes and return with panniers full and seething with the sluggish insects. To eat them, she said, you take a live one between thumb and forefinger, crush it in a dish of *salsa ranchera*—the ubiquitous sauce of fiery chili pepper, onion, and tomato—and ingest it. She didn't care for them herself, she said, but she would try to get me some.

Some days later she put a bowl of them before me. They were bugs in the strict sense—*hemiptera*. They were perhaps an inch long, black, and lethargic. I asked for the *salsa ranchera*, with a view to the prescribed routine, but the cook then took them away and brought them back as a paste, mashed up in the sauce. I manfully made away with it all, scooping it up with *tortillas*, but it was not good. The taste was the familiar bedbug smell, redolent of A Street, S.E., Washington, D.C. The taste came back, arising in fumes from my stomach, for a day afterward. Such are the rigors of semantics in the field.

Keeping faith with Velma Pickett, we turned up at the extraordinary institute of missionary linguistics in Mexico City. A score or more members were there, and they regaled me with reprints of articles and with talk of linguistics and high adventure. Some fifty Indian languages in Mexico had been studied by the group and reduced to writing or were in process. A zealous missionary trained in linguistics by Kenneth Pike at summer sessions in Norman, Oklahoma, would head into the hills on muleback with his zealous wife and a babe in arms, to pursue his science and ply their pious mission among a little-touched and little-known people for the foreseeable future.

Presently lunch was announced, and we moved into a hall

of many tables. Before eating, we all stood at our chairs for the singing of a hymn.

The volcano Paricutín had been growing and erupting for six years since its inception in a cornfield two hundred miles west of Mexico City; and had risen two thousand feet. We went out and watched it. The crater was spewing red fire upward in the night, interspersed with occasional black bodies that were masses of not quite incandescent rock. The eastern slope was emitting a red cascade.

Uruapan, nearby, was notable for lacquered trays and a colorful market, captured in a big watercolor of which I am fond. It was given us by the artist, Virginia Davidson, Don's gifted wife. Next we spent some days in Pátzcuaro and a week in Querétaro. I had been working nearly eleven hours most days in Taxco, but in Pátzcuaro and Querétaro I was working twelve and more. I was hoping to finish *Methods of Logic* before taking up my summer job in California, where I was booked for government work with Rand Corporation. Querétaro proved to be a trim and up-and-coming latter-day city with little claim to the picturesque. I seized the opportunity for tailor-made suits at low cost. I got three, including twelve trousers—that is, six pairs. Continuing north for 350 miles through increasingly dry country, we settled next in Saltillo. It was of passing interest, here as in Querétaro, to live in a workaday Mexican city of no concern to tourists. We had our own work to do.

Our car had New Hampshire plates, and so did that of one Jim Niles, a novice in the Catholic clergy. That was how we met. It transpired that we did not see the eternal verities eye to eye, but still, Jim astutely observed, it could do no harm to have a phial of holy water aboard when we made our imminent perilous descent from the high plateau. In the event the experiment fizzled, for the descent from Saltillo was unexpectedly gradual.

We went through Monclova, notable for the ugly statue of some Mexican statesman in a top hat. At the summer solstice, 1949, we crossed the Rio Grande from Piedras Negras to Eagle Pass after four and a quarter months south of the border.

We crossed the border reluctantly and hugged it as best we could from there to the Pacific. We parked the car in Del Rio and walked about Villa Acuña. We parked in El Paso and walked about Juárez. We parked in Nogales, Arizona, and walked about Nogales, Sonora. We walked about Algodones, west of Yuma, and Mexicali, across from Calexico, and Tecate, farther west, and finally Tijuana.

At Mexicali there was a *vega*, or dry floodplain, spanned by a causeway from which we looked out over an assemblage of neat cardboard cabins. The material came from discarded cartons. There were trim porch roofs supported by pillars of soup cans. The scene attested to the aridity of the Imperial Valley, that such structures could endure. It attested also to an abrupt economic gradient. Poor Mexicalenses were building from the prodigal Calexican dump.

Crossing a desert, we struck out on a dirt road that had two attractions: it hugged the border and it saved a few miles. The surface was firm except now and then when the road crossed a sandy draw, in one of which we got stuck. The main road was seven miles behind us, and the temperature, we later learned, would have been 104 in the shade if there had been shade. We had a little water with us. Carrying the water, we walked more than four of the seven miles, at which point a border patrol came along in a jeep, took us back to our car, and pulled it out of the sand. In the Los Angeles paper soon afterward we read of a similar but fatal case, evidently in the same place.

Since Saltillo the heat had been intense and unremitting. When at last we reached the sea, south of San Diego, the climate changed abruptly. It was a pleasure to take my jacket from the trunk of the car before continuing to Tijuana.

Rand, Fulbright, and Europe　　　　　　38

Rand Corporation was an intelligence facility in the service of national defense. It was agreeably situated in Santa Monica, a coastal suburb of Los Angeles. My summer job as consultant there was unprecedentedly remunerative, but apart from that it was a mistake. Despite my top-secret clearance in the Navy, fresh clearance was required—reasonably enough, since a staunch anti-Nazi could be a communist. My new clearance did not arrive in time, so I was put onto boondoggles. One of them concerned Kenneth Arrow's monograph on social reconciliation of individual preferences. My resulting memoranda included two theorems about Boolean functions, ultimately published in *Selected Logic Papers*. The other project was in game theory. My memorandum on this was subsequently incorporated by McKinsey and Krentel into an article under our three names.

We lived in a redwood bungalow backed against a cliff in Santa Monica Canyon at 34 Haldeman Road. We saw something of the Reichenbachs, who lived in an adjacent suburb, and more of Chen McKinsey, Norman Dalkey, Olaf Helmer, and Abe Kaplan, who worked at Rand. The latter three were young philosophers of the Carnap persuasion. Olaf had come from Germany on account of Hitler. He and his wife Lou lived on the rim of a canyon in a little house, precariously perched, to which they hauled up supplies by rope. Lou played a guitar and sang, notably "Careless Love."

Albert and Roberta Wohlstetter were living an abundant life in Hollywood Canyon. They threw a great breakfast party. There was caviar with the scrambled eggs, and copious champagne. From there we all migrated to the beach.

Morton and Zivia (Syrkin) Wurtele were teaching at U.C.L.A., he in meteorology and she in mathematics. I had been his tutor before the war, and she had distinguished herself in my course in mathematical logic. Morton's parents had lately moved from Kentucky to Los Angeles. His mother gave me an oil painting, the work of a friend, depicting the church and market at Taxco. The father served mint juleps.

Naomi and the girls were living in Los Angeles. Marge and I contrived an outing with the girls—a trip to Catalina Island.

I gave a lecture at the University of Southern California, "On ontologies," bits of which are in "Identity, ostension, and hypostasis." Just thirty years later I again lectured there on ontology. We agreed on the latter occasion to make a regular thing of it hereafter—every thirty years.

Ed Haskell was briefly in Los Angeles, and when the time came for us to drive back east, September 1, 1949, he came along. We stopped at the Grand Canyon and walked down into it as far as the rim of the Granite Gorge. That and the subsequent ascent made for a strenuous hike, but Marge let it be known in no uncertain terms that eight years earlier she had done the whole thing *including* the Granite Gorge.

The Carnaps had a house in the hills east of Santa Fe where they spent their trimesters away from Chicago. We visited them there, and Carnap got passes enabling us to visit Los Alamos. He and I argued at length about the supposed distinction between analytic and synthetic truths. Ed surreptitiously timed us and found that Carnap talked five and a quarter times as long as I.

We moved into a flat on Harvard Street, corner of Prescott, even nearer Harvard Yard by a few steps that my bachelor flat in Ware Street had been. I would set off to class only when I heard the bell strike the hour.

In December 1949, I gave the Delaguna Lecture at Bryn Mawr, an early version of "Identity, ostension, and hypostasis." Marge and I stayed at Milton Nahm's. The department gave us a party to which I wore my snug dinner jacket of college days. I split the seat of the pants, but nobody may have known.

I was elected to the American Academy of Arts and Sciences, held in their old house of tender memory in Boston's

Newbury Street, Back Bay. Philipp Frank, by then at Harvard, was sparking periodic meetings at the Academy in company with Bridgman, Gerry Holton, Smith Stevens, and others, somewhat in the way of a Vienna Circle in exile. The meeting of March 1950 was a major event, bringing Peter Hempel and Alonzo Church among others. My paper, in response and opposition to Church, was "Semantics and abstract objects." I was still pressing the cause of the schematic letter, ontologically innocent until proven guilty. The proof of guilt is in the quantifier.

· 1950

The Fulbright Committee had solicited my application for a grant to teach at Oxford during the next academic year, at Oxford's request. The financial arrangements were unsettled, but I was told to expect neither gain nor loss. I compromised on a half year. Despite my recent sabbatical, Harvard granted me a semester's leave without pay. By June 1950— seven months later—the Fulbright committee still had not notified me of my award, despite having asked me to apply. Marge and I were leaving for a summer in Europe. My department chairman phoned Washington and determined that I had the award; then he phoned Goodman, my intended stand-in, and got his acceptance.

In New York on June 15 we boarded a freighter for Liverpool on Marge's first trip to Europe. There were some young Navy men on board as we waited to be billeted. Among them there was a very young radioman second class, two of whose utterances have echoed in our recollections for thirty years. "Oo, de Gi'nts" [uːdədʒaˈnts], he exclaimed in a discussion of baseball. The other was "Was that heavy-set girl your sister?"

We were eleven days at sea. It seemed like a lazy time: I was surprised at how much writing I accomplished. In the last days the wind in the stays and tackle seemed increasingly to hum familiar tunes. They were familiar because I was unconsciously supplying them, and tiresome because my repertoire of chords was so rudimentary. I was relieved to find that the illusion lapsed when we landed.

We roamed the length and breadth of the Isle of Man.

Aunt Bess had told me whom to look up in Douglas so as to connect with kin. I felt obliged to do so, and was relieved to find no one there. We were on our own. We checked parish records at St. John's in the center of the island, where Grandpa Quine was born. His father was listed as Robert Quine, laborer, and his mother had been Ellen Stanford. On the Point of Ayr we found what may have been the ruins of their thatched stone cottage.

Thanks to its insulation—a seagirt land in a landgirt sea—the island is lush for its latitude. The main street of the main town, Douglas, was a two-mile crescent along the beach. It had the aspect of a modest Victorian holiday town with its guest houses interspersed among the other houses and shops. Ramsey in the north was a town of old stone houses, twisting streets, and quiet waterways. One little street was Quine's Court. One of the two castles, Rushen, in the south of the island, was a well-preserved specimen of the story-book genre.

I took Marge to Chester and on to London, where we were shocked and saddened by the aftermath of the Blitz. The tall, labyrinthine old slums between St. Paul's and the Old Bailey, which had so delighted me in 1929, were flat, and the old lanes showed only as paved walks, out in the open and surprisingly close to one another, with the pits of old cellars between. Karl and Henny Popper gave us a tour in their little car—to St. Alban's and Verulamium and to their house, "Fallowfield," Penn, Bucks.

In Paris I received at last the Fulbright papers and found, contrary to the original assurances, that they demanded a heavy financial sacrifice. It was to be a busy term of teaching, and I did not propose to pay for the privilege. I declined. I wrote to the Harvard dean explaining why I would not be putting my leave of absence to its intended use, and I wrote to Columbia and Chicago to see whether either of these universities, which had just recently made me generous offers of visiting appointments, was still in a budgetary state to take me on for a term. Failing that, I was prepared to live frugally and write, unpaid and unencumbered.

Southbound, we rode nine trains in two days and walked a dozen miles, much of it in the rain. We took in the medieval delights of nearby Chartres and remote Sarlat, also the Romanesque church at Moissac that I knew from Oberlin, and the Cro-Magnon cave paintings and cliff dwellings at Les Eyzies. The woman in charge there carried an oil lamp, to the detriment of the twenty-thousand-year-old likenesses of deer and buffalo.

Our southern destination was another of my coveted vest-pocket countries, Andorra. We went from Foix by bus, crossing the Pyrenees by a pass eight thousand feet high amid patches of snow. Andorra was a land of mountains, narrow fertile valleys, and villages of black stone houses with black slate roofs. Our balcony in the capital village looked across to a slope that reached up and up, variously forested and variously gouged and molded. It was strewn here and there with great black boulders, and faintly traced with black stone walls. A good share of our four days in Andorra went into admiring it, and vigorous hours went into climbing its slopes.

The capital had its French school and its Spanish school. Villagers would learn to read one language or the other, but what they spoke out of school was Catalan. Posted proclamations were in Catalan, but books were in French and Spanish. One post office sold stamps of "Andorre" for francs and another sold stamps of "Andorra" for pesetas. To enter France or Spain from Andorra you had to pass French or Spanish customs, but on entering Andorra there was none; Andorra was just a wide spot on the border between France and Spain.

We went on to Seo de Urgel, in Spain. It was a town of dark streets, broadly and heavily arcaded. There were donkeys, seedy soldiers, and an air of poverty. From a hilltop farther east we looked out over Llivia, three square miles of Spain separated from the rest of Spain by a half mile of France. It has since been ceded to France. We continued to Perpignan by a sinuous narrow-gauge mountain railway in an open, roofless car, through a panorama of peaks, cliffs, and gorges. Medieval villages were wedged into improbable niches.

A pouch of goatskin called a *bota* may be seen suspended from a native's belt, filled with wine. It has a narrow nozzle and emits a narrow stream when gently squeezed. The native holds it aloft, head back, mouth open, and deftly imbibes. It can be shared with no thought of contagion, there being no contact. But one is well advised, having imbibed, to stop squeezing before righting the *bota*. On the train a kind native offered me a drink and I spoiled my shirt.

The principle of the *bota* is extended to the carafes in restaurants. A long glass spout tapers to a small hole, and the carafe makes its sanitary rounds without wine glasses.

By rewarding stages through Provence, we made our way to Cagnes to visit Don and Ginny Davidson. The taxi driver who brought us from the station had been talking an unidentified Romance language with friends, and I asked him in French what language it was. "Oh," he said, "c'est la langue d'ici." I suppose the experts would call it Niçois. I imagine a Romance continuum from the Balearic Islands through Catalonia and Provence and perhaps across the Piedmont, to terminate in Rhaeto-Romansch—a continuum in which mutual intelligibility varies inversely with the separation in miles. If there had been no disruptions by conquest, the continuum would cover the whole of Romance Europe, subject only to gradations rather than language boundaries. The discontinuity of the overlying official languages, e.g. at the Franco-Italian border, is a politically induced collision of two Romance dialects that belong as far apart in the continuum as the Ile de France and Tuscany.

Cagnes is a steep tangle of twisting cobbled passageways crowning an abrupt hill and culminating in a castle. On the side overlooking the sea the Davidsons had rented a narrow old house, wedged in among others in the tight mass of medieval masonry. It had five floors with a room on each. After a few days with them, we went on to Monaco and walked all over the principality. Thence by bus over the Maritime Alps to Stresa, on Lago Maggiore, to enable me to recover from an attack of colic and heat prostration. The view over the water to the rugged peaks, and the view down on the three tight little Isole Borromee—one of them green with gardens, another white and red with tile-roofed houses and bell towers—lent joy to convalescence.

There followed a week in Venice, implausible as ever: a network of dry chasms, the footways, superimposed in a network of wet chasms, the canals. The Biennale di Venezia was on view in the park at the eastern point, and Jackson Pollock's work had not been accepted. Peggy Guggenheim had responded with an exhibit of his dribbled canvases in one of the palaces on the Piazza di San Marco. I thought how that Wyoming cowboy had taken Peggy Guggenheim for a ride. Posterity has seemed, unaccountably, not to bear me out.

From the heat of Venice we fled to Switzerland. Walking and riding, sometimes in snow, we saw chalet villages that looked too inaccessible to be lived in, and fields and pastures that looked too steep to hold their cows and farmhands. A dizzy crossing from Martigny brought us to Chamonix in High Savoy, where I canvassed seventeen hotels and found all of them full. I took a room in the last and fanciest.

We ventured into occupied Germany hoping to find my father's mother's birthplace near Kaiserslautern. The mission failed with a vengeance. Regulations imposed by the French occupation of the Palatinate forbade my changing travelers' checks unless I went to Speyer; and without cashing a check I had no cash for the trip either to Speyer or out of Germany. Panic mounted. In the end a decent old bank official came to the rescue and cashed a check. By then my one concern was to get out. We took a bus to Echternach, sacred to the memory of the Anglo-Saxon missionary St. Willibrord. Echternach is on the Moselle and safely across the border in Luxemburg.

So we were back in another of my vest-pocket countries. We traveled through the rugged northern part, new to me, and through Belgium and Holland. In Amsterdam we plied the canals in water busses and called on the philosopher Evert Beth and his wife Cori. At Antwerp we embarked for America. Bob and Helen Thackaberry were aboard—friends through my brother Bob. They taught English at Akron University and were bright and amusing company.

Family Man Again 39

On learning of the Fulbright fiasco, the Harvard administration surprised me by generously reactivating my salary and teaching duties. Oxford's loss of an extra hand was the Harvard department's gain, for we had Goodman for the term despite my being back. Chicago also came through, and for this, though declining, I was deeply grateful. I have kept clear, ever after, of Fulbright entanglement.

The Oxford philosophers had invited me to give the first John Locke Lectures during the spring of 1951 when I was expected there, and they had also organized a symposium "On what there is" for the meeting of the Aristotelian Society scheduled for Edinburgh in that interval. I had to decline the lectureship and to participate only by proxy in the symposium. My "Reply to Mr. Geach on what there is," bewilderingly misprinted, was read and ably defended, I can well believe, by Dreben at the eventual meeting.

I have long made a practice of noting down little verbal conceits and absurdities that cross my mind and strike my fancy. A page of examples will convey the spirit.

Kine low.
Foul regards.
Haff and hahf.
Matter incarnate.
Down with upstarts.
Bedfast in Belfast.
Ras Tafari on Safari.
Chartrousse langerée.
Orientation-oriented.

Gregory the Gregarious.
Ibides among the irides.
A troika for every woika.
The City of Brothelly Love.
A-settin' on the davenporch.
Lend an ear to a Lydian air.
It cleans while it cleanses.
"Welcome, stranger," he lied.
A self-styled God knows what.
The merest pingpong of phonemes.
The wind rose in the windrows.
The daïs is on the bias, Thaïs.
Like a cœlocanth on a terebinth.
As varicose as a blueberry blintz.
That sounds all very well on paper.
Fetch the wrench, you wretched wench.
A slovenly hovel at a heavenly level.
Yon cloistered orbs that ere the night. . .
Loaded question: "Will you ride or waddle?"
Life on a biodegradable sanitary landfill.
He lay there soaking in his own bath water.
The terrible parable of Clarabelle the Unbearable.
The American Kit & Caboodle Co.: kits & caboodles.
O'er the morn-misted dew with a fresh of spring buttercups.

    That fall, 1950, I took to gathering a lot of such bits into what purported to be a cross-purpose jumble of multiple conversation at a cocktail party. The three pages, entitled "It tastes like chicken," built up cryptically to an account of unrecognized cannibalism. It came out in a "little magazine" called *Furioso*. Taken aback in retrospect, I canceled my order for offprints.

    Russell came to Harvard that November for a public lecture. Marge and I picked him up at Mrs. Whitehead's, where he had been paying his respects. Crowded into our coupé, we drove to his lecture. Our way was blocked in Kirkland Street by a young throng running across from New Lecture Hall to Sanders Theater, where there was more room for Russell's unexpectedly large audience. What with the girls' colorful dresses and sweaters flying in the wind, it was a bright homage, and Russell was pleased.

Mrs. Whitehead told Irving Singer afterward that she had been reluctant to receive Russell and had resolved to give him a piece of her mind, but that when he came his sprightly talk and engaging way had charmed her resentment away.

It was ten years since Tarski and I had argued in vain with Carnap against the distinction, so basic to his thought, between analytic and synthetic truth. Morton White, drawn into the issue by Goodman, had launched a triangular correspondence on it with Goodman and me. Over the decade the issue was widely aired. I was invited to address the American Philosophical Association on it. My paper was "Two dogmas of empiricism," and the meeting was scheduled for Toronto in the last days of December 1950.

Our son was born on December 20, the last autumn day of the first half of the century. We named him Douglas, wanting a Gaelic name to go with "Quine" and thinking also of the Manx town. The three of us celebrated Christmas in the hospital. Next day I brought Marge and Doug home and left for Toronto.

Frozen water lines delayed the train five hours. Breakfast was served on board after noon. Passengers queued for it for more than three hours, and one woman fainted. The return trip was better. I had the company of my Harvard colleague Donald Williams and George Burch of Tufts, both of them witty, erudite, and philosophically provocative. I slept in a roomette. The logistics were under control and the train was less than three hours late. The snow-covered hills and ice-covered trees were dazzling under a blue sky. George said he thought he would retire to a roomette.

· 1951 There was a meeting on "Two dogmas" in California in April, and there were two sessions on it at a convention in Boston in June. Articles in response to it proliferated over the years; even books. The essay has been anthologized dozens of times, outpacing "On what there is."

I went to a meeting of Carnap's seminar in Chicago that

spring to join issues with him on another topic: ontology. I argued that numbers and other abstract objects, if admitted as values of bound variables, were full-fledged assumptions on a par with physical objects. He gave them a privileged status, on grounds involving his purported distinction between the analytic and the synthetic. Feigl was there and requested my piece for his journal, *Philosophical Studies*. It appeared as "On Carnap's views on ontology." It had been preceded by my "Ontology and ideology," a requested response to Gustav Bergmann's contention that the predicates of a theory commit us directly to an ontology of corresponding properties. Between Bergmann's excessive acknowledgments of abstract objects and Carnap's disavowals of them, I was midway. *Da stehe ich, ich kann nicht anderes.*

Gonzalo Zubieta wanted me to present a paper to the Sociedad Matemática Mexicana. Recurring to my quest of 1948 for an algorithm for simplifying truth functions, I presented *in absentia* "Two theorems about truth functions." Six months later Jim Oliver, formerly my top-notch teaching assistant, phoned me in desperation from Florida to say that as program chairman for the Association for Symbolic Logic he had been let down by his main speaker. I turned again to that theme and prepared a paper on "The problem of simplifying truth functions," which came to be called Quine's Problem. Many contributors to engineering journals cited my paper and took up my terminology.

Prompted by a query from Leblanc, I wrote "On an application of Tarski's theory of truth" to show how narrowly the system of my *Mathematical Logic* escapes the fate of affording a definition of its own truth predicate—a fate that is known from Tarski's work to spell inconsistency. It was an exercise in brinkmanship.

I was to address the Ann Arbor linguists in August 1951. We proposed to drive, take Douglas, and visit in Akron. At a motel on Lake George, Doug cried all night. Contrite over having disturbed other tenants, we gave up. Marge drove home with Doug and I went on. My paper, "The problem of meaning in linguistics," continued the struggle against the uncritical notion of meaning that I had waged in my attack on analyticity.

I began working toward a philosophy book that proved, nine years later, to be *Word and Object*. Roman Jakobson bespoke it for a series under his direction and got me Rockefeller money for secretarial help. I sensed that it would be a long pull and that I would do well meanwhile to spread the word by a little volume of my existing essays. Henry Aiken and I were with our wives in a night spot in Greenwich Village when we heard Harry Belafonte sing the Trinidad calypso that ends:

And so, from a logical *point of view,*
Always marry woman uglier than you.

That, Henry suggested, offered a title for my interim volume; and so it did.

Meanwhile the home scene had evolved. Our family of three being too much for our little flat, we had bought a brick house at School and Temple Streets in hither Belmont, three miles from Harvard Yard. In September my daughter Elizabeth came from California to live with us for the year and finish high school in Belmont. My sudden responsibility for a teenager found me awkward. I fancied neither a censorious role nor a permissive one. I resented the dilemma, and I showed it when without warning Elizabeth stayed out with her boy-friend Wendy until one. My anger was providential; Elizabeth was relieved and happy to see at last that I cared.

· 1952   In February I became chairman of the philosophy department. It was a chore of four years or so that was passed around, and duty called. So I hedged other duties by resigning my consulting editorship of the *Journal of Symbolic Logic*. Having steadily reviewed articles and books for the *Journal* from 1936 onward, except for the war years, I had reviewed more than anyone else except the prime mover, Alonzo Church. Relief from the burden was welcome, but in consequence the mounting activity in logic soon left me behind.

Family Man Again

In March 1952 I was offered a professorship at Berkeley. Salary, climate, and scenery favored it, but the teaching load did not. I was also offered the George Eastman Visiting Professorship at Oxford for 1953–1954, on terms that made up handsomely for the Fulbright fiasco. This I accepted. Berkeley I ultimately declined, in the face of a counter-offer from Harvard: I was given a raise, and it was agreed that after my year at Oxford I would receive the top Arts-and-Sciences salary, continuing with it if it rose. It was agreed further that I would never have to resume the chairmanship after Oxford. My stint as chairman was thus to be just a year and a half.

The electing of Junior Fellows to the Society of Fellows was heavy duty in season. I was also a Syndic of the Harvard University Press. We convened each month under Tom Wilson's genial direction to approve books for publication. If I were to share administrative duties at all, these were the two best. They were instructive activity, pursued in high-grade company. The fringe benefits in the one case were great, what with the Monday evenings, and not negligible in the other; for there was an occasional sumptuous dinner at the Club of Odd Volumes on Beacon Hill, and a copy of each Harvard book that one might care to have.

A lighter duty was that of adviser to the Harvard Corporation's committee on honorary degrees. In that capacity I pressed for honoring Gödel at the 1951 commencement. Let us do it now, I urged, rather than jump onto a subsequent bandwagon. I failed. In the following winter, Gödel was a joint recipient with von Neumann of the Einstein Prize. I told the Corporation's committee at their subsequent meeting that I had told them so, and let us now jump onto the bandwagon. We did.

I drove to Easton with Marge and Elizabeth to view again the house that I had had to buy for Naomi. When she abandoned it for California, furniture and books were left behind. Rats and weather were getting in and much was spoiled. We salvaged some. I was still trying to get Naomi to release the property for sale. It pained me to see it neglected and my alimony wasted.

Elizabeth graduated from high school after a happy year. She had made many friends and had the leading part in the school play. Fifty-odd schoolmates gave her a surprise party on the eve of her departure for California, and five of them went to the airport next day to see her off. Then Marge and I sailed with John Cooley for a week, returning in time to escort Gödel to his doctorate and to throw a party for him and his wife in Belmont.

"Kürtli," Mrs. Gödel asked, "wouldn't Cambridge be nice for a summer vacation?" Sweltering Cambridge! But they had once tried coastal New Jersey and he had found it too cold. Frail Gödel sought warmth in all seasons.

Taxco III and After   40

"To be perfectly bigging taken precisely *qua* bigging," Etienne Gilson once said, to the best of my detection, "is always and always *other*; always *different.*"

I failed to understand. *Being*, not *bigging*; does that help? Not much. Henry Bugbee might have understood. He reveled in being. Henry had joined our department in 1947 as an assistant professor for a five-year term. He brought his wife and children, but within a year, without visible effort, he was out on divorce. He was lean, contemplative, and best visualized in leather jacket with pipe, rod, reel, and creel. He had a mystical sense of the pure poetry of being. There was the poetry of what is, the poetry of the cabbage or rowboat, and also perhaps the poetry of being in the other sense: what it is like, on one's own part, to be. Henry, if anyone, could be poetically. And is being poetically the same as being poetic? Questions flood in.

Marge and I had just taken up residence in New Hampshire in September 1948 when we ran into Henry and Daphne, who were there getting their marriage licence. Daphne was an architecture student, exuberant and well turned out by Bonwit Teller. She and Henry subsequently imbibed our enthusiasm for Mexico, and by 1952 the tables had turned. They had come to know the ins and outs of Taxco, and found an idyllic retreat that we could rent for two months that summer.

We drove to Akron, taking Doug. After a few days with the parents and a weekend at Put-in-Bay with Bob and Rosalie, we flew to Mexico with Doug in tow, aged one and a half. Morning on a Lake Erie ferry, night in Mexico City.

Our house in Taxco was the home of Americans named King who were away in Paris. We were welcomed by Feliza, the Indian housekeeper and cook, and her niece Eugenia. The front that the property presented to the steep little cobblestone Calle Guadalupe was the usual noncommittal blank wall with a locked door, lest one surmise the glories inside. They comprised a rambling house and a lawn studded with palms, yucca, jacaranda, grapefruit trees, banana trees, avocado trees, and coffee plants. The fifteen-foot wall against intruders was hidden from within by a tangle of bright bougainvillea, but was surmounted by an artist's studio.

Lunch was served on a patio adjoining the garden, dinner in a dining room adjoining the big beamed living room, and breakfast on a terrace adjoining the declivity. From there we looked down over the red-tiled roofs and cobblestone streets and out to mountains. In the middle ground steeply below us was that loveliest of all Mexican plazas, so vividly remembered from other years for its Indian laurels and its glorious church. Looking up the slope behind us, we saw our narrow Calle de Guadalupe continuing its steep course between houses to the Guadalupe church in its precarious little courtyard. Footways and small houses straggled on upward and gave way little by little to the meadows and tropical forests of the upper slopes.

Doug spent much of each day on Eugenia's back in her rebozo, while she washed clothes or scrubbed floors or cultivated the garden. I sat long hours on the terrace, writing, reading novels, or daubing painstakingly at my primitive watercolor of the inspiring scene below.

I worked on a sequel to *Methods of Logic,* to be called *Higher Logic* and deal with the theory of proof. My deepened insight into Gödel's proof of the completeness of the logic of quantification and related matters owed a good deal to Dreben, and as I reflected on this debt, I was moved to drop the project and leave him a clear field. His first little paper on the subject appeared that summer. The admirable work of his that flowered twenty-five years later in collaboration with Warren Goldfarb concerns an aspect of proof theory with which, after all, my *Higher Logic* would have had little to do, but what mine would have covered has been more than adequately covered in books by others. One residue of my project was "Interpretations of sets of conditions" and another was the completeness proof in later editions of *Methods of Logic.*

We walked in the mountains and to neighboring Indian villages, and we consorted with a colorful international colony: a former wife of Sherwood Anderson, an exiled Polish ex-ambassador, a Hungarian baroness, the retired philosopher B. A. G. Fuller, and three artists. One of these, Charles Okerbloom of Columbus, Ohio, did a big Taxco scene, slightly cubistic, which I bought for a hundred dollars and continue to like.

Feliza would bring me a liter of *pulque* from the market on Sundays. It is the fermented juice of the *maguey,* or century plant, and its consumption antedated the Conquest. Broad plantations of giant maguey are given over to it. The heart of the plant, like an artichoke heart on a large scale, is cut open, and a dark fluid collects in it and is drawn off. It quickly turns chalky white when a culture is added, in the form of a bit of pulque from the day before. The stuff is best when fresh. This is why Feliza bought it for me only on Sundays; Indians brought fresh pulque over the mountains Saturday nights.

The alcoholic content is that of a fairly hearty beer. Pulque is drunk mostly by Indians, and not in ordinary bars or restaurants, but in *pulquerías.* A sign at the door excluded women, policemen, and (redundantly) men in uniform. A woman could bring a jug to a window at the sidewalk for pulque to take home. Inside there were drunken, dirty, barefoot Indians, eager to buy one a friendly glass. A big tumbler of pulque cost pennies. A gutter along the base of the bar served opportunely as a urinal.

Don Davidson and I first tried pulque in a pulquería in Cuernavaca in 1941. He sipped a little of his and I downed mine, but neither of us liked it. Mine came up later, explosively, without nausea.

But I liked the idea. Pre-Columbian. Indians remote from maguey made a somewhat similar drink from maize. I encountered and drank it in Chihuahua in 1941 under the name of *tesgüino;* in Peru it is *chicha.* It was in Guadalajara in 1947 that I encountered a pushcart *pulquero* who tempered his brew with chili powder and orange, thus cultivating my taste. In Taxco on Sundays in 1952, I was liking it without condiments. Marge's father, who flew out from Panama to visit us at Taxco, described its taste as somewhere between clam juice and sauerkraut juice.

Toward the end of our two months in Taxco, I fell desperately sick. A local doctor diagnosed it as typhoid, despite past inoculations, and plied the chloromycetin. It knocked out the fever, but then it knocks out various fevers. North American doctors have since claimed, on the basis of tests, that I did not have typhoid. Anyway, I was tottering when we left. We went the seventy miles to Mexico City by taxi, and when we got to the hotel where we were to stop overnight I could not walk up a flight of stairs; we went to another hotel. On this and other occasions in Mexico I have been the only one laid low, and we have wondered why. Maybe it was my handling of the money, or maybe it was pulque. *Tequila* is a wholesome post-Conquest distillate from pulque, but pulque is mild enough to harbor germs, which no doubt abound in the making.

Classes, department chairmanship, Society of Fellows, Syndics, and a bushel of mail awaited me in the fall. In November there was another session at the American Academy in Philipp Frank's series, and it called forth my little paper

"On mental entities." I was cheered by high praise of it from the astronomer Harlow Shapley, who had copies made for his students.

Back in 1944 a paradox had made its way from Berkeley to Washington and was exercising the mathematicians in the cryptanalysis room below my office. It was the one about the man who was condemned to be hanged on an unspecified one of the next seven days. I found it to be a soluble paradox rather than an antinomy. I wrote up my solution and circulated it among my friends, to their apparent satisfaction. In the fall of 1952 I was surprised to find that the paradox was going strong, sometimes in the form I had known and sometimes as a paradox about a surprise examination, and that it had called forth a flurry of papers in *Mind* of varying degrees of absurdity. I published my solution in *Mind*. It is clear to me that I solved the puzzle, but it is still perhaps not clear to all concerned.

Barkley Rosser, president of the Association for Symbolic Logic, urged me to succeed him in January 1953. I had declined twice in earlier years, and this time I declined with what I thought an ironclad excuse: I would be in Oxford for a year. Rosser took it up with the Council and reported back that they found this no obstacle, since the Association was meant to be international. I had ventured all on that single excuse, so I reluctantly began a three-year term.

Marge and I went to New York for the annual philosophy convention in the last days of December 1952. We went with Henry Aiken and his current wife Lillian in their old Packard, making a lark of it. It was a vigorous congress, in which I introduced as many of our incipient Ph.D.s as possible to as many potential employers. Recreation was vigorous too, what with dancing at El Chico, listening to Phil Napoleon's jazz band somewhere else, and partying at some friend's flat in Greenwich Village. Our return to Boston was beset by a storm. Henry's vision was impaired by a cold with streaming eyes, so I drove the Packard over icy roads through snow and sleet to Boston. We had no chains and no snow tires. We made it, passing many roadside wrecks. I then lapsed into a bout of bronchitis.

Gonzalo Zubieta was at Harvard, and so was a graduate student in philosophy from Costa Rica named Roger Chacón. Marge and I arranged a party for them and two Spanish-speaking couples from outlying towns. I brought Zubieta and Chacón early in my car, and then a blizzard struck. Two guests were snowed out. Zubieta and Chacón stayed overnight and helped me shovel out of the three-foot accumulation the next morning. It was a novel experience for a Tabasqueño and a Costarricense.

I accepted Gilbert Ryle's invitation to review Strawson's *Introduction to Logical Theory*, because I foresaw my review as a manifesto with which to herald my arrival at Oxford. I was arriving to beard the British lion of ordinary-language philosophy in his den, and Peter Strawson, if anyone, was that lion. Gilbert caught the spirit and published the review as the lead article in the October 1953 issue of *Mind*, simultaneously with my accession to the Eastman chair.

Installation at Oxford   41

We rented our house to Charles Stevenson, who would be visiting at Harvard. I sent the wardrobe trunk to shipboard along with a quantity of books and papers and a hundred and fifty pounds of canned food to allay the lingering wartime rationing. We sailed for Southampton on the *Queen Elizabeth* on July 1, 1953.

The Eastman chair, founded with Kodak money in 1930, is an annual visiting professorship for an American in any subject. A house has been built for the Eastman Professor, but in my day there was a flat. My predecessor, the physiologist George Corner, would not be vacating it until mid-August, so we settled temporarily in a little residential hotel called Linton Lodge, in a dull Victorian northern quarter of

Oxford. It had a garden with gravel walks, croquet, and tennis. The maidservants were middle-aged and the permanent residents were old.

One of the former asked one of the latter, "How was your tea?"

"I've *had* my tea," was the answer.

"I said, '*How* was your tea?'"

"Well, it didn't *taste* like tea, you know. It had all sorts of bits and scrapings in it. It makes me ill, you know."

An Englishman is thankful, be it for ever so little. A clerk or waiter thanks for a request, thanks again when he hands over the goods, again of course when he takes the money, and again when he returns the change. I heard the Oxford operator ask for Trafalgar double eight double eao; and what did the London operator have to say to that? "Thank you very much." I heard someone in the Broad ask a passer-by if it was the Broad. "Yes." "Thank you *very much*." The double thank is not infrequent: "Thank you very much, thank you." An American "You're welcome" could trigger another thank and set off a vicious regress.

Yet if you corrected someone who undercharged you, his thanks were casual; honesty was seen, in those days anyway, as a matter of course. It was a country where you told the bus conductor your fare. And, to complete the inversion, you added "Please."

Doug, aged two and a half, came down with a raging fever at Linton Lodge. It induced convulsions. Terrified, I rushed down the empty stairway in the dead of night yelling to rouse someone to call a doctor. Presently I found myself in the bright and populous private bar of the hotel, where lodgers are exempt from closing hours. There was a befuddled old doctor and a clear-headed younger one. We got Doug to the hospital, and he came through all right.

We were not fond of Linton Lodge, through no fault of the management. A temporary abode was found for us comprising two floors of a little seventeenth-century house at 14 Merton Street, in the cobblestone heart of old Oxford. The quarters were once those of Siegfried Sassoon. We hired a nanny to take care of Doug, and we bought a tiny old Austin in which to tour the countryside. Ranging from Warwick and Stratford to Stonehenge, Salisbury, and Winchester, we prized the Cotswold villages in their mellow blond limestone and the Berkshire villages with their thatched stone houses and Norman churches. While Marge and I admired the delicately fluted columns and graceful ribbed vaulting of Salisbury Cathedral, Doug marveled at the ugly little latter-day iron heaters in the side aisles.

There is a hamlet called Noke on the edge of Otmoor, northeast of Oxford. Its inhabitants in earlier times had a reputation for surliness, according to the Penguin Guide, as borne out by an old jingle:

I went to Noke and nobody spoke.
I went to Beckly and they answered directly.

We drove with Doug to Noke and stopped to admire a hog wallowing at the edge of a farmyard close to the road. Unfamiliar with hogs, Doug was fascinated. A woman came out of the house and established herself beside the hog, silently glaring. Anyone making away with her hog was evidently going to have to deal with her first. Tradition had endured.

Peter Viereck, the poet and historian, came to Oxford for a meeting. I had known him from Eliot House. I joined his group for a jolly evening at Magdalen College. Among them was Naipaul, a young East Indian from Trinidad, who sang some calypsos. He is now a celebrated writer.

In August I went to the world philosophical congress at Brussels. Walking in London's Oxford Street between trains, I overtook the Duke of Windsor, to all appearances, and a lady on his arm. A second look disclosed Akron's Bob and Helen Thackaberry. Bob strikingly resembled His Highness and sometime Majesty.

On the boat train to Harwich there was a bevy of American college girls one of whom asked, with cigarette poised, "Has anybody got a lighter working?" American vignette.

The young King Baudouin attended the opening session of the congress. Over the succeeding days I was frequently with Freddie Ayer and his former tutor Gilbert Ryle, tall and lean, of military mien. There were parties at the U.S. emb.ssy, at the handsome Gothic city hall, the Perelmans', the Barzuns', and the Devauxs'. Philippe Devaux took several of us to see Waterloo; the others were Tarski, Karl Popper, and Leroy, a French Berkeley scholar. The five of us were natives of five countries.

Robert Feys, canon and logician, chaired a panel on modal logic featuring my "Three grades of modal involvement." Bernays and Tarski participated vigorously in sessions on other logical topics. Bernays would go on at length in three languages. Speaking in French, he would be deflected by a loan word such as *Entscheidungsverfahren*, and continue thereafter in German until something switched him to English. Tarski lashed out unmercifully against Ferdinand Gonseth, whose generalities Tarski found empty of content. Gonseth was a blind philosopher of science at Zurich and something of an empire-builder, one felt. He was Bernays's superior at Zurich, and it was evidently at Gonseth's behest that Bernays intervened the next day with a prepared speech in Gonseth's defense. There were other currents against Gonseth. At a meeting of the Institut International de Philosophie, in connection with the Congress, the Dutch philosopher Evert Beth denounced Gonseth for his factional machinations and did what he could to counter them with factional machinations of his own.

After the congress, many proceeded to a logic meeting in Holland. Several of us went with Jean-Louis Destouches and his wife, Paulette Février, in their curious car. The steering wheel was not quite at the left, so that a passenger could sit on either side of the driver. At the Dutch border there was a bureaucratic impasse over Paulette's papers. I, unaccountably, was the one to come forward with vigorous representations and see her through. I had not pictured myself as the forceful type, nor the French as so retiring even on so nearly their native heath.

From Amsterdam we drove east over treeless lowlands to the Hoogland, or highland. It was a modest rise, but wooded, evidently because it was above sea level. Arend Heyting lived there and commuted to Amsterdam, a long way. We continued east to Amersfoort, the scene of the meeting. Tarski and I led two days of discussion. My theme was "Nominalism and platonism in modern logic."

I walked in Ghent, Bruges, Amsterdam, and Delft. Bruges was best, for the magic of its canals flanked with medieval buildings. It was prettier than Venice, what there was of it, but less exciting.

Back then to Oxford. Heads of colleges there—the master of Balliol, the president of Magdalen, the dean of Christ Church, the provost of Worcester, the warden of Merton, the principal of Jesus, the rector of Exeter, and the rest—were commonly accorded handsome lodgings. The house at 8 Merton Street, however, built about 1908 for Bowman the warden of Merton at his behest, was outsize even in its category. The warden had rattled about in it in starkest celibacy, with his retinue of servants, and never so much as entertained at tea. A fellow of Merton did come unbidden at teatime to pay his respects—on a bet, it is said—and stayed to observe the warden in the undivided enjoyment of his refreshment. The next warden, Muir the Hegelian, was a family man, but even so he found the spaciousness excessive and decreed a less stately pleasure dome at the far end of Merton gardens in Rose Lane. The house at 8 Merton Street was thereupon turned to other purposes, among which were the Chinese library and the Eastman flat.

A roofed flight of stone steps that has been likened to a giant coal chute slanted from the street up to the grand entrance. Here one entered the hallway of the Chinese library, above whose lofty ceilings was the Eastman flat. Our living room, dining room, study, bedroom, and kitchen all were big. There were further bedrooms, baths, and a colonnaded hall from which we looked through vast windows down the noble stairway to the Chinese library. My desk chair backed into an oriel window whose leaded panes commanded a view up and down the cobbled street and past the great square fourteenth-century tower of Merton chapel, so gracefully proportioned, to Christopher Wren's Tom Tower in Christ Church. There was a distinctive mellowness to the Merton chimes; hearing them twenty years later carried me vividly back in memory to my oriel window. But my chair migrated by degrees to the fireplace as the winter of 1953-1954 wore on. We depended for heat on coal fires in the fireplaces.

We looked across Merton Street to the wall of Merton College and onto the gardens and thirteenth-century buildings that the wall enclosed. From our back windows we looked across our bit of play yard and into University College. From our side windows we looked steeply down into a narrow old passage called, of all things, Logic Lane—a scene that inspired what I may describe with faint praise as my most successful watercolor. It is appalling to think of the hairs that have been split, the logic that has been chopped and mangled, the heresies that have been hatched and hunted in that lane and the adjacent acres.

A convenient approach to our flat was through a service entrance in Logic Lane, and it was there that the house numeral "8" hung; the front entrance bore "8A." Accordingly I tried using "8 Logic Lane" instead of "8 Merton Street" as postal address, and it worked. My business as president of the Association for Symbolic Logic was accordingly conducted for a year from 8 Logic Lane.

Gratifying segments of Oxford's city wall, from Norman times, are to be seen in the gardens of New College and Merton. These and the cloisters of New College and Magdalen, the medieval towers of Magdalen and Merton, the Gothic chapels, the sudden narrow passages, the mellow old pubs, did much to allay my chronic antiquity deficiency.

The gardens of Magdalen College made me see Oxford as a city inside out. You leave the traffic jam of the High by stepping through the porter's lodge; you pass through more doors and quads and a cloister, and you are in rural England. Woods, a cow pasture, a deer park, a trout stream, all are contrived with a cunning simulation of limitlessness. You are surprised when your country walk recovers its starting point. You have forgotten that factory workers live in mile on mile of streets outside the Magdalen walls.

Michaelmas Term and Morocco 42

The Eastman Professor is *ex officio* a supernumerary fellow of Balliol College. This means that he is welcome to attend college meetings and discuss the business but has no vote. I attended one meeting out of curiosity and was happy to be spared the obligation. I took frequent lunches in the common room and occasional dinners at high table. Now and then Marcus Dick and I would fetch pints of beer from the buttery and sit in the fellows' garden. Marcus had done outstanding work in my logic course as a Commonwealth Fellow at Harvard two years before.

Invitations abounded. Over the year I dined in thirteen Oxford colleges. On these and other occasions I met many public figures—Clement Atlee, Lord Beveridge, Lord Cherwell, Lord Elton, Sir Oliver Franks, C. S. Lewis, Lord Simon, C. P. Snow.

I was given an Oxford master's degree, without diploma or ceremony, so that I might wear an Oxford gown at lectures and at high table in college halls. I inherited a gown that had been bought by an earlier Eastman Professor and handed down.

I gave a lecture course in the Clarendon Physics Laboratory in South Parks Road during each of the three short terms. In the first or Michaelmas term I lectured on the philosophy of language. I was struggling to find the right structure for my work in progress, what was to become *Word and Object* in six years. My course at Harvard the term before had been recorded on tape and transcribed by a graduate student, Alice Koller, to a length rivaling this autobiography, but I set that all aside, lest my quest for the right structure be obstructed by excessive detail. Better to let the transcript lie for a year or two and then mine it for supplementary substance when the structure was in hand. I even dreaded broaching it, what with my spoken hems and haws, my false starts and infelicities. When at last I did, years later, I found a smooth and finished text, book length. Alice had done a masterly job. Still, I was glad I had kept it under wraps until achieving a better structure.

Three eager auditors of my lectures in Michaelmas term were a Prize Fellow of All Souls, a Scholar from New Zealand, and a Privatdozent on leave from Innsbruck: Michael Dummett, Jonathan Bennett, and Wolfgang Stegmüller. The three would compare notes, prepare questions, and then meet with me for discussion. The three have since become eminent philosophers at Oxford, Syracuse, and Munich.

While at Oxford I received some thirty invitations to lecture or meet discussion groups in outlying places, but I evidently did an unusually good job of declining. In the Michaelmas term I gave only one outside lecture. It was at Bristol, though Shepherdson was away. The reigning mathematician drove me out to admire the dramatic gorge of one of Britain's four Avons.

I declined to represent Harvard at the Leeds jubilee, for I would have had to rent tails because of royalty. Little arrangements require such effort in England, what with queuing and coming back "in a fortnight's time," and "Sorry, sir, but I don't quite see how we can possibly . . . ," and all that, that you get to nipping the buds. But in the end I did rent tails for the Commem Ball at Balliol.

Once, wanting to get two books bound, it occurred to me that I might beat the system—if "system" is the word I want—by taking them to the binder on the eve of departing for three weeks abroad. Thus for once I could take the dread word "fortnight" in my stride. But did I hear it? No; six months!

In preceding years I had had some discouraging exchanges on logical matters with Peter Geach. He was a reader at Birmingham but lived in Oxford, where his wife, Elizabeth Anscombe, was a fellow of Somerville College. I foresaw tiresome times with him but learned otherwise, walking back with him one evening from a meeting in Magdalen College of the Philosophical Society. He had perceptive new things to say about Curry's Paradox, something related to the ancient Paradox of the Liar. We became firm friends.

Peter Geach, Ted Palmer, and Alonzo Church have something basic in common, something glandular. They are big-boned men, deliberate in speech and movement, keen on detail, strong on tradition, and drawn to history and to logic. Peter, like Ted, has a taste for the quaint and curious. He is interested in oddities of language and origins of words, and is vastly erudite.

He and Elizabeth and their brood lived in a lively house in St. John's Road off Wellington Square. One occasion there was memorable, in those days of lingering shortages, for a succulent side of venison baked caked in clay. Our friendship has flourished down the decades, enlivened by visits as occasion offers. My file of Peter's letters, approaching two hundred, is a treasury of wit, logical insights, animadversions, odd observations, and verbal virtuosity.

Peter Geach and Max Black had brought out a volume of Frege's papers the year before, in English translation, with comments. Frege's proposal of 1903 for avoiding Russell's paradox was there represented as a significant anticipation of later proposals, mine in particular. The claim was unwarranted, and Heinrich Scholz wrote me from Münster in June 1953 urging me to assess the situation. Besides sorting out the tenuous relationships, which was easy, I succeeded in proving Frege's plan inconsistent. When I showed this to Peter in October, he told me that he had meanwhile found a 1949 report by Sobociński that Leśniewski had likewise proved Frege's scheme inconsistent. Leśniewski had thus anticipated me in this just as Łukasiewicz had aniticipated me in my maiden article of twenty-two years before. But whereas my piece on that occasion had lacked something of

Łukasiewicz's, my present result was a bit stronger than Leśniewski's. It appeared as "On Frege's way out."

Paul Arthur Schilpp of the Library of Living Philosophers conscripted me that fall for an essay in his volume on Carnap. I bent to the task and met his spring deadline with "Carnap and logical truth," not guessing that the volume might languish for another nine years. The essay was a timely contribution to the controversy that "Two dogmas of empiricism" had precipitated, and I was annoyed to see its timeliness sapped while it stayed under wraps. In 1956 Sidney Hook wanted something from me for his *American Philosophers at Work*, and with Schilpp's grudging consent I gave him a Carnap-free half of the essay under the title "Logical truth." In 1957 Nicola Abbagnano wanted to translate something of mine for his *Rivista di Filosofia*, and with Schlilpp's permission I gave him the whole essay. In 1959, Vuysje wanted something from me for an issue of *Synthese* honoring Carnap. Switching at last the onus of permission, I offered Vuysje the essay on condition that he permit Schilpp to reprint it if occasion arose. So it appeared in *Synthese* in 1960 and in Schilpp's volume in 1963.

The Oxford forces for law and order were on the alert on Guy Fawkes' night, November 4, for the students are then apt to be up to no good. The head proctor, Woozley, issued into the High Street from the thin cleft which is Oriel Street wearing his gown, mortarboard, wing collar, and flowing white tie. With and behind him were three bullers in black suits and bowlers. They turned west in the High. Ahead was a knot of eight students making for Carfax and the Cornmarket, where the thousands were. A word and a nod from Woozley, and two bullers peeled off on the run, holding their hats on. They gathered in and retracted the group of students, while Woozley and the third buller overtook them. An exchange of civilities and perhaps of credentials ensued.

Early one Sunday I was about to enter the High from the thin cleft which is Magpie Lane. An academic procession of two was entering the High from the other side. There was Warden Smith of New College, who was vice chancellor for

1953. He was decked out in full regalia like Woozley, above, plus hood, and he was preceded by his mace-bearer. They crossed the High, which was deserted except for an unobserved and unobserving cyclist who sped along my edge of the road. The mace-bearer serenely mounted the curb and the silent cyclist passed behind him, cutting off the vice chancellor, who reached out and had a nice but unsuccessful try at spilling the bike. No word was spoken. Evidently no one was aware of the little drama except the vice chancellor and me and he was unaware of me.

Toward the end of Michaelmas term we acquired Tecla, a vivacious *au pair* girl from Tremezzo. She prepared *tagliarini* admirably *al dente,* and introduced *uova ai pori*—eggs with leeks. She unearthed in the Oxford market a Gorgonzola that taught us the true genius of that genre. Oily and bitterly savory even apart from the blue, it had nothing to do with Roquefort.

Tecla was bright, dependable, and good with Doug, as was his daytime nanny. It meant that Marge and I could go abroad for the generous vacation between Michaelmas and Hilary terms. We flew on December 7, 1953, to Gibraltar and met my brother Bob, Rosalie, and their boys Rob and Van. Rob has since gained fame with his guitar. Van, for William Van Orman, is now a librarian.

The little airport at the foot of the Rock puts an implausible end to the thousand-mile flight. The whole country measures two square miles, and the uninhabitable Rock takes up most of it.

We engaged a chauffeur and quasi-guide with the Anglo-Portuguese name of Charles Mascarenhas, and seven strong we devoted five days to the circuit of Andalusia. We swept through Tarifa, at the southernmost tip of Europe, and on to sea-girt Cádiz, a grid of straight and narrow medieval streets cutting from sea to sea. At Jérez we visited Pedro Domecq's. The tireless and tiresome guide to the plant was nonplussed when we deserted him in mid-period, foregoing the samples that were said to await us at the end. Onward then to the Giralda and Alcázar at Seville, the Moorish bridge and great mosque at Córdoba, and the Alhambra at Granada. Gypsy dwellings are built into caves at Granada, and we went into one to watch the dancing. Bob and his family continued with Charles to France. Marge and I went by train and ship to Ceuta, which, though in Africa, was and is part of Spain. From there a bus took us across the guarded border into Spanish Morocco, and so to Tetuán.

In Tetuán the European *colonia* and the Moorish *medina* are startlingly contiguous. You walk along an utterly European street: Foto Such-and-Such, Dura Gloss, Farmacia, Tabacos, Surtido de one thing and another, Tintorería. One shop, called the Mango, is indeed European only to the degree that you overlook it. If you pause, you see that the customers are in fezzes or burnooses and that they recline somehow around the margins of the deep interior, perhaps sipping sweet tea from glasses stuffed with green sprigs of mint. Three doors farther along, if you turn in through the arched doorway, you plunge straightaway into a maze of teeming oriental passageways. You are launched on miles and hours of incredulous wandering, as discontinuous with its antecedents as Alice's beyond the looking glass. Cobblestone passages lead through series of arches or disappear into the dark, covered by upper stories. One passage was so narrow that it was best managed sideways. Some were so low that I had to stoop. Some ascend or descend a cascade of stone steps. The outdoor-indoor dichotomy becomes vague; thus there was a tiny square, lined with shops and a continuous balcony, that clearly was once the patio of a modest house. A hall into it and a hall out had been transformed into covered streets by the simple expedient of taking off the doors.

Hooded figures shimmer into the murk of a vaulted aperture and are gone, we hope, especially the black prognathous one with the scimitar. Fezzes, tarbooshes, turbans, burnooses, veils, red pantaloons, red slippers, squatting smiths, tinkers, stinkers, vendors, menders, mendicants, loungers, scroungers of baksheesh, smokers of hashish in long slim pipes—all vintage Sheherazade.

We looked in on Tangier and we went on to Lisbon for Christmas. I sensed the lifting of a linguistic taboo. In my many months in Spanish-speaking countries over the preceding ten years, I had been having effortfully to keep my Spanish clear of Portuguese.

In the heart of Lisbon there are three hills, each crowned by an old quarter: the Bairro Alto, the Mouraria, and the Alfama (= Spanish *Alhambra*). For steep little streets and old buildings the Alfama was the most rewarding, but Tetuán was a hard act to follow. We listened to *fados*, sad songs in a Moorish mode.

Hilary and Trinity Terms   43

· 1954

Richard the Lion-Hearted and our daughter Margaret were born in Walton Street, Oxford. Richard was born in Beaumont Palace, where Walton Street passes now. Margaret was born in the Radcliffe Infirmary, *ibid.*, compliments of National Health. She was born so early in February, 1954, that the cablegrams reached her grandparents in January; for there is a five-hour difference in clocks. Her birthday is February 1 in Europe and January 31 in America.

In that season I attended a weekly seminar in University College that was run jointly by Peter Strawson and his former tutor Paul Grice. There was a little gas fire at one end of the large room, and we sat in our overcoats. Peter and Paul alternated from week to week in the roles of speaker and commentator. The speaker would read his paper and then the commentator would read his prepared comments. "Toward the foot of page 9, I believe you said . . ." Considered judgment was of the essence; spontaneity was not. When in its final phase the meeting was opened to public discussion, Peter and Paul were not outgoing. "I'm not sure what to make of that question." "It depends, I should have thought, on what one means by . . ." "This is a point that I shall think further about before the next meeting."

Peter was fastidious in dress, manner, speech, and style of writing. He and Ann soon became two of our closest Oxford friends. Paul was shabby, though far from the hippy figure that he cuts in California today. His white hair was sparse and stringy, he was missing some teeth, and his clothes interested him little. He was vice-president of St John's College, and when I came as guest to a great annual feast there I was bewildered to encounter him impeccably decked out in white tie and tails, strictly fashion-plate.

Paul was a cricket fan. He sat with me at a playing field through a considerable part of a sultry afternoon watching a sedate match. He explained how it was done and what was happening. The excitement was low-keyed and did not prove contagious.

My lectures at Oxford during the second or Hilary term were on axiomatic set theory. I compared various systems and was pleased by the neatness of interconnections. I thought of making a short book of this forthwith, since my philosophical work in progress moved so slowly; but I subdued the impulse. *Word and Object* proved to take six more years, and the set-theory book followed three years later still, swollen beyond expectation.

In that same term I gave five lectures on ontology at University College in London, the Shearman Lectures. In them I pondered the Skolem-Löwenheim theorem, which tells us that any consistent theory admits of a reinterpretation in which the only objects assumed are natural numbers. It promised a Pythagorean ontology, recognizing natural numbers as the only reality. I cared little for the plan, and soon dropped it. Ten years later I argued in "Ontological reduction and the world of numbers" that the Skolem-Löwenheim theorem bore no such Pythagorean implications.

Freddie Ayer was the philosophy professor at London, so he sponsored my Shearman Lectures. Another friend in attendance was J. H. Woodger, biology professor at Middlesex Hospital. He championed mathematical logic and wrote a book organizing the concepts and principles of biology in the notation of *Principia Mathematica*. I had known him when he came to Yale on an abortive project of Clark L. Hull's in psychology. It had occurred to Hull to bring the power and precision of mathematical logic to bear on psychology, and he recruited Woodger as collaborator. By clarifying relationships, logic could contribute to the framing of hypotheses and the designing of experiments; such was Woodger's hope. On arriving, he was disillusioned to find that Hull was developing his theory unaided by logic and wanted Woodger merely to put it over into logical notation afterward for an appendix. Woodger refused and Hull found others for the exercise.

Woodger was a little man, and when I renewed our acquaintance at my Shearman Lectures he had white hair and a long white beard. His friends called him Socrates. He was selfless in his admiration of logic, Tarski, and Popper. He translated Tarski's papers and edited the volume of them. It was a service to the profession, and a big job—the more so as he patiently reworked the translations in response to Tarski's no-doubt reasonable objections. He also translated Popper's *Logik der Forschung*, a thankless job indeed; Popper found it hopeless and would have none of it. I can sympathize with all concerned.

Woodger and his wife Eden entertained Marge and me at their old stone country house in Epsom. He drove us to the neighboring village of Ockham by way of pious pilgrimage.

John Austin conducted a discussion group at Oxford on Saturday mornings. He was a lean man, dry and austere in mien and manner. His focus was usage, shades of meaning, distinctions. Instances were chosen with a view to philosophical illumination, but he was in no hurry to draw the philosophical consequences. The group consisted of dons, and it was said that he devised complex eligibility requirements in such a way as to exclude, in general terms, some specific individuals.

In March I lectured and conducted three discussion sessions at Manchester. The philosophy professor there was

Dorothy Emmet, a disciple of Whitehead. I was startled to hear the taxi driver call her "love." She put me up at the Brantford Private Hotel, where Michael Polanyi and his wife lived. They gave a dinner party. After my meeting the next afternoon, Dorothy Emmet and I stood long in the cold hoping for a bus to the bleak periphery where she lived. Ultimately she capitulated and hailed a taxi. Her little house was frigid. She made a fire in the grate. Guests at length arrived, notably Alan Turing, who had done great things in proof theory and the theory of computers. Like Dorothy Emmet, he lived alone in the bleak suburb. He committed suicide a few weeks later.

My lectures in Trinity term were on topics in logic. Also I wrote on "Logic, symbolic" for the *Encyclopedia Americana*. Their rate of three cents a word was not an inducement even in those days, but I wanted to see how much logic I could render generally intelligible in 5750 words. When I had finished a presentable draft I checked my time, out of curiosity, and found that the pay was reasonable; but then I thought of a new angle, and reworked the article. The pay dwindled to absurdity but the satisfaction abounded. My efforts yielded novel algorithms and proof procedures.

An amenity of Oxford was good theater within strolling distance. The D'Oyly Carte company came to town, and during the intermission in *Pirates*, Oscar Wood commiserated and admired us for being dutiful. He was a philosophy don at Magdalen and had done well in my course when he was a Commonwealth Fellow at Harvard. "How about you?" I asked. "Are you being dutiful?" "N-no," he replied. "I *like* it." "You over-estimate your insularity," I said.

In May I lectured at Aberystwyth, Leicester, London again, and Cambridge. Marge drove with me to Aberystwyth and we stayed at the Aarons'. Richard Aaron was the philosophy professor there, and staunchly Welsh. He had published philosophy in Welsh. Welsh was the language of their home when there were no foreigners to consider. Their children learned English only in school. Their youngest learned it in

America at the age of five, when Aaron was a visiting professor at Yale.

We meant to drive back to Oxford by way of grim Snowdon, but the rain discouraged us and we turned east. It let up when we got to Stokesay Castle, over the border in Shropshire. It is a fortified and moated manor house of the twelfth and thirteenth centuries, and naggingly picturesque in its overhangs and half-timberings and rakish decrepitude.

Marge drove with me also to Cambridge, where I addressed the Moral Sciences Club. We stayed with the Braithwaites two nights and came away exhausted, for Richard and Margaret (Masterson) were intense and indefatigable. Margaret was beside herself with communication theory and Chinese characters. One agendum that got crowded off the list was a meeting with C. D. Broad; I never met him. What was most rewarding was a lively conversation with Herman Bondi on the expanding universe and related matters. He invited me back in June for the King's College gaudy, but when the time came, to my great disappointment, I was immobilized by a bad cold.

Parties at Oxford succeeded one another at a dizzy rate, some in hall or common room for men, others in homes or, indeed, in colleges for men and wives. There were garden parties with shady hats, strawberries, and champagne. The philosophers gave us a farewell dinner at Magdalen and we gave them a party at Balliol. I had to buy a second dress shirt because of the rapid turnover. At the Balliol ball we frolicked until four, I in my rented tails.

H. H. Price, the Wykeham Professor of Logic though no logician, was interested in flying things: spooks, gliders, birds. He and his sister drove us up along the Cherwell one evening to a secluded pub to have supper and hear the nightingales in the adjacent hedges. Another time Marge and I drove to Cheltenham for an overnight visit with Jacob Bronowski and his wife in their imaginative modern house. And then one day we struck out on a longer drive, taking Doug along. We drove to Exeter and stayed the night in the Clarence, inside the cathedral close. Bound for Land's End the next day, we stopped to gaze seaward at castled St. Michael's Mount, hoary but humble counterpart of its glorious namesake across the English Channel. Presently a flat-bottomed vessel came ashore and amazed us by continuing across the beach, our first experience of an amphibious craft. The drive back to Oxford was marked by the Ancient Mariner's home port, the cathedral at Wells in its swan-bedecked waters, the intact Anglo-Saxon church at Bradford-on-Avon, a crumbling medieval inn called the George, and, in a downpour, Glastonbury. The trip was meant to test Doug for a jaunt to Scotland. He bore up admirably, even when the car broke down one dark night; but in the end we decided against Scotland because of persistent rain.

The close of the academic year was emphatically marked by the pomp and color of encaenia, Oxford's commencement, in the Sheldonian theater. The university orator and the vice chancellor, Sir Maurice Bowra, did their parts in the reconstructed Latin phonetics of [weːni] [wiːdi] [wiːki], and the chancellor, Lord Halifax, did his in the hallowed [viːnaɪ] [vaɪːdaɪ] [vaɪːsaɪ]. Afterward there was the vice chancellor's party in the garden of Wadham College.

Karl Compton, chancellor of Washington University, and his wife called on us on June 27. He wanted me to participate in a meeting that he would run the next day in Cambridge. Marge and I drove to Cambridge and were put up in Nuneham Grange. Lowry, president of Wooster College in Ohio, participated in the meeting, as did a grandson of Darwin and perhaps others. I have forgotten what it was about.

Continental Interludes   44

I had known Heinrich Scholz by correspondence since Nazi times, when he had worked courageously within Germany to save Poles. He had written to me on postcards, these being less closely scrutinized. In July 1954, I put our quasi-acquaintance to the service of young Michael Dummett. Michael had become interested in Frege, partly perhaps through my lectures, and wanted access to the Frege archives, which Scholz jealously guarded at Münster. I wrote to Scholz in Michael's behalf, and then Marge and I accompanied Michael to Münster. Seeds were sown for his big book on Frege of twenty years later.

While we were brooding on a lofty Romanesque church in Münster that had been bombed to great vertical splinters, a worker in a worker's cap and an aura of alcohol wheeled his bicycle over to us and said in German, "You have to be a philosopher." I responded unproductively. "You are a foreigner, aren't you?" he pursued. "Yes." "Well, then, you can't understand what it's like." "Have you seen London and Rotterdam?" I countered. "Yes," he said, "from the air." "Well, foreigners saw that too." "You are a journalist, aren't you?" he asked. "No." "What then?" "A philosopher." This was the perfect point for *auf Wiedersehen*.

After a day or two with Michael, Scholz, Hans Hermes, and young Gisbert Hasenjäger in Münster, Marge and I went to Bonn. The Conants had invited us to call on them; he was then High Commissioner for the United States in occupied Germany. We sat with them at tea on their broad lawn at Bad Godesburg and looked out on the gentle Siebengebirge across the Rhine.

We flew to Berlin, partly because Marge, keen on Egyptian antiquities, wanted to see the head of Nefertite. We stayed in a hotel called Alemannia, rebuilt behind a ruinous façade in the desolation east of the abandoned Anhalter Bahnhof. It was close to the as yet unwalled boundary of East Berlin, and two short blocks from what is now the notorious Checkpoint Charlie. Today the area is razed. We crossed a little angle of East Berlin and then, chary of further penetration of enemy territory on our own, we walked a mile and a half in the cold July rain to the Kurfürstendamm, West Berlin's rebuilt central thoroughfare, and repaired to a huge, rough tavern for a healing hot grog. There was an air of the old American frontier in West Berlin. Much as our frontiersmen hacked a home out of the wilderness, the Berliners were building a home out of the rubble. Our frontiersmen had hostile Indians close at hand to reckon with, and the Berliners had the Russians.

An industry flourished of grinding rubble to make sand to make cement, for the Russians obstructed importation of sand and gravel to West Berlin. Everywhere there was ruin and anywhere you might see men sorting rubble. The whole bricks were for further use, and the broken ones were for the sand mill.

Next morning we walked a few hundred yards northwest from our hotel onto an empty tract backed by towering, precarious ruins. Men were high in the ruins, dismantling them. Herr Nikolai, the boss of the demolition, told us that the empty area had been the garden of the Hohenzollern Palace. Its level had been raised six feet by grading the rubble of surrounding buildings, smashed by ground artillery. Some two thousand Russians had lain dead on that garden. The last opponents of the Russians had been Latvians, who could not surrender to the Russians on pain of being shot as renegades. The wreckage of Hitler's last command bunker was there, a concrete slab a hundred feet long and six feet thick sagging over a rubble-chocked abyss.

The ruin that was being dismantled had been the Gestapo headquarters. Nikolai showed us cells in the cellar big enough only for one man to stand in, and shaped to prevent leaning. Other cells were porcelain, so that blood could be washed away. There were cells, admitting some sixty men each, that were completely dark when closed. He led me up to a fragmentary upper story of the ruin and into what he said had been Himmler's office. There were patches of brocade on what remained of the walls. A small street along the back of the building had become the boundary with East Berlin, and Nikolai pointed out a building just beyond as the Berlin headquarters of the Soviet secret police. We were leaning over what had been a windowsill, viewing the scene; but on Nikolai's advice we did not linger. The Russians, he said, had been known to shoot across; they had been touchy since the bloody uprising of thirteen months ago.

We had a tour of East Berlin in a jeep of the U. S. Army. Streets were almost deserted, shops dingy, display windows virtually empty, in startling contrast to the bright and merry bustle of the Kurfürstendamm. We returned to West Berlin through the Brandenburg Gate and the Tiergarten, which was in West Berlin except for an enclave that contained a Soviet war monument and was Soviet ground. A soldier from our jeep took a picture of the monument and a Soviet soldier confiscated his camera.

Nefertite was not in Berlin. She was said to be temporarily in Frankfurt. In Frankfurt we were told that she was in neighboring Wiesbaden, and there she was. We then cruised down the castled Rhine to Cologne, drinking pleasant white wine from ugly chalices.

Next we went to Bavaria. Between trains in Würzburg we hurried across town for a quick look at the castle. We meant to take a taxi back, but there were none. We ran all the way and barely caught the train, hating every minute. But we were consoled by Rothenburg-ob-der-Taube, a town of medieval houses surrounded by a high wall, intact. We made the circuit on a wooden catwalk along the parapets.

An Australian woman had a message for her tour driver, and did her best: "Mein husband ist zurück des omnibus."

Thence to Füssen, near the border of the Austrian Tyrol. Mad Ludwig's Schloss Neuschwanstein, that glorious caricature of the wildest dreams of chivalry, stands close at hand. Above the castle there looms a mountain known as Tegelberg. At a restaurant below the mountain, trout swam in a basin. Marge and I made our selection and the cook broiled them to perfection. The delicacy of flavor, the faint bitterness of the gray-green, crisp, tissue-thin skin, have lingered long in fond memory.

We proceeded up the mountain. The trail made zigzags to ease the grade, and I took to short-cutting them, walking steeply from switchback to switchback after next. Marge objected; any Girl Scout knows, she said, that you should stay on a trail. One of the zigzags, a long one, passed out of my sight before doubling back. I went directly up as usual to the visible top of the next leg of it, and waited for Marge. She did not appear. I descended the trail the long way and inquired at the restaurant. Then I climbed to the top of the mountain.

On the way I overtook a young couple. The woman signaled silence. *"Gemse,"* she murmured, pointing. It was a splendid chamois on the brink, fifty yards away. But no, they had not seen Marge. In the hut at the summit the story was the same. I went down and inquired again at the restaurant. I walked back to Füssen and alerted the authorities. A search party went out.

She got to the hotel in Füssen in the night. At the switchback beyond my range of vision she had mistakenly continued ahead on a lesser path instead of switching back. It dwindled and she made for the summit without a path. I had come and gone. Two boys conducted her down the mountain the quick way, as they called it. It was rather the adventurous, precipitous way, and it terminated behind the mountain. The boys got three bicycles and saw her to Füssen. It was a black day in the annals of the Girl Scouts of America.

We spent a night at Landeck in the Tyrol, and then walked twenty-five miles southeastward up the Inn and the Kaunertal. This brought us near the foot of the Gepatsch glacier, in the high Alps bordering Italy. People in Landeck had insisted that I needed stout boots for the walk, until at last I foolishly let myself be bullied into buying heavy shoes; boots no. The shoes hurt my feet, and I ended up carrying them all the way in my knapsack and wearing my sneakers. I should have trusted my own experience as walker.

We bunked in the Gepatschhaus. There was a guitar and singing. They sang *"Ein freies deutsches Südtirol,"* an irredentist song for Austrian territory awarded to Italy in 1918. The youth hostel for the youth hostile. Next day we walked to the glacier and then back down to Landeck, still carrying the new shoes.

Our next stop was Liechtenstein. My enthusiasm of 1929 for the place had not abated when I walked with Naomi to all its *Gemeinden* in 1932, but it abated now. The prosperity that the principality had gained as a tax shelter had given it the aspect of a prosperous suburb. Something lingered too, incongruously, of the old bucolic air. I guessed the natives might feel disoriented.

Our hotel in Zurich, the Stork (Storch, Cigogne), looked out on the picturesque old center of town straddling the river Limmat. We walked up to the Eidgenossische Technische Hochschule and called on Bernays.

Five days of academic activity still awaited me in August in England. The Chicago philosopher Richard McKeon had arranged a colloquium at Cumberland Lodge in the Great Park of Windsor Castle. He proposed an experimental case study of philosophical communication. A traditional philosophical issue was to be discussed for a few days, and the process was to be observed and subsequently discussed in turn. Isaiah Berlin had the good sense to decline. Popper, who lived near enough for easy commuting, tried it for a day. Among the steadies were Freddie Ayer, the old-line philosophers Ewing and Paton from Cambridge, Popper's articulate young disciple John Watkins, and Sir Walter Moberly, who ran Cumberland Lodge.

The session opened with a reception. Sherry, a small glass; that terminated the conviviality for the five days. The nearest beer was in a remote pub. The meals were predominantly starch—potato, rice, bread, bread pudding—laced with trace elements of meatier character. The intellectual fare was comparable. The traditional philosophical issue chosen for the case study was free will versus determinism. McKeon distributed selections on the subject from classical philosophers, salvaged perhaps from the project of a *Syntopicon* that Mortimer Adler was directing. The discussion droned on for days in an undisciplined way. Arguments that had been made and answered would be made again. Critical review of what we had been up to was scarcely ventured, however, and came to nothing. I wondered why Freddie, in particular, had stayed. Perhaps we all suffered from a vitamin deficiency. As a foreigner I could not decorously make the break. Then it struck me: it was an American show, McKeon's, and I could indeed! And so I did, but it was too near the end to matter.

Marge and I went back to the Continent for a mathematics congress in Amsterdam. The Flemish logician Joseph Dopp accompanied us to the old-fashioned fishing town of Vollendam and the Isle of Marken. Traditional caps, peaked bonnets, baggy trousers, wooden shoes, old buildings, narrow passages, and windmills fulfilled every preconception.

Two Years on Home Ground 45

On September 9, 1954, as we were about to board the *Queen Elizabeth* for America, we met John and Magdalena Finley. John was a professor of Greek at Harvard and the master of Eliot House. He was succeeding me as Eastman Professor, and when I got back to Eliot House I would find the poet Archie MacLeish standing in as master.

When we were a day or two at sea, Doug came with a message: "The pursuer said to assemble at the tourist-class mustard station." I can imagine him adding "They are expecting a tycoon," but happily it was only a drill.

The Columbia Bicentennial was celebrated in October with a program of lectures at Arden House, the Harriman mansion at Tuxedo Park. The final banquet, at the Waldorf Astoria, was adorned by the Queen Mother. I penciled a surreptitious portrait of her maternal majesty. My lecture, "The scope and language of science," was a prospectus for my eventual *Word and Object*. The editor of the bicentennial volume made a plaything of my quotation marks, obliterating crucial distinctions between use and mention at some points and reversing them at others. J. O. Wisdom kindly published the original text in the *British Journal for Philosophy of*

Science, after I wrested a grudging permission from the president and trustees of Columbia University.

Gilbert Ryle visited us for a week in November, homeward bound from Adelaide. We gave a party, and Henry Aiken and Morty White were there. As was often the way, especially with Henry's help, it lasted into the small hours. Next day, nevertheless, Morty, Gilbert, Henry, and I proceeded as planned and climbed Mount Monadnock.

· 1955   In June 1955 Marge and I went to Oberlin for my twenty-fifth reunion. It was my first reunion, more accurately, and the twenty-fifth of my class, and I was getting my first honorary degree. I became acquainted with Adlai Stevenson and James Reston, fellow honorands. The reunion was a happy occasion also apart from all that, and I resolved to go more often, but in vain; my next reunion was the fiftieth.

Having Doug and Margaret, we wanted a summer home. Tidewater appealed with its ebb and flow and its *fruits de mer,* but it was too cold for pleasant swimming unless you were south of Cape Cod, which was inconveniently far away. I studied the map for lakes and found one in the town of Harvard, confusingly so called, thirty miles from Harvard Yard by road; twenty-five as the crow flies, west by north. It is called Bare Hill Pond and averages a mile long and a half mile wide. It is set among low wooded hills, despite its name, and its shores are not oppressively built up. The village, close at hand, is vintage New England, many of its sixty houses dating from the eighteenth century. We sought out the real-estate agent, Commander Turner, Ret., who showed us a plot of two wooded acres at the shore. I promptly pressed a check on him by way of deposit. I sensed that his wife wanted him to hold off. "Who, after all, are these people?" she wordlessly asked. "We have the neighbors to consider." But I prevailed; Marge and I were likewise old naval officers, after all.

Our land stretches four hundred feet uphill from the water to a little dirt road. With increased familiarity, I am struck by analogies with Ellan Vannin. The lakes are about the same size. The property in both cases is on the southeast shore, with a bay continuing southward and a little cove just to the north. In both cases there is a peninsula opposite, beyond which the lake makes, in both cases, its major southward sweep. Bare Hill Pond has the advantage, over the East Reservoir of my boyhood, of being less built up, but the disadvantage of being landlocked.

I drew plans for our summer cottage. It was to be of one story, eight by ten yards, with twenty-two windows, four outside doors, a stone fireplace, and a low-pitched, broadeaved roof inspired by Tech-Built Houses. Technicalities that arose in the drawing were instructive: which way to swing a door, and which edge to hang it on, so as not to interfere with another door or a window; how big a window could be, and how low it could be cut, and still admit of being opened by lowering it to the floor; where to drill a well; how to cluster the plumbing; how to shutter the windows in winter; how to space them to please the eye. Our architect friend Daphne Bugbee congratulated me on this last point when she saw the house a year later, and I agree with her.

The sides, in dark brown, are of vertical boards with battens over the seams. Each window is a framed pane of stock size suspended on spring pins and opened by sliding to the floor. Fly screen is nailed outside the window, and outside that a shutter, homogeneous with the outside wall, is hinged to flop open. The shutters were cut from the wall itself. We visited the house in May 1956 when the walls were still unbroken; the only access was where the fireplace was to be. We watched the carpenter cut a slit in the wall for the bottom of a window, screw hinges over it, cut slits for the other three sides of the window, and finally push the excised square out, where it flopped into place as an open shutter. The outside doors were likewise hinged pieces of the walls. Closed in winter, the house looks impervious.

Marge and I drove off in September 1955 to prowl the northern fringe of Maine and farther lands. The northernmost point of Maine could be reached only by driving along the Canadian side of the St. John and St. Francis Rivers; our side settled into unbroken forest. The town is Estcourt, Quebec. From it you could see the northwest boundary of Maine, the international boundary, cutting southwestward over the hills. You could see it because it was the boundary between Canadian fields and our forest.

I was puzzled by a sign in Estcourt pointing to a U.S. customs house. For what? Yes, the cleared ground did broach the frontier, barely. The last little street, with perhaps five little houses, was in Maine, and the last house was that of the customs officer. He and his wife spoke no French, and the natives no English; but his wife spoke loudly enough to the natives to compensate. A resident of the little street was putting some Estcourt tile pipe into his yard and had to pay duty on it. One of the five houses had a shop in it, to which cigarettes and canned goods were brought through Canada under seal from the main body of Maine. Our customs officer deplored what the Canadians across the street were getting away with, buying in this shop and not paying Canadian duty.

We rounded the Gaspé and drove home to a cellar flooded knee-deep, in the aftermath of a hurricane. It was still September 1955 when Michael Dummett visited us for a week. September also consummated my seven-year effort to get Naomi to release the abandoned Easton house and avail herself of the dwindling proceeds.

My address in December as retiring president of the Association for Symbolic Logic was "Unification of universes in set theory," and it drew me back for a while to my deferred project of a book on comparative set theory. Mostly, however, in that year and succeeding ones, I was groping toward *Word and Object*.

· 1956   Someone's chance remark in January 1956 led me to the discovery that the top salary in Arts and Sciences at Harvard had risen to seventeen thousand dollars. Mine was still fifteen, contrary to Dean Buck's promise of 1952 to keep me at the rising maximum. I confronted Buck's successor, Mc-

George Bundy. Mac checked Buck's letter, and interpreted it as a promise merely to pay me the maximum of 1954. I had been aware of the ambiguity of Buck's letter, but I knew the intent and had preferred not to fuss. I told Mac I had no choice but to try to reactivate the California offer of 1952. When I told Buck about it, he bore me out and took Mac to task. Mac restored me to the moving front. The Harvard budget forbade making up the preceding year's deficit, he said, and I mistakenly acquiesced, happy with the raise.

I received a demand for unpaid Federal income tax. A space was provided for filling in numbers from the back of my cancelled check as proof of payment. I ransacked the attic, found the check, and filled in the numbers. It did no good; the demand was renewed. I sent a photostat of the canceled check. It was ignored, and threats ensued. I took my canceled check to the tax office in Boston and waited my turn. A political employee named Conway looked at the check and said it would be taken under advisement by his superior. In a few days I was notified by telephone that the police were coming for me. I telephoned the tax office, demanded to speak to someone in authority, and reported my persecution in tones of desperation and outrage. He reassured me and called off the police. Thereafter, however, my income tax was audited every year; I was on the crook list. After a few years I took to the shelter of a reputable tax accountant, and there I remain.

In July 1956 I became Edgar Pierce Professor of Philosophy. Ralph Barton Perry had been the first one and Clarence Lewis the second. When philosophy and psychology separated, in Perry's day, a matching Edgar Pierce Professorship of Psychology was declared. I thus shared the Edgar Pierce chair or love seat with Edwin Garrigues Boring, who was later succeeded by Fred Skinner.

Andes   46

The American Philosophical Association found funds to send
me 5225 miles due south as delegate to an Inter-American
Philosophical Congress at Santiago de Chile in the summer
of 1956. Marge came too. From Jamaica we flew to Colombia
and then up the broad, brown Magdalena River and into the
Andes, ending at Bogotá. It was a big city and is said to be
three times as big now, despite its altitude of 8600 feet. It
occupied an edge of a plateau rimmed by mountains which
rose another three thousand feet. High above the city there
was a shrine called Monserrat, as such shrines often are.
From there we looked steeply down through a foreground of
trees and saw, thus leafily framed, the city of stucco houses
under red tile roofs. I find a special charm in such an abrupt
view of a city through trees or rocks from high above. It
owes its magic to the extravagant discontinuity. We enjoyed
a similar view of Quito in Ecuador a few days later, from an
adjacent little mountain called the Panecillo. Quito was
higher still than Bogotá, and its population was more colorfully Indian; costumes abounded.

In the plane from Lima to Cuzco there was an oxygen
tube at each seat, for the intervening mountains are high.
Cuzco itself stands at eleven thousand feet. Under the Incas
it had been a city of massive masonry, the huge blocks fitting
together in snug perfection. Spanish superstructures have
been toppled by earthquakes, but the Inca masonry has
held. Seen from above, Cuzco's roofs of glazed purple tiles
give the impression of a porcelain city. Such is the view from
Sacsayhuamán, a parade ground fortified with Inca walls. An
Indian boy of perhaps ten with a flat, circular, dark face sat
high on a wall of Sacsayhuamán playing a simple pipe such
as I had seen a shepherd blowing in 1932 on the plains of
Bulgaria.

When I asked someone in Cuzco about *chicha*, the traditional drink fermented from maize, I was directed to an inconspicuous passage between two buildings. It opened into a long wasteland flanked by the backs of the buildings on the surrounding streets. I came to a humble tavern bearing a crude sign with a word or two in Quechua and a figure of the sun. I went in and drank *chicha*, which was what I had found in Chihuahua in 1941 under the name of *tesgüino*.

Abruptly below Cuzco on the east there is the deep valley of the Urubamba, a headstream of the Amazon. On its far bank is the Quechua town of Pisac, backed by a steep mountainside meticulously terraced for agriculture in Inca times. The inhabitants wear bright ponchos and hats similar in structure to the academic mortar-boards, but round like halos and more colorful than either. A procession came out of the church led by three gaily caparisoned little men carrying maces; they were said to be the mayors of Pisac and adjoining villages.

The narrow-gauge railway from Cuzco to Machu Picchu crossed scrubby uplands, where llamas grazed, and then descended to the Urubamba by literal switchbacks. The train would head diagonally downward across the slope to a dead end of track; then a switch would be thrown behind the train, allowing the train to back out and downward across the slope on an opposite tack. This backward tack would end at length in another dead end, and a switch would be thrown in front of the train; and so on for several switchbacks. After reaching the river, we continued for fifty miles along its bank. A bus then made the zigzag ascent to the great ruins thousands of feet above.

In the lower portion of the ruined city the stones of the houses were fitted with the classic precision of Sacsayhuamán. In the upper levels the masonry was less meticulous. Higher still, the serried ranks of ruined houses gave way to terraces for agriculture. The region was one of steep, wild, forested mountains. The ruins are on the brow of a peak that drops off almost sheer on three sides to the river a half mile below. From the ruins a saddle extends down, over, and up to a higher peak shaped like a sugar loaf, on which we could see traces of further terraces.

After Peru, Bolivia. From Puno on Lake Titicaca we voyaged for sixteen hours to Guaqui—the loftiest navigation on earth. The vessel had been built in Glasgow, transported to a Pacific port, dismembered as far as possible, and wrestled up over the Andes. From the shore of the lake, 12,500 feet above sea level, snowy mountains rise 10,000 feet higher still. Fishermen ply the lake in reed boats, which are also to be seen drying on the bank. They become waterlogged.

From Guaqui we crossed the high plain to La Paz by train, passing the remains of a tower of the Tihuanaca culture, ancestor to that of the Incas. At an altitude of twelve thousand feet at the bottom of its canyon, La Paz is the highest capital anywhere. Wandering in it the first day, we were at some pains not to waste altitude and have to regain it. By the second day, acclimatized, we ranged blithely to the top of the town and the canyon's rim a thousand feet above. Natives up there were playing basketball.

La Paz is chilly. The round-faced Indian women in their derby hats were the chunkier for their many layers of clothing. Some men wore tan woolen headpieces that nearly encompassed the head and neck and culminated in a peak reminiscent of pointy-headed Martians. Women spun yarn, suspending a bobbin as they walked or sat in the sun. Broad baskets brimming with coca leaves contributed the pale green component to the colorful markets, where the dominant color was the orange of a million oranges from lowlands in the northeast.

The Bolivian monetary unit is the *sucre*. Sucres were twelve cents a thousand and falling. Luxurious quarters in the capital's best hotel cost us $4.70 a night, and filet mignon in a top restaurant cost twenty-four cents.

From La Paz we flew over vast empty salt flats in western Bolivia and alongside lofty Sajama. My plane in 1942 could climb no higher than a precarious eighteen thousand feet; but in 1956 we were doing better. By a wide and effortless margin we cleared the hump of the Andes and saw the rainless coast of northern Chile. In a little while Argentina rose off our port bow in the unmistakable form of Aconcagua, the highest peak in the Western Hemisphere.

On this flight we had the company of a prominent American philosopher of science who was bound for the same meeting. He spoke of *Limá*. Somehow this absurd hypercosmopolitanism struck our fancy. We are kicking it around to this day.

On reaching Santiago we stopped at a lunch counter and discovered the *loco*, possibly a small, thick abalone. We hailed it as a happy find, but we had had more than enough of it before the week was over. Hospitable Chileans kept proudly pressing *loco* on us from every side, anticipating our pleased surprise over this distinctively Chilean delicacy. On the other hand an abundant Chilean delicacy that never cloyed was *palta rellena*, which was avocado (ugh!) filled with tiny shrimp. I shudder not at the delicious fruit, but at our outrageous corruption of *aguacate*. Lawyer indeed! But what else can we say? Alligator pear, perhaps. Or, indeed, *Persea gratissima*.

There was an abrupt hill in the middle of Santiago, called Santa Lucía. It was a park, and its ruggedness had inspired fanciful follies—temples, synthetic ruins, stairways, arches, and fragmentary castles. Openings in the lush growth of trees and vines framed tasteful vignettes of the surrounding city. For the rest, Santiago was visually dull. After ten in the morning the distant mountains were occulted by the polluted air. But we were able to improve our acquaintance with Aconcagua by going to a village northeast of town.

The star of the philosophical congress was Mario Bunge, an energetic and articulate young Argentinian of broad background and broad, if headlong, intellectual concerns. He seemed to feel that the burden of bringing South America up to a northern scientific and intellectual level rested on his shoulders. He intervened eloquently in the discussion of almost every paper.

He proposed translating *O Sentido da nova lógica* into Spanish for publication in Argentina, and I happily concurred.

Translations of books of mine now number forty-four; it is curious that the first of my books to be translated is the only one that has never appeared in English.

A few years later Mario despaired of Argentinian politics and moved to North America, ending up at McGill in Montreal. His output of books has been staggering.

Selected members of the congress were entertained at the ballet in Santiago and received by the president of the republic, Ibañez, in his palace. For the concluding festivities we were all transported to Viña del Mar, a resort near Valparaiso.

Marge and I wanted to get over to Mendoza, in what would have been my sixty-second country, Argentina. But the trains were immobilized by snow in the passes, and the planes were booked up far ahead.

Flying home, we were regaled with unprecedented mountain splendor between Lima and Ecuador. The pilot deviated east toward Peru's highest, Huascarán, and its range. Snow was continuous for over a hundred miles, pink in the sunset glow, and there was one appalling matterhorn after another, each higher than its eponym. Glaciers gleamed and glacial lakes lay shelf on shelf, one green, the next one blue.

Prinstitute and Royaumont   47

By July 22, 1956, we had made our way from chilly Chile to summer at Bare Hill. A prefabricated cabin, eight by ten feet with eight windows, was set up at a distance from the house to serve as my study, and I put a slab of plywood across one end for a desk. I have written hundreds of thousands of words there in the ensuing twenty-five years.

I was invited to the Institute for Advanced Study at Princeton for the academic year 1956–1957. We rented our house in Belmont to the Hyneks. Alan Hynek, prominent today in flying-saucer circles, was to be at Harvard on

"Moonwatch," a project prompted by the expectation that Russia would launch a satellite.

I devoted the year serenely to *Word and Object*. We were given a guest house in Maxwell Lane, a few minutes' walk across the grass from my office. The grounds of the Institute were wooded and suited to meditative strolling, and a towpath led farther afield. Friends abounded and proliferated. We saw something of Gödel and more of Robert Oppenheimer, Alexander Koyré, Prince Orsini, Harold Cherniss, Sir Llewellyn Woodward, Marston Morse, and Hassler Whitney. Georg Kreisel undertook to tell me a new result in logic each day at tea, weekends excepted. I had known him at Oxford when he was a reader at Reading—an office calculated to inspire a limerick.

Our circle transcended the Institute to embrace the Charles Gillispies, the Oskar Morgensterns, the Sidney Ratners, our old friends the Hempels, and, from Navy days, the Borgerhoffs. Evert Beth of the rank cigars and his bright, amiable, alarmingly fat wife Cori were visiting Princeton from Amsterdam. Luncheon parties glittered at Paul and Gabrielle Oppenheim's. Jim Sell, clown of old Ἄϱθϱον, worked for a nearby drug firm, so we had jolly sessions with him and his Slovak wife Terry. Jim made a box kite for Doug that soared like a dream.

I had long since been getting ideas for a revised edition of *Methods of Logic*. Charles Madison at Holt was to alert me when a new printing might be due, so that I could bring my revisions up to the minute. I now went ahead at last with the revisions and sent them in, feeling that the time must be getting ripe. It was more than ripe; it was rotten. While Madison was on vacation a subordinate had put through a new printing that would last for years. What grieved me most was the postponement of an appendix containing an unprecedentedly concise and transparent rendering of Gödel's proof of the completeness of the logic of quantification, and as a corollary the Skolem-Löwenheim theorem. The publisher made partial amends by printing the appendix as a pamphlet for insertion in the unsold books. I never knew it to turn up in a copy of the book, but I distributed it privately.

The publisher Nueva Visión in Buenos Aires wrote me that Bunge's Spanish translation of *O Sentido da nova lógica* was at hand in typescript. I insisted on seeing it before printing. The publisher protested that there was only one copy, and this confirmed me in my insistence. To have made only one copy was a presumption of slapdash job. I got them to send me a microfilm and the presumption was confirmed. The blunders were those of a headlong rush. Especially in the last part of the book, fraught with formulas, the symbols were a shambles. My corrections of those pages would clearly be too much for proper execution without two rounds of printer's proofs. But no; the publisher had no time for that. It is odd but not unusual that a publisher will take on a relatively unremunerative scientific book for the sake of prestige or as a service to culture, and then not prize and exploit the author's cooperation in making it come out right. So it came out wrong. And financially? Well, I had my hundred-dollar advance from Nueva Visión and did not hear from them again.

· 1957   I became president of the American Philosophical Association, Eastern Division, for 1957. I was elected also to the unphilosophical American Philosophical Society, an exclusive academy of scientists and scholars that was founded by Benjamin Franklin and meets twice a year for two or three days of lectures and happy association with distinguished company. Its eighteenth-century building, designed by Franklin, shares the grounds of Independence Hall in Philadelphia.

I went to St. John's College in Annapolis to discuss with faculty members who had been studying my work. The town was a gem. The eighteenth-century statehouse with its great dome was a wonder for the America of its time. Much of that century lingered in Annapolis, and every turn revealed another little cove of Chesapeake Bay. It was reminiscent of what Boston must have been before its landfills. St. John's was pursuing its new plan, centering on the hundred great books. A further innovation was the freshman seminar.

The callow youth had been reading Dostoievsky and Plato. Julius Klein was eliciting their unguarded impressions and silly judgments with skill and tact and no sign of embarrassment.

Our summer of 1957 at Bare Hill was interrupted by a trip to Ohio State University for my second honorary doctorate and by meetings at Cornell and Washington. A Summer Institute of Mathematics was raging at Cornell on mathematical logic. Characteristically of mathematics meetings, it was an exhausting affair, featuring complex constructions and badly expounded proofs. I was content to leave after a week, called to Washington for an Inter-American Congress of Philosophy. I opened it as president of the Eastern Division of the Philosophical Association. Parties were held in the Pan-American Union, the Library of Congress, and the National Gallery. A Watergate concert by the Navy Band was dedicated to the Inter-American Congress, as was a show of Latin-American songs and dances in the outdoor Sylvan Theater. The United Nations provided simultaneous translation of the papers.

At that meeting I was able to indulge my curiosity about zombies. William Seabrook and Faustin Wirkus had written credulously of them. During the war I met a girl who had lived in Haiti when her father was on naval duty there, and she told me of seeing a procession of zombies being led to some work detail. I had read a Haitian novel, Philippe Thoby-Marcelin's *Canapé Vert*, that dealt with zombies. At the Washington meeting at last I met two Haitians. One, Lhérisson, was a medical man and evidently the leader of Haiti's organized science, such as it might be. He vouched for zombies. The other was, of all people, the author of *Canapé Vert*. No, he did not really believe in zombies.

A delegate from Paraguay took me to a house where eight Paraguayans lived who were on missions to Washington. Knowing that the Paraguayans are bilingual, speaking Spanish and Guaraní, I was surprised to learn that they are nevertheless mostly of Spanish stock. The fostering of Guaraní was the good work of the Jesuit missionaries. The Paraguayans talked Guaraní for me and played native records. They said that Spanish was their language for science and Guaraní was for sentiment and song.

Expectation of a Russian satellite was mounting. After we reoccupied our Belmont house I was twice awakened in the dead of night by a telephone call from the *New York Times* for our recent tenant, Alan Hynek of "Moonwatch." I regretted not having the ready wit to play a hoax. On October 4, 1957, Sputnik went into orbit. Marge, Doug, and I went across the street to the school yard and saw the starlike speck moving across the night sky.

I stood in for Crane Brinton as chairman of the Society of Fellows for the ensuing academic year. It was a duty that I did not relish, and in later years I declined the permanent chairmanship.

The philosophy convention in December 1957 was in Boston. The banquet was held in the hall at Eliot House, appropriately, for it was the occasion of my presidential address. I gave "Speaking of objects," which foreshadowed *Word and Object*.

When Marge and I chose in 1951 to live in Belmont, it was because of its superior public schools. Ironically, by the time Doug was in school we were thinking of moving and facing the expense of private schools. Our house was convenient and the school was all right, but the scene could be that of any American suburb. We resolved to find a house with one of three attractions: the old-world look of Beacon Hill, proximity to Harvard Yard, or, if in Belmont, a view over Boston. We ended up in a brick town house of 1820 at 38 Chestnut Street on Beacon Hill. It is only twenty-two feet wide, but has five full stories puls a sub-cellar for the furnaces and a small unfinished attic with a hatchway to the roof. Sitting in this hatchway with some student's doctoral dissertation on my lap, and looking out over the jumble of old rooftops and chimney pots to the white sails on the blue of the Charles River Basin, would tend to mitigate the chores of spring.

We bought the house in November 1957. By February 20,

1958, the remodeling was done and the mover was due. Then a blizzard struck, and the police forbade the move. We had to unpack and settle back into the Belmont house, paying rent to the new owner and awaiting a thaw.

We had two Chevrolets, but the move to Boston meant cutting back, for there is nowhere to leave a car but the street. I tried selling the coupé of 1948, which had carried us nearly to Guatemala and to California and back and was still working beautifully. A dealer offered me too little for it, so I gave it to Marshall Cohen, who was then a graduate student in our department. Later he passed it along to Morty White's son Nick.

I was invited to the Colloque de Royaumont, an annual philosophical event north of Paris. I rearranged my teaching to clear the required week. It immediately followed Harvard's April recess, so I could be gone seventeen days. It was my sixth trip to Europe, my first by air, and my most casual. With my small suitcase I walked across Boston Common from my house to the subway—five minutes—and in twenty minutes I was at the airport. This has been my way ever since, when alone.

In Paris I luxuriated in ten days of unstructured leisure. I ran into my former junior colleague Hiram McLendon and we walked and talked, ranging widely. I dined in the homes of three philosophers—Jean Wahl, Aimé Patrie, and Ferdinand Alquié.

The colloquium was held in what was left of a picturesque and ruinous monastery. A few miles away is the tinselly Chateau de Chantilly, doubly dazzling by dint of its reflection in the lake. The topic of the colloquium was *philosophie analytique*, and the participants from outside France were mostly friends of mine from Oxford. Our papers were translated into French, mimeographed, and distributed. The translator was a stylist and innocent of philosophy. I corrected my paper, "Le mythe de la signification," before the mimeographing, but in the discussions, with our stylist as interpreter, communication languished. At the final session, despairing, I burst extempore into French. I held forth at length and communicated. I learned anew what I knew in Brazil sixteen years before: speak, if you can, the local language, even if badly.

My plane for Boston was out of order. Air France transferred me to London and lodged me there, pending a flight a day later. I thus missed further engagements at Harvard, but I accepted my lot philosophically as a lucky break. I went out for a look at Hampstead, something I had never before got around to doing, and walked back through Hampstead Heath to Soho for an Indian lunch.

Child Development   48

When we crossed to England in 1953, Doug was two and a half. The foghorn on board emitted an awful blast when the three of us were too near it. Doug's word for a big ship thereafter was "hornboat."

When Marge and I left Oxford for Gibraltar, he was nearly three and was speaking in two ways: British and American, with the typical intonation of each. When we got back to him twenty-four days later, he had turned three and strictly British. His company meanwhile had comprised his English nanny, our Italian girl Tecla, and two little English neighbor boys. I think the timing was crucial: just when Doug's phonemes were due to crystallize. This thought is supported by other observations. Walking in Christ Church Meadow in the fall of 1953, Doug and I met a dog that barked in greeting, and Doug responded in kind. Walking there again in the spring of 1954, we again met a dog that barked in greeting, and this time Doug's response, from his rigid new repertoire of phonemes, was little better than "Bow wow."

In June 1954, aged three and a half, Doug became chary of strange food and averse to mixtures. He wanted a clean dish for each course. Also an uncanny faculty for orientation and way-finding emerged. Reports on other children seem to agree. Do these emergent traits derive by natural selection from life in the forest, when children at that age tended to stray off the compound?

Early that fall, back again in Belmont, Marge spoke of Doug to a woman at his nursery school. "Oh, there must be two Douglases. The one I know is a little English boy." But by December he was as American as any.

In October I said something quietly and Doug was reminded that Marge and I had been talking quietly in the "hornboat." He said he had then been drawing through a stencil (described, not named) and cutting with scissors, and that the boat was rocking and he had been sick. It was a flood of details from thirteen months earlier, of which I remembered nothing. "Why had you been talking quietly?" he asked.

He raised a startling question in November: "Why don't people like targets?"

Gilbert Ryle was erect, gaunt, chinful, rather like Ed Haskell, but a bit older. When Gilbert visited us that November, 1954, Doug's first move was to suggest that Gilbert take him across the street to the school playground—something Ed had done months before. Gilbert, distant in juvenile contacts, did not rise to the suggestion. Later, undaunted, Doug suggested that Gilbert play with him in Doug's room, a plan that succeeded somewhat. Before the first day was over, Doug trotted into the living room with the poker chips— things never used except in Ed's presence.

When Gilbert left, my parents visited us for a week. Reacting to the emptiness after they too had left, Doug asked, "Where's that young man?" He meant Gilbert, and was still confusing him with Ed; for he went on to ask, "What was that other man's name who was here?" and added, to keep the record straight, "The *young* man's name was Head." Head Rascal, Ed Haskell.

About then, hence well before turning four, Doug was practicing contrary-to-fact conditionals: "What would you say if . . . ?"

One thing he wanted that Christmas was a baby doll. He

declared it a boy and named it Mike Margaret. He took it to nursery school and evidently someone there teased him. Nothing more was seen or heard of the doll.

Doug remarked in January 1955, aged four, that he remembered the red book, pointing to Whitaker's Almanac. Among hundreds of books, he recognized this one from the preceding summer at Oxford. What did he remember about it? A picture. Of what? Hesitation, and then, "A steamer . . . tipped over." It was the first time I had heard him say "steamer." When he had last seen the book, his word had been "hornboat."

Two days later, my words "coming from Mexico" suggested to Doug "coming from Exeter." He went on to recall how our little old Austin had broken down on a bleak night after Exeter. He volunteered many details. Clearly that had been an impressive occasion for him, six months before. I had lit out on foot, and he and Marge were sitting in the dark in the car when I came back with help. He got out to watch the repair and was trembling with the tension and cold.

As late as March 1955, Doug would slip back toward his English way of talking when he was sick or tired. Having been given the polychrome pencil that he had seen on my desk and coveted, he said, "I jolly like it"—a queer new corruption. "Because it's so special."

Crawling with Margaret, he said, "We're twins, but I'm a dog. We both came out of Mommie's tummy, but I turned out to be a dog." Perhaps the similarity of "Doug" and "dog" contributed.

Other quotations from the spring of 1955: "I'll last longer than you," to us, "because I'm already a child." "Taking down the stormy windows and putting up the screams." "Jelly jelly bean," sung, "I wonder what you mean." "Mommie, what temp'ature is it when it's a five and a round one?"

He was pushing an unfamiliar wheel toy with a gong. "When you push it slowly," he said, "it sounds like bells in Oxford." So he had internalized the bells of Merton Tower, just as I found twenty years later that I had done.

He extrapolated his observation that big people know more than small ones. "Daddy, if there were giants, they would know more than you, wouldn't they?"

He was explaining what he had learned at nursery school: that the earth is round. "And what's the earth, Doug?" "It's a round thing up in the clouds."

Until he saw a movie film projected, Doug thought the purpose of a movie camera was to spare the subjects the trouble of holding still.

He remarked that Mrs. Abe Klein's hair was black like Tecla's. He had last seen Tecla nearly nine months before.

Puzzled by a picture, I said, "I don't dig it." "What does that mean?" Doug asked. "It means I don't understand." "Marge," Doug called, "Daddy does not dig it." "What does 'understand' mean, Dougie?" "It means that you know what it means."

In June 1955, aged four and a half, he asked me, "How is a mouse born from its mother?" "Like you from Mommy." "How is the mouse's mother born?" "From its mother, like Mommy for her mother." "How was the first person born?"

Marge told him she would get him some sandals. "Get a kind that won't hurt," Doug said. This evinced a ten-month-old memory of England.

In August, Doug said, "Daddy?" "Yes, Doug?" "The following." Silence ensued. Then he asked, "What does 'the following' mean?"

Marge told him that she and I would be going away. "Where?" "Canada," I said. "Where is that?" he asked. "That's where Raymond is," I explained. "Oh," Doug promptly replied. "Who *is* Raymond?" I pursued. "Tecla's friend." Doug had not seen Raymond for over a year and could have scarcely heard of him meanwhile.

Doug got to talking again in August of our engine trouble "coming from Exeter" a full year before. Marge told him he need not have worried, since she takes care of him, and I of both. "And who takes care of Daddy?" Doug asked. "You and I." But Doug had a different idea. "God is in the sky, and takes care of me and Johnny and everybody." That was

Johnny Burch of pious parentage, though Doug claimed not to remember where he got these ideas.

Then he went on to wonder how God eats, since nobody sees him. "He must come down from the sky at night to do his shopping."

He asked Marge, "Do you wish your father were my grand one who has the farm?"

Doug: "Is it any fun digging holes?" Marge: "Why, I should think it was." Doug: "Well do you know what? A man said it wasn't."

Doug: "I know how to count to *one* very easily. One,." Rising inflection. We are now in September 1955.

"There are two kinds of *so*, aren't there? You *sew* something, and *so there*."

"Is there really a heaven?" Doug asked. Marge: "I don't think so." Doug: "Yup." "What?" "*Yup*, there is." "Where is it?" "Way up norse. Norse *pool*."

He had turned five and was sixteen months removed from his English nanny when he dredged this up: "Mary Mary white con*chary* had a little garden with silver bells and cockle shells and little girls all in a row."

There were nice crossings of words: "squirld"; "persimminon"; "arrescued by the police."

Without my glasses I could not read the little cheese package, so Doug spelled it out: "For house, for elephant, *r*, *k*, ..." At that point I got it: Herkimer.

On viewing a printed portrait of P. M. Roget, Doug asked: "What's wrong with him?" "Little." "How little is he?"

Seeing me stalled at the typewriter, Doug said, "If you want to remember something afterward, just sing it to yourself." It recalled the primeval mnemonic function of verse. Pressed, he said he had "thought it up."

"You know teachers mean a lot to little children," Doug told me. "That's why you mean a lot to me."

"Isn't it curious," Doug observed. "Little children remember better than big people even though their brains are smaller. Maybe it's because their brains are newer and work better."

Margaret at sixteen months took to applying "bahbu," for "baby," to her doll and appropriate pictures. Within the next two months she was saying "Hello, Doug. Dougie, come. Come in. Mommy, Daddy, come!" Even at two years, however, she would say [ā wā baʕ:map dɑ:dɑ], "I want button up, Rhoda." "Milk" was still [nə:kə] at two, and evolved into [no:uk]. Evidently *m* was troublesome; thus "witten" for "mittens." She persisted in putting an aspirate for *f*, as in Japanese and old Spanish, and for *s* as in Greek; thus "hinga" and "whetta" for "finger" and "sweater." Her *s* was still a problem at nearly five; Peninsula School was "plintha thkool." Yet she had no such trouble over her snow suit, "snow snoot," or her bathing suit, "baby suit." She went "slimming in her baby suit."

Already at two she was being creative semantically. The telephone, the chair, the pram, and my corduroy jacket were the hello, the sitdown, the bye-bye, and the work. She said "Button it" of a book, meaning that it be closed. She took a bold line in syntax too. "The knife didn't sharp me." She said "I don't want it Dougie cookie" for "Dougie doesn't want cookie."

She was just two and a half when Marge and I got back from our month in South America. She stood looking solemn and thoughtful and presently, without change in facial expression, announced her hypothesis: "Daddy." Marge got recognized more gradually.

Margaret was three when Marge asked her, "What did Daddy say when you told him he was absurd?" "He didn't nast me. He just [wæft]."

Further selections: "The nuts are going to get all gone up." "Here's your cup and sausage." "I am very nangry." "But how will I be bable to get into my clowset?"

She was still three when we took her and Doug to Mount Monadnock. Doug and I forged ahead up the mountain, not expecting Margaret to get far. It is a model mountain on a moderate scale. It is steep and has a tree line, due not to altitude but to the onset of rocky terrain. Doug and I had got to the tree line and were sitting on a ledge admiring the view when we heard the approaching chatter of a very young voice. It was Margaret, ascending the steep trail on all fours and never pausing in her chatter to catch her breath. Marge was behind her, and the four of us continued to the top. Margaret was in lively good spirits all the way home and through her late supper and into bed.

A year later, when she came to know my daughter Norma, Margaret identified her as "Dougie's half-sister." I wonder if she thought that sister and brother were converses, so that only boys had sisters and only girls had brothers.

She pretended reading: "Sally said, 'We will be there now.'" Soon she was really reading. We were in California; next chapter. Margaret was ineligible for kindergarten, being under five, so she went to Peninsula School, a nursery school in Menlo Park. She and her little contemporary Catharine Pease sequestered themselves under a table there and taught themselves to read.

Mexico and Stanford 49

· 1958 Late in June 1958 I gave three lectures to the computer engineers at Ann Arbor on simplifying truth functions. My paper "On cores and prime implicants" came out of those lectures, and a remote effect was what engineers now call the Quine-McCluskey method. A few weeks after Ann Arbor, having been back in Massachusetts only a year and on Beacon Hill only a few months, we were off again for a year away. I was to spend 1958–1959 at Stanford as a fellow of the Center for Advanced Study in the Behavioral Sciences. We rented our house in Boston to Mason and Florence Hammond, he a Boston Brahmin and she a New Orleans belle. Mason was a Latin professor at Harvard, newly retired from the mastership of Kirkland House and waiting to resume possession of his venerable Cambridge house in Brattle Street.

We drove to New York and boarded the Norwegian freighter *Bennestvet Brovig,* car and all, for Vera Cruz. We were taking the long way to California. The ship was detained in the East River by a dock strike, with us on board. We were grateful for the unexpected sojourn in New York, and in such choice lodgings. I tried while there to buy a Norwegian grammar, but the bookstores were closed on Saturday, even Brentano's, so I went to New York University in Washington Square and tried the library. They lent me the book, unaffiliated though I was. I mailed it back to them from Mexico.

We four were the only passengers, and we took our meals with Captain Abrahamson and his chief engineer. I was given the use of what had been a radio room and there I worked at *Word and Object,* scanning the sea for inspiration from paragraph to paragraph.

We spent three leisurely days driving from Vera Cruz up and over to Mexico City, where we picked Norma up at the airport. She had just finished college in California and was joining us for our trip back to California through Mexico.

The streets of Mexico City were clogged with a glutinous mass of vehicles and humanity. We were hours crossing it, but at last we settled into a west-side hotel and kept a rendezvous with Gonzalo Zubieta in the Café Tacuba.

We enjoyed anew the picturesqueness and grandeur of the towns and country from there to Guadalajara, and we were glad as always to get back to the *tacos, tamales,* refried beans, and Spanish. I spotted a *pulquería* and had a *pulque,* still not having sorted out my earlier experiences to the point of appreciating my rashness in so doing.

The country beyond Guadalajara, running up to the Gulf of California and all along it, was new to us, and unlike the familiar uplands it was hot. We lingered at Mazatlán for the swimming and seafood. We lingered also at Nogales, reluctant to leave Mexico, but we crossed frequently on foot for an American chocolate milk shake.

Thence we drove to Needles and across the Mojave Desert. At Altadena we visited Jane and Frank Goddard. She was our Jane Thornton of Navy days, and he was a rocket engineer at Cal Tech. We all drove to Anaheim and were entranced by the illusions of Disneyland. When the crocodile reared up alongside out little jungle boat and our white hunter, in split-second reaction, discharged his rifle into the creature's cavernous maw, Margaret grew up a little.

The Carnaps were in Los Angeles; he had moved to U.C.L.A. We did not call on them, for I would soon be back, perhaps with Marge, and without the children. I was slated to give a lecture there. However, it was not to be. We moved into our house at 743 Cooksey Lane, Stanford, and within a few days I had hepatitis. It may have been the pulque.

After five weeks in bed, two of them in the hospital, I was allowed to sit in our yard. The spacious lawn focused upon a little pool that was choked with tall pampas grass and shaded by a clump of redwoods. Georg Kreisel, Don Davidson, and John Austin were among my solicitous visitors; Georg and Don were on the Stanford faculty and John was visiting at Berkeley.

During much of my illness I was able to write. On October 30, 1958, still convalescing in the yard, I reached the end of *Word and Object*. I foresaw months of polishing and revising, and a pleasant prospect it was; the struggle was over. In Oxford five years before I had been seeking a structure, trying to devise a suitable scaffold or skeleton or, in a less lugubrious metaphor, Christmas tree, upon which to arrange the many things I wanted to say. The problem had long endured.

Four days later I started going to my office. From home to office, when I grew stronger, was an agreeable mile. The last bit was a shortcut up a steep, wooded slope of buffalo grass. In the dry season the grass was tan and slippery. After climbing a bit, I would stop to catch my breath and admire the view over the red tile roofs of the university and Palo Alto beyond. When I next stopped for breath, my view had grown; I looked out upon the blue waters of the southern end of San Francisco Bay and on to the distant hills. When I stopped the third time, I was in my office at the top of the slope and the view out my picture window was superb. I would settle down to my desk in the blissful state of having nothing to do but what I wanted most, to rewrite *Word and Object*.

The offices, in blocks of two, were scattered motel-fashion through a grove of gnarled live oaks. A central building housed the administration, a secreterial staff, and seminar rooms. Another central building was for lunch, and its tables spilled over into the plaza. The profile was low and the architecture rustic. Tea and coffee flowed at ten and at four in the plaza, if one was in the mood for a break and a bit of bright chatter.

The only other philosopher was Joe Schwab, in philosophy of education. That suited me; I battened on linguistics, ethnography, and psychology when I was away from my desk. The linguists were the Africanist Joe Greenberg and, in the second term, Roman Jakobson and Alf Sommerfelt. The ethnographers were Cora Dubois, Fred Eggan, the New Zealander Raymond Firth, and the South African Meyer Fortes. The psychologists were Gene Galanter, George Miller, Charles Osgood, the brain psychologist Karl Pribram, and the psychiatrist Jerome Frank. There were also two literary figures, Dan Aaron and Mark Schorer, and two sociologists, Dan Bell and Ed Shils.

One was allowed to nominate a scholar from outside as an assistant. I got Don Davidson. He read my evolving draft and discussed it with me to good effect. He and Ginny had designed a little house on the Coast Range, overlooking Stanford and further stretches of the North American continent from a dizzy height. Other Stanford University company were my old friends John and Nancy Goheen and our new musical friends Sandor and Priscilla Salgo. We had some evenings with my old teacher and colleague Clarence Lewis and his bright and gracious wife Mabel; they had retired to Yale Avenue, no less, in Menlo Park a few doors from Palo Alto. She has since lived to a hundred.

· 1959   We persuaded my father and mother to visit us. He had not been west of St. Louis, nor she of Encinal. They came luxuriously by rail—Vista Dome. We drove them north as far as Healdsburg, where my father renewed a boyhood friendship, and south as far as the windblown pines of Monterey and the Spanish mission of Carmel.

I took a weekend jaunt with Karl Pribram, Dan Aaron, and Jerome Frank to Volcano, a ghost town in the mother lode. We found a town of a hundred and stayed in its hotel, a relic of the gold rush. There once had been seventeen hotels, thirty saloons, and six temperance societies. We drove up to where the road was snowed in. The walking, climbing, and talking were good, but three of us were glad to get back to Stanford even so, for Karl was a demon driver.

The second edition of *Methods and Logic,* so grievously delayed, was at last going into print. Charles Madison of Holt proudly sent me the colorful new dust jacket, impatient to have me see it without awaiting the bound book. I was grateful for his impatience, but it would have been better still if he had sent me an advance proof; for the blurb was a disgrace. It had me claiming an extension of Gödel's theorem. I telegraphed him in horror. It must be said to his credit that he scrapped the whole stock of jackets and printed a new supply with an acceptable text.

That spring I gave five lectures at Stanford University and a sixth at Berkeley, the annual Howison Lecture, all drawn from the nascent *Word and Object.* Early in June 1959 I got the book off to the publisher. It was well, for on June 9 I was off to the

Jack Smart, the Scottish professor of philosophy at Adelaide in South Australia, had invited me thither as Gavin David Young Lecturer. Through John Goheen I was also invited to the University of Tokyo. I accepted both invitations. Marge would fly to Boston with the children, leave them with our faithful sitter, and join me in Tokyo. But first we had to get rid of our car. This involved skeins of California red tape, besides finding a buyer. In the end good Preston Cutler, deputy director of the Center, solved all by taking custody and finding me a buyer among the next year's Fellows.

I stopped in Honolulu. I went up over the rocky spine of Oahu for a look at the other side and then returned to Waikiki to stay the night in a waterfront hotel, so called because it boasted a pedestrian right-of-way leading from the hotel all the way to the beach. I swam and sat in a *lanai* for a *luau* and watched the *hula hula* and heard the *ukelele*.

I flew from this Polynesian corner of the United States to Melanesia, more particularly the Fiji Islands, specifically Viti Levu (Big Fiji), more particularly the town of Nadi, pronounced Nandi, which is peopled by Indians who grow rice. On the advice of Raymond Firth at Stanford, who had consulted Cyril Belshor, I proceeded to the hotel at Korolevu Beach on the south coast and inquired for Joseteke, of Vatua, who would take me to a *sevu sevu*. It is a welcoming ceremony.

Joseteke was a waiter. He was black and bushy-haired and wore a *lava lava*, which is to say a kilt. We were to go to a *sevu sevu* in each of two villages, so we went to a rustic store and bought two pounds of *yaqona*, pronounced yangona. It is the root of a pepper, and said to be mildly narcotic. We drove to Koniave, a cluster of *bure* or thatched bamboo houses scattered roadlessly through a coconut grove from roadside to beach. The headman, Joseteke's uncle, was a big non-bushy black who spoke no English. At the doorless entrance of the largest house, Joseteke stepped out of his sandals, so I took off my shoes. It was a single great room, tapering to the ridgepole. The columns and beams were poles, tied with coconut rope. The floor was made of bamboo slats ornamentally woven and partly covered with palm mats.

Nine of us squatted in circular formation on a large mat. A vessel of *kava*, the liquid pressed from the *yaqona*, was in the center, and a length of coconut rope next to it pointed to me as guest of honor. Several more men were squatting or lying outside the circle, and beyond them were two bushy-haired women. The headman orated for some minutes in Fijian. Joseteke occasionally interjected something. At points there was a rhythmic clapping, or the word *naka*, short for *vinaka* (with bilabial *v*), meaning "good" or "thanks." Sometimes the response was a sustained open *e*, crescendo. At length a young man filled half a coconut shell with *kava* and served it to me, cupping it with both hands and dropping to his knees. I drained it—having been briefed—while all solemnly watched. The Ganymede said "Ah, *matha*," [maːða], meaning "empty," and clapped three times. Then he served the headman, and so on to all present, except the two women, evidently in a fixed order. The routine was the same for each, even to the "Ah, *matha*," except that each man clapped his hands once before taking the cup, or, if shy a hand, slapped an arm.

For my second *sevu sevu* we drove to Tagaqe, pronounced [taŋaŋkɛ]. Here I saw how the *kava* was pressed from the *yaqona*. A hollowed stump was the mortar, and the pestle had a long handle so that the woman worked in a standing position. The headman of Tagaqe was the *buli vakacegu* (*c* for theta), that is, the retired *buli*, of the entire *tikina* of Baravi. His English was good, but did not intrude on the ceremony, which proceeded as at Koniave, except that this time I knew to clap before receiving the bowl. At Tagaqe there was a second round of *kava*, making three for me altogether. It had a musty taste, little more, and I detected no effect.

Viti Levu is the top of a huge submerged volcano, and the coral reef that rings it is a mile offshore. The mountainous interior is wooded and scarcely inhabited. I occupied a cabin at the beach and swam in the lagoon.

I remember two vignettes: a native climbing a high palm and tossing down a coconut; natives building a *bure*, the traditional hut.

From Melanesia I returned to Polynesia, in a sense, by flying to New Zealand; for the Maori are Polynesian. In Auckland I had an evening with a little group gathered by the local ethnographer Ralph Piddington, who had been alerted by Meyer Fortes. Some of them were about to visit a New Guinea people whose language was unknown to linguists and perhaps without known affinities.

I flew in a small plane to Rotorua, in the center of the North Island, a land of pasture and gentle green mountains. The spectacular peaks are on the South Island, but my time was too short for that. Rotorua, my farthest south, offers hot springs and Maori culture. Maori women wash their clothes and boil their dinners in the steaming streams. Maori architecture is on display: stockades, wood sculptures, and meeting houses.

At Canberra, Australia, I stopped overnight with the Passmores. John had friends in to meet me, young Harsanyi among others. John gave me a tour of the growing capital, which recalled a painting of our capital in its early days. Some stately structures were complete, among them the Academy. It was an inverted bowl, incalculably heavy but conveying the impression of being pinioned to the ground and straining to take off. From a vantage point above the town he showed me where, in the fullness of time, there would be a lake.

I then flew via Melbourne to Adelaide. Through his father-in-law, a retired justice of the Supreme Court of Australia, Jack Smart had arranged for me to stay at the posh Adelaide Club. With its dark paneling and deft waiters, it was the epitome of the traditional London club. Ironically, when Jack called for me he had to cool his heels in a waiting room until I could get to him and graciously invite him into the sacred precincts.

Downtown Adelaide was ringed by park, which was ringed in turn by the suburbs. The city had a Victorian air, with horse-drawn carriages and wagons.

It was luxurious to have *Word and Object* complete but free to draw upon, being still at press. I crowded the eight lectures into half a month, for I was due in Japan in the middle of July and meant to see things on the way. A weekend was found, even so, for an excursion out back. C. F. Presley, called Val, and his wife Evelyn took me to the Flinders Range in their car, along with his colleague Charlie Martin, an expatriated Bostonian. The country resembled Arizona, with the addition of kangaroos. As we drove, a kangaroo appeared on the plain and kept pace with us, effortlessly leaping on a parallel course.

My next destination was Singapore. It meant a day's flight across Australia from south to north, and then a night flight. The terrain from Adelaide to Darwin was mostly fierce desert. The gum tree or eucalyptus is Australia's dominant tree, capable of impressive proportions; and groves of it penetrated the arid lands, ever shrinking, until on the fringes of the driest deserts it had shrunk to patches of mere ground cover, recognizable as eucalyptus still by its hue of dusty green.

Our first stop was Alice Springs, on the Tropic of Capricorn and at the center of the continent. It was a village of a few thousand souls, the biggest town within five hundred miles. There was just a pale green hint of moisture about. We also put down at lesser desert outposts—Tennant Creek, Daly Waters, Katharine. I saw an Australian aborigine now and then, in shirt and pants, working at one and another air station. I walked about Darwin and saw many black natives, presumably not the characteristic Australian aborigine; there would have been an admixture from New Guinea.

It was frustrating to fly over Indonesia on a moonless night. I had to choose some countries over others, and I eliminated Indonesia in view of the hostile atmosphere at the time. But the plane did touch at Djakarta, and I walked about the terminal in the dead of night, chalking up my sixty-fifth country.

Through the kindness again of Raymond Firth, I was met at Singapore by a young English ethnographer, Michael Swift, a professor at the local university. He showed me around the city, which was largely Chinese but had an occasional garish Indian temple. He took me across the bridge into Johore Bahru, capital of the Sultanate of Johore. Up the hill was the sultan's palace, a romantic Moslem pile reminiscent of one of the better postage stamps, and at the foot of the hill was the Malay market, where we enjoyed a curious crisp pastry. The little wooden Malay houses were elevated on stilts as a precaution against water and wildlife. We went back to Singapore and had tea in Swift's flat. The walls were bare of pictures, for his wife was a Malay and therefore Moslem. I stayed the night in the Raffles Hotel, outpost of empire.

My plane for Bangkok put down at Kuala Lumpur, the capital of Malaya, and flew over Penang, which I recognized by its position on its island. It lies in 100° east longitude, and still marks my farthest west. Meanwhile my east has crept to 88° east, at Calcutta. I have girdled the globe the hard way, forwards and backwards, minus the 975 miles from Calcutta to Bangkok (which is less than from Calcutta to Penang).

The drive from the Bangkok airport was enlivened with garish billboards. They screamed their enigmatic messages in the outlandish Thai characters, inducing a vivid sense of being away from home. After settling into my hotel in an uninteresting quarter, I wanted to see the center of town. I hailed a pedicab, but I could not communicate. Then I thought of *wat*, which apparently means temple, at least in Cambodia if not in Siam; and a temple might well be at the center of town, or even be rewarding in itself. I sounded the magic word, and we were off to a temple.

Temple is putting it mildly. There are great Buddhist campuses, each cluttered with the wildest extravaganzas. There is one temple after another, in gilt or shining marble, with dazzling red or green tile roofs that taper to soaring finials at the corners and gable ends. There are fantastic varicolored pagodas, intricately modeled, and grotesque statues of giants in bright regalia. Walt Disney would have reveled in it, and perhaps did.

Another lively aspect of Bangkok was the river life. Huts stood on stilts along the banks and in the water. The river was cluttered with the boats of vendors and buyers, a floating market. Other boats were in their small way floating homes.

On a tip from an Englishman at my hotel, I went to a boxing match. There were the familiar fisticuffs and there was fast footwork, indeed footwork with a vengeance; the kick in the face. It was a quick upswing of a straight leg, a pirouette, and a canvas shoe smack against a cheek. There were several hits of that kind, though all the knockouts were manual. The best of the show was sidelong: the rapt, frantic faces and gesticulations of the Siamese fans. Oriental with a vengeance, yet scrutable to a fault.

I soon was on a plane for Siem Reap, in Cambodia. It was a big plane, but I was the only passenger. Siem Reap is the village near Angkor Wat. Its hotel, the Grand Hôtel d'Angkor, was a wooden French colonial structure with prominent verandas. The village houses were of withes, closely woven, and some of them were on stilts. The village straddled a river in which there was an occasional waterwheel, like a miniature Ferris wheel five yards high, fitted with paddles and at one point a tub. The paddles caused the wheel to rotate with the current, and the tub scooped up water, subsequently spilling it into an overhead trough that conveyed it ashore. Water was pumped by its own power.

Angkor Wat occupies a mile-square plot which is bounded by a broad moat in the jungle. The complex of walls and courts, enclosures within enclosures, bristles with beehive towers intricately carved to the last inch, lush as the jungle. Unlike garish Bangkok, all is monochrome: gray stone. A half mile of bas-reliefs eight feet high depict gods, wars, and daily life of twelfth-century Cambodia. Elsewhere in the

jungle, a monstrous carved gateway topped with three beehive domes and three huge, smiling faces opens onto the ruinous old capital, Angkor Thom, which abounds in heroic
statues and is dominated by a great stone temple, lavishly
carved. Angkor Thom's Cabin it is not.

After Siem Reap, I prowled Saigon, as we called it then,
and its big Chinese suburb, Cholon. South Vietnam was
what I had known from maps in my childhood as Cochin-
China. The Vietnamese women were a chic and dainty lot,
smartly fitted in tunics and trim white trousers.

In Hong Kong I stayed in the Peninsula Hotel, that Victorian transplant that plays Raffles to Hong Kong's Singapore.
It is in Kowloon, on the mainland, overlooking the ferry that
serves the island of Hong Kong. The island comprehends
the capital, Victoria, and the rugged mountains to which
Hong Kong owes its second place, after Rio de Janeiro,
among the scenic seaports of the world. Rather a close second, one feels, gazing all unrepelled into mountain-girt Re-
pulse Bay, strewn with square-rigged junks and sampans. I
had a notable Chinese dinner in a floating restaurant on that
bay. In the evening, exploring upper reaches of the dense,
steep city, I saw Chinese arranging their bedding on the
street for the night. The housing shortage was desperate, despite the enormous housing project that the British had built
and were continuing to build in the New Territories behind
Kowloon. The flood of refugees from Communist China exceeded all measures.

I took a small ship to Macao. The berths were little more
than the *couchettes* of the old French trains, and cheap; by
booking two, I had a room to myself. It was a mere forty-odd
miles, but one could continue to sleep after docking.

I explored Macao's six square miles. The Portuguese element was recessive there, as was the English in Hong Kong.
Macao gave me the experience of a small Chinese city, as
Hong Kong gave me that of a great one. Macao was old-fashioned. Streets would break needlessly and heedlessly into
steps; wheeled traffic had small claims.

Red China was in the foreground as I looked out from the

docked ship or from the town. I walked up the street toward the international gate and guardhouses, to see how near I could get. Not near. Black soldiers with fixed bayonets, Angolese perhaps, waved me away.

From Hong Kong I flew in a Cat, for Cathay, to Taipeh, in Taiwan, the Formosa of my youth, Nationalist China. The Grand Hotel was a rambling, palatial, Chinese-red product of Mme. Chiang's creative imagination. The streets of Taipeh with their small wooden houses were like the streets in the surviving old quarters of Tokyo, as I later observed. It is ironical that the routed government of China should have come to rest in a land that had been shunted for fifty years into Japanese ways.

From there I flew to Tokyo, touching at the temporarily American island of Okinawa. Marge joined me in Tokyo and we settled into the Hilltop Hotel, or *Yama no Ue Hoteru*, on July 12, 1959.

Japan   51

In the ensuing month I put in fully fifty hours of lecture and scheduled discussion at the University of Tokyo, plus a lecture at Keio University and many hours of unscheduled discussion in homes and cafés. The time ran long because most of my lectures, as well as the responses, had to be filtered through translation. Hiromichi Takeda did most of the translating; Shozo Ohmori did some. Each minute that I talked took two or three in translation. I would lend the translator my typescript a day ahead so that he could study it; this was easy for me, since it was a typescript of *Word and Object*. I would also place it so that he could follow it while I spoke. But there was no diminishing the ratio.

At these meetings, we all sat at the outer side of a circle of tables. At the center there was a metal stand in which rested a huge prism of clear ice with a bouquet frozen inside it.

The sweltering heat was probably somewhat mitigated by the expedient, and the eye was gratified. By the end of the two-hour session, the ice had dwindled almost to the flowers. Next day it was pristine again.

My later lectures were addressed to mathematicians under the auspices of Shigekatsu Kuroda and were held in an air-conditioned building. They were on set theory, and constituted one more step toward the book that I had conceived at Oxford and had postponed for the sake of *Word and Object*. Kuroda felt we might dispense with translation in view of the nature of the subject, the visual aid of the blackboard, and everyone's presumed knowledge of English to some degree. My lectures elicited little discussion and few questions. Apparently, my effort to communicate had been either a complete success or a hopeless failure.

The philosophy lectures, translated, had elicited lively discussion. Philosophy does. The discussion was largely vague and somewhat off the point, but in philosophy that is not unusual even on home ground. Were my philosophy lectures then well understood, thanks to my hard-working translators? Recalling misunderstandings I have known even on home ground, I can guess.

Our Japanese hosts were solicitous. A university chauffeur took me to each of my lectures. Miyo, the attractive wife of the senior philosopher Hideo Kishimoto, looked to Marge's interests. We were entertained in many homes.

We were given a banquet in a sumptuous Buddhist restaurant overlooking a large and meticulously landscaped private park. It was hard to believe that the food, excellent and unidentifiable, was vegetarian. There were twenty-odd guests, among them an old woman and an old man who had not met. The woman was probably a professor's widow, and the man a scholar whom her husband had revered; for, when they were introduced, the woman so far exceeded the customary Japanese bow as to drop to her knees and touch the floor with her forehead.

We squatted on cushions at a single long table some fourteen inches high. One's legs were decorously folded under the haunches; no sprawling. Rising after a long dinner was excruciating.

Another occasion was a reception to meet the students. We all stood around in a big room drinking beer, until presently the students were marshaled shoulder to shoulder along the walls of the room and Marge and I were taken the rounds to meet them one by one. Each student was to say his name. Some were so shy that they could not emit the familiar syllables.

Ohmori and two other young philosophers—Natsuhiko Yoshida and Makoto Yamamoto—took me to the Shinjuku quarter for an evening on the town. We went to a tiny bar room. There were tables for perhaps a dozen customers, and a little bar across one corner. Behind the bar were two attractive barmaids, one in kimono and the other in European dress. We four drank standing at the bar. Yoshida suggested singing and invited me to begin with something from America. Well, hardly. Then he burst into a song from Hokkaido, where he lived. Next Ohmori sang a song, and Yamamoto. A curious combination, the shy, retiring Japanese manner and the readiness to sing unaccompanied in public. Alcohol was no factor; there had been little. The barmaids, cultivated girls, were included in the conversation by excursions into Japanese, and one of them joined in the singing when she knew the song. It was a social occasion. The Japanese bar provides the gentleman at loose ends with an hour of easy contact at his own polite level.

Marge and I went to an intimate little *bistro* where the tablecloths were red and white checked and a little Japanese *chanteuse* sang *chansons* in the authentic throaty way, utterly French except for *r* and *l*. I tried opening a conversation with her between numbers, but she spoke no French.

We visited a strikingly cross-cultural little *tempura* bar. It was a circular counter, and the cook sat at the center in a slowly rotating apparatus with his pots. With chopsticks he would put a tidbit on each customer's plate as he made the rounds. One time it would be a sprig of asparagus, delicately fried in thin batter; next time around, a shrimp; next perhaps a fried bit of cauliflower; next a piece of fish. The apparatus was made by the Otis Elevator Co.

From a rapid transit we saw a big house in full flame, as imposing as the perpetual blockhouse fire in Disneyland. We got off at the next station and hurried back, to find it totally extinguished in the intervening minutes.

Tokyo surrounds the extensive walled compound of the Imperial Palace. Permission was arranged for us to visit parts of it. We marveled at the *bonsai,* potted dwarfed cypresses, extravagantly contorted and centuries old. Waitaru Kuroda took us to his home suburb, Kamakura, to see the towering, brooding Buddha. A longer excursion was northward to Nikko. Dominated again by a Buddha, it is a rich concentration of temples, shrines, and pagodas to which, what with the shortness of time and a miserable rain, we did less than justice. Semantical note: temples are Buddhist, shrines are Shinto.

Our second month in Japan went to sightseeing, except for a lecture at Kyoto. Katsuji Ono, a hulking mathematician and logician whom I had known when he was at M.I.T., showed us his city of Nagoya and the cormorant fishing at Gifu. The cormorants are on leash, tied too tightly at the throat to permit them to swallow the fish for which they dive. They are hauled back to the boats with their catch.

At Ise we saw the sort of shrine that antedated the advent of Chinese culture and curly-cornered roofs. These shrines are built of cypress, supported by myriad stilts. The roof is thickly thatched in the smoothest coiffure and weighted down by a succession of cylindrical timbers balanced transveresely on the ridgepole. Rafters at the gable ends are crossed, extending beyond the ridge. These shrines are maintained in identical pairs, by rebuilding first one and then the other, every twenty years. This has gone on, they say, since the seventh century.

We visited the pearl farm. Acres of floating frames are loaded with oysters in each of which a seed has been planted to serve as the nucleus of an eventual pearl. The so-called seeds proved to be pretty big. Calling the product a cultured pearl, rather than a pearl-plated marble, is a triumph of enlightened modern merchandising.

In Tokyo, what with the heat and hard work, a western-style hotel with its air conditioning and familiar arrangements had seemed a wise choice. In Kyoto, however, we were delighted with life in a Japanese inn, the *Hiragiya* or Holly House, and regretted not having lived that way in Tokyo. In the vestibule we docked our shoes and stepped ashore, as it were, on the matted floor. When we had padded through the corridors to our room, we mounted a new level of matted elegance: soft, padded, and resilient. White walls were trimmed in burnished wood. Sliding screens were paneled with rice paper. The focus of the room was the *tokonoma*, a recess in which a scroll was displayed, or a vase of flowers. The maid in a kimono pulled out a broad drawer at bedtime and spread rolls of bedding on the soft floor. In the morning she came with a tray and knelt opposite us at the low table where we squatted to breakfast. She served us strange delicacies, including various kinds of fish, some raw, and seaweed, each a discrete tidbit tastefully separated from its neighbors. There was a variegated plum, strong in pepper, that helped to alert one to the dawn of a new day.

The scene out the window, when she had pushed the *shoji* or screen aside, was a miniature Japanese garden with its pool and steep bridge and its painstaking disarray of stones, gravel, and asymmetrical cypresses. In the room one wore a *yukata*, a simple kimono, which was provided by the inn. I did some writing in the room, and got on very well without chair or table. I sat on a cushion, leaning against a door jamb. I could sprawl indecorously and strew my papers about me on the matted floor. I had some sort of board on my legs to write against. I recalled that Shigekatsu Kuroda had a western-style writing room in his otherwise oriental house in Tokyo, but perhaps there was no need of it.

Takeda had returned to Kyoto, where he lived and taught. We got on well, for he was given, like Peter Pezzati, to the congenial sport of playing with languages, of which we shared several. He showed us Kyoto—palaces, tea gardens, a gilded pavilion in a pond, a Zen garden of raked sand and rocks. We deployed to Nara and Horyuji, holy towns. Nara's bronze seated Buddha would be seventy feet tall if he stood up, but would still be dwarfed by the ornate pagoda. The temple at Horyuji boasts wooden buildings from the seventh century. The octagonal Hall of Dreams, in burnished wood, was built for a thoughtful prince, who would sit in the center and meditate. He still was sitting, serenely, in wooden effigy.

Takeda had been commissioned to guide us on our further travels. We plied the Inland Sea, threading our way among abrupt little wooded islands, steep and deeply green. After a stay at a luxurious inn near Takematsu, on Shikoku, we sailed on to Miyajima. A great red *torii*, a symbolic gateway, stood in the tidewater and marked the way to a monastery, whose red wooden buildings were ranged over a parkland of cypresses, maples, ponds, and steep bridges. Our inn, the *Momijiya* or Maple House, was at the foot of a well-groomed wooded mountain.

Marge and I wanted to be alone, free of social responsibility toward our friend and guide, but we were chary of hurting his feelings and reluctant to deprive him of the rest of what was perhaps a welcome junket at institutional expense. Somehow I succeeded in conveying our wishes without offence, and we were alone. In the cool of the evening, people strolled in the village—we among them—in the distinctive yukatas of the several inns. We were the only visible occidentals.

At the Center in Stanford I had found some time for working on Japanese. Books were recommended by my orientalist friends Joe Levinson and Don Shively. Japanese is written in Chinese characters, supplemented by two Japanese syllabaries, one for grammatical particles and another for foreign words. I did not venture the limitless task of learning to read Japanese, but my dim memories of my brief study of Chinese a dozen years before enabled me to do some playful speculating on characters. My manuals of Japanese used our Latin alphabet, as did my pocket dictionary. I did not aspire to a serviceable command even of the spoken langauge, but I wanted to get some idea of it. I had occasion to put my little knowledge to work after all, eked out by the dictionary; for the man from whom I bought our passage from Miyajima spoke only Japanese.

We took a ship overnight to Beppu, on Kyushu. We and the other passengers slept on mats on the floor of the saloon or on a cushioned bench that encircled the room. Beppu boasts hot springs and a moderately giant Buddha. A backdrop of wooded mountains abounds in friendly apes.

When we returned to Tokyo, philosopher friends took us to Hakone and Lake Ashi and lodged us in an inn with a view over the lake and, weather permitting, Fuji. It never permitted, but we cruised the wild waters.

In a Japanese inn you get clean in a shower and then soak chin-deep in a king-size tub in which the water has been kept hot by a thick wooden lid. Successive bathers soak in the same water, having considerately showered. So sumptuous was the inn at Lake Ashi, however, that we had a private king-size tub, full of hot water under its lid.

We went to a stonecutter in Tokyo and bought nearly a ton of his wares. They were shipped to Boston in nineteen crates. There was a four-foot *ishidoro* or stone lantern that I cemented to a rock at Bare Hill; also four squat *ishidoro* for our relatives, and two old knee-high Buddhist sculptures, one a gift for the Burches.

Korea, Alaska, Europe   52

Flying from Tokyo to Korea for a weekend, we surprised Fuji. The peak had been hidden by overcast throughout our stay, but above the clouds it was exposed in all its symmetrical, snow-capped grandeur.

Sidney and Ann Hook had been staying in Tokyo, and went to Korea when we did. He was scheduled to lecture; I was unheralded. But evidently Sidney spread the word, for a gathering of professors and a journalist or two were assembled around me at the university for informal discussion.

Sidney was to visit Panmunjom at the hostile border. There was room for one more, and I was eager. But no; Ann's priority was indisputable.

Old temples and palaces in Seoul were roofed with hemicylindrical tiles in the traditional way of east and west, but gray tiles rather than red, and closed at the eaves with ornamental half disks. Women wore voluminous flowing garments, impeccably white, and particularly striking on the dusty roads. Old-fashioned men with straggly beards wore high black hats like opera hats but absurdly slim. The streets were badly smashed up, as was much of the city. There were no cars but jeeps, and no street lamps.

Korean for "Korea" is *Han*. Korean for "China" is also *Han*, but with a different character, when Chinese characters are used rather than the Korean alphabet. Korean for "big" is also *han*, the character this time being the same as the one for—guess which—"Korea." The Koreans can also say *te* for "big," answering to the Chinese *dai*. The official name for Korea is *Te Han Ming Wha*, "Big Big People's Land." I suppose the reason for *Te Han* is the need of indicating in speech that the *han* intended is the one for "big" (and "Korea") rather than the one for "China." *Han* in Korean can also mean "river," but this is a third character. The great river near Seoul is Great River, or Hangan for *Han Han*.

We were to fly from Tokyo to Boston by way of Arasuka, which is Japanese for Alaska. We booked a stopover at Anchorage and a side trip through Alaska to Point Barrow, the northernmost point of the North American continent, but when we got to Anchorage on September 11 the plane to Barrow had been cancelled because of upheaval of the landing strip by frost. We lowered our sights to Kotzebue, on the Arctic Ocean just north of the Arctic Circle.

The terrain around Anchorage supported scrubby larch woodland in the swampy areas and scrubby birch, already autumn gold, where the ground was dry. As we flew northwest the larch was more stunted. Presently it was growing only where a glint showed standing water. By then even the birch, more stunted, was growing only in low and presumably moist places. As we pressed yet further north, the larch disappeared and the birch, reduced to the merest yellow ground cover, grew only amid the glint of water. For the rest, tundra.

We flew within thirty miles of the snowy glaciated massif that culminates in Mount McKinley. The whole appalling white bulk of it dominated the barren landscape to starboard, clear as crystal. We put down at outposts called McGrath and Unalakleet and crossed part of the Bering Sea to Nome, passing over a small gold mine on the beach.

Nome had a frontier look, as well it might. Its sketchy little main street was lined with scattered one-story shops and houses, a two-story wooden hotel, and a lunch room, where we ate reindeer. On the beach there was the hulk of an old whaler. Scattered over the tundra were Eskimo shacks of rough lumber, propped up on stones and usually askew; for the land buckles each spring when the surface thaws above the permafrost.

It seemed bitter cold. The landlady in the hotel agreed. She said she was always glad when the Bering Sea freezes; it reduces the humidity and therewith the discomfort.

We flew north across the mountainous backbone of the Seward Peninsula, the headland nearest Siberia, and swooped down over an arm of the Arctic Ocean to Kotzebue. A little seaplane was moored to a big whalebone on the beach. A stocky Eskimo woman with a circular face was dressed in a handsome sealskin parka and mukluks. The noonday sun was low. We sensed a wholesome Arctic aura about the tiny village that contrasted with the perhaps misleadingly squalid look of Nome.

We flew to Fairbanks, crossing the broad Yukon River and leaving tundra for woodland. The streets of sub-arctic Fairbanks, with their two- and three-story houses and yards, could have been in some modest older neighborhood in Akron. We sadly flew over part of Yukon Territory and the whole of the scenic Alaska panhandle in the dead of night. By September 18, 1959, we were home.

For me the attraction of Beacon Hill had been partly its own old-world charm and partly its contiguity to more of the same. I could walk over the hill into the largely picturesque West End and on to the best and oldest, the North End. There were little streets, an unexpected pushcart around the next turn, a foreign language. Just before we moved to Beacon Hill, some old streets on the nearer edge of the North End had to my sorrow been bulldozed for an ugly elevated highway. But the full tragedy, the sack of Boston, had been raging during our fifteen months away. The West End had been converted to hills of rubble and ragged remnants of half-demolished houses. The scene was that of a bombed European city. Boston's two city fathers, the mayor and the urban renewer, had envied the Europeans' opportunity for a building program and had created their own desolation, ignoring the public outcry.

My Japanese friends wanted me represented in a volume of theirs. I shared the sentiment and still I did not want to bury a significant piece in an inaccessible volume. I sent them "Posits and reality," an opening section of *Word and Object* that had dropped out in the course of my revisions. I had persistently rewritten that book for fear of harping unduly on the obvious, and Dreben tells me that I overdid those precautions. He and others have found "Posits and reality" helpful as orientation to the book, and it has accordingly been accessibly reprinted.

Another loose end carried over from Japan was a hernia. It was as if my fabric had melted in the humid heat. The Christmas vacation lent itself to the operation at the hands of my friend Jack Fine.

· 1960   Roman Jakobson drew me into a meeting in New York on mathematics in linguistics. My paper was "Logic as a source of syntactical insights." To my delighted surprise I found Fred Cassidy there. We walked the streets of New York, so walkworthy in those days, and talked at length.

I happily consented to address Philadelphia's American

Philosophical Society. My audience there would represent all fields, philosophy least of all. Still I wanted my piece to be new in content. I thought back to "Toward a calculus of concepts," my early venture in algebraizing the logic of quantification. That apparatus was not exactly intertranslatable with quantification and the truth functions, but I now devised one that was. It is what I have since called predicate-functor logic or term-functor logic. My paper was "Variables explained away."

The dignitaries at the Harvard commencement in June 1960 included Spaak, Menzies, J. F. Kennedy, the Patriarch of Armenia, and Nelson Rockefeller.

It was Jean Piaget's custom, at his institute in Geneva, to hold a five-day seminar each June at which his researchers would report their findings, and a few outsiders would be imported for critical discussion. I worked it into a well-packed trip of eighteen days.

I stopped for twenty-four hours on the island of Santa Maria in the Azores. Talking with the proprietor of a little roadside wine shop, I remarked on the green fertility of the countryside, the profusion of flowers, and the serene beauty of the little white and red farmhouses, plaster and roof tile, nestled among the trees. Philosophizing as is my wont, I said that people on such an island once felt deprived in their remoteness from the great centers, but that in the present era of shortages, congestion, unrest, and bomb scares, they in the peace and plenty of their sequestered isle are perhaps the lucky ones. Mine host quietly adduced data—that a pair of shoes might cost the farmer a month's income, that he might eat meat but once a week, and that he might afford an egg from his own hen only once in two or three days. A poignant reminder of the apparent incompatibility between the poetic and the abundant life.

The western half of the island is flat—hence the airport—and the eastern half is suddenly mountainous. I walked to the principal town, Vila do Porto, and then across to the precipitous east coast to look steeply down and down to the rock-girt little bay and islet of São Lourenço. Night was falling when I got to Santo Espírito and its great squarish black and white church, old, baroque, yet strangely surrealist. A taxi took me back ten miles to the airport hotel. In Lisbon, my next stop, I arose early for a walk in the steep, twisting old streets of the Alfama and the Mouraria before emplaning for Geneva.

Piaget was a robust and fine-looking old man with abundant white hair. He presided ably over the research reports. Afterward I contrived a quick visit to Mont Blanc for a walk on the gritty ice of the Mer de Glace and then set out for a few days in Paris, but was frustrated by an airline strike. I substituted Copenhagen, my further objective being Norway.

Dagfinn Føllesdal, successively my student, assistant, and colleague, had sketched a route across southern Norway for me. At the Oslo airport a woman in the government tourist service took his route in hand and swiftly arranged everything: hotel reservations, train, bus, and ship connections, a complex sequence.

Oslo was notable for a Viking ship, a restored village with blooming sod roofs, and Frogner Park with Gustav Vigeland's exuberant nude sculptures—a hundred individuals and families in acrobatic abandon, bigger than life. I stayed the night at Arne Naess's home.

Crossing Norway I visited two stave churches, those wild wooden caricatures of Gothic architecture from the dawn of Norse Christianity. At a fork in Sogne Fjord my ship and two others met and were lashed together to transfer passengers according to destination. At another point a young government guide was detailed at no extra charge to accompany me from ship to bus and from bus to train.

From Bergen I took an excursion to Lys Fjord, to the south, where the ship went to the very cliff; I could touch it from the deck. It rose a thousand feet sheer from the water, and dropped perhaps a thousand sheer below.

I flew from Stavanger to Iceland. It was early July and light all night. Walking in Reykjavik, I felt again as I had in Fairbanks: the houses could have been those of a humble older quarter of Akron. But on closer look a difference emerged: they were made of corrugated iron, painted. There is no timber in Iceland. I flew on to the States the next day and did justice to the sights in Iceland only twenty years later.

Four Years at Home 53

For four solid years, from July 1960 onward, I never strayed more than nine score leagues from Beacon Hill. (Akron is nine score leagues away as the crow flies.) I devoted two of the years to my set-theory book, so far as teaching and lesser projects permitted. At Bare Hill I was at it as many as fourteen hours a day, struggling with problems and taking satisfaction in neat maneuvers. It was a welcome relief from the inconclusiveness of philosophical speculation and exposition. I gained much from consultations with Burt Dreben.

My envisaged comparison of set theories encountered a curious expository problem. I needed to brief the reader on central themes, notably the infinite ordinals and cardinals and transfinite induction, if he was to appreciate the objectives and advantages of the various axiom systems. Such briefing needs some deductive structure, to lend plausibility to unintuitive properties. But deduction from mere uncodified plausibles is ill-suited to this domain, for it leads to paradox; we need the constraint of explicit axioms. Thus we are caught up, expositorily, in a circle. I coped with the predicament by beginning with weak axioms. To keep them weak, I exploited the virtual theory of classes and relations (chapter 30 above), which I integrated with the real theory of classes as a source of virtual supplementation. As the preliminary matter developed, parsimony and perspicuity jostled as rival objectives. The thickening book came to stress the logic at the bottom no less than the systems slated for comparion at the top. Logic was doing double duty in the virtual theory, which is just set theory logically simulated. Logic cried out for recognition in the title; hence *Set Theory and Its Logic*.

In May 1961 I was back in the hospital with a painful bout of pleurisy. I had been prone to colds, and the irritation caused by my excessive pipe-smoking was a factor. In Oxford I had compromised with the doctor by cutting down, only to resume my old ways when I got back to the pressures of Harvard life. The pleurisy, however, settled matters. While it continued, smoking was unthinkable; air was too painfully come by. This gave abstention a head start. When the pain was over, the memory of it lingered as a salutary warning. A smoking habit of thirty-five years thus ended.

I had long preferred the pipe to cigarettes, but I had inhaled it; the addiction was real. I smoked at work; tobacco fueled my output. After stopping, my work habits changed. There was less tendency to push a bad idea doggedly to a dead end; more tendency to pace the floor and descry the dead end from afar. The pipe had fostered compulsiveness by subduing a healthy impatience.

It occurred to me at the Society of Fellows the following year, as the cigars were passed around, that I was in the position of being able to savor a good cigar, as one is not whose taste is deadened by constant smoking. I smoked one, with moderate enjoyment at best. A week later I took one again, but stumped it in mid-career; it had no appeal. It was striking evidence of a lasting cure.

My efforts in set theory were interrupted again in the fall of 1961 by an invitation to speak at the University of Akron. In loyalty to the hometown it was a command performance. I had to be intelligible to non-specialists, so the natural topic was paradox. Later in the year my turn came to address our Shop Club at Harvard, and again I had to be intelligible to non-specialists; so I repeated my talk. Months afterward my fellow Shopclubman Jack Fine was still praising that talk and advising me to publish it. His season for polite response had passed, so I took him seriously and sent it to the *Scientific American*. Two years later I was invited to participate in a mathematics issue of that journal. Both papers reappeared in my collection *The Ways of Paradox* and in a book by *Scientific American*. Such were the consequences of a sentimental journey home.

· 1962   I gave three lectures at Bowdoin College in July 1962 on the history of modern logic. Reinhard Korgen provided us with a cottage for the week on Merepoint Neck facing Maquoit Bay. The rest of the summer, at Bare Hill, was marked by a doubling of our fleet: Marge supplemented the canoe with a Sailfish for my birthday.

I occasionally accepted a professional invitation for the sake of a reunion with Ed Haskell or Fred or Harold Cassidy. Thus it was that I spoke on logic in a Yale program on Frontiers in Philosophy that fall, and thus it was that I chaired a session at the philosophy congress in New York after Christmas. Those last days of 1962 were plagued with zero temperature, Fahrenheit, and incessant gales. My train back from New York got me to Boston at 5:30 on New Year's Eve and I walked home, the taxi drivers having fled the cold. We had a quiet evening and allowed the children to

· 1963   see 1963 in. A few minutes later a ceiling fell, followed by a torrent from a pipe that had burst in the attic. The very lighting fixtures were dripping. I turned off all power and water. The children took refuge with a neighbor.

Set Theory and Its Logic left my hands in April and I was aware for the first time in decades of not being at work on a book. It was in this propitious season that Robert Silvers of the *New York Review of Books* phoned to see if I would review Freddie Ayer's *Concept of a Person*. I was still disinclined to review anything, and had not heard of the *New York Review of Books*. Silvers named some illustrious contributors, and in their reflected light it was left that he would send me proofs of Freddie's book and I would see whether I was moved to write something. I read and annotated them as I lay drifting in my canoe on Bare Hill Pond, a way I had of reading on a summer day. In the end I found the book ill-suited to a review for a lay public. To console me for wasted time, Silvers sent me the new *National Geographic Atlas*; someone had told him I like maps. He said he would be glad if I felt moved to write about it, and as I idled over the rich pages the hint took hold. It was a fun review, gaily outside my field. I reviewed another atlas for him in a few months. Someone told him that I also like words, and he asked me to review the fat posthumous edition of Mencken's *American Language*. I already had an early edition, bristling with marginalia from my college days. By checking them against the new edition, I generated a lively review. In the next five years I took on a few more such unprofessional reviews—thus a history of cartography and two dictionaries for Silvers and an atlas for the *Chicago Tribune*. When these excursions from my main business lost their novelty, I stopped.

Hao Wang was back with us at Harvard. His was a persistently unhappy life amid success and good fortune. When I first heard from him, in 1942, he was unhappy in China and wanted to be brought to America. As a brilliant graduate student at Harvard he was unhappy in his insecurity. Publication and a Ph. D., he felt, would make all the difference. Both were forthcoming, as well as a Junior Fellowship in the Society of Fellows. Unhappy in his celibacy, he married an attractive and capable young geologist, Yenking. He was again unhappy, and they separated. He spent the third year of his Junior Fellowship at Zurich with Bernays, and from there he wrote me that any hope of happiness hinged on a post in philosophy at Harvard. We appointed him. He was not called on to teach anything off his beat, but he was unhappy. He arranged a year's leave to work at Burroughs and see how he liked the computer industry. At length he accepted a readership at Oxford. He and Yenking, reunited, were perhaps happy there, but after some years he was lured back to a chair at Harvard in computer theory. Such was his

· 1964   post in the spring of 1964, when we collaborated briefly on neat ways of generating the infinite ordinals. By then he was outspokenly bitter about the West and staunch for Red China. His move to Rockefeller University was still to come.

He was a gifted mathematical logician. His rehabilitation of my *Mathematical Logic* and his proof of relative consistency (chapter 25) were two notable results among many. He did deep and significant work on proof theory and the relative strength of deductive systems.

I had spent only three of the six academic years 1953–1959 teaching at Harvard, but all of the next five. My past publications had meanwhile imposed an increasing burden of upkeep; there were corrections to prepare for new printings, translations to check, and voluminous correspondence with readers. The problem of combining teaching with scholarly production was thus aggravated. Teaching loads were kept equal across ranks, with the result that my past productivity was penalized rather than rewarded. I put the matter to President Pusey without success, so by 1964 I was receptive again to outside offers.

There was a generous one again from Penn. Marge and I visited Duncan Luce's little town house in one of Philadelphia's refurbished mews to get a sense of the amenities. From New York I had the offer of one of the fabled Schweitzer chairs. My office would have been in Forty-second Street across from the Public Library, in the incipient graduate center of the City University of New York. It was on a fine spring day that I walked from Penn Station to Forty-second Street to confer with the chancellor and P. P. Wiener. Spanish was the prevalent language of passers-by, and it warmed my heart. But I was alarmed by an appropriation that would be put at my disposal. I would feel negligent in not putting it to use, and I had no desire to run a miniature institute.

My friends Ray Nelson and Mortimer Kadish invited me to Case Western Reserve in Cleveland on lavish terms: high salary, duties at my discretion. Academic contacts would be meagerer than around Boston, New York, or Philadelphia, but there was the attraction of the native heath.

My sabbatical leave from Harvard, 1964–1965, was at hand. I could hope in the course of it for a perspective in which to set the gains over against the losses in leaving Harvard. I did not want to keep Penn or C.U.N.Y. in suspense meanwhile; for my Cleveland friends, on the other hand, time was no consideration. So, having Western Reserve in reserve, I declined Penn and C.U.N.Y.

Six Characters in Search   54

Marge and I proposed to spend the first term of the sabbatical traveling with Doug and Margaret in Europe and the Near East, and the second at the Center for Advanced Study at Wesleyan College.

Remembering our trip across Mexico with my daughter Norma six years before, I reflected that I might well do something with Elizabeth. I wrote to her in California inviting her to come at my expense with her daughter Melissa and her husband Chuck O'Brien, if he could get away, to spend a month or so with us at Bare Hill before we sailed. In response I learned that she and Chuck had separated. I then proposed instead that she and Melissa come later and accompany us on our great trip.

We were Melissa, Margaret, Doug, Elizabeth, Marge, and I, aged 9, 10, 13, 29, 46, and 56. Doug flew to Geneva a month early to visit Swiss friends. At the end of August 1964 I contrived to stow our car and a load of gear at Wesleyan for the spring term and then maneuver the five of us and our nine suitcases to the SS *Hanseatic* in New York. To my weary eyes the receding skyline was a gratifying scene, enhanced by the sight of champagne from Bob and Rosalie and flowers from Elsa Sturenburg of Bare Hill.

The crossing was luxurious, even in our lowly class, except for the tail of hurricane Cleo. It had the ship rolling and put us fifty miles off course. The mountainous waves were a glorious sight for all who did not sicken. The storm was raging when we passed the Grand Banks in the night and saw the lights of as many as six vessels at once—fishermen or Russian observers, stout fellow either way.

As soon as we had immigrated at Southampton, we sought out such bits of the old city as had weathered the Blitz; for I was impatient to give Elizabeth, Margaret, and Melissa the excitement of medieval scenes. Thence by train twelve miles to Winchester for the night. The thirteenth-century school and cathedral, the city gate with the chapel on top, and the generous lengths of medieval streets gladdened our hearts and gratefully eased our antiquity deficiency.

Off then to acquaint Margaret with her native Oxford, where Doug joined us. We lodged in the Mitre, which was still unspoiled, a blend of quiet elegance and hoary antiquity. Its crooked corridors traversed the upper stories of a succession of old buildings along the High and the Turl.

We were lionized. Peter Geach and Elizabeth Anscombe had the six of us to dinner, along with their small children and their grown-up son John and his girl. The children from Doug down played a game that had them clattering up and down through the lofty house. I prized John's way of excusing himself for a few moments from his girl: "Be brave."

Marcus Dick drove the six of us one day to a splendid dinner at an inn in the picturesque stone village of Aynho, in the southwest corner of Northamptonshire. The Dummetts had us all to tea, and we admired the delicate sandwiches of watercress and banana. We dined at the Strawsons', at the Urmsons', at Gilbert Ryle's, and at Philippa Foot's. Paul Streeten took me to dinner at Balliol, and lent me his car so that we could drive through the villages of Wiltshire and Berkshire to Stonehenge. I had good walks and talks in Oxford with Peters Geach and Strawson.

Such were our ten tight days in Oxford. It was relaxing to disappear into Stratford and Warwick. We walked on to Kenilworth, whose thirteenth-century castle would be rather like Warwick's were it not a towering ruin. It is sad that this circumstance adds to its romantic impact.

During our week in London, Woodger came in from Epsom to talk logic with me, and I went out to Penn to see Popper. Antiquity deepened in Canterbury with its seventh-century Christian buildings in salvaged Roman brick, and in

Dover with its octagonal Roman tower, Norse church, and massive Norman castle.

And so to Paris, with hotel memoranda gathered from friends. Off-season as we were, I would make the rounds and choose on the spot. I left Doug at the Gare du Nord with sandwiches and suitcases, and shepherded the girls and ladies by Métro to the Latin Quarter.

We proved to be the grudging butts of a tired Fortune's forced hilarity. We tried two of the recommended hotels; both were full. We deployed our forces and canvassed twenty little hotels of the district indiscriminately and in vain, in the rain. I tried the Restaurant de la Méditerranée, in the Place de l'Odéon, thinking in my haste that there was a hotel in connection. The proprietor proved to be a *grand restaurateur*, a friend of Bemelmans and host to princes. He seated my four charges and plied them with refreshments while I tried further hotels that he suggested, again in vain. At length he found a room for Marge and me in a minimal establishment called St.-Sulpice, and the landlady squeezed a cot in for Doug. Elizabeth, Melissa, and Margaret he accommodated in a flat of his own. I fetched poor Doug and his cargo by taxi in the rain and the five o'clock traffic. Next morning I resumed the quest, and by eleven we were all ensconced in the Hôtel de la Faculté for two nights.

So I resolved to show my descendants what they needed to see of Paris in under two days and then to clear gratefully out. On foot and by Métro we did swift justice to the top of Montmartre, the top of the Eiffel Tower, and the dozen best sights in between. We threaded the old streets of the Left Bank and spent hours in the Louvre. The rain moderated and occasionally stopped. Several of us concluded our last evening with a fast walk around the three-mile quadrilateral formed by Boulevards St.-Germain, Raspail, Montparnasse, and St.-Michel. The rain changed to a brisk tailwind in time to blow us home.

At Dijon we collapsed easily into an ugly hotel within lugging distance of the station. Next morning Elizabeth, Melissa, and I walked five miles south to the narrow-streeted, steep-roofed stone village of Couchey and its little Hôtel du Luxembourg. After engaging rooms for the six of us for the next few days, we walked five miles back to home base in an unusually heavy rain.

Our ways subsequently parted. Marge, Doug, and Margaret went to Geneva to visit the Renolds, our Swiss friends with whom Doug had so recently spent a month. Albert Renold is a physiologist, head of a research laboratory on diabetes; they had been our next neighbors on Beacon Hill. Scrupling to impose all six of us on their hospitality, Elizabeth, Melissa, and I made for Montreux at the far end of the lake. The dreamlike splendor of the snowy Savoy Alps over the glittering lake blended with the dreamlike efficiency of the Swiss hotelier and the dreamlike impeccability of his hotel to make of Montreux a haven and a heaven.

We took the cog trailway to the Rochers de Naye, a mile higher than the lake. For a moment the clouds parted and revealed the abyss, a chastening glimpse. So as not to wade in the snow, we rode back down to a village at the snow line and descended on foot from there. Torrential rain overtook us, as was its wont. Next morning we ranged up the slopes again, through a gorge and green forests and above noisy white water to a dizzy old village called Sanzier, a tight cluster of stone chalets decked out with heavy timber eaves and galleries.

Marge, Doug, and Margaret joined us in Montreux. At the Castle of Chillon we relished the romantic scene that is graven in the memory of everyone who looks at calendars, postcards, or jigsaw puzzles, and shuddered to see where the prisoner had been chained. From Montreux we ascended by train the Alp-girt Rhone past castle-studded Sion and other sightly towns until, at Brig, we veered underground. We emerged from the Simplon Tunnel in Italy, skirted Lago Maggiore, and soon were in Milan.

Four of us went to Lake Como to see Tecla, our *au pair* girl
of eleven years before in Oxford. Her village of Volesio was
a medieval maze. In its intermittently covered passages, as
in those of Tetuán, one was indoors as much as out.

On another day we six went on to Venice. It is like a Japanese house, where you step out of your shoes in a vestibule
and step into a domain untouched by grit and grime of the
outer world. In Venice it is a matter not of shoes but of cars,
and the vestibule is the Piazzale di Roma. For a whole serene week we saw no cars and heard none, except on two
brief occasions. One was when, on an ill-starred impulse,
three of us stayed on the *vaporetto* to the end of the line, at
the Lido. The other time was when we went to the Piazzale
itself, that outpost of hell, to book seats for Ravenna.

The magic of Venice was undampened even by the flood.
But flood there was, what with the secular subsiding of the
city and the seasonal rain and east wind. Boardwalks were
laid on St. Mark's Square, and in the entrance to the cathedral the water was almost knee deep.

The Venetian dialect emerges on street signs. There was
de for *di*, *de la* for *della*, *dei* for *degli*. It is soft. For "Che
bella" I heard "Che bea," like Mexican Spanish. And there
is the curious *z*: *Zulian* for *Giuliano*. *Zanipolo* for *Gian e
Paolo*.

The bus to Ravenna crossed the Po delta, serving Chiog-
gia, which was a foil to the Venice it is said to resemble. It
has a good canal, some creditable passageways, and much of
Venice in its houses, but it is a town of drivable streets,
blighted by cars.

There was no inkling of the wonders of Ravenna as we approached the city through a new hell of heavy industry and
got off the bus between parking lot and rail station. I settled
my five charges on a bench with the luggage, as so often,

and sought a hotel with balconies over an old-world square, only to end up in the new Jolly Hotel overlooking a parking lot. But the city improved in our evening walk. There were streets without sidewalks, and they were lined with old houses. There were Early Christian churches, even in excess of the short Michelin guide. The impact of the mosaics next day banished all reservations.

I scratched San Marino. It would have been my third visit and a welcome one, but my charges showed no eagerness, and time was wasting. They would see other hill towns, and my special predilection for small countries was perhaps not shared. I learned only in the Vatican City that it was shared and that San Marino was regretted.

In order to cross the Appenines and reach Florence by day, we broke the journey from Ravenna at Brisighella. A long, winding two-story street there was reminiscent of the rows at Chester, but with an irregularity that enhanced the air of mystery. A church and campanile crowned a startlingly abrupt hill, and a castle crowned another. The implausible hills shown by early Venetian painters reflected, I had supposed, a Venetian's ignorance of hills, but Brisighella was a vindication.

As we were making the rounds of the Florentine wonders, we ran into Myron Gilmore. He wafted us to Berenson's palace, I Tatti, where he was director. On another day we took train and bus to San Gimignano, a walled hilltop town bristling with absurdly tall medieval towers. For lunch the family went up to a little ruined tower at the top, *la Rocca*, with their cheese and tomatoes, while I shopped for wine and warm bread. When I made to join them, a witch at the wicket said no eating. So I shouted my family down from the tower and we had our picnic at the wicket.

Prowling the town, we were overtaken by a lonely old bore with heart of gold who was bent on showing us around. Leaving my family to cope with him, I vanished and gleefully probed all passages. At length and of itself our family of six fell together and we returned to Florence.

To get us to Rome I bought into a Florence-Rome sightseeing bus. When it had taken us as far as Perugia, it pulled in at the Hotel Excelsior for an optional subscription lunch. We six emphatically declined the option, so as to use the time for climbing to the top of the old city; we would grab a quick snack on foot in the course of our explorations.

Perugia was big and its medievalism was abundant, luxurious. It crowded in on you, towered over you, and piled up and up. You could lean on it, wallow in it. You could hurry through it and not be caught short, not end up presently in the fields with the dream behind you.

We started back to the Hotel Excelsior to join the bus. Elizabeth would take the children the shortest way, which I indicated, so as to get the girls to the bathroom. Marge and I, exploiting our adult bladders, would make a more devious and picturesque descent. As we descended, Marge questioned my orientation. I inquired and turned out to be wrong. The children were getting ever farther down the back of the mountain. We got to the bus at the appointed time, and the children were not there. I circulated in a taxi looking for them. When I got back, they had arrived, breathless. It was much to their credit, given the strange land and language. "They should be spanked," said an American passenger, indignant of the delay. Wrong, madam, I should be spanked. And the bathroom? Well, some other time.

Next stop: Assisi. The compact town tapers into a western bastion or forecastle which is the church of St. Francis. Its back walls drop sheer to the fields below the town. We toured the great church and its Giottos, but I regretted not prowling the inviting old streets again.

We plunged into Spoleto at its very heart and were benighted in a tunnel. Trevi I recognized from afar as in 1929 and 1933—a single mass of masonry capping a conical mountain. So to Rome and to bed in the Albergo del Senato.

In the morning we looked across from our window to the colonnaded façade of the miraculously intact Pantheon with its 27 B.C. credit line to M. Agrippa. We soon had crossed Piazza Navona and the Tiber to Hadrian's hulking tomb and continued to the Vatican, lured by the boundary and, for Elizabeth, Sunday mass in St. Peter's.

Off then to the swaggering white monument to Vittorio Emmanuele II, beyond which the eye comes to grateful rest upon the Campidoglio, or Capitoline Hill. Equestrian Marcus Aurelius, larger than life, shares the scene and the view of the tasteful symmetries and proportions wrought by Michelangelo. Beyond are the brick-red expanses and masses of Roman antiquity. The fora are backed by ruined temples and basilicas and by the dashing, steep palace of the crusading Knights of Malta, and faced by the Palatine Hill with its gardens and ruined palaces of emperors. The Colosseum looms in the offing, and the arch that celebrates Titus for his conquest of Jerusalem.

What I have called my antiquity deficiency might better have been diagnosed as a medievality deficiency; for I unconsciously resisted Rome in 1929 and was apathetic in 1933, apparently in consequence of my odd old distaste for schoolwork. By 1964, in any event, antiquity came into its own, and I eagerly studied the guidebook as we made the rounds.

This despite a miserable cold and fever. I did forgo two walks, and was still in a bad way when we entrained for Brindisi, at Italy's remote heel, bound for Greece. In the train we peopled a compartment of six *couchettes*. They were transverse planks stacked in threes: lower, middle, upper. Each had a small blanket and a wisp of sheet. What with my coughing and frequent retiring to the *ritirata* to cope with my phlegm and rheum, the six of us had a rough night. We were roused at Bari, and so observed the remaining miles of Apulian olive groves. Thick, gnarled trunks leaned and divided fantastically.

We found our way to the proper dock in Brindisi at eleven and expected to board ship at noon. We were kept waiting, little by little, for seven hours. After two hours I took my descendants to lunch; Marge stayed with the luggage, professing to want only an apple and cheese that we might bring back. Obtruding his helpfulness, a native marshaled us to a *pizzeria* and made a point of being noticed by the proprietress. I asked her for a list, remembering shady practices in Ravenna and elsewhere. She produced none, but tried to seem motherly. I would have moved on, but it was Sunday and restaurants were not in evidence. We ordered modestly. I estimated a thousand lire; she charged five. I said I would go to the *questura*. She said four. I went, and came back with troops: two uniformed officers in a car, one on a bicycle, and one on foot. The bill was adjusted to a midpoint, 2500, which I suppose is the way. I was still cheated, but had given the villainous proprietress a bad moment. Her husband may have pursued an unsympathetic line of his own when we had gone.

Brindisi felt Balkan. Greek signs were frequent, and Italian faces no longer predominated. The plastered little houses in the back streets suggested the Near East, or Mexico.

Greece Again 56

It was a hell ship called the Κυπρός, of Cypriot registry. The bungled beginning was in character. The cabin boy spoke no language west of Greek, but I beckoned him down the passage and pointed to the clogged washbowls and the unapproachable toilets. By the next morning someone had done the Augean labor that I had hinted at. We passed Ithaca and other sunlit Ionian isles and the length of the mountain-girt gulf to the Corinth Canal. This ancient engineering achievement is a sea-level ditch, one ship wide, a steep vee in cross-section, and straight as a die. Sighting along it, you do not expect it to be four miles long nor its sides to rise over three hundred feet at midpassage.

I had selected the Adrian Hotel in Athens from a government pamphlet on the strength of its position on the map; for it appeared to be in the quarter under the Acropolis that I remembered from thirty-two years before for its medieval aspect. The sloping old quarter is called the Plaka, we learned, and ours was a good little hotel with a view up to the Acropolis from our back windows and views of Hadrian's Library and the Roman Forum from other sides.

I remembered a miniature Byzantine church halfway up the slope. We now found two more below. All have the squat Orthodox dome and are built of polychrome blocks, red to brown, of brick and granite. You have to stoop, almost, to enter.

The gem of the Plaka is the elegant little octagonal marble Tower of the Winds, from the first century B.C., with festoons in delicate relief around the sides and personified winds around the cornices. The central square of the Plaka is Hadrian's Square, an earthen rectangle faced by our hotel. There are folding chairs, and if you sit there a man materializes and takes your order for Turkish coffee.

For dinner we would go to a *taverna*, usually the Seven Brothers, near the Tower of the Winds, and make our selections from the steaming pots and platters. For lunch we would go to a stand at the foot of the Plaka, where a cylinder of succulent lamb some two feet high and eight inches thick was mounted on a vertical spit alongside a rack of burning charcoal. The cook would turn it and deftly cut thin, bubbling slices into a generous cone of unleavened bread, adding onions, lettuce, tomato, and yogurt. The result, sheer perfection, was called a νδώνηρ, *doner,* and cost thirteen cents.

One evening we tried a restaurant called Kewpie. Here there was no bank of pots and platters to peer into; a menu was brought. One of us sensed that the figures ran higher than those posted down at the sidewalk. I went down to look. The proprietor emerged too, so I rounded the corner as if on an errand. When he had gone in, I checked and found substantial discrepancies. I summoned my five charges and we filed out. Already the typewritten menu at the sidewalk had been deftly supplanted by a handwritten one matching the one we had been shown. The substitute was still there days later, despite being less calculated to draw customers. The man was afraid he had been reported. Weeks later the original was restored. I am the scourge of shady *restaurateurs.*

The Greeks are an intent and unselfconscious lot. They jostle you a bit on the crowded sidewalk with neither rancor nor apology. Occasionally a fight breaks out. One in the Seven Brothers was dissolved by the proprietress, who ejected the combatants bare-handed.

Don and Ginny Davidson were living in a flat at the foot of Lycabettus, an abrupt little mountain in the midst of Athens. All six of us went to them for an evening of Eastern food and drink and Western conversation. Don's recent pupil John Wallace was there.

On November 21, 1964, I joined Don and John for a day's jaunt to Mount Pentele. We rode a bus to a monastery from which the mountain was visible. The monks were under a vow of silence, so we proceded by dead reckoning, but were at length turned back by a sentry. Another lane brought us to a series of quarries, where inquiries in Don's incipient modern Greek netted us some inconsistent counsel and a truck ride up the slope. Continuing upward on foot through the rain and scrub and over jagged scraps of marble and into a rain cloud, we came to a guarded gate. The guards let us through to warmth and shelter but gave us only the vaguest instructions as to how to get down the other side of the mountain. Shivering with cold, we picked our way down the steep and stony slope toward the invisible gulf in the clouds below. Finally a quarry road led us out of our wet cloud into the temperate lowland. In the village of Dionysus we sat in a café, thawed, talked, and drank *retsina;* thence by bus to Athens. Apart from some constructive discussion along the way, centering on the concept of stimulation in *Word and Object,* the outing was poor.

After nine days in Athens, we went south by bus. A stop yielded a view of Acrocorinth, the theopolis of ancient Corinth. Pressing on through the Peleponnesus, we came as close as the bus would get to Mycenae. Here a boy put me onto a busline employee, who put me onto a telephone man, who shouted into the phone for a taxi, which took us to the Xenia Hotel, which was booked up. We moved into the Mycenae Palace, a shabby Balkan dwelling with rooms to rent. Ours was strong in icons and weak in illumination and the bed was hard. The water supply was cut off before we could get to our evening ablutions. There was no buzzer and no identifiable door to knock at, so I stood in the hall and yelled until a man came and turned the pump back on.

We were on a trajectory into ever deepening antiquity: from California to New England for two of us, then on to England, Ravenna, Rome, Athens, and Mycenae. Crete and Egypt were in the offing. From Periclean Athens to Mycenae was alone an ascent of a thousand years. Agamemnon's Tomb, alias the Treasury of Atreus, is an intact building of 3500 summers, an earth-covered beehive tomb thirty-odd feet high, smoothly lined with meticulously fitted stone. Its vaulting is a thousand-year anticipation of the touted Roman arch, if we waive a technicality having to do with flanges on the keystones. "Look," Rome exulted, "no hands!"

A narrow stone road penetrates the city wall of the Mycenaean acropolis through the Lion Gate, which is topped by a bas-relief in dark stone of two lions rampant with an altar between. The acropolis is laden with utter ruins tier on tier, but the encircling wall stands firm and harbors doorways with sudden stairs. One flight goes down into the blackness a hundred steps.

We rode a bus to Argos, seven miles, and paid cursory respects to the Argive acropolis. The next bus took us three more miles to scenic Nauplion, on the Aegean. Abruptly seaward of center there rises a granite peak topped with a monastery. An islet in the bay is crowned with a crusaders' castle. We settled into a wooden hotel in an old quarter by the sea.

A local bus took us to Tiryns, where King Eurytheus is said to have assigned Hercules his Herculean labors, and a long-range bus took us to Poros, up and down dizzy slopes and along tortuous brinks. The scene was grand, and more gratifying, if less thrilling, such times as the driver was facing and driving in the same direction. It was still bright day when we dropped to the narrow sound that separates Poros from the mainland and were pleased to find no bridge such as the map had shown. Poros was a free island, free of any leash, and we were rowed to it. We climbed steps to a little hotel at the bold corner of a village that was tightly packed between slope and sea. Streets were squeezed narrow and close to avoid or minimize the climb; other streets climbed by steps.

Several little ships serve Poros, each with its agent in one or another shop or café on the quay. The *Mario* for Hydra docked at noon and was immediately ready to go. I had to run for it, newly acquired tickets in hand. My family had been allowed aboard and the gangplank had been lifted, but it was let down for me.

Steep mountainsides flank the narrow harbor of Hydra, and a steep whitewashed town cups the end of the inlet. The whitewash is slapped thick onto the fat plaster sides of the little houses and continues for a foot out onto the pavement, where it terminates in a neat line to leave an unwhitened path for foot traffic. Narrow streets twist their devious ways up the slopes among white houses, opening startling vistas.

Elizabeth decided to settle with Melissa on Hydra for an indefinite period. She found a pleasant little house for seventeen dollars a month, a figure compatible with her slender alimony. Reduced thus to four, we returned by way of Aegina to Athens. Our ship Χάρα from Aegina to Piraeus rolled through fully forty degrees and the crests of the waves washed the deck. Doug was miserable, and Marge was sure then and in retrospect that we were in grave danger.

I sent Elizabeth a bank draft from Athens, canceled her flight and Melissa's to Egypt, collected the refund, and postponed their passage to America. As we walked back at last toward the hotel at about six, I felt something pass my ankle. My wallet was on the sidewalk, containing the refund. It was high time to get my tattered pocket replaced. I found a tailor near the hotel. Having got his price—rather high—

and his promise to have my trousers for me next morning, I went to our room, changed trousers, and brought him the bad ones. By then he had raised his price and his time estimate. I asked a cobbler where I could find another tailor. He sent me up a neighboring stairway to a top floor. I showed a man what I wanted, and he talked at length to another man, who, it developed, would take me to a tailor on his way home. He led me on a devious course through a mile of crowded streets and turned me over to a janitor, who took me up an elevator and across a roof and through an unposted door into a big room where tailors and seamstresses were working. A man quoted a low price and promised to finish by the same time next evening. I went back to the street, noted its name and those of neighboring streets, and took a taxi to the hotel. Margaret came with me next evening. We were kept waiting and meanwhile were plied with lemonade and coffee and the schoolgirl English of the tailor's daughter, while the mother eagerly witnessed the English exercise.

On December 3 the Davidsons saw us off to Cairo on the first and last flight in our five months of travel.

Egypt   57

Egypt had fascinated Marge ever since her school days. She knew what sites she wanted to see. I knew no Arabic, and mistrusted Egyptians; so, despite my usual distaste for conducted tours, I had put the whole affair into the hands of the Egyptian government tourist agency Eastmar. They tailored us a private tour, with much retracing because of the problem of finding available space.

A black driver from Eastmar met our plane, saw us through the bureaucracy, and drove us to the Semiramis Hotel in the night. Big servants in gaudy flowing garments and turbans took us through lofty red-carpeted halls to our absurdly large bedrooms, anterooms, and balconies. There was an excess of garish easy chairs and ornate tables, and of cabinets and chests into which to distribute one's poor effects if one were staying. Four of the gaudy barbarians arrived with the luggage and stood their ground pending a round of tips.

We were up before six and southbound at 7:30 in a luxurious train built in Soviet Hungary. Metropolis gave way to green, flat countryside bordered with palms. Water buffaloes wallowed in ditches or pulled plows. Gowned natives stood, walked, or rode donkeys. Camels carried loads of sugarcane or dried palm fronds. Villages were of adobe. Many houses were piled high with fronds, which were used for fuel and served meanwhile as insulation from the sun. There was a *shadouf* here and there for spilling Nile water into ditches. It is a pole with a bucket at one end and a weight at the other. A man stood in the ditch and plied it. Water wheels, serving the same purpose on a larger scale, were run by rotary power provided by a man, buffalo, or donkey walking round and round. Mills were similarly operated. Beyond the lush and populous green, the sands and barren hills of the desert were visible to the east and west; irrigation made the difference.

From Minya, 130 miles upstream from Cairo, we were taken by car into the western desert to see Tuna el Gabal, where a cliff depicts Ikhnaton and his family in bas-relief. Catacombs were lined with the mummies of thousands of monkeys and ibes, or ibides, but the environs were alive with buffalo and colorful natives on camels.

We drove back to the Nile and our guide whistled for a broad, battered motor ferry run by two turbaned wild men. A plank was put out from deck to mud. We were met at the other shore by a riot of color and a riot. Boys with donkeys clamored to transport us. A guard in flowing white, with a rifle slung from his shoulder, was menacing the boys with a long switch and beating the donkeys to clear our way. It was a scramble of some thirty natives, ten donkeys, and two guards. We walked to a village, accompanied by the rabble as closely as the guards with their flicking switches would permit, and then continued by jeep to the flat ruins of Ikhnaton's mud-brick palace.

A sleeping car conveyed us from Minya to Aswan, where Nubia, in black Africa, begins: the First Cataract. A small Nubian drove us to the old Cataract Hotel, which played the Peninsula, Raffles, and Shepheard's to Aswan's Hong Kong, Singapore, and Cairo. A plaster palace in subdued pink, it sat its hill easily, its soft lines further softened by palms and sycamores. Winding walks descended its steep tropical garden to a turbulent Nile studded with rocks and islands. Black and rounded by water and windblown sand, the rocks suggested elephants.

Towering feluccas, lateen-rigged with triangular sails like my Sailfish, scudded among the rocks and islets, each manned by a single Nubian. To furl his sail for the night or reef it against strong wind, the sailor hoisted the lower hem of his gown to his teeth and climbed the dizzy mast and yard as he might a coconut palm.

We were driven across the Nile on the old Aswan dam, nearly two miles long, and then south through desert hills until we were upstream from the high dam that the Russians were building. The dam was to continue rising for two more years, and Lake Nasser with it. We boarded an old side-wheeler, the *Star of Alexandria*, and steamed up through Nubia for twenty-seven hours to Abu Simbel, just short of the Sudan border. The course was 170 miles of narrow lake or swollen Nile, typically a mile wide, flanked by sandy desert and tan mountains. On the bank we saw from time to time a row or two of Nubian houses, painted perhaps with crude designs on and about the door. Always deserted, these were the hindmost houses of villages whose forward houses had already dissolved, as adobe will, into the rising waters.

At length bunches of green appeared in midstream. They were the tops of tall palms standing on what had been the irrigated land beside the Nile. Continuing south, we saw whole crowns of palms above water. All the green of Nubia was submerged and gone except these palm tops; there was just lake and desert. The water was destined still to rise twice as high. Inhabited Nubia was wiped out, except at Aswan, and its inhabitants were resettled downstream. Our driver in Aswan told us that he and his parents had been happy in a village on the Sudan border and now they were paupers in a foreign land.

The *Star of Alexandria* anchored at Abu Simbel. A coffer dam shielded the two temples from the rising Nile while the operation began of cutting them out of the bedrock block by block, in preparation for reassembling them above the cliff. Sand was being heaped about the façades and interior walls to cushion the fall of a precious block in case of a fumble. Little Nubian *fellahin* were spooning the sand with hand shovels. Seen against the colossal backdrop, it seemed a hopeless labor. Thus far the great portal of the larger temple had been partly blocked with sand and scaffolds. It was flanked by four statues of Ramses II, sixty-six feet high, carved out of bedrock and knee-deep in sand. The cliff façade behind them bore a big relief of hawk-headed Horus and, higher up, a cornice of bas-relief baboons. We entered the portal through a large tube of corrugated iron. The halls, hewn out of the mountain, were scrupulously finished and adorned with painted reliefs and with seated statues of the deified Ramses and other gods.

There were two young ship's officers in European garb on board the *Star of Alexandria*, and two waiters in the flowing raiment of the East. Doug and Margaret worked with them at Arabic alphabet and vocabulary during our three days afloat. The pilot and sailors were little Nubians in desert dress. For much of its course the ship zigzagged on the broad water. What with the palms that occasionally met the surface, and those that did not, the zigzags were not gratuitous. The pilot continued his uncanny navigation in the night, with the saloon curtains drawn so as not to impair his night vision. His only shore clues were modulations of the desert hills.

Kalabsha, a noble temple begun under the Ptolemies and finished under Augustus, had already been wrested from the rising waters and reassembled near Aswan. A group of Ptolemaic and Roman temples, Philae, lay submerged between the old and new dams. We were rowed to Philae by four Nubians and a boy at the tiller. They chanted to time their strokes. We beached on the roof of a temple, of which only the twin pylons stuck out of the water. Nearby was a quasi-Grecian temple due to Rome's Trajan, of which just the roof and the upper quarter of the columns were exposed.

Our guide in Aswan was a dark mixture named Abd el Wahab Gaddos. The first part means *father* of Wahab—a curious custom of honoring one's son. He showed us a quarry, the source of granite for temples built two hundred miles downstream. Granite had been cut by drilling holes, driving sycamore into them, and expanding it by wetting. The greatest of all obelisks lay there, still *in situ*, cut half free in ancient times and then abandoned because of a crack. The ancients would excise an obelisk, then excavate so as to balance it, and cut a ramp for it in the bedrock. They would ease the obelisk down the ramp and onto a barge in a canal dug for the purpose.

A felucca bore us swiftly to the islands. On Elephantine Island a stone stairway was cut in the bedrock and calibrated in cubits to measure the height of the annual flood water. Out beyond an expanse of ruins on the island there was a living Nubian village, a tight little tangle of narrow ways which I explored. The black inhabitants seemed surprised, but when I said "Salaam aleicum" they relaxed and responded in kind.

We flew north to the awesome temples of Luxor. A mile-long avenue of sphinxes leads on to Karnak, where the temple of Amon Ra was intermittently abuilding for two thousand years. Passing between its high pylons and its colossi of omnipresent Ramses II, one enters Hypostyle Hall—a gross or dozen dozen, almost, of crowded columns sixty feet high and ten feet thick. The builder spaced them within reach of his roof slabs, not knowing about vaulting. The walls depict Seti's Syrian campaign. Hit the Hittites, smite the Semites.

Across the Nile is the Theban city of the dead. In the sandy Valley of the Kings the bases of the barren mountains are honeycombed with secret royal tombs. Corridors lead deep into the earth, branching and opening into chambers supported by columns carved *in situ* out of the bedrock. Walls are delicately carved or frescoed with scenes of the spirit world and its wrong-headed deities—hawk-headed Horus, jackal-headed Anubis, and the rest.

For the next few days we steamed south in the gleaming vessel *Nefertari* and visited great later temples. One at Edfu, Ptolemaic, is hemmed about by an enormous wall, just a few feet from the temple itself, that is covered with pictures and hieroglyphs in relief—a voluminous illustrated record of the life of the time. The temple at Esna is mainly Greco-Roman, its reliefs incongruous in their juxtaposition of Egyptian gods and Roman emperors. In Esna we walked through the narrow and largely covered streets of a bazaar to the gentle swish of the beggars' *"Bakshish, bakshish!"* When we got back to the boat a piper was charming his cobra at the bank.

The *bakshish* litany was ubiquitous in Egypt; even museum guards begged. Other Arab countries that I have seen are not thus plagued. The white Moslem Egyptians call themselves Arabs to distinguish themselves from Nubians and Copts, but surely there is more of old Egypt than of Arabia in their blood.

On the *Nefertari* there was a somehow repulsive young German with a plain Spanish consort whom he thought beautiful and kept photographing. There were a French couple, a Franco-Italian couple, and three lively Italian couples, including the sculptor Coccia. The guide, Aboudi, was a dark man in native dress who made a study of being a memorable character and regrettably succeeded.

We flew back to Cairo and put Doug and Margaret to bed with a fever. By December 20, Doug's birthday, they were well enough for a trip to the pyramids. We began at the beginning: Zoser's stepped pyramid at Saqqara, 2750 B.C. Thence to the proverbial pyramids and sphinx at Giza and the camel ride. The Egyptians from these earliest dynasties onward were gifted artists, brilliant engineers, indefatigable workers, and insane. Dazzling wealth, much of the economy of the world's richest country, was buried forever, once in each reign, in a hidden and forgotten hole in the Theban desert or squandered on the fastidious megalithic masonry of a useless pyramid. It must be significant, somehow, that civilization at its first great height was so irrational.

We were pestered about the registering of our passports. I had had an agent register them in Minya on our second day in Egypt, but at Aswan the hotel manager called on me again to register them and to fill out twelve big cards, three for each of us. I showed him that we had registered them in Minya, but I complied. It seems that a triangular rubber stamp on the passport is meant to show registration, but the office in Minya had had no stamp. The Aswan police detected, even so, that the passports had already been registered, so they came back still unstamped. When we boarded the *Nefertari* in Luxor, the stewardess called upon us anew to fill out the twelve big cards and register the passports. I showed her that we had registered them in Minya. In Cairo, finally, while I was off on other business, the police closed in on Marge; no more stalling about registration of passports. Again she managed to bring the Minya inscription to their attention. The authorities then applied the triangular stamp.

There was the question of whither next. We had a vague engagement in Crete with the Davidsons for New Year's Eve. Should we see the Levant meanwhile, or, surfeited with touring, should we relax early into Crete? If the Levant, how would we get from the Arab countries into Israel? Inquiry in a succession of offices yielded at length the perfect solution: a luxurious Italian ship from Alexandria to Crete by way of six eastern ports. We could loaf on shipboard and do restrained sight-seeing when in port.

From our hotel in Alexandria we looked out over the East Harbor to the Mameluke fort of Kait Bey. That was where the tall lighthouse stood, the Pharos, before the Arabs moved in. Its name became the word for "lighthouse" in Romance languages, but it had been the name rather of the locality, which had been an island. We walked out to it along the curving esplanade that was still open sea in the days when, according to Homer, Proteus ruled the Isle of Pharos. The name has been linked with "pharaoh."

In the old quarter south of the bazaar the narrow streets were toilets and the houses were tall, sinister, and shabby. When I was about to photograph a crowded, colorful street with an old minaret tastefully placed at one side, an officious Egyptian nationalist shouted and came forward to stay my hand. I had had a similar contretemps in Aswan. Nationalists take pride in dull esplanades, highways, and twelve-story skyscrapers, and would shield their fair land from slanderous photographs of backward conditions. The present case in Alexandria, however, had a rewarding sequel. Another young Egyptian, a merchant who had already greeted me in German, sided with me and told me to go ahead and photograph what I pleased. I was content to step back and let the two confront each other. They were on the verge of blows. Bystanders gathered. Some seemed even to show a participatory interest. A lively spectacle promised, but it died down and I withdrew inconspicuously with my picture.

Strictly by Sea 58

Our ship, the *Bernina*, was white, immaculate, and tastefully decorated. It was committed to first class and freight, and was well staffed by lively Italians. Our eleven fellow passengers were German. The ship's company staged a festive Christmas Eve, and we docked at Beirut on Christmas, 1964. The four of us went over the mile-high mountain of Lebanon to Baalbek, sharing a car with a cultivated couple from the ship: the Baron and Baroness de la Roche, German despite the name. After each great zigzag of the ascent, Beirut reappeared ever more startlingly below us—a great cape, white with a hundred thousand houses, in a blue sea. The high slopes were dotted with villages and summer palaces, notably those of the Sultans of Kuwait and Qatar.

Baalbek was built by the Romans to impress their eastern subjects and neighbors, and dedicated to the glory of Baal and Jupiter, thanks to an identification. One is stunned to think how the temple looked when the towering columns were all intact and topped with the full complement of carved pediments and architraves. Then one is counter-stunned to reflect that the columns of the Hypostyle Hall at Karnak are equally high, two and a half times as numerous, three times as thick, almost twice as old, and all standing. Anyway the temple of Baal and the adjacent temple of Bacchus are carved abundantly with lions and luxuriant foliage, and the limestone building blocks, of staggering size, are fitted with jewel-like precision.

On returning to Beirut we contrived a quick further excursion south to Sidon. There were no Phoenician monuments; the attraction was an intact little castle of the Crusaders, a hundred yards offshore and reached by a narrow stone causeway.

It was still Christmas when we were aboard again and bound for Famagusta, on Cyprus. Walking past a guard and a barbed-wire barrier there the next morning, we found ourselves in the Turkish quarter. Two stone churches were in ruins and a third, damaged, bore a superimposed minaret. The streets, houses, and shops were those of a village. Swedish soldiers in United Nations uniforms patrolled the streets and were visible on the roof of a fort. At an adjacent smaller fort, dating from the Crusaders and the Venetian occupation, we were received by a Turk, Fadil Fettin, and shown through the old tunnels, halls, ramps, and towers. He recounted a history of intolerance under the Crusaders, the French, and the bloody Venetians, who were dislodged in 1460 by the tolerant Turks. I easily deflected him to current affairs. Greek soldiers killed Turkish civilians in Nikosia in the thirties, he said, and Greek aggression and legislative oppression had continued. Turks dared not venture out of their quarter. The Greeks opened their mail and restricted the flow of goods. He was serving as clerk of an unauthorized Turkish court. He gave me a pamphlet, but gave me his name on a separate piece of paper, lest the Greeks associate him with propaganda. Faces that we passed in the Turkish streets wore an expression of mistrust and anxiety. Those in the Greek quarter seemed jolly and carefree.

We docked next at Latakia, Syria, and joined a tour to the excavations of Ugarit, Canaanite birthplace of the alphabet. It was leveled by a lava flow in 1200 B.C. We saw beehive tombs reminiscent of Mycenae, and traces of cultures dating back nine thousand years. After lunch on shipboard we threaded the old streets and arched passages of Latakia on our own.

We steamed into the Turkish port of Mersin, in St. Paul's Cilicia. It was a dusty town with three minarets and a shabby shanty quarter occupied by Armenian refugees from Russia. I picture Armenian refugees crossing the Russo-Turkish border in both directions, or trying to. Gaily caparisoned horses drew two-wheeled carts in which men stood as if in chariots.

In the market a whetstone hawker demonstrated his product. He held his stone in one hand and a cutlass in the other, and with swift arm-length strokes, chattering the while and scarcely watching, he put an edge on the cutlass that would sever a slip of paper held by one end in his fingers. Then, with the same extravagant strokes and disregard of the threat to his wrists and fingers, he blunted the cutlass and proved its bluntness by drawing it across his throat. This left him in a position to sharpen it again from well-attested scratch. Lively sales ensued, and I was glad.

We watched a woman rolling and frying great ballooning sheets of unleavened bread. She gave us some, and we enjoyed it as we walked back to the ship.

We squeezed through between the Asiatic land mass and the sightly port of Rhodes, and on December 30 we docked at Smyrna, where we joined the Baron and Baroness in an excursion to Ephesus. It was a scenic ride up and over from gulf to gulf, crossing the inland hilt of the Clazomenae. We dropped to a dwindled stream which, emptying at Ephesus, had to be the ancient Caÿster. Our Turkish driver called it the Menderes, or Mæander, but that really had to be the next river south, emptying at Miletus. The National Geographic map called them both Menderes, and the government pamphlet *Your Holiday in Turkey* had the Mæander emptying at Ephesus. Heraclitus of Ephesus had had an identity problem about his river, and in a way it has lingered.

The Temple of Diana at Ephesus, sometime wonder of the world, had disappeared. Justinian's big basilica of St. John was a ruin. What were rewarding were the remains of the ancient paved streets and the remains of the houses, temples, and offices, mostly Roman, that lined them. The scene recalled Pompeii. The cosmopolitan character of old Ephesus was evinced by a temple to the Ptolemaic tandem god Serapis, built by the Egyptian minority.

A Roman temple here was converted by Constantine into the first of the Mary churches, and it was at the Council of Ephesus here in 431 that Mary was proclaimed Mother of God. It is significant, the Baron suggested, that the Mary cult began where the greatest goddess shrine had been.

From Smyrna we cruised among Aegean islands, finally passing close under the precipitous shoulder of Thera *sive* Santorin. Soon we docked at Candia *sive* Heraklion, metropolis of Candia *sive* Crete. We were sorry to leave the *Bernina* but hopeful of seeing the Davidsons, for it was the eve of · 1965   1965. We inquired for them in the next few days in vain, but learned afterward that they had been there January 1–3. A letter of mine had not reached them.

Rooms in the best hotel were cramped and warm water was intermittent. We stayed a week, looking down on two hundred acres of close-packed white houses that sloped convexly to the blue sea. To the right was the Venetian fort commanding the entrance to the harbor, and beyond was the silhouette of Mount Juktas, called the profile of dead Zeus. To the left a distant bold shoreline extended abruptly outward. Halfway up it and halfway out was the village of Rogdhia, a white smear on the gray-green slope, five miles from where we sat. Farther to the left were the distant snowy wastes of Mount Ida, framed by nearer dark mountains.

Heraklion was a maze of crooked, narrow streets, overlaid by a loose grid of straighter and wider streets that carried the wheeled traffic and were lined by the shops. The city was still ringed by the heavy Venetian wall. Part of the wall was topped with houses, and whitewashed cottages were huddled against its base.

The lively market district was cluttered with shops that were sorted in the Arab way: a string of knife shops, a string of shoe shops, a string of little taverns where we dined. Racked up overhead in a tavern there were big barrels of *retsina* or resinated wine, filled by hose from a tank truck in the street. Sometimes in a tavern a customer would go through the slow steps, slaps, kicks, and gyrations of a native dance, to the recorded accompaniment of a male voice singing a Middle Eastern tune. Once a man danced with a bottle on his head and a half-full glass balanced on the bottle; but usually there was no stunt, just a spontaneous and earnest exercise, viewed respectfully by the other customers.

We sometimes lunched on *souvlaki* and yogurt in a twist of flat bread, in an establishment that had two tables in an outdoor arcade and a basement kitchen reached by a stairway down the block. Another restaurant specialized in fritters, another in *bogotsa*, which is a pastry of sheep cheese. A proprietor would send out for coffee or yogurt or beer as required. A waiter might run from a basement kitchen to an overflow dining room on an upper floor with three loaded plates on an arm and a plate in his other hand. One restaurant had wings on two streets and a unit across the way. The broiling was done in one window and other cooking across the street, and the waiters bustled back and forth.

Occasionally we saw a rustic in regional costume: shirt, jacket, baggy jodhpurs terminating in shin-high boots, a broad black headband, a sash, and sometimes a cape.

On January 6 the waters of the harbor were to be blessed in commemoration of the baptism of Jesus. From ten until noon the streets and quays blackened with the arriving hordes. Boats were full to standing capacity, as were the walls of the fort. A boat at anchor had a decorated platform over its cabin. It was mounted, to the accompaniment of a band, by bearded priests in bright robes and inverted stovepipe hats, and then by the Metropolitan himself in brighter robes, a torrential gray beard, and a high gold crown. He wore a jeweled cross of gold, which he threw into the wintry sea. Boys in swimming trunks dived for it from the deck. One of them retrieved it, and the ceremony was repeated twice. Sacred music and a long, intoned prayer were hoarsely amplified by faltering electronics.

Cnossus is two miles east of Heraklion. The ruins of the Minoan palace are labyrinthine, to apply a Minoan word. Underground storehouses survive, with lead-lined casks and serried ranks of amphorae; also a drainage system under the old pavements. There were indoor pools and austere little thrones. The superstructure has undergone wildly imaginative reconstruction.

During the night of January 8, 1965, we voyaged to Piraeus in a four-bunk stateroom on the Καναρης, forgoing dinner because of a violent sea. Then we boarded the *San Giorgio*, sister ship of the *Bernina*, for a luxurious two-day passage to Naples.

Our cabin steward showed us his coin collection. It was strange to see coins with star and crescent that antedated Islam. They were Sassanid, from Turkestan. He had perfect silver coins of Philip of Macedon. He followed up with his tale of woe, torrential and enduring. His early professional aspirations had been spiked by his Fascist record. We tired of it, I for want of sympathy and Marge for want of Italian.

Negotiating the Straits of Messina twixt Scylla and Charybdis, we made extravagant angles in the ample waters, as did the ship before us, though no obstacles could be seen. At dusk we passed close beside Stromboli. Looking high up the looming dim cone, we saw an intermittent volcanic glow.

In Naples we settled into a new slough of bureaucracy. Winter luggage shipped from the *Hanseatic* had to be put aboard the *Vulcania* for America, along with further luggage that I had sent from Milan. From both lots I had to recover Elizabeth's portion and ship it to Hydra. An inquiry at the Italian line and two queues at the rail station netted me a Mr. Cuocolo, who took me to successive offices for payments and paper work. At last I saw two of our suitcases. Then there were more offices, windows, papers, and more waiting while an official went away. A four-hundred-lira stamp had to be fetched by motorcycle. By the end of the day I got the two suitcases, but the other luggage involved a different office, which was closed all day. I went to it next morning, to be told, again, *"Domani."* I expostulated over the continuing persecution, and prevailed.

We had hoped to get to Capri, which we had glimpsed from afar, and Amalfi; but time had run out. We settled for Pompeii, renewing my faded memory. Excavation had meanwhile augmented the ancient city by half. Outward from a colonnaded forum there were street after paved street, a mile this way and a mile that, solidly built with ancient houses and shrines. Out beyond were the colonnaded barracks of the gladiators this way, the theaters that. Intersections were fitted with high stepping-stones that kept the pedestrians clear of the puddles while letting the chariot wheels through.

We boarded the *Vulcania* on January 14, 1965. She had been new when she bore me across the Atlantic from Ponta Delgada in another stormy January, twenty-six years before; now she was ending her days. She was gratifyingly dilatory about engaging the fury of the ocean sea. We had a generous stop at Palermo and another at Lisbon, and touched briefly meanwhile at Gibraltar.

Palermo, viewed again after thirty-two years, kindled new appreciation. The vaulted ceilings of the chapel in the great Arabo-Norman palace are covered with mosaics of the time of those in St. Mark's, but more splendid. Each interrupting ridge or arch is rounded in gold, engendering a continuous jewel-like perfection. The cathedral in Monreale, which houses yet more celebrated mosaics, perches on its lofty brink a mere suicide's leap from solid Palermo. From Monreale the cliff rises sheer to a yet dizzier height, with an old church clinging to its face.

At Lisbon we transcended old scenes, taking a taxi through Estoril and Cascais and up the slopes to three-dimensional Sintra. Its crooked streets, lined with bright houses, scale a cluster of steep hills crowned with palaces: the great royal palace, the lesser Palácio dos Sete Ais, and above all an eleventh-century walled Moorish castle on the mountaintop. The bed chamber of Manoel I in the royal palace is a tiled beehive vault forty feet high. The kitchen is two beehive vaults a hundred feet high and open to the sky. Cooking was done on a colossal spit in the middle of the room.

The crossing to Halifax was rough and enjoyable. At the end we were startled at the number of strange faces hidden in bunks all week. After a cold stroll in Halifax we sailed on to New York. We had been gone five months.

Middletown, London, St. Martin 59

In Middletown, Connecticut, we enjoyed for the next five months the generosity of Wesleyan's Center for Advanced Studies. Our trim little house in Home Avenue at the wooded edge of town was a pleasant mile from my office. The Center's director was Paul Horgan, a prize-winning historian and novelist, a patron of music and painting in Santa Fe, a pillar of the Catholic church, and genial, engaging company. The Fellows included the historian Herbert Butterfield, the poet and critic Sir Herbert Read, the Jesuit Father d'Arcy, the philosopher Hans Jonas, the recent ambassador to the Dominican Republic—John Martin by name—and the writers Jean Stafford and Edmund Wilson. We met for dinner Mondays and a Fellow would read a paper; mine was "Meaning and the alien mind." To a senior faculty group called the Apostles I spoke, strange to say, on "Logic and possible worlds."

We had hospitable friends on the Wesleyan faculty, notably Phil Hallie, who had taken his doctorate with us at Harvard a dozen years before. His wife Doris was an amiable Italian-American, adept at her ancestral cuisine. There were also Frank Reeves, young novelist and English professor, and his Russian wife. Frank took Marge and me cruising down the Connecticut in their sloop. Others were Victor Butterfield, president of Wesleyan; Burton Hallowell, future president of Tufts; and Dick Wilbur, poet, whom I had once helped elect to the Society of Fellows.

There was a young Egyptian, Ihab Hassan, with a beautiful Dutch wife. He was dark and merry, she blond and retiring. He was a professor of English and had gained notoriety for his nihilistic stance in literary criticism. He invited me to join him and his colleagues Peter Boynton, Alvin Kibel, and one or two others in a recurrent poker game. For years I had shunned cards, except for nostalgic poker games with the old Arthrites, lest I be pressed to give too much time to that barren recreation. In this case, however, thanks to my transiency, there could be no long commitment; so I happily joined in. Stakes ran higher than with the Arthrites, but not to my sorrow, for I usually won.

Six months earlier I had carried abroad with me the question whether to break with Harvard. Case Western Reserve, my fallback, now gave way to an offer of a university professorship at the University of Chicago. The pay was high, the duty light. I went out and talked with President Beadle, a fellow former Eastman Professor; Provost Levy, a future Attorney General; and several old friends—Ted and Mary Silverstein, Benedict Einarson, Manley Thompson, Ruth Marcus. It could be a good life, with half of each year free for other climes. I painfully decided to prefer it to Harvard failing a course reduction, and notified Harvard accordingly. To my relief I was accorded the reduction and was responsible thenceforward for one course each term.

A publisher's proposal to reprint my little old *Elementary Logic* set me thinking rather of a revised edition. It went to press, half new, that spring. Dagfinn Føllesdal's proposal to include papers of mine in an anthology for Random House set me thinking rather of some collecting on my own part, and I prepared *Selected Logic Papers* and *The Ways of Paradox* for Random House.

I lectured at Amherst, Ann Arbor, Chicago, and Urbana, and in July 1965 I flew back to Europe for Karl Popper's logic symposium at Bedford College in Regent's Park. The occasion was memorable for the combined presence, after all those years, of Carnap, Tarski, and Bernays. Old László Kalmár came from Budapest and Andrzej Mostowski from Warsaw. The contingent from America included Church, Curry, Kreisel, Ruth Marcus, Grover Maxwell, and Wolfgang Yourgrau; and there were many Englishmen.

Popper was counting on a confrontation of Titans. Carnap's latest work was his ponderous one on induction. The first volume had appeared and the second was in progress. Popper decried induction, and he meant to settle the matter. I sensed that he was deploying his henchmen, Imre Lakatos and John Watkins, with military precision as the three of them undertook preliminary skirmishes. But the last scheduled session drew to an end without the anticipated culmination. Popper accordingly declared an additional session, next morning, for all who could see their way to staying. It was strictly Popper vs. Carnap, with an audience of twenty-odd in a seminar room. I was carried back to Carnap's confrontation of Lovejoy in Baltimore thirty years before. Again he met vehemence with the mild but ready answer, the same old cool, unruffled reason. It is my splendid last memory of Carnap.

There is an odd firmness in English conventions. The card table set up by motorists at a lay-by, complete with tablecloth and a teakettle steaming atop a spirit lamp, is part of a broader picture. There is the shunning of marmalade until after the meat and eggs. This escaped me during the year in Oxford, for I saw little breakfast society. I first noticed it in 1959 at the Adelaide Club, when a neighbor at table declined my offer of marmalade at first and asked for it later. In Middletown, Sir Herbert Read mentioned the convention in some connection. It was now borne in on me at my London hotel, when the boy tried to carry away my remaining sausage because I was in the marmalade.

On one of the days of Popper's colloquium, Freddie Ayer

took me to his flat near Regent's Park to meet Lady Ayer. She was Dee Wells, an American writer of radical tracts and bawdy books. It was cocktail time, so what would I have? Whisky. Freddie mixed me a whisky and soda, but there was talk of Pimm's Cup; had I tried it? Dee pushed it. After one of them, I made to retrieve my whisky. Dee insisted that I go on with Pimm's; she would drink my whisky after dinner. I was not dining there that night, but I did so the next; and again I was asked, before dinner, what to drink. Whisky, I replied, slow to learn. Freddie asked if I wouldn't like a Bloody Mary; he was going to have one. It dawned on me only in retrospect that whisky belongs after dinner and that deviation makes a proper Englishman uncomfortable. What impresses and pleases me in these conventions is not their content, but their specificity and the sense that they matter.

My teaching, gratifyingly lightened, resumed in September 1965. I received *in absentia* an honorary degree from Lille in October, went to Akron for another in December, and to St. Louis for yet another in May. I went lecturing at Brown, Amherst, Rensselaer, East Lansing, New York, and Denver. · 1966 The Denver affair was a symposium in May 1966 on Physics, Logic, and History organized—so to speak—by Wolfgang Yourgrau. There were distinguished physicists: George Gamow, Alfred Landé, and Sir Herman Bondi, whose company I had enjoyed twelve years before. In logic and philosophy there were Karl Popper, Georg Kreisel, Czesław Lejewski, Imre Lakatos, Jaakko Hintikka, André Mercier, Arne Naess, and David Kaplan, among others.

Kreisel has been known to subject a speaker to an oddly savage attack. His victim was meek Mostowski at Popper's colloquium the year before, but this time it was Lakatos, who parried thrust with witty thrust and gave us a good show.

After visiting my cousing Norma and Thalia and their progeny in Denver, I flew home for a surprise party that the Society of Fellows was staging for retiring chairman Crane Brinton. His wife Ceecee was to bring him on some fabricated errand. The security was so utter that she assumed the plan had been dropped, and out of delicacy she forbore to inquire. The guests were met, the feast was set, at the top of Holyoke Center. Current Fellows were there, and old Fellows from far and near, but no Crane and no Ceecee. They were tooling northward to their summer place in Vermont. For all its ill-starred inception, the year-end feast became an annual affair.

David Dushkin of Random House urged me that spring to write about evidence and sound thinking for a thin paperback in a series for freshman English. When I protested that I was not in touch with the freshman mind, he suggested that I collaborate with some former student. I thought of Joe Ullian (more properly Quartullian, Joe has modestly conjectured, deferring to Tertullian as his illustrious predecessor). Negotiations were begun that were to issue in *The Web of Belief*. They were threatened six months later, however, when Random House brought out my *Selected Logic Papers* and *Ways of Paradox*; for Jim Oliver informed me from South Carolina that *Ways of Paradox* was straightway being reported out of print. Outraged, I refused to sign the contract for *The Web of Belief*. A contrite vice-president, Jesse Stein, attributed the mishap to a computer error that could never happen again. At length I relented and signed. The computer error recurred in a few weeks, but I was hooked.

My intervening summer at Bare Hill was brightened by a little Arthric reunion but painfully interrupted by a double hernia operation. Jack Fine's repair of six years before had let go, and the other side to boot.

That same summer, 1966, I was inspired by suggestions from Charles Parsons, Burt Dreben, David Kaplan, and others to begin a much improved second edition of *Set Theory and Its Logic*. Natuhiko Yosida and Akira Ohe, visiting from Japan, attended my set-theory course that fall, and at the outset Ohe told me with satisfaction that he had delivered his translation of *Set Theory and Its Logic* to the publisher, Iwanami Shoten. I answered in consternation that I was finishing a drastic revision. Ohe undertook to resume his labor of translation, much to his credit, and the publisher, much to his credit, revised his production schedule. The improved book consequently came out in Japanese before it came out in English. It incorporates improvements by both Ohe and Yosida.

I was to give the opening address in a colloquium at London, Ontario, November 4. James and Judy (Jarvis) Thomson and I emplaned for Buffalo, where we would change planes, but a blizzard forced us down at Rochester. A girl at the counter took up our problem and returned triumphant: she had booked us to London via New York. Resourceful, I thought: off to New York and then clear back to Ontario, leaping the blizzard. *Reculer pour mieux sauter.* She had our reservations to London but not yet to New York; however, she said, preference is given to passengers who are booked through to London. A doubt dawned, and I imprudently voiced it: "*Which* London?" If I had held my counsel, we might have been flown to New York and then continued painlessly home to Boston. Instead, the airline dispatched us and two other passengers to a Buffalo hotel in a taxi, which ran out of gas. James, Judy, and I hitchhiked down the icy road, past numerous disabled cars, to Buffalo. We got no farther. Margolis read my address, "Existence and quantification," to the colloquium, having had the foresight to ask for a copy. I presented it in Princeton the following spring.

The annual philosophy convention was held at the end of 1966 in Philadelphia, and I was slated for a panel on Russell. We went *en famille*, for we were to continue to St. Martin for a week's holiday. I was drawn to this Lesser Antille by its political oddity, for two-thirds of the island is part of the Netherlands Antilles and one-third is part of the French *département* of Guadeloupe.

Doug fainted in Philadelphia. Alarmingly, it had to do with his heart. The doctor there advised us to go ahead with our Caribbean jaunt. Subsequent tests in Boston, repeated annually, have allayed our fears.

We had a cabin at a beach hotel on Lille Baai, Sint-Maarten. The island was hilly and semiarid, with big cactus and maguey. We looked out on little Philipsburg, the chief town, and its big lagoon where salt was leached from sea water. I stood on a bluff watching a pelican. The great white bird would plunge and stay down unconscionably long. When he emerged he was the merest shadow of his former self. His feathers, no longer fluffy, were clinging to his puny wet sides.

On crossing the island to the French town, Marigot, we could look north to the British island of Anguilla. The four of us took passage thither on a shabby, clattering launch, operated by black natives and patronized, except for us, by neighborly black youths who lolled on the engine housing. We walked over Anguilla to the airstrip, and were able after a while to get a flight back. The local pilot had an errand on St. Kitts and dropped us off, figuratively speaking, on St. Martin along the way.

Perhaps a majority of the men on St. Martin were trilingual. Five languages were in evidence: Dutch from one school, French from the other, Papiamentu from migrant work in Curaçao, Spanish from migrant work in the Dominican Republic, and English from everybody.

· 1967 The day of reckoning at Lille Baai was an eye-opener. The bill was several times what I had reckoned on through my travel agent. It turned out that the hotel leaflet had been inadvertently ambiguous. My agent had read it as I did, and his letter of reservation to the hotel had read unambiguously our way. The hotel manager acknowledged this and accepted the agreed amount. We had been enjoying a great bargain unawares.

Ohio, Canada, New York 60

We got home to Boston on January 6, 1967. After a whirl in my office I was off again, hurtled in a roomette to Columbus. My week there was devoted to vigorous engagement with graduate students and faculty at Ohio State. Virgil Hinshaw had been preparing the students with an intensive seminar on my philosophy, and they bristled with questions. Lectures alternated with discussion sessions, and discussion spilled over into unscheduled hours. The sustained impact was effective. When I corrected Bob Trumbull's misunderstanding of my position, I sensed that he took my correction as the familiar sort of face-saving verbalism; but when the point came up again the next day and I belabored it further, I could see comprehension abruptly dawn. I had a similar experience with Herbert Hochberg, to the extent of reaching a common understanding of our differences. Among the graduate students, along with many eager and untendentious questioners, there were perhaps two militant opponents, and it was gratifying to see them come around to my view as the week wore on. The experience encouraged me to accept five similar invitations elsewhere in subsequent years.

From Columbus an allstop Greyhound bus bore me to Akron at its petty pace. After a brief visit I flew to Boston, only to fly back two weeks later: for on February 1, 1967, just as Margaret entered her teens, my father died. He was eighty-five. He had worked in his orchard on weekends through the fall and had gone regularly to his office until within a week of his death, though Bob had become president of the firm. Then he awoke sick and multiple failures quickly ensued.

In the light of a prospectus from the editor of the series for freshman English, Joe Ullian ventured a rough draft of *The Web of Belief* to spark my revisions and elaborations. I produced an improved and extended text for his consideration and further embellishment. Such was our desultory collaboration back and forth over the thousand miles for the next year and a half.

May netted me another degree. This one, from Chicago, was the more moving in view of the previous kindnesses of that university and my failure to rise to them. There had been a teaching invitation in 1949, its renewal in my moment of need in 1950, and the lavish offer of 1965.

I gave a short early version of "Ontological relativity" at Chicago and again at Yale. I mark my lectures page by page with estimates of minutes required, and on starting I set my watch on the hour, meaning to correct it afterward. At Yale I was taken to dinner, and at length I feared missing my train. I forwent dessert and so did poor Rulon Wells, who drove me to the station. We were a half hour early; I had forgotten to correct my watch. My dinner companions must have put me down for a nervous wreck.

In June we were off *en famille* for an Inter-American Philosophical Congress in Quebec. My slight contribution there was a reply to Joseph Owens, S. J., on matters of ontology. He remembered my birthday in subsequent years with anti-Christmas cards.

Mario Bunge's paper at the congress was distributed in English but delivered in Spanish. The Argentine accent is hard for me to follow, but I found that with the English text before me the Spanish words came through with utter clarity. It is uncanny how the semantic link between phonetically unrelated phrases clarifies the phonetics without conscious translation.

After a congressional outing to sightly Montmorency Falls and horrid Ste.-Anne de Beaupré, I drove my three charges upstream to the world's fair at Montreal. One of a number of architectural pleasures there was the Habitat with its randomly and precipitously poised little habitable parallelipipeds, reminiscent somehow of the Taos pueblo. Another was Buckminster Fuller's great spherical pavilion. Our appetite for the exotic was titillated by the pavilions of new African republics. But the greatest wonder was a little thing, the hologram. Here was a two-dimensional depiction of three dimensions so complete as to provide parallax. Vision and touch were put utterly at odds.

Early in September 1967 I went to a huge meeting of the American Psychological Association in Washington to participate in an ill-conceived psychophilosophical panel with Michael Polanyi, Tom Kuhn, and Michael Scriven. I spoke on "Logic and the learning of language." While in Washington I spent an exhilarating afternoon with Harry Cooper, an urbane Virginian whose company I had enjoyed when he was a naval officer in my command. He had stayed on in intelligence and spent harrowing years abroad with the C.I.A. He had retired early and written a thriller, *Cave with Two Exits*, in the light of his experiences.

In October I spoke at Long Island University in Brooklyn on "Kinds." I began the day with Ed Haskell, and we happily walked the hundred-odd blocks from his flat off Riverside Drive to the Manhattan Bridge, to find that we had to take a subway train in order to cross the bridge to my lecture. Pedestrians not allowed.

Academic life was abruptly deteriorating. Student disorders, blandly indulged at Berkeley, were spreading. The threat of disruption reached Harvard, condoned or encouraged by the weaker or more radical professors. My own tolerance bidding fair to be brief, I bethought me of a standing offer from Rockefeller University. There were just a handful of students there, handpicked and highly subsidized, and the teaching duties were said to be slight. I arranged for unpaid leave from Harvard for the spring term and accepted a visiting professorship at Rockefeller. I did not propose to cut my Harvard ties unless the administration failed to contain the mounting disorders, but meanwhile I wanted to sample life in the New York archipelago with a view to that contingency.

· 1968   I moved to Rockefeller at the end of January 1968 and entrained next day for little-known Brockport-by-Rochester, in continental New York, where they were staging month by month an oddly ambitious International Philosophical Year. I presented "Philosophical progress in language theory." The other speakers on my occasion were Paul Ziff, Arne Naess, and Max Black.

I agreed to stay three months at Rockefeller. Leaving my family meanwhile in Boston, I settled into a little flat on the Rockefeller campus. This is a campus of grass, walks, driveways, buildings, and parking lot, extending for four midtown blocks along York Avenue and backed by the East River. In a sense, though, it is a roof garden and its buildings are penthouses; for there is a basement beneath it all, which even has a full complement of windows looking out over the Franklin Delano Roosevelt *sive* East River Drive to the water. In bad weather one threads one's way from building to building underground.

The philosophers were Harry Frankfurt, Joel Feinberg, Sidney Shoemaker, Hao Wang, Saul Kripke, Bob Nozick, and John Nolan, and, in a visiting status, Marshall Cohen and Sidney Morgenbesser. They outnumbered their students two to one. I had two eminent Dutch colleagues in physics: Sam Goudsmit, a great wit, and Abraham Pais, who shared my admiration of his compatriot Escher. I lectured twice, received an occasional student for discussion, and attended lectures by passing visitors.

At Columbia I gave the inaugural pair of John Dewey Lectures: "Ontological relativity," expanding what I had given at Chicago and Yale. I began by saying that I had heard John Dewey give the first of the William James Lectures. I saw Marshall Cohen laugh, and asked him afterward why. "We wondered who would give the first Willard Quine Lecture," he said. I was alarmed at so immodest an implication of my innocent remark, and the more so that the laughter came so quickly.

The thesis of "Ontological relativity" is a natural sequel to my "Ontological reduction and the world of numbers" of 1964. Proxy functions, as I called them, map one ontology onto another. They served in 1964 to disqualify certain shifts of ontology, but they serve equally to change the ontology of a theory at will, without disturbing any sentences or any supporting evidence. Such was ontological relativity, but it was still foggy in my Dewey Lectures.

Columbia had publication rights. Thirty-three pages make a poor sort of book, so we included a few other essays. One was "Epistemology naturalized," which I wrote that spring for presentation in Vienna in September and presented meanwhile at the New School for Social Research.

The student miniterror struck Columbia. Low Library and Philosophy Hall were occupied. I went up with Reuben

Abel, and as we walked around the outside of the library he tried to reason with students in the windows. I did not.

I saw Ed Haskell often and joined him on hikes of the Appalachian Mountain Club. I enjoyed the company of philosophers from neighboring institutions—Charles Parsons, Leigh Cauman, George Boolos, Sam Coleman, Mary Mothersill, Tom Nagel, Gil Harman, and, as far away as Princeton, Don Davidson and Peter Hempel. There were parties, and I reciprocated at Rockefeller. Marge visited with and without the children, and we enjoyed the resources of the island: the circumnavigation, the Empire State Building, foreign restaurants, plays, concerts, museums.

My generous friends Don Davidson and Jaakko Hintikka assembled a volume, *Words and Objections*, of essays on my philosophy. I prepared replies. It was satisfying writing, for I was no longer addressing a faceless public and having to guess what most needed to be stressed or clarified.

When I had returned to Boston, a chance encounter with Peter Pezzati revived our friendship of the thirties. He said he would like to paint my portrait, with no obligation on my part. They were long and leisurely sittings, with much lively talk, largely about words. The portrait is a fine painting, and I hoped Marge would like it, whereupon I would talk with Peter about price. But she felt that it did not capture me. I got opinions from Ed Haskell, Bob, Rosalie, and Marge's sister and brother-in-law, but no encouragement.

I took on a three-week stint at Southampton, Long Island, in the Summer Institute of Philosophy. Jean van Heijenoort summered near there, so he met my ferry at Orient Point and drove me over. Fifty teachers from obscure colleges came on fellowships to hear Sellars, Chisholm, Plantinga, and me in those weeks and others in other weeks. We four lectured, conducted discussions, and attended one another's lectures. Sellars and his wife lived away; Chisholm, Plantinga, and I shared a college house and made merry. I relished their lectures for their acuteness, despite disapproving of *necessitas de re et de dicto*, or metaphysical necessity and analyticity. It is a game one can be drawn into.

I explored the surroundings by bicycle, and Rod Chisholm drove some of us to Montauk Point. That eastern extreme of Long Island had stirred my childhood imagination; I had placed one of my imaginary towns and great houses nearby. What had been Lake Wyandanee to me back then, and remained so for fifty years, proved to be Wyandance. There had been a misprint or smudge in an atlas.

Italy, Dalmatia, Vienna 61

I was to be in Vienna in September 1968 to represent the American Philosophical Association at the quinquennial World Congress of Philosophy. We made it a family vacation. We flew to Europe by the Iceland line, for three reasons: it was cheaper, it touched down in a country—Iceland—that was new to the rest of the family, and it ended up in Luxemburg.

The middle of the capital of Luxemburg is an abrupt depression, the Grund. Its high walls, stone bridges, and narrow streets lined with medieval stone houses did justice to my fond memories. Great bastions and stone stairways at one side rose to the Grand Duchess's palace, which fronted on a square in the upper town. Three of its balconies overhung the square, where two guardsmen patrolled and sustained the Graustark air.

We looked in on Arlon so as to put Doug and Margaret in Belgium, and then flew to Milan, where we ran into Jerry Buckley of Harvard and his wife, stranded by loss of luggage. Having better luck, we took a bus to town through torrential rain, hail, and gale. The next plane crashed, with heavy casualties.

We went on by train to Lugano, in Ticino, the Italian-speaking canton of Switzerland. I thought Ticino might be a good place to retire to when retirement came due. I liked Italian temperament, language, and cuisine, and Swiss honesty and efficiency. Intellectual centers of four countries were within easy reach. Hans Epstein had retired to Miglieglia, above Lugano, and we meant to visit him.

Hans was a former Junior Fellow with whom I had shared a study in Eliot House. He had taken a well-paid job in the C.I.A. with early retirement, married a rich girl, and decreed a dream house with a view. Half of it was centuries old and half was imaginatively modern but deftly harmonious. There were built-in butterfly racks; Hans, like his friend and my acquaintance Nabokov, was an ardent amateur lepidopterist. There was a built-in aquarium, its glass panel flush to the wall, for Hans's love of natural history extended to fish. Hans and Cathleen reviewed books. Lugano lay a dozen steep and tortuous miles below them—"just a few minutes away." True, as Hans drove it, but it was a chastening experience.

My brief glimpse of narrow streets in Genoa thirty-nine years earlier had made a lasting impression. Acting on it, we stopped in Genoa and enjoyed its medieval quarter in deliberate leisure.

Fabrizio Mondadori, of the publisher's family, had written his dissertation at Milan on my philosophy and then had come to Harvard for further study. He was translating *Word and Object*. He picked us up at Genoa and took us to Sori for a supper party at his uncle's house, dramatically poised on the brink of a sea cliff. Its roof terrace, flush with the road, commanded a magnificent coastal panorama to Portofino.

We settled at La Spezia for sorties into the Cinque Terre. These are five steep old towns along the coast, crowded from behind by mountains. The highway, in the heights, misses some of the towns and leaves them free of cars; they are linked rather by paths and by a tunneling railway. Each day we took a train from La Spezia to one of the five, explored it, walked to another, and took a train back.

Skipping Pisa and Florence this time, we visited the walled city of Lucca and went on to Bologna, memorable for its miles of arcaded sidewalks and its leaning towers. Such was our route to San Marino, where I expiated my sin of omission of four years before. The years from 1929 to 1933 had treated San Marino kindly, but subsequent years proved to have been cruel. An ugly big casino had been built just outside the capital village, and a full-scale road had been built up the mountain to serve it. The village and the nearest of the three mountaintop towers swarmed with tourists. At one point, to avoid having to make my way through a crowd, I jumped down from one rock to another and landed too hard, injuring the transverse arch of one foot.

A few days in Ravenna, then, and Venice. Bound for Trieste, we contrived a visit to Palma Nuova, a planned town that had aroused my curiosity. It dated from 1593. Its wall was a regular enneagon, with a turret at each of the nine vertices. Eighteen streets radiated to the sides and vertices from the central *piazza*. Cross streets intervened at regular intervals to describe concentric enneagons.

Trieste had suffered war damage, but there were still some medieval streets to explore. Then we crossed into Yugoslavia. At Opatija, the Abbazia of Italian days, we boarded the *Aleksa Santič* for a week's cruise of Dalmatia.

The seven ports of call allowed for exploratory walks. The first was Rijeka. Before 1918 it had been Hungary's one point of contact with the sea, and in later years it had been Gabriele d'Annunzio's vest-pocket fascist sovereign state, Fiume of the triangular postage stamp. Our farthest port was Kotor, or Cattaro, at the end of its dark fiord beneath the mountains of Montenegro. Along the way were Split and Dubrovnik. Split, the Spalato of the Italians, invites the false etymology 'Ex-Palazzo', for its old part occupies the palace of Diocletian. The walls of the palace became the walls of the old town, and the corridors became the streets. Rooms of the palace, all in stone, became the major buildings. It takes a big palace to make a small town, and a small town it is—but a palatial one. The modern city spreads out from it over the countryside.

Dubrovnik had been a little republic—Ragusa—with its legate in Washington in Federalist times. Its mighty city wall is intact, and the old city that fills it is a continuous mass of heavy stone masonry. The Middle Ages take on a gratifying air of permanence in the narrow streets of Dubrovnik.

We went on then to the Congress of Vienna. The mood of Vienna had changed mightily in the thirty-five years that I had been away. My sojourn, antedating even the Nazi horrors, had been a period of drab poverty and depression. What we found now was bustling prosperity.

I chaired a logic session at the congress and spoke "On the limits of decision," exploring the interface between the algorithm of truth functions and the algorithm-resistant logic of quantification. In a public address a week later, "Epistemology naturalized," I indulged my mood of reminiscence, pitting naturalism against phenomenalism in a historical perspective.

Russians invaded Czechoslovakia. Refugees arrived in Vienna. Members of the congress joined in protesting Russian imperialism and in forming committees to place refugee scholars.

Dirk Siefke, a young *Dozent* at Heidelberg who had been engaged to translate *Methods of Logic*, wrote to me hoping to confer on problems of translation. I arranged a meeting in Luxemburg, our takeoff point for America. Our conference began alarmingly. I had touched the philosophy of logic only lightly in the book, but I had been at pains to present the logic in such a way as not to encourage various murky views of the subject that were all too prevalent in the tradition. Thus I had avoided intensional logic, I had avoided positing abstract objects before they were needed, and I had tried tacitly to deflect the reader from common misconceptions of the relation between pure and applied mathematics. Now what was alarming was that Siefke planned to annotate the book with critical comments injecting just the familiar viruses that I had been intent on keeping clear of. I would have none of it. It was my book, and he could express his views under separate cover.

The project then proceeded smoothly. He consulted me by mail from time to time on problems strictly of translation. When I perused the handsome finished product a year later, entitled *Grundzüge der Logik,* I had a strange and unforeseen feeling that my logic had become official. German had been for me the language of revelation in logic, after 1932, and it stamped my book as authoritative.

But I was soon preparing a third English edition. The publisher had urged me to it as publishers will, and my ideas had evolved. I developed the logic of one-place predicates algebraically, postponing quantification. For quantification I developed a multiplicity of proof procedures. They afforded varied perspectives, deepening one's understanding of logical theory.

Publishers' eyes are sometimes bigger than their stomachs. When the new edition was ready for publication, it took a year of prodding to get Holt to start production. *The Web of Belief* fared somewhat similarly at Random House: the manuscript remained unacknowledged for four months. The eagerness of Dushkin and Stein in 1966 had served its fleeting purpose.

Prentice-Hall meanwhile engaged me in another project, *Philosophy of Logic,* for another series of thin paperbacks. By coincidence the Collège de France invited me to give a dozen lectures on that same subject.

· 1969 In January 1969 I flew to Tucson and answered questions sent in advance by students of my work. I stayed with Frank Raab, a philosopher and amateur naturalist. He lived in the desert, where I walked among the giant cacti in summer heat.

Harvard Down, Paris Up 62

Disorders mounted at Harvard. Students occupied University Hall, ejected the authorities, and rifled the confidential files. President Pusey was compelled to call in the police, after many hours of waiting and warning. He was unduly apologetic afterward about having acted thus responsibly, and the culprits were set loose on further mischief in the service of their headlong ideals.

Emerson Hall had lately been remodeled and cleared of social scientists, affording the philosophers excessive office space. It is said that when Bolivian uplanders are transported to the lowlands, their disused lung capacity soon harbors tuberculosis. Something analogous proved true of office capacity. Through connivance on the part of some of our professors and unawareness on the part of others, offices in the upper reaches of Emerson Hall had become headquarters for the activists' councils, recruiting, and underground press. The violence peaked with the fire-bombing of a center for international politics in old Divinity Hall.

There were demonstrations of solidarity with the Viet Cong; demands for severing the Reserve Officers Training Corps; demands for student participation in staffing the faculty, planning the curriculum, and planning the courses; demands for abolishing grades and for abolishing general examinations; demands for amnesty of apprehended activists. The demands for amnesty were crowned with success, to the detriment of any self-image of heroism on the activists' part. So was the demand for severance of the R.O.T.C., and so were other demands in varying degrees. Feeling ran high in the faculty between a radical caucus at one edge, which backed the vocal students, and a conservative caucus at the other edge, in which Oscar Handlin played a leading role and I an ineffectual one. Attendance at faculty meetings exceeded all bounds; we had to move them from the faculty room in University Hall to the Loeb Theater. In previous years I had seldom attended, but now duty called.

At one of these crowded faculty meetings, two shabby black undergraduates demanded to be admitted and heard. Henry Rosovsky had done a conscientious job of devising a program of Black Studies that might accommodate the new racism without serious abdication of scholarly standards; but the two black youths demanded more radical provisions, on pain, they hinted, of fire and destruction. The serried ranks of faculty, flecked with eminent scholars and Nobel laureates, were cowed—a bare majority of them—by the two frail, bumbling figures and voted as directed. What price scholarly standards, what price self-respect?

Standards sank in various departments. The preliminary examinations for the Ph.D. had been the major hurdle in our department, and they were dropped by direction of the Students for a Democratic Society, who had found that the exams induced anxiety. Personal relations deteriorated. Professors who had shared their students' intellectual concerns in a friendly or paternal way were put off by the strident talk of students' rights and put to calculating their own rights and the limits of their obligations. The loss in rapport and fellow-feeling, as well as in academic standards, was not soon to be made up.

I was thankful to have given Rockefeller University a try and to have found the life acceptable. Perhaps I would go. But the Collège de France was in the immediate offing, and the larger decision could wait another term or two.

By April 1969 I finished a draft of *Philosophy of Logic*. I represented logic as exploring the truth conditions of sentences in the light of how the sentences are grammatically constructed. "Logic chases truth up the tree of grammar." Tarski's logical analysis of the concept of truth portrays this arboreal pursuit in a recursive formula. My little book included, accordingly, a capsule philosophy of grammar and a streamlined rendering of Tarski's analysis.

I proceeded to turn this first draft of the book into French lectures. Having helped Mondadori with his Italian translation of *Word and Object*, I knew I was hard to translate, but now I luxuriated in the freedom that a self-translator enjoys. If a sentence is sticky, he is free to say something else to the same long-run purpose. There were other changes, too, to suit the material to the lecture hall, and there were substantive afterthoughts. The French text was an improvement and a significant further step toward a final English version.

I submitted my first two lectures to van Heijenoort's kind criticism and emendation. It was a chastening language lesson. French stalwartly withstands extrapolation. It offers the adjectives *descendant* and *ascendant* and the verb *descendre*, but no *ascendre*; we must say *monter*. There is the noun *descente*, but no *ascente*; there is *ascension*; but no *descension*. There is an appalling mess when you want to treat of reference in the semantic sense, as is my wont: reference to objects. One verb might serve that purpose in one context, another in another, and the nouns built on those verbs might serve it in neither.

Jean van Heijenoort is Parisian and, unlike his name, utterly French. In his youth he was ally and secretary to Trotsky, first in Turkey and then in Mexico. He had edited Trotsky's *Diary in Exile* and written a book about his years with Trotsky. He became a professor of philosophy at Brandeis and did a major service to logic with his monumental source book *From Frege to Gödel*. He has a house and Mexican wife in the state of Morelos, Mexico, and in retirement he divides his time between Morelos, his native Paris, and Cambridge, Massachusetts.

On May 2, 1969, I settled in the Hôtel des Sts.-Pères, in the *rue* of that name in the Faubourg St.-Germain. From there to the Collège de France was a pleasant walk through a succession of back streets roughly parelleling the busy Boulevard St.-Germain. The Collège is adjacent to the Sorbonne, but more prestigious. There are no students. Its professors give lectures that are open to the public, and pursue their experiments in the laboratory if, like François Jacob and Jacques Monod, they are scientists. Twice a week I went to the professors' room, signed the book, and was conducted to my classroom by the *huissier*, who meanwhile had seen to details such as chalk and clean blackboard.

Professor Jules Vuillemin, my colleague and sponsor, told me after my second lecture that my turnout was the largest in philosophy at the Collège since Henri Bergson. "Well," I countered, or "Eh bien," the number had certainly fallen off from the first to the second. No, he explained, it was a different room the second time. The first one was too small.

Between lectures I was busy in my hotel room preparing them. At first I passed each to Vuillemin in advance for emendation of language; but his emendations dwindled encouragingly, and soon I was on my own. My French had improved, but I also suspect that Vuillemin was more permissive than van Heijenoort.

Some instructors from Rennes, Mlle. Imbert and Francis Jacques among them, were in regular attendance. I was flattered that they would come all the way from Brittany, until I learned that they lived in Paris and commuted to Rennes. They arranged with me to join them for questions after one of my lectures, for there was no regular provision for questions and discussion. We repaired to Derrida's office in the Ecole Normale Supérieure for two vigorous and exhausting hours.

Georg Kreisel was dividing his time between Stanford and Paris in those years, and he attended some of my lectures. Afterward he wrote a paper in which he took issue with what he wrongly took to be my views. When I set him right, he cheerfully adjusted his paper by ascribing the views to a fictitious character.

One of my regular auditors, Eric Thom, talked with me twice at length on semantics. His ideas seemed discouragingly foggy, but Kreisel told me he was an outstanding topologist. He is now famous for his theory of catastrophe.

Violence had rocked the neighborhood a year earlier. Things were now quiet, but police vans and *gendarmes* were standing daily at the Lycée Louis-le-Grand, up the street from the Collège de France, just in case. To me, newly arrived from the strife of Harvard and the ugly plague of hippies in Cambridge and Boston, the serenity of Paris and the respectability and courtesy of its inhabitants were deeply refreshing.

In the beginnings of the Rue de Grenelle there was a tiny restaurant of the same name. It was close to my Hôtel des Sts.-Pères, and I went back day after day for the *moules marinières* until I was driven to another hotel by the noise and dust of renovations. Kreisel put me onto the Hôtel de Nice et des Beaux-Arts. Its street, the Rue des Beaux-Arts, is one long block in length and a delight to the eye. Each side is a row of uniform light gray houses with mansard roofs and tastefully spaced windows with slatted shutters. The view is closed at one end of the street by the monumental Ecole des Beaux-Arts and at the other end by the bustling and colorful Rue de Seine.

Whereas Rennes philosophers lived in Paris, the Paris philosophers lived outside. Roger Martin, the professor of logic at the Sorbonne, had me to dinner at his home far to the south, near the end of the Ligne de Sceaux. Vuillemin lived fully forty miles south, in a seventeenth-century palace that had been Talleyrand's. The grounds embrace a manicured forest, lawns, a sheet of water or *pièce d'eau,* and two palaces. The newer one, dating from the eighteenth century, is occupied by Talleyrand's descendant, who divided the older palace into flats for distinguished tenants such as Vuillemin. Though lecturing on Monday and Tuesday, Vuillemin would make the trip home even for the intervening night. His wife would meet his train. For her own part, she taught at far away Cologne, and made the international trip each week. For the six months each year when they were free of academic duty, they would disappear into their retreat in the Jura on the Swiss border. The French, some of them, are as mobile as Californians.

Vuillemin took me to dinner at his Talleyrand palace, where I met the philosophers Althusser and Foucault. When the Collège de France closed for the summer, he and his wife headed for the Jura and dropped me off in Burgundy. I went to Vézelay and Autun for their Romanesque cathedrals, remembered from college studies. Vézelay is a sinuous old town, clustered along a street that scales a little mountain to the cathedral at the top. In Beaune I walked the city walls and admired the hospital. Its building has been mercifully preserved over five centuries, while the procedures within it have mercifully progressed.

Before going back to America, I had a jaunt with my daughters Elizabeth and Norma, who now lived in London. Elizabeth and her daughter Melissa had moved in 1965 from Hydra to Israel, where Elizabeth was admitted to a kibbutz and Melissa to a boarding school. Perhaps they were the first O'Briens to learn Hebrew. There followed an interlude back home with Naomi in California. Then they moved to London and Elizabeth married a young English engineer, Mike Roberts, whom she knew from the kibbutz. They established a thriving business servicing electronic equipment. Norma, meanwhile, modeled fashions in California. She was brought to fashion centers in Dallas, New York, and London, and at length was made manager of the London branch of Israel's Beged-Or. The Israeli connection of the two girls was a coincidence, and so was their ending up in London.

A woman on a Manx newspaper saw some publicity about Norma and recognized "Quine" as Manx. She volunteered to track down our relatives on the island. Thus it was that on June 12, 1969, I joined Norma and Elizabeth in London and took them to the Isle of Man to meet unknown relatives and admire an ancestral land. The forging of family links that I had shirked in 1950 was congenial now that someone else had the initiative. The nearest relative encountered was William Shimmin, in Peel, my father's first cousin. He arranged a gathering where there were elderly widows who had been Quines.

We made the rounds of the island and stayed in a great house at Tholt y Will, in a wild glen in the shadow of Snaefell, the island's peak. Our host was a strange lord named Lord Strange, hearty and garrulous, who saw his way to taking paying guests.

Soon afterward I was with Bob and Rosalie in Akron dismantling the house in Orchard Road. Our mother had lost her memory and was in a nursing home. She died seven months later, aged ninety-five.

Don Davidson and Gil Harman staged a cozy cross-cultural colloquium at Stanford in August to spark mutual appreciation and enlightenment between logicians and structural linguists. The other logicians or philosophers were Geach, David Kaplan, and two Dutchmen, Staal and Vermazen. The linguists were Barbara Partee, George Lakoff, Jim McCawley, Emmon Bach, and Charles Fillmore.

Geach had been tinkering with Ajdukiewicz's scheme of syntactic categories, a sophisticated successor to parts of speech. Geach's resulting system was neat and powerful, but the linguists showed no appreciation. Two were over-eager to amuse us with whimsical examples having nothing to do with the case. The next speaker was McCawley, who told how he was able to handle some grammatical problems by positing propositions, or intensional sentence meanings. Geach managed to intervene and briefly indicate how with his apparatus of categories he had been able to handle the same problems without McCawley's resort to cumbersome and obscure auxiliaries. Ah, I thought, now McCawley, at least, will spot the pearls. But no; he courteously held his peace until Geach had had his say, and then picked up where he had been interrupted.

I had looked forward to Don Davidson's talk, but there was no time for it, what with the chatter and clowning. The project failed miserably; Don and Gil had led the horses to water and that was that. I suspect that Barbara Partee grieved silently the while, for she is a linguist with a proper grasp of logic. She took my graduate course at Harvard when she was a student at M.I.T.

I thought of a family holiday in Bermuda as the winter re-
· 1970 cesses drew near, but bookings were tight, so we settled for a long weekend in Charleston. Its little streets lined with rows of old town houses had the Federalist charm of Georgetown and Beacon Hill, and its avenues of stately mansions recalled gracious ante-bellum days.

In May 1970 I spoke at Calgary. Two young philosophers drove me up among the jagged, snowy peaks into British Columbia and part way back, where we stopped for a walk at Lake Louise. After a half mile the crust of the snow began to give way, obliging us to wade back in wet snow knee-deep. When we got to the car, I produced dry socks from my suitcase, happily three pairs. The young men then established me in the turreted Scottish castle which is the Banff Springs Hotel.

I spoke twice at Edmonton, the northernmost big city in

the hemisphere. ("Big" means a half million.) Three days later I was in St. Louis to comment on a paper on the sterile subject of relevance logic and to introduce one of Peter Hempel's Paul Carus Lectures. I muffed the latter; its place had been changed and I waited in the wrong room. When I found the place, Peter was lecturing. I was determined to unleash my encomium, so when he finished I seized the floor, made my excuses, and instead of introducing I extroduced. My next stop, Notre Dame, was longer: May 11–15. There I laid sustained siege, as at Columbus three and a half years before.

Honors accreted in the next weeks. I received the Nicholas Murray Butler gold medal at Columbia University and an honorary degree at Temple, and I was slated for another at Oxford on June 24. We had not meant to go to Europe that summer, but the Oxford degree settled it. Dagfinn Føllesdal then embroidered on it: how about touring Norway with him? The Davidsons embroidered further: how about East Africa? Plans were laid on a heroic scale.

Northern Climes 63

I took my gold medal home from Columbia University on June 2, 1970, and emplaned next day for a rendezvous at Helsinki with Dagfinn. He arrived from Oslo in his big station wagon and we drove swiftly northward through heavy forests of spruce and pine alternating with farms and clear lakes dotted with wooded islands. It was like northern Michigan or Maine, even to the straggling villages of wooden buildings. Occasional signs in wildly alien Finnish struck an abruptly contrasting note.

Dagfinn communicated in Norwegian with speakers of Swedish, but they were scarce in northern Finland. At Oulu, where the hotel was full, we wanted the clerk to phone ahead and clinch rooms for us at Kemi. She awakened the manageress, who had learned some German in school, and thus we communicated. So we found haven at midnight in Kemi, at the northern tip of the Gulf of Bothnia, having driven five hundred miles in a day. It was a bright midnight, blending sunset with dawn.

Next day we drove north along the broad river Tornio, looking across it into Sweden. We crossed the Arctic Circle, but forest and farms continued. Pine gave way to birch as we moved north from Finnish Lapland into Norwegian Lapland, and the birch became scrubby as we gained altitude on Finnmarks Vidda. In its freedom from underbrush the scene recalled the mesquite country in southern Texas. A Lapp in ornate red garb, surmounted by a cylindrical red hat, drove by in a jeep.

At Kautokeino, Norway's largest Lapp village, a young Lapp whom I met alluded easily to a couple of passages in my writings. He was Keskytalo, M.A., a recent pupil of Dagfinn's. Eight people were living in his modern cottage: his two brothers, his parents, his grandmother, and an uncle and cousin who were visiting from the Olympic Peninsula in Washington. The mother and grandmother were present only to serve tea, salmonberries, and cake. The grandmother spoke only in Lapp, the parents spoke also Norwegian, and the father could handle also Finnish and English. The uncle had grown up in a colony of Norwegian and Finnish expatriates, his father having brought the first herd of reindeer to Nome from Lapland. Keskytalo took us to a neat log cabin of his at a lake shore. We broiled slabs of reindeer on forks at the fireplace and toured the lake by outboard motor as far as the ice permitted.

Spring came in the sunlit night, and the scrub birches, bare the day before, showed hints of green. The Lapps turned out for Sunday church in traditional regalia. They were the very young, the female, and the old; for the ablebodied males, apart from a rare cosmopolite such as Keskytalo, were following the reindeer herd.

The reindeer live outdoors all winter, eating the brittle, pale gray reindeer moss from under the snow and starving only if the snow thaws and then freezes to form a crust. Their instinctive northward migration in summer prevents depletion of the next winter's supply of moss on the home ground. They migrate at will and the herdsmen follow.

We likewise continued north. With decrease of altitude the forests became heavier and birch gave way again to pine. Ponds were still icy, but children bathed in them. At Alta, a busy town of six thousand on the Arctic Ocean, we walked up an abrupt little mountain and admired the rugged, snowy peaks that rim the fiord. Isnesstoften, a headland a dozen miles northwest of Alta, was our northermost point: 70°7'. A farming hamlet there is dominated by a rocky hill honeycombed with Nazi bunkers and gun emplacements. Mountainous snowy islands line the waters to the north.

Our road southwestward twisted from one fiord's end to the next. Twice it took the bit in its teeth and zigzagged up and over the snowy backbone of a peninsula. We saw Lapp huts, conical and sod-covered, and conical tents, but no big encampment. We learned that the herd had swum out in the Arctic Ocean to one of the islands, followed by the herdsmen in boats.

Dagfinn handled his big Volvo deftly, driving rather fast on the narrow, crooked roads, ever ready with his brakes when a car emerged at a bend. He did all the driving. My spelling him could only have slowed our progress or courted disaster.

Late in the sunny night, a single day out of Kautokeino, we retired into a *gjestgiveri* at Nordreisa. Next morning we drove twenty miles up the rugged valley of the Reisa and engaged a boatman, boat, and outboard motor. We ascended rapids and negotiated shallows through the slightest of apertures. One of the rapids could be circumvented only by charging the bank and bounding off it; Dagfinn was at the bow with a pole for the purpose. The propeller often clinked bottom. We carried a spare.

The river flowed through a gorge a half mile wide, between cliffs a half mile high. Midway in our ascent we beached to gaze at a waterfall. More than half of its half-mile tumble was free fall.

Great boulders marked the head of navigation beyond per-adventure. Dagfinn and I continued upstream for an hour on foot, clambering over *ur*, or scree, picking our way across swift tributaries, scaling cliffs, and threading surprisingly lush forest. Pines in this Arctic nook grow to twenty inches thick. We reached another waterfall, more voluminous than the first. Here the river Reisa itself thundered down into a misty chaos of clefts and chasms into which we peered from cliffs hundreds of feet above.

We saw a big white reindeer at close range. He fled before my camera was ready. Dagfinn ran out on a circuit to shunt the deer back, but the only effect was that I got to wondering whether I would see either of them again.

The return cruise was swift and wild. Our agile steersman shot the rapids with hairbreadth precision. At the crucial moment Dagfinn was at the bow again to deflect us around our point of inflection.

We drove north again and west. The Lyngfjord Alps. abrupt and snowy, resembled the Canadian Rockies of five weeks before and were doubled by reflection in the fiord. In the Signaldal, farther west, vertical canyon walls framed the view of a towering matterhorn, gracefully accented in the foreground by a sod-roofed farmstead. At length a high bridge brought us into Tromsø, a surprisingly sprawling city for 69°45′N. We took three rooms in the Grand Hotel and drove to the airport to collect Marge, Doug, and Margaret, fresh out of Boston. We caught them as they were boarding the bus. "Can I help you with that bag?"

On our way south on back roads we saw five Lapps dis-mantling their two tepees and stowing the deerskins and other gear into a pickup truck. Soon we were south of the raindeer moss, where hay becomes a major concern. Strings are strung on upright poles like clotheslines, row on parallel row, and hay is laboriously draped across them, stalk by stalk, to dry. The wet climate precludes letting it dry on the ground.

Around a noisy cascade a salmon ladder had been built. It is a hierarchy of pools, spaced at intervals that a salmon can leap. Some are made of unabashedly artificial concrete basins, but this one was cunningly contrived of local rock and readily confused with the natural scene.

Narvik was an anomalously Arctic center of heavy industry. Trains brought iron ore from Kiruna in Arctic Sweden. Heavy hoists traveled on high beams. Broad steps led to tunnels a hundred feet below. Traces of an earlier phase of Arctic culture were visible high above Narvik, where petroglyphs depicting deer had been cut in the glacier-smoothed rock four thousand years ago. A farmhouse nearby was secured against Arctic gales by heavy chains that reached to the eaves from buried blocks of concrete.

We tunneled and skirted cliffs comparable to El Capitan, often at fiord's edge. Lemmings ran across the road and a gull flew by with one in his beak. At our exit from the Arctic the road climbed into tundra and snow and passed a ceremonial circle of boulders contrived by Lapps in the Middle Ages. A bare peak a mile from the road defined an angle of the Swedish border.

Mountain passes are heralded by pikes, which are turned to close the road when the snow is deep. Windswept stretches are shielded at a distance by snow fences, not in the flimsy American style, but high and built of planks. Sometimes two or three are built in parallel to share the load.

At Majavatn, a lake mirroring snowy mountains, we detoured into a Lapp hamlet comprising an old sod-roofed log cabin on stilts of tree trunks, several new cedar cabins, a tepee, a wooden bell tower with a room below, and a simple rectangular wooden church with curtained windows. A reindeer looked on.

A hundred miles south of the Arctic we entered Viking country. Burial mounds with large trees on them were conspicuous in the fields, for it is forbidden to till them. Near a little thirteenth-century stone church, a gull in a tree feared for her eggs and came screaming and diving at us. We encountered stave churches again, those fantastic wooden ventures in Gothic flamboyance. Trondhjem, a six-digit city, boasts one of the great Gothic cathedrals of Europe, and much of it, like the stave churches, dates from the early years of Gothic. One is tempted to link the Gothic to the Goths after all.

We skirted a narrow fiord between vertiginous cliffs that were draped at intervals with white cataracts. Fallen boulders as big as cabins crowded the road, which was posted with an 'M' from time to time to indicate where there was room for two cars to meet and pass. A winding course of milky green glacial streams and a dizzy stack of switchback—Trollsteig—brought us up two thousand feet to snow and a frozen lake and then down to the little gorge of the Gudbrandsjov, where the water has drilled its own drain.

At Geiranger we boarded a ferry for a mountain cruise. We were in the heart of mountainous Norway, threading our sinuous way between towering cliffs on deep sea water many devious miles from the open sea. Repeatedly the ship headed stubbornly for a mountain wall at the apparent end of the fiord, only to open an abrupt bend in the chasm and a breathtaking new vista. Sea birds and land birds swooped down the dizzy slopes and circled the ship. We penetrated to the genuine end, from which, resuming our car, we drove over the heights to Hornindalvatn, Europe's deepest lake: 1700 feet deep and flanked by cliffs to match.

Thence we continued to Europe's largest glacier, the Jøstedalbre: three hundred square miles. We approached it from a somber fiord-end that had suffered three disasters from rockslides in the past three generations. The last one precipitated a tidal wave that drowned most of the inhabitants. The survivors moved away, except for one stubborn man. In the sunlit evening we walked five miles from there to the edge of a grimy blue-green curtain, a tongue of the glacier.

Dagfinn's mother was born at Innvik Fjord. He pointed to a spot, atop the opposite precipice, where a cow had imprudently grazed backwards and fallen, ungrazed, two thousand feet to the water. The morning yielded us a bright succession of scenes: glaciers, mirrored snowy matterhorns, steep spruce forests, steep flowery meadows, and a seemingly Japanese lake scene with island and asymmetrical conifers.

The head of Lustra Fjord, belying its name, is a gloomy recess in the mountains. Its steep, dark expanse of forest is accented at one remote point by a white waterfall, and near it are the remains of a cabin in which Wittgenstein spent some summers.

One morning we set out to climb Fannaråk. Its summit, 6800 feet above sea level, stood 4000 feet above the beginning of our walk—a steep walk, with some clambering. Midway we heard a cuckoo, for all the world like a clock. We came to snow, which deepened as we climbed. Doug left the trail and fell eight feet through the crust.

From the summit we looked across at the Jøstedal glacier, down at a fiord, and out at black peaks and pinnacles to either side. The back of the mountain dropped off a thousand sheer feet to another glacier. There is a weather station near the brink, from which, in a blinding snowstorn two years before, a weatherman stepped off to his death.

Dagfinn had a key to the *hytte* at the summit, in which a cache of canned goods was maintained by semiannual helicopter. Toward midnight we watched the sun go gaudily down and the moon come up. We retired to bunks in the *hytte* under heavy blankets which Dagfinn lined with sheets from his knapsack.

We breakfasted in the *hytte* on reindeer stew, soggy flatbread, canned pineapple, and coffee, and made the vigorous descent to the car, obliged to get to faraway Oslo before the morrow. The road thither climbed high again among frozen lakes and snowy mountains. Farming country ensued, and the rich Gudbrandsdal. The traditional farm houses are long and white, the barns red and sod-roofed. A usual adjunct is the *tabbur*, a sod-roofed granary on piles, often ornamented with painstaking woodwork. A side road yielded cabins, sodded and windowless. By midnight we were installed in Stefanshotellet, Oslo, and Dagfinn was at home in suburban Sandvik.

A Scandinavian logic colloquium started the next morning, June 18, 1970, defraying part of the cost of our summer travels. The participants included Abraham Robinson, Georg Kreisel, Bill Tait, Bill Boone, and Jean van Heijenoort from America, Stig Kanger and Dag Pravitz from Sweden, and some young Scandinavian mathematicians. We were all given a supper cruise on the Oslo Fjord. My paper was on predicate-functor logic.

Dagfinn and his wife Vera entertained us in their imaginative house, designed by him and poised on a bluff among giant pines. They took us to dinner at a showplace in a northern suburb overlooking Oslo, which is sealed by a belt of forest and rugged hills. The Norwegians have planned well against cultural blight.

Dick and Catherine Hare met our plane at Heathrow, drove us to their old brick house in old Ewelme for a swim and lunch, and thence to Oxford. Dinner at the Quintons', dinner at the Strawsons', a reception at Balliol, and dinner at the Berlins' noble Headington House ensued. Marge and I were lodged at Headington House along with the French ambassador Courcel and the historian Momigliano and their wives. Both men were likewise getting degrees.

June 24: breakfast in bed in the Berlins' luxurious ménage and then off to Brasenose College to join the other honorands and be robed, regaled with strawberries and champagne, and marshaled into the procession. It was headed by the chancellor, old Harold Macmillan, in flowing robe and long gold-braided black train carried by a page. As we approached the Sheldonian Theater, a few communists irrupted to abuse the prime minister of Malaysia, but some agile guards restored order.

Macmillan was enthroned in the Sheldonian. Each honorand was led forward and addressed in Latin by the university orator, Colin Hardie. Each of these eight orations ran to some four hundred words of a biographical nature, a skillful blend of fact, praise, and wit, and withal a gem, I trust, of

ornate classical prose. After each, the orator led the honor-
and to the throne to be addressed more briefly in Latin by
the chancellor and given the diploma. Sir Maurice Bowra, a
fellow honorand, remarked that two Eliot House boys had
now made good. He was attached to Eliot when he was
Charles Eliot Norton Lecturer in 1948.

Macmillan presided at the Christ Church gaudy, sitting
where Charles I had held his last court. Behind him hung
Holbein's Henry VIII. Guests at high table included the
eight honorands, also chancellor Hogg of the exchequer, Sir
Roy Harrod, and Gilbert Ryle. Harrod talked to me of his
new translation of Nicod on induction; the earlier version
had been the subject forty years earlier on my first scholarly
publication. Courcel spirited me away in his ambassadorial
car to join in the aftermath of a concurrent dinner party at
the Berlins'.

Ethiopia   64

On my sixty-second birthday next morning I shipped off our
Arctic garb and dinner clothes and my Oxford robe. Tony
Kenny took me to lunch at Balliol and Dick Hare drove us to
our channel steamer at Southampton, with time out to stroll
and dine in Winchester. After a short night in steamer chairs
we rented a Renault in Cherbourg. Doug driving, we dallied
for a few days in western Normandy and eastern Brittany
looking at turreted castles, Gothic and Romanesque
churches and abbeys, medieval streets, stone villages, and
thatched stone barns. We walked up the steep street of
Mont St.-Michel and on up the dreamlike pile that domi-
nates it—a visit long overdue. Such was our progress to the
Paris airport. Then we flew to Rome, where we boarded an
Ethiopian plane.

Dawn revealed red desert, desolate mountains, and a great
gorge in the eastern Sudan. The desolation continued into

Ethiopia. We alighted at Asmara and settled in the White Hotel. Soon Don and Ginny Davidson and their thirteen-year-old Elizabeth arrived from Israel, and our rendezvous was achieved. Don and Ginny had laid out the ensuing six weeks meticulously and knowledgeably for the two families and reserved all lodgings, flights, and car rentals.

Asmara had been the capital of Italy's Eritrea and still retained a dull latter-day Italian look except for the signs and the people. We got our first inkling of the system behind the Amharic syllabary, in which the signs are written, from Coca Cola; the character for *ca* shared one recognizable feature with the sign for *co* and another with the sign for *la*. The people were black, but many had Semitic features. Some walked in white robes, others in polychrome African garb. The approach to Haile Selassie's local palace was jealously guarded; the sentry menaced us and turned us back when we were still a block away.

The seven of us arose early and boarded the single car on the narrow-gauge track for sweltering Massawa on the Red Sea. Our altitude was 7500 feet, and the intervening escarpment was the west wall of the Great Rift. We zigzagged down slopes that were green with Mexico's prickly pear, alternating with groves of Australia's eucalyptus. Trees obtruded that could pass for Mexican *pitahaya*, a giant cactus, but were really euphorbia and strictly African. A lone grizzled baboon sat under a tree and squinted as we passed. Camels munched on prickly pear. Soldiers boarded the car midway in our descent and searched the native passengers, for there was trouble with guerrillas who sought an independent Eritrea. It was Eritrean Moslems against Abyssinian Christians.

Terraces near sea level were planted with henequin, another Mexican touch. Leveling out, we crossed a flat desert dotted with oases and finally crossed the blue water of the Red Sea by causeway to insular Massawa. Houses in the old Moslem town bore capacious wooden balconies, elaborately carved, that reminded us of Lima. But we were closer now to where such things began.

We went back up to Asmara by bus. The route was even more tortuous, there being no tunnels. The bus was crowded and we sat on folding seats in the aisle. Some passengers had rings in their ears, others had them in their noses. Some faces were veiled, others tattooed. An old black Moslem woman and her white-skullcapped son vomited sporadically out a window, until the woman disappeared to the floor between the crowded seats. One pair of double seats, built for four, was occupied by a family of ten little people of various generations. We passed a settlement of huts occupied by refugees from a village that had been burned by government troops, we were told, in reprisal for aid given to Eritrean separatists. Tanks, army trucks, and soldiers were in evidence along the route. Our ascent was capped by a monastery on a pinnacle above the escarpment.

We were sad to miss the ancient monastery and rock-hewn church of Lalibela; the airstrip there had dissolved that very day for the duration of the rainy season. So we booked instead for the ancient Ethiopian capital of Axum, which some identify with Sheba. It was a mere half-hour flight, but we checked out of the hotel and turned up at noon with all our luggage, for we were not coming back. Delays ensued, and we learned that the plane had been commandeered. The authorities wanted to lodge us in a hotel and transport us the next day, but this would have played havoc with our continuing schedule. We insisted and succeeded: the airline transported us by road in a small private bus.

It was better than flying. We passed clusters of cylindrical huts with thatched conical tops. Suddenly we came to the brink of an escarpment, perhaps two thousand feet high, commanding a branch of the Great Rift. Strange mountains rose to the southeast, broad but thin, like stage sets. One great dome resembled Rio's Sugar Loaf; other mountains divided into extravagant pinnacles. We zigzagged down to the arid valley floor, which was littered with rounded black stones, some as big as houses, some poised precariously on others. On crossing the river Merab we left Eritrea and entered the Abyssinia of the atlases of my youth. The road was alive with donkeys, goats, zebus, and men carrying plows and yokes. We were stopped at dusk by guerrillas, but our driver and his armed companion talked our way through.

Axum's empire reached its height and turned Christian, like Rome, in the fourth century. The main remnants are stelae as tall as a hundred feet, carved with representations of doors and windows. Notches suggest that the monoliths were extracted from the rock with the help of wooden plugs as in Egypt. A royal tomb carved in the bedrock, with a carved stair and several burial recesses, dates from the time of Jesus. A modern church houses the crown jewels and robes, which women visitors can view only from the atrium through a grill.

Mosquitoes had made for a bad night, but in the day they gave way to swarms of flies. Brushing could not be relaxed. Pedlars and beggars swarmed persistently too. But the eye rested gratefully on the bevies of beringed, bedizened, and brightly bedight black belles at the village wells.

We were seven of the eleven passengers in the little plane for Gondar, 150 miles southwest. We flew over barren mountains, dry valleys, and palisaded compounds, again of round thatched huts. Then the terrain broke into a chaos of canyons with buttes and mesas towering over abysses a mile and a half deep. At length order prevailed: the ground leveled off at 7300 feet, Lake Tana glittered in the offing, and we alighted.

Festive arches bore witness to the emperor's recent visit. He had conferred degrees at the local Haile Selassie I University and Public Health College the day before, accounting for the commandeering of our plane out of Asmara.

Our hotel in Gondar looked out on an odd campus of four stone palaces. They were medieval without being old, for Gondar dates only from 1632. The palace of King Fasilidas was partly Portuguese in spirit and partly archaic fancy. Later kings built further palaces progressively northward. The last of them dates from around 1820, but the age of jousts and chivalry pervades them all.

We walked past huts of mud and wattles, thatched or

roofed with tin, to the seventeenth-century church of Debra Berhan Selassie, which is to say, Mons Sanctissimae Trinitatis. It was a high, narrow parallelipiped with square windows. For protection the whole had lately been encased in a tin-roofed, four-square portico. We left our shoes and entered onto guady straw mats. The timbered ceiling was painted with row on row of identical winged faces, and the walls were hung with painted canvas depicting Bible stories. Scenes were rendered in squares, as in comic strips, with boundaries drawn between. A human figure might lean against a boundary, or reach around it. There was a strain of Early Christian naïveté reminiscent of Ravenna, but darkly Ethiopian: full-front faces, black and brown, with big black eyes. Natives standing near us bore living proof that the eyes were scarcely an exaggeration.

Off again, then, for a short hop across Lake Tana to Bahar Dar. A native passenger ahead of us had been frisked for weapons—another reminder, before the era of hijacking, that there was unrest. As we approached our landing south of the lake we saw where the Blue Nile emerges, filtering away between islands and headlands at the southeast corner of the lake.

The flowery lawn of our hotel bordered the lake and backed up to the little bungalows that were the bedrooms. At the shore there were great grotesque trees, called sycamore fig perhaps, whose fat, smooth branches, low and bulbous, invited one to climb as if onto an elephant. A baboon was chained to one of the huge trunks.

The town market was a large field thronged with colorful natives with ringed ears or noses, odd headgear, and flowing garments; black Africa to the full. We walked past a Russian technical school, a straw in the wind, and came to a marsh that teemed with herons, hornbills, and great implausible marabou storks. Brilliant little birds formed serried ranks on the telegraph lines. Continuing to the brown waters of the Blue Nile, we encoutered papyrus in abundance, and ibides. Perhaps the Nile preserves a certain character over its four thousand miles. A procession of natives crossed the Nile bridge, and two of them stopped to kiss the cross worn by a black priest.

A skipper at a crude stone jetty took the seven of us in a launch to an island church, Debra Marian. A path through the heavily wooded island led past two populous round wattle huts and brought us to the crude little church. Its central structure was of rough stone with a broad door of hewn timber. The whole was enclosed, for protection, in a round outer casing of poles and thatch. A thin, black old priest sat in the doorway of the inner building, which we were not permitted to enter, and showed us page by page the treasure of the place: an early manuscript of the gospel with each evangelist depicted at his writing. As we cast off from the island a storm broke. The rain blew into the boat in slanting sheets. The lightning was brilliant and the thunder deafening, and white-capped waves buffeted the boat. Capsizing was doubly to be dreaded because the water was infested with bilharzia. We made port drenched, but only with wholesome rain.

Midway in our flight to the capital, Addis Ababa, or New Flower, two hundred miles to the southeast, we crossed the Blue Nile's gorge, of which Alan Moorhead has written that no one can thread its bottom. It is perhaps twice as deep as the Grand Canyon, and the swift river fills its floor. The region is a chaos of dizzy canyons, with an occasional palisaded compound of round huts perched on a breathtaking promontory over an abyss. At length the uplands solidified into a firm plateau again, and Addis Ababa was spread below us, silver and white: white plaster and tin roofs.

At the Hotel Ras we were called on by a Canadian named Crummie, of the local faculty, who had been alerted by our Boston friends Sam and Betsy Putnam, old Ethiopia hands. Crummie and his brother took the seven of us to a native restaurant. The walls of the large round room were hung with necklaces, weapons, and other artifacts. We sat on sofas at a low table. To each table was brought a large wicker tray topped with a large inverted circular basket, the whole swathed in yards of flowered cloth. The waiter in flowing robes authoritatively whisked off the cloth and the basket as if there were some point to them, and exposed sheets of spongy sour unleavened bread lying on another great cloth. The bread, called *injera*, is made from *tef*, which is perhaps millet, and fermented. Then a woman in flowing robes ladled *wat* onto the *injera*, *wat* being a wet stew of mutton, beef, and/or chicken. It is prepared in *ghee*, or clarified butter, and mercifully peppered and spiced. We tore off slabs of *injera* with which to spoon up the *wat*. The plan is reminiscent of Mexico, but the soggy *injera* is sloppier than a *tortilla*, and less agreeable to ingest. Everyone was served a decanter of sweet mead, called *tedj*, to mitigate and wash down the *injera* and *wat*. One drank from one's decanter, and further decanters arrived as required. When we had done, the waiter bundled off the sodden leavings in the underlying cloth.

Next day Marge visited a nursery school with Mrs. Crummie, Don retired with colic, and Ginny and I walked to the extensive but dull and squalid market quarter. One alley, relatively exotic, called for a photograph, but a black chauvinist interfered. Someone stole my spectacles from my breast pocket during the brief altercation. I bought a passable replacement.

We all went to a buffet supper at the Crummies'. The approach to their house was a hundred yards of rough private lane between bamboo palisades. This terminated at a locked enclosure surrounding their house. The guests included an adventurous young English couple named Nerrish, likewise academic, who had spend two years in Siam before Ethiopia; also a local professor of philosophy named Grünfeld, who has since moved on to America.

On July 8, 1970, laden and seven strong, we moved to the airport for our scheduled flight to Kenya, only to face a repetition of the Asmara fiasco: a long delay culminating in cancellation. Air India transferred us to a hotel for the night, during which Marge and I came down with colic. Next day at noon, Margaret alerted us all for frantic packing and immediate departure; she had got the word accidentally in the street. We took off for Nairobi.

Kenya 65

Through a rift in the clouds I glimpsed a vertical half of Mount Kenya, rocky below and snowy above, as we crossed the equator. An agent of Brooke Bond Travel met our plane at Nairobi and took us to day rooms in one of the bungalows of Nairobi's sprawling Norfolk Hotel, which plays the Raffles, the Peninsula, Shepheard's, and the Cataract to Nairobi's Singapore, Hong Kong, Cairo, and Aswan. In the evening a propeller plane wafted us to Mombasa, where our rented Volkswagen microbus waited. We drove twenty miles northeast along coastal roads to Whispering Palms, a luxurious resort in a district called Kikambala. It was midnight, but sandwiches awaited us.

Each cabin had an end wall of heavy stone and a high, steep roof of smooth, dark thatch. A porch gave onto a broad lawn shaded by coconut palms. They were notched for natives who would effortlessly scale them to prune or reap. Beyond was the white beach, the blue Indian Ocean, and, a mile out, a coral reef with surf visibly breaking. Strange bright shells and starfish lured one into the shallow lagoon, to one's abrupt and excruciating regret. The sea urchin is a bristling ball of poison. I stepped on one, was felled by the pain, and came down on another with my hand. I sidled crabwise to the beach. The worst was over in ten minutes, but traces lingered for weeks. One must wear sneakers or swim in the pool.

The beach was interrupted at intervals by bold wooded ridges of coral, forty feet high, projecting across from the high ground to the sea and cavernously undermined by the tides. An absurd baobab, vast in the trunk and skimpy in the crown, stood in midair on the side of one of these ridges, supported from behind by roots that reached back into the bluff. Another of the ridges sheltered at its inland end an inviting nook of beach, suitable for pirates, in which we found two curious large wicker fish traps. From there a shoulder-wide path, clear and sandy underfoot, wound mysteriously for half a mile through eye-high brush and led nowhere.

A straight path of more evident utility was flanked by fences at the boundary of Whispering Palms. Evidently a public footway to the sea, it was trodden by head-laden natives in traditional garb, some of them bewilderingly steatopygous.

A wild dog called a *guiriama* frequented the grounds. He was black and fan-eared and croaked like a crow. He slunk, bullied by a domestic dog that was egged on by the cruel son of the white landlord.

At low tide we walked across the lagoon to the reef, and at high tide we sailed the lagoon in the hotel's little boat. Farther afield, we engaged a French boatman named McConnel and went snorkling over submerged coral in the crystal-clear sea. The vessel was a jerry-built catamaran with an engine in each hull—a thoughtful precaution, for one of them failed.

So playful a six-day sojourn was out of character, and occasioned only by our having missed our booked flight to Zanzibar through the hang-up in Addis Ababa. Unable to book another, we enjoyed the *dolce vita*.

Some streets of Mombasa had an Arab look, with closed balconies as at Massawa; others were lined with free-standing cabins. Fort Jesus, built in 1599 to buttress Portugal's crumbling empire, had medieval charm beyond its years. We were vouchsafed an aerial reconnaissance of Zanzibar as we flew low over its forests on the way to the Tanzanian capital, Dar-es-Salaam, Port of Peace. A rented Land Rover awaited us there, in 7°S. I had spanned seventy-seven degrees, from the Arctic Ocean, in thirty-eight days.

Natives in the market of Dar-es-Salaam were notable for their bright costumes, their brass anklets, and their artificially distended earlobes, suggesting pretzels. Msasane, up the coast, was a village of palm-thatched mud huts strewn along the beach and back among the palms, bananas, and baobabs. On the beach there were dugout canoes with bilateral outriggers. Men were mending nets.

Flying back to Nairobi we had a close view of Kibo, the part of Kilimanjaro that was above the clouds. It was steep to the top and then abruptly flat and snowy at 19,342 feet. As we approached Nairobi we saw farmsteads, each with its trees and green gardens, set off by enclosures from the tan grasslands. The tan gave way here and there to land black from burning.

Our third car, a Volkswagen microbus, awaited us at Nairobi but proved defective. While Brooke Bond sought a replacement, an employee drove us through an animal reserve. Excitement began with Thompson's gazelles and baboons, and mounted as we espied giraffes slanted across the horizon between the thorn trees. Zebras moved in herds, interspersed with gnus. The uncouth mien of the gnus was a foil for the grace and bandbox elegance of the zebras. Self-conscious warthogs averted their ugly faces and hurried off, tails high. Lithe impalas leaped about and fenced with their lyre-shaped horns. The hartebeest was unsettling; his straight horns and upright ears gave a doubling effect that made one feel astigmatic. Bushbucks abounded, and there was an occasional waterbuck, as big as a cow but better looking. Of the plentiful birds the most striking was the crowned crane, or, as our native driver explained, the clowned, or clested, clane.

A viable microbus awaited us across from the great mosque of Nairobi. We drove north through grassland punctuated with tall euphorbia. We passed fields of coffee and of white daisies that produce an insecticide; then miles of sisal, whose tall stalks made a sketchy forest. The huts, round and plastered, had conical black roofs. Natives were head-laden and draped with beads.

We boarded the Ark, a game lodge in the Aberdare Reserve. It had the projecting curved roof that Noah seems to have fancied, and galleries like decks. Occupants were

Kenya

shielded from wild beasts, which in turn were shielded from human emanations that might upset the tenor of their ways. We were thirty yards from one end of a water hole, an open patch of marsh in the forest. A dozen Cape Buffalo grazed and drank and were succeeded by another dozen. They gave way as a muddy, oversized bull buffalo moved unswervingly through their midst. His heavy horns, parting at the middle of his broad forehead, gave a combined impression of menace and murky, effortful, low-browed meditation. Occasionally a rhinoceros moved in, likewise self-absorbed and unswerving, and the buffaloes gave way. Two rhinocerotes confronted each other in a hostile way, snouts down and little pig eyes upward blinking, but at length they backed off. Hyenas came, and giant forest hogs. There were crowned cranes again, sacred ibises, Egyptian geese, hammerheads, and the ubiquitous weavers, whose hanging nests the color of parchment and the size of a grapefruit will deck a thorn tree with the lavishness of a Christmas tree.

Next day we zigzagged along the equator and then veered south to Lake Nakuru. Millions of flamingoes covered great expanses of lake like pink frosting. They crowded the beach, pacing fastidiously, lifting each leg and laying its distal segment flat on the sand. Interspersed among their millions there were thousands of white pelicans, clumsily wading or chugging through the air, leading with their Adam's apples. Round little hyraxes scurried up the rocks, and a troop of baboons ambled by.

We moved southwest through plantations of trim green tea bushes and slept at Brooke Bond's Tea Hotel at Kericho. Brooke Bond is primarily in tea, not tourism. Kericho is an outpost with unpaved streets, roofed sidewalks, and wooden shop fronts. The shopkeepers are Indian, the employees Negro.

Soon we were moving among the Masai. They are rather Caucasian in features and coppery in skin, and they redden their hair with henna. Occasionally a herd of cattle passed, tended by a slim Masai draped in a brown or red cape and carrying a spear. Once we stopped and I photographed such a scene, standing in the opening in the car's roof. The young Masai ran to us, furious. I gestured with coins from behind the glass, but he would have none of it. He made a feint for the camera through the opening in the roof, and then brandished his spear at the glass. Don was daydreaming at the wheel, but I got him going. Evidently the Masai think their cattle, which are their wealth, are sickened by photography. Later, when a Masai boy frantically gestured me not to photograph his herd, I sympathetically desisted, despite the interesting horns.

We passed a herd of goats and their youthful goatherd, whose dusty drapery hung from a shoulder along with his bow and arrow. Herds of zebras, mixed with gnus, roamed the grasslands. Impalas bounded like rocking horses, and eighteen giraffes sloped within our ken, though we were not yet in an animal reserve. Robed Masai stood about with their spears. Their cattle grazed amid the wildlife.

We entered the vast Mara-Masai Game Reserve. One had to show proof of reservations in the safety of Keekorek Lodge. The fauna observed outside the reserve were supplemented now by buffalo and, in brief succession, eleven elephants. We came to a confluence where hippopotami were submerged, their long faces presented flush with the surface of the lively current. Next we saw a baby rhinoceros and its mother. We picked up a nature guide who spoke only "small English" but, on Don's supplying the Swahili word *simba*, guided us unswervingly over the grass to a pair of lions lying under an acacia. They take no umbrage if one stays in a car. The male gave us a bored look, yawned, roused the female with his paw, and mounted her while we photographed from five yards away. The native then steered us to where five lions were lying. They seemed unaware of being photographed at two yards.

We jostled back onto the road and overtook two hyenas, who veered off and alarmed two giraffes, who fled headlong with their tails out. We saw a giraffe wade into a herd of zebras and gnus, without much disruption. But another time such a herd broke into a stampede, aware perhaps of a lion.

The species sorted themselves: zebras this way, gnus that. Perhaps it is because gnus defend themselves with their foreheads and zebras with their hind legs.

A great ugly marabou stork took flight from a pool, an awesome sight, his white wings slowly sweeping. Then two jackals slunk away from the pool.

More Africa 66

We crossed the boundary between the Mara-Masai Reserve and Serengeti Park, reentering Tanzania as fourteen elephants trooped across our road. We settled into Lobo Lodge, on a *kopje,* which is an isolated hill of irregularly fissured rock rising abruptly a hundred feet or so above the plain. The lodge was an imaginative mixture of levels and of indoors and out, wood and rock. Each bedroom bore an abstract painting with a motto in Swahili. Ours read *Mtu ni nduga mke ni rafiki.* Construed by means of my Swahili manual, this seems to say "Man is kinsman, woman is friend." Folk wisdom, if any.

Pressing onward the next day, we saw five lions move across a hill. Antelopes faced them from afar, watchful and motionless. Farther on, vultures were wheeling and more vultures were quarreling under the trees; there I found the remains of a hartebeest. A parade of strangely dark giraffes moved along the skyline. Fifteen zebras filed by, as evenly spaced as their stripes.

We quietly pulled into a meadow alongside two watchful cars to see what they had found. A spotted cheetah was nursing her cub. Later we passed this information to a man who, in return, directed us to a leopardess and her cub. They were lying on a bough of a thorn tree, and the cub was trying to get his teeth into the carcass of an impala that the mother had wedged into a crotch of the bough. The cub mewed in frustration and presently dislodged the carcass, which splashed into a brook below. The bored mother walked down the bough, dropped to the ground, and disappeared. After some splashing she reappeared with the dripping impala in her teeth. She fixed it firmly into the crotch of the bough again and lay down on the ground while the cub resumed its efforts.

Seronera Lodge was in a drier part of the Serengeti Plain. The thorn trees were scrawny and the termite castles were taller than I. The lodge consisted of tents. Each was porched and zippered, with a zippered bath. A pail of water was poised to spill into the shower. A gazelle passed between our tents in the night, and a buffalo was ruminating in the yard by morning.

We struck out on back roads for Olduvai Gorge, setting our course by the Shell map. Twice it had proved wrong, and so it was again. Roads divided and dwindled and we wandered far afield with only the sun to reckon by. We got there, and a native who worked for Leakey pointed out strata in the cliffs that were associated with our various forebears of a million years and more ago.

On then to Ngorongoro, at 7600 feet again. The grassy floor of the crater, dotted with blue alkaline lakes, was two thousand feet below us and ten miles across. We made the steep, tortuous, bumpy descent. A marsh teemed with the various great birds that we had already admired and many new ones, notably the angular and overdressed secretary bird. Moping rhinocerotes stumped by with oxpeckers or tickbirds on their backs, and elephants with cargoes of egrets. We came upon ten sleeping lionesses and many cubs, and on fording a stream we met the sire, a dark-maned lion with surprisingly visible ribs for one so well staffed for predation. His harem evidently slept too much and hunted too little. He ambled to the stream and drank and drank until we were the ones that were bored.

Hyenas ran by in their headlong, head-down way. We came to a herd of zebras, two of which were fighting. Each tried to bite the other's neck and kick his face Siamese fashion with a hind leg. Ten hippopotami basked in a pond, nearly submerged. They differed from black rocks in their responsiveness to sudden noises, bestirring themselves like annoyed clubmen.

Our next lodging was on the edge of the escarpment over-looking Lake Manyara in the Rift. The game park, skirting the lake for twenty miles, was a heavy forest of grotesquely bottom-heavy baobabs, thick and extravagantly contorted sycamore-fig trees, and heavy twisted acacias. A lion would sleep on an acacia bough, lying limp with legs dangling on either side of the branch like a lionskin rug draped to dry. An elephant would engage an acacia, trunk to trunk, tear it out of the ground, and mull it over for edible bark. The elephant is a great lumbering beast in two senses.

Elephants gleaming black and huge with gleaming white tusks emerged from the heavy green of the jungle and blocked our car. One of them snorted, raised his ears, and visibly contemplated a lunge at us from fifteen feet, while we, with cameras poised and engine running, were on the alert to back up as best we might if the tension were to snap. But it subsided.

We continued east across the Rift, which was studded with docile conical volcanoes. One, Meru, soars to fifteen thousand feet. At a market where hundreds of Masai were gathered, my six companions got out to prowl while I stayed in the car with a view to furtive snapshots of stragglers. Instead I became a center of attention. The copper-skinned natives with their hennaed hair and their brass necklaces and festoons of beads kept rapping on the windows hoping to sell things. I would ignore them and they would drift away and be succeeded by others.

I bought a Masai spear in Arusha. We spent the night in a tent camp just across the Kenya border, at the foot of a fog-bound Kilimanjaro. We were in the Amboseli Game Reserve, and it yielded the accustomed complement of wildlife. An addition was an odd gazelle, the wispy gerenuk, with long, thin legs and neck and negligible head. We watched a shiny elephant at his mud bath and then drove off into some brush to observe three rhinos, or, to persist, rhinocerotes, one of which moved toward us, foursquare and head down, fixing us with his pig-eyed upward regard. Our car refused to retreat for a nervous minute, but Doug maneuvered us free.

We drove back to Nairobi, closing a nine-hundred-mile loop. Masai were on the road, some in pink and red, others in dark robes and headbands with ostrich feathers. Men washed clothes in a water hole while six marabou storks looked on from a thorn tree. At Nairobi we surrendered the car and emplaned for Uganda.

At midnight we alighted at Entebbe, the former capital, on Victoria Nyanza. Which is the biggest fresh lake in the world, this or Lake Superior? Sources vacillated down the years. I am reminded of the rival claims of Peirce and Dedekind to have invented the ancestral function, when Frege had anticipated them both. Far and away the biggest fresh lake is Huron-Michigan, whose status as a single continuous flat lake is indisputable.

In our fourth rented car we took vague leave of Entebbe, which, with its scattered embassies, had the air of an ill-defined garden suburb. The native houses on the twenty-mile road to Kampala were of adobe, withes, and thatch. Bananas, coffee, and flowering shrubs flourished on the red land. Kampala, the new and hilly capital, was partly a modern town of modest business blocks and partly a pioneer town of wooden Indian shops and shaded sidewalks. Women wore long full blouses tied at the waist, full skirts to the ground, and extravagant headdresses, all in brightly patterned cloth, matching or contrasting.

We traveled northwest. Neatly symmetrical adobe houses with sloping thatched roofs were painted in pale colors. Men wore white gowns, topped sometimes with European jackets. Pods like big sausages hung from umbrella-shaped trees.

The mighty White Nile had sprung full grown from the head of Victoria Nyanza. At Murchison Falls a hundred miles downstream the swift, white water curled over the brink and crashed into a roaring chaos of whirl and spray. The cloud of spray was refreshing under the equatorial sun.

Thirteen elephants enlivened the scene as we continued downstream to the ferry. A panel of scowling buffaloes looked on as from a gallery, ranged in a row as is their wont. Presently two elephants scuffled in the papyrus. One put his trunk over the other's head, they tangled tusk to tusk, one jabbed the other in the rump with a tusk, and there was peace.

Paraa Lodge, where we lodged, was just beyond the tip of Lake Albert. A launch cruise back up the Nile to the falls was prodigal in hippopotami and crocodiles. Hippos by the dozens soaked in the water, their heads and backs shining pink, purple, and brown. Surfacing, they would blow water from their nostrils. Several would surface together, making waves that rocked the boat. Crocodiles gaped motionless on the beach and occasionally a bird stepped into the gap and picked the teeth.

Musicians at the lodge played *ndongoli* of assorted sizes, each consisting of eight or more flat prongs of iron in assorted lengths mounted on a sounding box. The smallest of them were played within gourds, for more resonance.

A family of five elephants moved in on the guests at breakfast. The baby elephant headed for the garbage pit and was deflected by the mother to the veranda, where the mother, pursuing, knocked over a chair and precipitated a flurry of photography.

The next leg of our journey was southwestward to Fort Portal. A turbaned woman was walking in the road with an axe balanced on her head, blade this side, handle that. Ruwenzori, the Mountains of the Moon, towered over us unobserved, such being the weather.

A native king's tomb in Fort Portal was wrought delicately in reeds and thatch. Fragrant dried grass was strewn on the floor and the king's clay pipe, meat knife, gourds, and other utensils were ranged about. It was reminiscent of the ways of ancient Egypt in its small way, and it dated back only forty-odd years.

Queen Elizabeth II National Park, the last game reserve in our great safari, lies between Lake George and Lake Edward and straddles the broad Kazinga Channel that connects them. Lions and elephants were abundant and the gaudy birds were bewildering. Hippopotami cluttered Lake George, egrets on their backs. The clumsy beasts tussled, two by two, each trying to clamp the other's jaw and snout in his maw and always failing. A neighboring mudhole was paved with hippoes, contentedly prone in the muck. At length the leader disliked our proximity. He effortfully roused himself and lumbered over to another mudhole. One by one his retinue followed, stepping and sinking, oozing mud, squealing and grunting. The second mudhole was slightly smaller, so that the last comer found no place on the bottom and had to start a second layer.

The Republic of the Congo lay near at hand. It has since been named Zaïre to resolve the ambiguity of two Congoes. It was the Congo Free State or Belgian Congo in my youth. Its name epitomized Central Africa, black Africa at its darkest. We decided to broach it, though we had no visas. Our exit from Uganda was beset with formalities relating to currency, car, and cameras. The formalities on entering the Congo were comparable, and sufficient evidently to cause the official to forget to look for visas on stamping our passports. We were in.

The houses were square, of mud and thatch. Some were painted with broad horizontal bands, others with stick figures of people. Round straw corncribs stood on stilts. Anthills and reeds stood as high as the houses. A headman's stone mansion, surrounded by guardhouses and big trees with whitewashed trunks, was heralded by a sign, "Le Grand Chef Bwisha." Women wore robes, dusty red like the land, and their heads bristled with tiny stiff braids. Some carried baskets on their heads, or blackened pots, or oil tins filled with water.

Our southward drive of thirty miles through the Congo brought us to the mud and thatch village of Rutshuru, where we turned east for Uganda. We went through a thick forest of banana, or, more probably, the tasteless local plantain, which, however, if skillfully fried in brown sugar, can be rendered almost as palatable as brown sugar. Perhaps the plantain is also the basis of so-called banana beer and banana brandy, further improvements of man upon nature.

Around a hut in a clearing among the plantains, a crowd of natives watched some young dancers. Two girls stirred a big pot with long poles. We were invited in French to join the wedding party. It would have been awkward in our ignorance of native etiquette, and risky on the score of food and drink; so we demurred. No proper ethnographers we.

Conical volcanoes loomed on either side as we approached the border. The Congolese officer noticed the lack of visas. "We thought transit passengers didn't need them." "*L'ambassade à Kampala était fermée.*" The official nodded and said "*Allez.*" Not to be implicated, he withheld his rubber stamp.

Reentry into Uganda was routine. Our Ugandan money, which was not supposed to have left the country, was hidden in Margaret's shoes, hurting her feet. We were welcomed by sixteen crested cranes, Uganda's national bird.

At Kisoro, a few miles east, we turned south up a mountainside to another Central African republic: Rwanda. Again we had no visas, but we parked at the barrier, which was open, and walked through. The uniformed guards were affable and unconcerned. I thought it rash of Marge and our young people to go over to the immigration hut for the sake of a souvenir in their passports, but they got them stamped.

Above us to the west, just over the Congo border, rose the great dark cone of the volcano Virunga, said to harbor Africa's greatest gorilla population, along with a fuller complement of chimpanzees.

Proceeding east from Kisoro, we passed a forest of giant bamboo, each stalk as thick as one's lower leg and as close to its neighbors as the thickness of a man's chest. It was called the Impenetrable Forest, and was said to abound in chimpanzees. We climbed by hairpin turns and looked out on rich, green, open country reminiscent of the gently mountainous reaches of northern Switzerland. I felt that Uganda was the most promising country of the region—the Switzerland of East Africa, as Lebanon was the Switzerland of the Middle East. The metaphor was soon and tragically confuted in Uganda by Idi Amin. It took longer in Lebanon.

Children were sliding down a hill on banana leaves. A causeway carried us across a banana swamp into a eucalyptus forest. Kabale, with its Gospel Church of reeds and tin roof and its golf club in the best Scottish tradition, admitted us to its White Horse Inn for the night.

Next day we drove over the mountains and the equator to Kampala and turned in our fourth rented car, closing another loop of nine hundred miles. On August 8, 1970, we took leave of the Davidsons and emplaned for America. We put down in Nigeria, Ghana, Liberia, and Senegal on the way, but gleaned little of those implausible and far-flung lands.

The Year of the Islands   67

· 1971   My last sabbatical began a year later, in the fall of 1971. Having ranged from arctic fiords to equatorial jungles only a year before, Marge and I were content to settle for a home base and intermittent travel. We visited islands.

We began modestly in September in Nantucket. In October we went to the Florida Keys with a party from the New England Aquarium, where Marge had been doing volunteer work. Our base was varicolored Isla Morada, magenta in its bougainvillea, orange in its hibiscus, green in its coconut palms. Off Key Largo we boated amid green thickets of mangrove, communed with fish through a glass bottom, and snorkled over pink coral such time as the squalls and torrential rains were in abeyance. The clarity of the water compared unfavorably with Kikambala. Key West, that intriguing dot on the map that puts a period to Dixie, was a rugged old fishing town with somewhat the air of Nantucket.

Miami's Seaquarium was something intermediate between a three-ring circus and a world's fair. Dolphins leapt for fish held by their trainer. Porpoises played basketball, jumped through hoops, and played the piano. Sea lions balanced balls with their noses. The two-ton killer whale wriggled out of his half-million-gallon tank and the trainer sat on his back while flamingoes and roseate spoonbills looked on.

Our Bostonians went home, but we flew fifty miles in an amphibian plane to another country, the Bahamas. We deposited one passenger on Cat Cay and then splashed down again at Bimini, where we mounted the runway into Alice Town. The island is long and narrow, running on for mile after wooded mile between white beaches. The town is short and just wide enough for two closely parallel streets. It is a predominatly Negro village with two inns, a string of one-room buildings for shops, and a few dozen pastel-tinted cottages, dominated by an all-purpose government building.

In November we left Boston with our two shoulder bags and flew to another nearby country, Bermuda. Hamilton is a town of white plaster houses with roofs of stepped slabs of limestone. Cisterns on the roofs hoard rainwater. The soil on the coral is thin, causing the roots of a big rubber tree to roam the surface for a hundred yards. In our Waterloo House and the adjacent streets, shops, and tea rooms, the color and indolent grace of a subtropical isle blended with the niceties of English ways—a blend on which the sun never used to set. A bobby in helmet and Bermuda shorts directed traffic in a birdcage kiosk at Queen and Front Streets. Fort Hamilton, up beyond, was girded by a deep moat cut vertically into the coral and serving nowadays as an exotic tropical garden, out of the wind. There was a tavern in the town named "Chez When."

The five main islands are joined by bridges and causeways. St. George's Island, in the north, boasts a spacious, lacy coral cavern in which there is a lake so clear that its bottom is visible forty feet down. There I had the satisfaction of interpreting for two bewildered young Italians from the crew of a ship in the harbor. That day we walked nine miles, and the next day we rode motor bicycles thirty miles, spanning the archipelago. The clam chowder along the way was memorable—fish stock instead of milk.

At the end of December, our island was Manhattan. Doug and Margaret were home from Princeton and Wellesley for vacation, so we took them. We lodged in Rockefeller University. Marge, Doug, and Margaret frequented opera and musea while I went about my business, which was the annual philosophy convention. I gave my three Paul Carus Lectures, whereof more anon. Goodman introduced me at the first one, Davidson at the second, and Dreben at the last. The great hall was tightly packed for the first two and pretty full for the third.

· 1972   The biggest trip of our island year began in February 1972 and was directed upon Madeira and the Canary Islands. We had to fly clear to Lisbon and then out to Madeira after an interval of four hours, which we improved by threading again the steep old streets of the Alfama and the Mouraria.

Funchal in Madeira is a compact, traditional city with straight, narrow streets overhung with balconies. The sea stretches before it and a mountain towers behind. We climbed the slope by stairs and cobblestone pavements to the church of Nossa Senhora do Monte, altitude 1800 feet, and hired a *carro* for the descent. It was a two-passenger basket on runners for sliding down the cobblestone streets to the city, an exhilarating mile and more. Two men operated it. Where the grade was gentle, one man pulled us by a rope and the other pushed. Where it was steep, so that our sled skimmed swiftly over the round tops of the stones, the front man ran beside us with the rope and the rear man stood on the ends of the runners to make more friction.

The coast west of Funchal is bold. Cabo Girão rises 1800 feet—that number again—sheer from the waves. Buses, punctual and cheap go everywhere. One of them took us around the stern and rockbound eastern cape and up the side of the huge volcano, through village after precarious village, to the very rim at 3400 feet; then over the rim and down into the verdant crater to a village, Curral das Freiras, 1100 feet below. Prior to the recent building of the road, some villagers lived out their lives without ever venturing over the rim to the outside world.

On, then, to the Canaries. Las Palmas, on Gran Canaria, is Spain's busiest port. Serried ranks of high apartment houses topped by thickets of antennas dominate its western approaches. The surviving bit of the medieval town, which Columbus knew, does little to leaven the lump. Maspalomas, at the opposite tip of Gran Canaria, is a nightmare of tall hotels and apartment houses and swarming beaches. The Spaniards have been weaker than the Portuguese in the face of the depredations of tourism. But unspoiled old villages are plentiful still, along the coasts and amid the rugged, fertile mountains. Grottoes dug into a mountainside date farther back, to the Guanches—mysterious white aborigines who were absorbed by the Spaniards.

The islands to the east, Lanzarote and Fuerteventura, are detached fragments of the Sahara. Lanzarote seethes with two hundred little volcanoes, some of whose slopes are hot. A guide scooped into the sand and fried an egg; he scooped further, threw in some tumbleweed, and it ignited. A castle on a promontory commands the port, Arrecife, which has an Arab look. Camels are in use. Yet there is viticulture, each vine sheltered in a little pit. Malmsey comes out.

We flew south to La Güera, a tropical outpost on Cabo Blanco, the southwest tip of what was then the Spanish Sahara. The scene was tan sand dunes and blue sea. A taxi took us to Nouadhibou, formerly Port Etienne, in the Islamic Republic of Mauritania. It was a straggling town of dusty streets, shacks, and wooden establishments inscribed in Arabic and wavering French. On some fronts the message was conveyed pictorially—with a crude sketch of an electric iron and cord, or of clothes on a line, or of a head being washed, or of a table set with food. Gaunt, dark natives wore flowing robes of blue, black, or white. An occasional Negro, Senegalese perhaps, appeared in more brightly variegated garb.

When we went back to Las Palmas we were joined by Bob and Rosalie. With them we continued our exploration of

Gran Canaria and even flew back to Spanish Sahara on a day's tour to its new, white little capital, El Aiuun, in the northwest corner of the country. We were taken out to a lush, deep green oasis of date palms among the sand dunes. Seated at tables in a big tent, we were served *couscous* in great tureens, family style. A big German tourist was at pains to corner all the chicken for himself and his dependents, good provider that he was, leaving the rice for us. It is uncanny, what with elbowing into queues and the like, how unfavorably many touring Germans compare with their courteous compatriots who stay at home.

The second city of the Canaries is Santa Cruz, on Tenerife. Our ship thither from Las Palmas carried crates of carrier pigeons, to be released for the return flight. The pigeons were numbered and bets were placed.

What had mainly drawn me to the Canaries was Teide, the high point of Tenerife, which stands twelve thousand feet above the nearby sea. Its conical regularity understates its scale, rendering the mountain less awesome than I expected.

We lunched with Bob and Rosalie on the Santa Cruz waterfront when they were about to leave us. Boarding time loomed and we could not get a taxi. The four of us hurried toward the ship with their luggage, but time was too short. Marge flew to the rescue: she flagged down a passing car and got a ride for the two of them and their bags. In minutes they were at sea.

A letter from Manuel Garrido in Valencia was forwarded to me, inviting me to address his pioneer group of logicians and scientific philosophers when I might next be in Europe. I replied that I was already in Spain, in a sense, and was willing to come for the marginal further expense. So I prepared a lecture in Spanish, my first ever, by translating a paper "Philosophical reflections on language learning" that I was to present at Bloomington, Princeton, and Tufts later in the spring.

On the way to Valencia we stopped in Madrid. The bit around the Puerto del Sol and the Plaza Mayor was appealingly old. At the Prado, I suffered a surfeit of El Greco, whom I had admired in small doses. We walked all over medieval Avila, in its heroic walls, and all over medieval Toledo, which was indeed straight out of El Greco, but a delight.

Carmen and Manolo (for Manuel) Garrido entertained us royally in and about Valencia. They showed us Sagunto, where Roman remains are overlaid by Moorish ones, and then established us in a seaside palace that had been converted to a luxurious government hotel or *parador*. Manolo and his young colleagues surrounded me there for a long discussion session the day after my lecture in Valencia. We flew home on April 6, 1972—a long day with multiple stops and changes.

To round out my year of the islands I got Fred Cassidy to join me in a June jaunt to Jamaica, his native land. Our rendezvous and point of departure was a lexicography conference at the New York Academy of Sciences, where he spoke on his monumental work in progress, the *Dictionary of American Regional English,* and I spoke on "Vagaries of definition." Kenneth Pike was there, the evangelical linguist behind the missionary project that had so impressed me in Mexico in 1949. He had a whimsical hobby of exotic headgear, and turned up in a different bizarre specimen at each session. Another participant was old Martin Joos, whom I had known at Ann Arbor twenty-one years before; I well remembered his remarkable oscillograms that revealed how a consonant influences the sounds uttered before and after it. A discussion interval was brightened by a witty woman from Charleston who deplored, in a vintage Charleston accent at its loveliest, the sorry state of English speech outside her native heath.

In Kingston, Jamaica, we stayed with Fred's spinster sister Helen, whom I had known when she was a baby in Akron, "Rice and peas" proved disconcertingly red and white; beans are locally called peas. Another chromatic surprise, flourishing at the roadside, was a yellow raspberry.

We climbed Blue Mountain, Jamaica's highest. This

meant a drive to an upland inn and three days on foot, largely in the rain. Wet and cold, we contrived a little fire in a shelter at the summit, where the wind and rain were fierce and the view was clouded out. But we had good talk along the way, and intermittent panoramas of tropical splendor. Fred had told me of the trees, shrubs, and fruits of his exotic homeland forty-odd years before, and we had hoped for the day, now at hand, when he could identify them for me. Another source of pleasure was his expertise in Jamaican Creole English; for he is the top man in it. The backland blacks were friendly, and their chatter with Fred, translucent to apaque, proceeded apace. There were hints of truculence in town, but not to compare with subsequent years. Racial hostility finally forced Helen Cassidy, Jamaican born and bred and devoted to good works, to give up her modest home and take refuge in Florida.

Interstitial Years   68

The Paul Carus Lectureship calls for three lectures and an eventual book, of which the lectures are a résumé; hence *The Roots of Reference*. I gave the lectures midway in my sabbatical Year of the Islands, as noted. I was busy with the book during much of that year and the two years of teaching, 1970–1971 and the 1972–1973, that preceded and followed it.

Word and Object had been a deepened and extended development of the ideas of "Two dogmas of empiricism." *Roots of Reference* was to be a deepened and extended development of the ideas of Chapter 3 of *Word and Object*. I had argued that cognitive language at its most primitive consists of expressions that can be acquired by direct conditioning, and that these should be viewed initially as sentences, however brief, rather than as terms. Terms purport to refer, and reference emerges only when one has progressively mastered idioms tantamount to the use of bound variables in quantification. One root, I now argued, is the relative clause, and another is categorical predication: 'All S is P', 'Some S is P'. I carried the message to Yale and Cincinnati under the quasi-Schopenhauerian title "The two-fold root of quantification."

A competing interest intruded. My renewed activity in predicate functors, reported at Oslo the summer before, had been sparked by discussions with Davidson of Tarski's theory of truth; for predicate functors seemed to offer a simplification of it. I came to see that this was an illusion, but I felt

· 1970 moved to write both a study of predicate-functor logic and kindred systems and a study of the adaptation of Tarski's truth theory to various systems. I contributed the one, "Algebraic logic and predicate functors," to a *Festschrift* for Goodman; the publisher also issued it in advance as a pamphlet. I read the other, "Truth and disquotation," at Ohio State and again, more appropriately, at a week-long sympos-

· 1971 ium that was held in honor of Tarski at Berkeley in June 1971.

Later that summer I flew to California for a second time, for a Summer Institute of Philosophy held at Irvine. As on Long Island three years before, I lectured and listened for three of six weeks. Davidson, Harman, David Kaplan, and Strawson were active, and briefly Kripke. Thanks to some stretching of mandate, the stipendiaries were not all from obscure faculties. They included Richmond Thomasson, Oswaldo Chateaubriand, Stephen Stich, Robert Vogelin, Peter Unger, James McGilvary, John King-Farlow, Edwin Martin, Michael Levin, Herbert Bohnert, and Helen Cartwright. We lecturers attended not only one another's lectures but also one another's discussion sessions, such was the level. My lectures were a first draft of *The Roots of Reference*, and my brilliant audience worked wonders in deflecting me from error. (They made me appreciate that substitutional quantification is not suited to impredicative classes.)

The university at Irvine is a big ring of modern buildings in an artificial oasis. One of the philosophers drove me over the arid hinterland to Fallbrook, where my retired colleague Donald Williams and his wife Katherine lived in a lone cottage on a little peak above an avocado plantation. Katherine seemed frailer, but Donald was still his same bright, sprightly, pink-faced self. He had just killed a rattlesnake.

Twice a crowd of us drove southwest from Irvine to San Onofrio Beach. Don Davidson, an expert on the surfboard, coached some of us in the art. I lay prone on the heavy board, clinging, while Jack Nelson pushed me out to the breakers and turned me around. Riding the waves in, I could not even stay prone on the board, and it was exhausting climbing back on in the big waves beyond my depth. So I was impressed with young Gareth Evans, off by himself earnestly working at his surfboard. By the end of our second outing he was standing on his board and riding the waves.

Gareth was a black-haired young Welshman, vigorous, ebullient, and with a fierce glint in the eye. He had spent the preceding term at the University of Minnesota and had driven from there to Irvine in a big car. Future years back at Oxford would be time enough for little cars; he was doing the American thing now. He had installed a tape player for his long drive, and had stocked it with tapes of his choice; not for him the potluck of radio. He lived intensely, doggedly. His mastery of the surfboard was in character, and so was his philosophy. He went after hard analytic issues, tooth and nail. He was a bright light among the young Oxford philosophers when his short life ended in 1980.

· 1972   I participates in yet another Summer Institute of Philosophy the year after, to the extent of a single recital at Amherst on the theory of knowledge, contrapuntal to the more classical harmonies of Rodericks Chisholm and Firth.

Erwin Saxl had been a fellow student of Gödel, Feigl, and Gustav Bergmann in Vienna. In middle life he married Lucretia Hildreth and settled on Hildreth lands near Bare Hill. Adjoining their woodland home he had a small machine shop where he produced instruments for testing tension in textiles. As an amateur scientist he had also devised a sensitive pendulum and recording apparatus, with which he monitored gravity with a view to establishing a theory at variance with Einstein's. He had published a little report or two in a physics journal, and evidently regretted his lack of renown. I thought of the maverick Turkish physicist Hüseyin Yilmaz, likewise alien to academia, whose exuberant theories likewise diverged from Einstein's on gravitation. If Erwin and Hüseyin were to meet, they might prove to be kindred spirits. A scientific event might supervene. We had them and their wives to dinner on Beacon Hill in October 1972, and I took the two scientists up to my study afterward. Hüseyin, animated as always, gave freely of his ideas, but Erwin disappointingly held his counsel.

I had long appreciated that the notation of class abstraction, amounting to the words 'the class of all objects x such that', can profitably be used without assuming classes. Such was my so-called virtual theory of classes (chapters 30, 53). Assumption of classes is an additional step, needed for some purposes, and it is made when we allow substitution of the abstraction expression itself for variables. But it dawned on me only in 1972 that there was no call to represent the virtual theory even as a simulation of classes. The abstraction notation is better interpreted simply as 'x such that . . .', a mere relative clause, conceived as a general term. In a paper on "The variable," which inaugurated a new program of logic lectures at Boston University, I made this point and argued further that this innocent abstraction, rather than quantification, is best seen as the basic context of the bound variable.

In November 1972 I held forth under the improbable joint auspices of Ed Haskell and Sun Myung Moon. Ed had fallen in with Moonies and had admired their attitudes, notably their anti-communism. The contact had led to Moon's being impressed by Ed's ambitious theory of unified science, to the point of underwriting a First International Congress thereof, held at the Waldorf Astoria. Out of friendship I contributed a slight paper on hierarchic structures, this being a topic that figures in Ed's theory but admits of neutral treatment. Fred and Harold Cassidy came. Harold, indeed, had been working earnestly with Ed down the years, bringing scientific knowledge and restraint to bear. The Congress was to be an annual event; Ed's endeavors over the years were crowned with success at last. He had hit the big time, but not for long. Moon was advised against letting Ed's theory dominate the Second Congress, held in Japan the next year. Ed participated in it and then broke with Moon. The congresses have continued without him.

· 1973   I was to give the Hägerström Lectures, six in number, at Uppsala. Again I had a finished and unpublished book to lecture from, *The Roots of Reference*. Winter was an odd season for a sojourn in Sweden, but there were my Harvard duties to consider. Marge and I flew before dawn on January 5, 1973, after an eight-hour delay at the Boston airport, and stopped at Copenhagen for a weekend among its spires and palaces. Its corkscrew steeples flaunt a false etymology of spiral spires. Stig Kanger met us at the Stockholm airport, drove us to Uppsala, and lodged us under the eaves of the university's old guest house.

We had hoped for cross-country skiing, but there was no snow. This was unusual, and the Swedes found it depressing; for the daylight hours are few, and without snow the dark is unrelieved.

The university is ranged up a hillside that slopes from the old town to a battlemented castle. A spacious hall in the university's eighteenth-century Carolina Rediviva is lined from floor to high ceiling with bindings of tooled leather or parchment, accesible by tall ladders, and here the fourth-century Gothic gospel of Ulfilas is on display, the earliest Germanic document. Another old building, the Gustavianum, houses in its dome an elegant little round surgical theater, the earliest ever. True antiquity sets in at Gamla (Old) Uppsala, six miles north, with an eleventh-century church and a hundred burial mounds dating back to the Goths.

Dagfinn Føllesdal drove over from Oslo with eight students and colleagues to attend my lectures. I began with a paragraph that I prepared in Swedish. When I said that I would have to switch to my *modersprák* there was a burst of applause, either for my attempt at Swedish or for my decision to switch.

Denmark and Sweden were new countries for Marge. We netted her a third, Finland, by boarding the *Botnia* at Norttalje, east of Uppsala, and cruising fifty miles to Mariehamn, in Finland's Åland Islands. Wooden houses of one or two stories stood close to the streets and simple one-story commercial buildings were strewn along the shore. The language was Swedish; Finnish appeared only in the customhouse.

We went to "Rigoletto" in Stockholm and stayed to explore the city. Arms of the sea make an archipelago of it and provide dramatic settings for the rich baroque churches, palaces, and monuments. The sailing ship *Wasa*, raised from the depths, was undergoing restoration and dripping with preservatives. I was amazed at what size and towering grandeur a ship could aspire to in 1628.

The government taxes liquor prohibitively but purveys French wine at moderate price. At parties Stig would hand each guest a whole bottle of burgundy to cleave to and swig from. But the department extended itself with our farewell dinner at the municipal hotel, what with liquors and many toasts. We got back to our lodgings at 1:30; Stig got home at 4:30. Another great dinner was given by Professor and Fru Hidenius in their villa, illuminated outside by flaming torches. The Dahlquists, the Marc-Wogaus, and the Åqvists also showed us much kindness.

In Amsterdam we walked the old streets again, cruised the canals, and went to a concert. The litter in the canals and the insistent promotion of pornography marked a change from the fastidious Amsterdam we remembered. American hippies had made the scene.

Three days later we were in New Orleans. As Amsterdam cowers behind its dikes, so does New Orleans below its brimming levees. Mollusk shells serve as gravel in this muddy land. Streets bristle with "shotgun" houses in the Caribbean tradition, each little façade backed by a single file of square rooms. Pillared antebellum gentility shines forth now and then amid gnarled live oaks and magnolias. In the balconied Vieux Carré, a French quarter with a Spanish air, we listened to Dixieland music in Preservation Hall. I lectured on "The variable" again at Tulane, and Andy Reck plied us with Creole delicacies at the Commander's Palace.

Other engagements followed fast. A colloquium at Storrs featured Davidson, Dummett, Kripke, David Lewis, Charles Parsons, and Sellars—all old students of mine in varying degress. At Evanston and at Nashville, elaborating on an idea of Geach's, I showed how the concept of identity could be accounted for by construing many of our one-place predicates, e.g. 'dog', as two-place mass terms. (*Roots of References*, 57f.)

In Evanston the notable sight was a spherical studio that Sam Todes had built on a scaffolding in his back yard. In Nashville the notable sight, apart from Andrew Jackson's Hermitage, was the Parthenon. It defers to the original in respect of antiquity and in the respect in which concrete is inferior to marble, but it is in full possession of its Elgins. From Nashville we visited Harold and Kathryn Cassidy, who had retired to the brink of the wooded gorge of the broad Ohio River at Hanover, Indiana.

George Berry gave a seminar course on my philosophy at Boston University that spring. I conducted its last meeting, responding to questions sent in advance. Afterward we all repaired to Joyce Chen's restaurant for a Pekinese dinner. This routine became an institution, repeated year after year.

At Wayne University I lectured and discussed as I had done at Ohio State and Notre Dame in 1966 and 1970. I lectured "On learning," "On learning to speak," and "On learning to speak of objects." Our summer was brightened at Princeton by Doug's graduation and at Bare Hill by an Arthric reunion and a visit by Peter Geach.

At age forty beside
Emerson Hall,
Harvard.

My daughters
Elizabeth and
Norma near Los
Angeles, 1949.

With Carnap in
New Mexico, 1949.

On the Concord
River with Marjorie
and Douglas, 1951.

John Cooley, left,
and Saunders
MacLane, aboard
the *Linnet* off
Maine, 1951.

With my nephew
William Van Orman
Quine in Granada,
1953.

Joseph and Eden
Woodger at home in
Surrey, 1954.

Marjorie Quine,
about 1955.

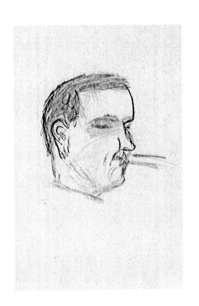

HERMAN AUTREY
1955

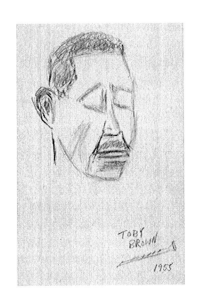

TOBY
BROWN
1955

My sketches while
enjoying jazz at the
Savoy, Boston,
1955.

My sketches of 1955–58.

Jerome Green

Nathan Pusey

E. G. Boring

Manley Thompson

Tillman Merritt

Vladimir Nabokov

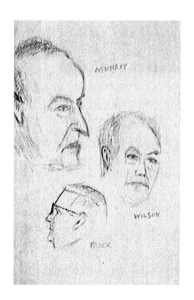

Harry Murray
Thomas J. Wilson
Paul Buck

J. O. Brew

On the deck of our camp at Bare Hill about 1962.

My son Douglas, daughter Margaret, and mother-in-law Alice P. Boynton in Meriden, 1965.

Oil portrait of me by
Pietro Pezzati, 1968.

Arthron reunion,
1971. From left:
Townsend Lodge,
Ed Haskell, self,
and Harold Cassidy.

Willard

Chestnut St,
Boston, 1977

My sketches from
my window, 38
Chestnut Street,
Beacon Hill,
Boston.

My brother Bob and
his wife Rosalie in
Chestnut Street.

Leaving 38
Chestnut Street for
a Harvard
commencement
with my Oxford
robe and Lille
épitoge.

At an after-lecture
reception, Oberlin,
1974.

From left: Fred
Simons, Peter and
Ann Strawson, and I
at Jericho, 1976.

With Marjorie and
Fred Cassidy at
Oberlin, 1980.

With laurel wreath
from degree at
Uppsala, Sweden,
1980.

Marjorie Quine and
Hilary and Ruth
Anna Putnam in our
Boston house, 1981.

Harvard
commencement,
1984. From left:
self, Eduard Sekler
(architecture), and
Samuel Thorne
(medieval law).

From left:
Morton White,
Marjorie Quine,
Burton Dreben,
self,
Lucia White.
Bare Hill, 1984.

Donald Davidson
(left), self, and
Dagfinn Føllesdal.
Oxford, 1984.

In my Harvard
study, Emerson 201
(photograph © K.
Kelly Wise).

I was to be Sir Henry Savile Fellow of Merton College, Oxford, for 1973–1974. The terms were generous and I was the first incumbent. It was twenty years after my year at Oxford as Eastman Professor. We sailed on the SS *France* and were met at Southampton by my daughter Elizabeth and her husband Mike in a rented station wagon. They took us to lunch at Romsey, which has a good Norman church and twelfth-century houses.

In Oxford we took possession of 9 Holywell Street, a narrow three-story row house of the seventeeth century. The street was one that I had admired twenty years before. Its slight curve renders the entire long succession of squeezed old façades visible as a single, foreshortened whole. New College, of medieval vintage, lines the other side of the street, and one of its gates faced our house.

Merton has Oxford's oldest college buildings. Several date from the thirteenth century. Its chapel, with the broad tower of serene proportions and the memorable mellow bells, had been built as the mere apse, unusually large, of a projected cathedral of vast extent; but the nave was never built, and Corpus Christi College stands in its site. In Merton's old library, a loft with gambrel ceiling and rows of dormer windows, volumes were chained to the long table centuries ago. I saw several still chained in 1953, but even chains decrepitate at last; only one remained twenty years later. It was my spiritual patron Sir Henry Savile that decreed the dormer windows and instituted book stacks, around 1590, setting the precedent for the Bodleian.

John Lucas was on leave and I was assigned his study, which housed a clutter of books, heavy furniture, Japanese armor, and classical plaster casts. It commanded a view of the fellows' garden and part of the twelfth-century city wall.

Two days after our arrival we went to a meeting and

sumptuous lunch in Stationers' Hall, London, as guests of our bibliophile Boston neighbor Rollo Silver and his wife Alice, the "older woman" in a mystery novel *Murder in Mount Vernon Street*. Three days later we showed them around Oxford and took them to lunch at the Turf, an ancient pub that leans against the high old city wall and is reached only by a narrow passage that links our Holywell Street with New College Lane. We dined at La Sorbonne, in a seventeenth-century building reached only by another narrow passage, off the High Street. Bob and Rosalie came four days later, October 4, and we put them through the same routine. On the morrow the four of us headed north for a week in Bob's rented station wagon.

At York the Norman walls and gates and the minster were noble sights, but best of all was the Shambles, its half-timbered houses sagging and bulging over the street. At Coxwold a big dog, fiercely barking, bade us unwelcome at the two-story stone house where Laurence Sterne, curate, wrote *Tristram Shandy*. At Durham a winding ascent from the tightly encircling gorge of the river Wear brought us to England's most glorious hilltop, crowned by a Norman castle and cathedral. The Normans were late comers; the foundation dates from the early Christians of Lindisfarne. We paused over the tomb of the Venerable Bede, born an even thirteen centuries before. The castle now houses the university, and the ultimate in Norman cathedrals makes a nice chapel.

Medieval villages gave way anachronistically to Roman ruins that culminated in Hadrian's Wall. We walked a few of its seventy miles, where its fifteen feet of height were the fortified fringe of an already redoubtable escarpment. *Castella* surmounted the wall at intervals of a Roman mile.

The mountainous Lake Country of Westmoreland was grander than expected, and the moors of Yorkshire were as empty as Wyoming. We probed ruined castles and ruined abbeys and took pious note of the lodgings of Wordsworth, Coleridge, and the Brontës. In the hill town of Shrewsbury I had my last flurry of intensive photography, for in Worcester I lost my camera. Thinking of the thousands of slides that I had projected but once, and a few hundred twice, and was unlikely to project again. I decided not to replace the camera. I can now admire a scene unaided by a viewfinder and unconcerned with whether and how to take the picture.

We got back to Oxford just in time for me to put on dinner clothes and my borrowed academic gown and attend a state dinner at Merton. I had brought my resplendent crimson Oxford robe back from America only to learn that its use is restricted to a few pompous occasions such as encaenia and that the black gown is called for at high table and lectures.

The four of us drove to a noonday cocktail party at Gwil and Sally Owen's in Rousham, a stone village on the Cherwell north of Oxford. Iris Murdoch and Gilbert Ryle were among the guests. Afterward Bob and Rosalie drove back to Oxford, but Marge and I walked the twelve miles back on the towpath of the canal, occasionally lending a hand at the locks.

The English, far from looking upon pedestrianism as prima facie evidence of vagrancy, have been at pains to accommodate it. Footpaths are laid out across country from village to village, kept open by law. They are mapped, but can be hard to recapture where the plowman has erased a segment. Marge and I set ourselves a course of footpaths one Sunday with indifferent success. We walked to the circular swamp called Otmoor, and to the traditionally inhospitable hamlet of Noke where Doug had wondered at the hostile native's hog twenty years before. We were counting on a pub lunch, but the pub in Noke was closed Sundays. We hurried on to Islip and arrived at its old stone pub just as it was closing. English drinking hours are no trifling matter. We finished our thirteen-mile loop parched, famished, and frustrated.

A series of Herbert Spencer Lectures that fall brought a succession of friends to town—Fred Skinner, Dick Pipes, John Wheeler, Karl Popper, and Herman Bondi. New friends emerged among my colleagues at Merton, especially Roger Highfield, Michael Wallace-Hadrill, Rex Richards the

Warden, Norman Davis in Old English, and the young philosopher David Bostock. We saw much of our compatriot Dana Scott, whom I knew from America, and his Viennese wife, Irene, a concert pianist.

Highfield and Wallace-Hadrill were historians. Highfield was the authority on the history of Merton, and was particularly solicitous. Wallace-Hadrill and his wife lived in Cassington, a village northwest of Oxford. Part of their house dated from the sixteenth century; the rest perhaps from the eighteenth. They had a moat and a spacious stone dovecote. He told with amusement of an American professor who looked out in admiration on these grounds and said, "What a back yard!" A back yard to Wallace-Hadrill would be a cluttered area of dustbins and clotheslines, something less than a kitchen garden.

Davidson was in Oxford for the year, and Føllesdal for a term. Freddie Ayer's Play Group, as Ann Strawson called it, met Thursdays in the college rooms of one or another member. A paper would be read, followed by drinks and discussion. Ayer, Davidson, Strawson, Dummett, Pears, Mackie, Parfit, Wiggins, Evans, Woods, McDowell, and Foster were regulars.

In November a conference was held at Cumberland Lodge, in the Great Park at Windsor. Times had changed in twenty years; scoutmasterly Sir Walter had been succeeded, the food had improved, wine was served, the duration of the conference had shrunk to a long weekend, the papers were respectable, and my only duty was to listen and comment when so moved. We bicycled about the park with the Strawsons.

My Marett Lecture at Exeter College, Oxford, a few days later was an affair of high ceremony. We were a procession of four in full regalia: the Provost, his mace bearer, the Rector of Exeter, and I. I lectured in the Hall, which had been cleared of tables and packed with chairs and people. My subject was substitutional quantification and I had banked on a blackboard, but the Hall was darkened. Few of the indulgent throng could have caught the drift. Cocktails ensued in the Rector's Lodgings, dinner at the High Table in Hall, and port and its alternatives in the Common Room. Marge and the Rector's wife were included—a chink in the armor of tradition. Marge was similarly privileged at Magdalen.

Alex Orenstein came to Oxford and we had talks in preparation for the book that he named after me. Schilpp had by then launched plans for his big volume on the same subject, for his Library of Living Philosophers. I had begun an intellectual autobiography for it, such being the established pattern. Remembering the unconscionable delay of the Carnap volume, I had no lively expectations regarding this one; but I was regrettably slow to appreciate that in consenting to it I had been unkind to the friends and colleagues whose contributed essays would be kept so long under wraps.

Iberia, Tuscany, Persia 70

Michaelmas term ran its short course, and in December we sailed to Bilbao. At Burgos we visited the great Gothic cathedral, so unlike Spain. The Goths indeed had their day in Spain, but the power of etymology has its limits. At Santillana del Mar, a stone town in a green land, Carmen and Manolo Garrido awaited us as planned. The cottages, tower houses, and austere palaces that lined the cobbled streets were two to seven centuries old, but the main attraction was the meandering caves of Altamira. Where daylight never penetrated, unless by mirrors, Cro-Magnon man had scratched and painted some 150 masterly likenesses of bison, deer, boar, and horses twenty thousand years ago.

With the Garridos we rented a car and drove west through the lush valleys, upland pastures, and crags of Asturias. At Covadonga we walked up to a rocky spur at the dizzy brink of a precipitous, wild gorge. From a black cave in the cliff behind us a stream rushed out and tumbled roaring into the depths. It was here in 718 that Pelayo is said to have turned the Moors back, seven years after they first entered Spain.

At Oviedo, thanks to Pelayo's repulsion of the infidel, churches sprang up early. Two small ones date from the ninth century, and parts of larger ones. At Oviedo the Garridos entrained for Valencia and we embussed for Galicia, where the vernacular is a dialect of Portuguese. We negotiated each *ria* or estuary through a colorful fishing village at its head, and subsided in the mightily walled city of Lugo.

Our next destination was the destination of countless pilgrims for a thousand years: Santiago de Compostela. Our hotel there was surely the most lavish of the government *paradores,* the palace of Ferdinand and Isabela. It embraces four cloisters with high verandas and a graceful chapel. Arches around the dining room are two stories high and the stone partitions of the rooms are a yard thick. In front is the broad plaza, flanked by a stone monastery and the cathedral. The latter, with its varied portals, its two-ply façade, its nave, choir, chapels, and crypt, is a congeries of architectural styles accreted over eight centuries—eleventh through eighteenth.

It was a dark and stormy night when we got off the train at Tuy, a river's width from Portugal. The station was deserted. When at last a policeman had telephoned for a taxi and we got to a distant *parador,* we were told that there was no room. But we prevailed.

For information on trains next morning, we would have to cross the broad Miño *sive* Minho to Portugal. A kind Portuguese, bound for home, offered to take us across in his car and ended up taking us all the way to Coimbra, where he ran an insurance firm.

Doug and Margaret flew over for Christmas and we converged at Lisbon. It was my third Portuguese Christmas: 1938 in Ponta Delgada, 1953 in Lisbon, and now 1973 in the walled city of Evora. York in Latin was Eboracum, so I suppose Evora is Portugal's York—both names being ultimately Celtic. The cathedral and the bishop's palace rise dramatically between earlier Moorish buildings. Narrow arched streets, balconies, and blue-tiled walls retain a Moorish aspect, and antiquity lingers in a Roman temple, walls, and aqueduct.

We bussed circuitously after a week to Nazaré, a populous fishing town. From our hotel we looked over the red tile roofs of the close-packed houses to the beach and headlands, white with foam and spray. Oxen dragged heavy, varicolored fishing boats up the steep beach from the surf. Fifteen men and boys rhythmically hauled at a net for an hour, some of them standing in the cold sea. Bad luck: just two buckets of fish, two octopoda, and a jellyfish. Black-shawled women, broad in their multiple skirts, cut the fish and arranged them on drying racks or sat gossiping over their crocheting.

Part of the town crowns a cliff. A chapel at the dizzy brink was where Vasco da Gama successfully prayed before rounding farthest Africa. We looked down 360 precipitous feet to the wild sea, which in its fury licked the top of a fifty-foot rock and the thresholds of waterfront shops.

In the walled town of Obidos we settled into a little castle that had become a *pousada,* the Portuguese equivalent of a *parador.* We made the circuit of the town on top of the wall, which ranged high by dint of cliffs and outcroppings at its base. Red tile roofs were interspersed with laden orange trees and green gardens with marble benches. One church was hexagonal; another was resplendent in blue tiles. A pillory stood in the square.

On January 14, 1974, Doug flew back to America, Margaret entrained for Spain to join Wellesley classmates for adventurous further travel, and Marge and I flew home to a dim Oxford. Shortage of fuel had darkened the streets and shops and shortened the hours of business. Some stores used "paraffin" (coal oil, kerosene) lamps or candles. A garment had to be carried to the door to determine its color. Merchants worked in coats and gloves.

Wolfson College sponsored public lectures by Anscombe, Davidson, Dummett, Føllesdal, Geach, and me, on Mind and Language. They drew vast audiences. I wrote "Mind and verbal dispositions" for the series, but then I observed that other speakers were dwelling so much on my work that I might do better to present a more central statement of my philosophical position. So I wrote and presented "The nature of natural knowledge," but both were printed in the volume of lectures. A session for discussion of my lecture was arranged, based on written questions gathered and edited for me by Dana Scott and Christopher Peacocke.

After each lecture, we and our wives all dined with the Wolfson dons and philosophy students. The college had just moved into its new buildings up the Cherwell. The ensemble was imaginative modern with a touch of the Japanese. It did not clash with old Oxford, being out of visual range.

Marge went to New England to celebrate her parents' eighty-ninth and ninetieth birthdays. I went to Birmingham for an unprepared session of responding to questions, and to Cambridge to address the Moral Sciences Club "On the individuation of attributes." Elizabeth Anscombe, by then a Cambridge professor, had been in Oxford for her Wolfson Lecture, and drove me to Cambridge in a traditional London cab that she had bought. We sat in the open front, on the driver's seat and the luggage box.

A typescript by Imre Lakatos on empiricism in mathematics reached my hands, and I liked it. I could see that he did not know my *Set Theory and Its Logic*, and that he would find parts of it congenial; so I tried to send him a copy. It proved to be unobtainable in Oxford, despite the fact that the Oxford University Press was the agent for the book in Britain. It took them ten days to get me a copy. On the day I mailed it I read of his death.

Soon I was telephoned from Utrecht, where Imre had been scheduled to address a group of philosophically minded scientists. I went over and lectured in his place, using my Wolfson Lecture. Everyone at the meeting was Dutch except a Viennese physicist and me, yet the whole meeting was conducted in English. The presiding mathematician, DeJongh, told me this was their way even in the absence of foreigners.

Boston friends stayed with us: first Betty Burch and then

Cyril and Alice Smith, he a metallurgical archaeologist and she a classmate of Betty's and future editor of Robert Oppenheimer's letters. Jerry and Blanche Bruner, Harvard expatriates in psychology, entertained us in their new home up the Cherwell. Jerry was finding his professional responsibilities far more burdensome than the statutory stint leads one to expect, and so was Dana Scott. Both have since repatriated. As Eastman Professor I had experienced no such burden, for a visitor is spared.

As a corresponding fellow of the British Academy since 1959, I had been invited each March to the dinner. At last I could accept. We dined formally and well in the great timbered hall of Lincoln's Inn, in London, and toasted the Queen and the Prince of Wales in worthy wine.

Florence, like Utrecht, had its group of philosophically minded scientists. Giuliano Toraldo di Francia invited me to address them. They expected to hear English, but I decided to try my hand at an Italian version of "The nature of natural knowledge." If a speaker takes the trouble to prepare his paper in the audience's language, he gets the linguistic considerations out of the way on his own time and frees the auditor for his brief hour of philosophy unalloyed. Foreign accent, within limits, is no impediment.

But it was a venture. I had lectured in five languages, but Italian was for me a weak sixth, mainly a reading language. So I deployed the manuals. The excessive time spent was not wasted, for I was learning more Italian. When my best effort was complete, I got Ron Laura to correct it. It was "Teoria ed osservazione."

Ron was a graduate student in philosophy at Oxford. He was born in the Italian North End of Boston and is utterly bilingual, to say the least. He also speaks Chinese, having learned it from his father, a distinguished chef and admirer of Chinese cuisine. Ron also learned Arabic, from an Arab roommate, and somehow he picked up Japanese and Portuguese. He is a former bandleader, an ex-champion weight lifter, and a gourmet cook. He and his wife regaled Marge, Don Davidson, and me with a notable Italian dinner.

Marge and I flew to Pisa and revisited the incomparable cluster of cathedral, baptistery, and leaning tower. In Florence after my lecture, Giuliano and an attractive young philosopher, Marisa dalla Chiara, took us to dinner with colleagues. Someone said *"Ciao"* as the guests dispersed, and Giuliano asked me if I knew the origin of the word. "Yes," I said, *"schiavo,"* and slipped into the line from "Rigoletto," *"Schiavo son dei vezzi tuoi."* This catalyzed Giuliano and Marisa, who, it turned out, made a hobby of singing operatic arias together. They sang beautifully, and as we drove about Florence they ran through a great repertoire. What with the joy of their singing and the delight they took in the bridges, towers, passages, *piazze*, and *loggie* of their incomparable city that they knew so well, it was a rare evening.

Marge and I spent the weekend seeing Siena and then headed for Oxford. On the train to Pisa the conductor asked if I wasn't Professor Quine. He had been to my lecture.

After two short days in Oxford, we were queuing in the railway station again. "Where are you off to?" a friend asked. I told him, and he looked puzzled. "What? I thought you said 'Persia.'" I had. It was a Swan tour, April 10–24. Prowling is more fun than being herded, but has disadvantages if the language is opaque and the time is short.

The hot plains of Elam, in Arab country continuous with Mesopotamia, yielded the oldest ruins—3000 to 600 B.C. We saw ziggurats, streets of half-standing houses, and the flat ruins of a great palace of Darius. Aesthetic impact was reserved for the next period, 600 B.C. to 600 A.D., in the uplands from Shiraz to Persepolis and Pasagardae. The Achaemenid and Sassanian reliefs on palace walls and smoothed cliffs, depicting lion hunts, battles, and the abasement of the Emperor Valerian, are a delight to the eye independently of the mind. And it is in the utterly different culture of the last period, 600–1600, that mindless delight comes fully into its own, with the dazzling mosques and palaces of enameled mosaic in Isfahan.

Deserts, black except for occasional Bedouin camps or camels, were dominated by vertical mountains. We threaded bazaars and labyrinthine mud villages and peered into *qanats*. These are broad, cool subterranean aqueducts, maintained for untold centuries, in which one can walk a hundred miles, stamina and low water permitting. We saw a dervish whirling at a roadside like a waterspout. We passed costumed Kurds and Lars and looked in on a festive Kurdish outdoor wedding.

As we approached Hamadan, the Ekbatana of the ancients and the home of Avicenna, I was inspired with snatches of potential song hits—thus "Ekbatana baby, don't you try to two-time me" and

When it's Ramadan in Hamadan
I'll be coming home to you.

Our fellow tourist Sir Lionel Brett caught the inspiration and awoke at four the next morning with this:

A tourist from old Alabama'd an
Affair with a lady of Hamadan.
They say Avicenna
Was furious when a
Reminder was born the next Ramadan.

In May I lectured in Manchester, London, Leeds, and as far afield as Aberystwyth in Wales and Edinburgh and St. Andrews in Scotland, talking mostly again of identity. It was our first visit to Scotland. Leslie Stevenson at St. Andrews drove us north beyond the Highland Line, which was a startling boundary; rolling meadows, tilled fields, and villages gave way abruptly to a tilted forest wilderness.

At Steve Graubard's request I wrote "Paradoxes of plenty," a brief reflection on the troubles of the late sixties and their aftermath. In it I ventured the wry thesis that academic affluence can impair standards by attracting people to the profession who would not have been drawn to it by scholarly vocation alone. I imagined economy-minded deans hailing this thesis with an ominous glint in the eye, and pay-minded professors bristling with indignation. But I was unprepared for the reaction of one Graham Bird in a *London Times* review of my collection *Theories and Things* eight years later. "It is difficult," he writes, "not to understand this as a regret that so few philosophers have been prepared to work simply within his own framework." If it is indeed difficult, let me help. I have been overwhelmed by the appreciative recognition that my work has enjoyed, especially from the middle sixties onward. Personal pique has no place in the picture.

One of many parties that June was a picnic at Yarnton with the Quintons. We walked with big Tony Quinton, now Lord Quinton, to his double brick garage in Mansfield Road to fetch his big Cadillac, and saw him enter the car through a big ragged hole that he had hacked, for the purpose, through the middle brick partition. There had not been room to open the door of the car.

We flew back to Spain for a symposium on my philosophy led by Garrido at the beach resort Cullera. It was tiring, for I alone of the eight participants was not a native speaker, and I was the one who had to hear all and respond. Nor was I spared by the long siestas, for I would be drawn then by one or two participants into an informal discussion. Sessions wore on until the effete Spanish dinner hour of ten—a contrived effeteness in point of fact, for the clocks are advanced two hours in double daylight-saving time. But the effort was in a welcome cause. The papers were readied afterward for publication and sent to me in America, where I wrote up my replies. Hence the volume *Aspectos de la filosofía de W. V. Quine.*

After three days in Paris and a flying visit to Oxford to retrieve our year's luggage, we sailed for home in the same stateroom that had brought us to England.

I had reached the age at which Harvard's president could retire a professor or invite him to continue for two, three, or
four years on half or full time. Derek Bok consulted my
wishes and I chose the maximum, my full load having long
been so attractively light. So in September 1974 I began my
pre-antepenultimate year of teaching, barely missing a new
statute that would have limited me to two years or half time.
In the course of the year I gave outside lectures in Boston,
West Chester, Oberlin, Iowa City, Norman, Dallas, Salt
· 1975   Lake City, and Tucson. Sometimes it was "Mentalistic foundations for physicalism," a *tour de force* in which I traced
steps by which a phenomenalist, moved by his own standards, might be shunted into physicalism. Sometimes it was
"On empirically equivalent systems of the world," in which I
undertook to sharpen my thesis that natural science is under-
determined by all possible data. This involved me in settling
on a criterion of sameness of theories, a question that I now
see as insignificant. We can talk of theory formulations and
skip the notion of theory.

There were further diversions: several short articles, an
enlarged edition of *Ways of Paradox*, visits by Vuillemin from
France and Toraldo di Francia from Italy, and Margaret's
graduation from Wellesley.

By August 10 we were at Bellagio, enviably ensconced in
the Villa Serbelloni and gazing down, out, and up at the
Lago di Como and the Alps of Lombardy. The great eighteenth-century villa had been given to the Rockefeller Foundation by a Princess of Thurn and Taxis who inherited
Hiram Walker's whiskey fortune. The Foundation was using
it as a five-week retreat for eleven thrice-blest scholars and
their spouses and as a four-day center for colloquia.

The Lake of Como comprises the stem and one branch of
a wye, whose other branch is called the Lago di Lecco. A

bold hill or little mountain at the tip of the promontory between the two branches was once dear to Pliny and is now
the domain of the villa. An olive grove, an orchard, vegetable gardens, and formal gardens of slim, dark cypresses and
meticulous topiary shrubbery occupy its lower slopes, and an
exotic forest clothes its upper slopes and summit. Ten miles
of gravel paths thread the woods, but the woods are so dense
that one is unaware of the proximity of one path to another.
Ruins of an eleventh-century castle crown the hill. A tunnel
pierces the summit and vertiginous paths cling to the precipitous eastern face.

My study was a medieval stone guardhouse on the brink
of the north slope. Its heavy door opened with a six-inch
key. The walls were two feet thick, but inside there was just
room for two chairs, a built-in slab of oak by way of a desk,
and an electric heater. I put in six to eight hours there most
days, writing my replies to critics for the Library of Living
Philosophers, and as I weighed my sentences I looked out
on a noble panorama. High mountains flanked the long stem
of the lake, and Switzerland closed off the distant end.
When a question called for more pondering than writing, I
stepped outside and walked with it over the magic little
round mountain, my celestial hemisphere.

From our bedroom window in the villa we looked steeply
down on the village of Bellagio, its little streets and squares
packed tight with tile-roofed houses. The town is crammed
between the escarpment and the waterfront. Ferries plied
the lake to a succession of handsome old towns on either
shore.

Bill and Betsy Olson were gracious hosts. Before meals we
all stood about in the garden enjoying aperitifs, conversation,
and the view. Meals were good; the varied *pasta*, in particular, a dream. Evenings most of us sat in the big living room
at chess, backgammon, scrabble, or unimplemented dialogue. We enjoyed the company of the Lebanese historian
Albert Hourani of Oxford and his wife Odile; of Tony
Camps, master of Pembroke in Cambridge, and his American wife Miriam, née Camp; of Max Black, Masso Neri to

me, and his Israeli wife Michal; and of Bill and Inge Griffith, he a globe-trotting political sociologist from M.I.T.

Sir Peter Medawar arrived with a retinue of symposiasts for a four-day session on immunology. We remembered each other from a good conversation at the Society of Fellows many years before. Toraldo di Francia came to see me, bringing the philosopher Magnani. Bryan Magee came, whom I knew from All Souls'. He is a man of many talents: member of parliament, novelist, music critic, philosopher, impresario. His books include a thick novel, books about Schopenhauer, Popper, and Richard Wagner, and two volumes of philosophical interviews conducted over B.B.C.

Bob and Rosalie came to Bellagio. We made the rounds of the lake ports, and when they left we drove with them to Bergamo to explore the steep old city. It took Marge and me three trains to get back to Bellagio, each on its last run prior to a strike at midnight. The intermittent strikes were a persistent hazard. Marge went to Turin three times to study the Egyptian collection, and always on the brink of a strike or at the end of one. Our flight to Italy had been switched to Swissair because of an Alitalia strike.

Octogenarian George Corner was brought to the villa for lunch. He had preceded me at Oxford as Eastman Professor 1952–1953, and since retiring from the Johns Hopkins medical school he had been ably managing the American Philosophical Society. His retirement from those duties was now looming, and he was visiting Menaggio, across the lake, to sit for a bust that the Society had commissioned. We ferried over with George to meet the sculptress, Joy Buba, and admire the work in progress and others of her pieces. She and her husband Peter had a Renaissance palace, Villa Evelyn, at the water's edge. It looked like an idyllic retirement, but it was not. They had trouble getting help and trouble making things work or getting them mended, and they felt short of intellectual contacts. What with the Villa Serbelloni just across the water at Bellagio and and a retreat for theoretical physicists just across the water at Varenna, the intellectual isolation seemed less than desperate, but at any rate the Bubas talked of unloading their palace and moving to America. My old idea of retiring someday to the Swiss-Italian lakes had faded in seven years, and this finished it.

Further amenities at the Villa Serbelloni included a library, secretarial help, and, for pleasure seekers, a bathing beach and a tennis court. 'Bellagio', after all, means fair ease. Marge and I would spend an hour on the court in the morning clumsily lobbing and volleying, not having played for decades.

The institution has been criticized on the grounds that it is an abuse of Foundation money to run a pleasure dome. I disagree. I accomplished a lot and I expect others did. Anyway I think the Foundation has taken the wrong line in billing the villa primarily as a haven for serene scholarly production away from the distractions of home ground. It is that, but that is not its importance; one can devise serene working conditions on home ground by disconnecting the telephone and sending the children to camp. I would bill the villa rather as a prize five weeks' vacation in recognition of past achievement. Those who deserve the award are not happy on a long unproductive holiday, so facilities are laid on to enable them to combine as much work as they like with the pleasures of the beach, the court, the scene, the sylvan walks, the salon, the beaker, and the table. Such are the specifications for the ideal vacation for an earnest and productive scholar. The Foundation is wrong in requiring a statement of a project. If care is taken to elect residents only of distinction and proved accomplishment, they can be counted on to do creditable work of their own accord during their stay in almost every case; and, in the rare exception, the resident will still have deserved the prize. It must be said that such a standard of selection has not altogether been maintained, so an occasional resident has enjoyed a five-week vacation that was neither earned nor productive. The standard of selection is the thing to work on.

The meetings of the Philosophical Association are unwieldy and preoccupied with the finding or filling of jobs. A group of philosophers reacted admirably in the sixties by establishing an annual meeting of moderate size at Chapel Hill strictly for carefully programmed philosophy. I attended their meeting in October 1975 to comment on Charles Parsons on my philosophy of mathematics. His lecture was his essay for the Library of Living Philosophers, and my reply was fresh out of Bellagio. The meeting was run by my former student Mike Resnik, a professor at Chapel Hill. He and his family lived in an old farmhouse where he was able to indulge his fondness for horses. He had become a licensed farrier.

Two weeks after my trip to Mike's University of North Carolina, I went to a meeting on pragmatism, at Jim Oliver's University of South Carolina. I had been identified with pragmatism, but it was not clear to me what it took to be a pragmatist. In my paper I examined the card-carrying pragmatists on each of a succession of tenets to which I subscribed as an empiricist.

Ernest Gellner of London is a social anthropologist and philosopher who shone in my courses at Harvard long ago as a Commonwealth Fellow. An article by him about me under the title "The last pragmatist" dominated a 1975 issue of the *Times Literary Supplement,* so he was on the program at South Carolina. He had misunderstood my position, and in the public discussion I undertook to clarify matters. A few days later he spoke at Boston University, and I attended with a view again to warding off misconceptions. He said apologetically that he would be repeating and thus wasting my time. He gallantly ad-libbed some novelty into his talk for my sake, and I still found enough to disavow or clarify.

Peter Hempel had retired from Princeton, and a colloquium was held there in his honor in November. I spoke again "On empirically equivalent systems of the world." A week later Marge and I were at the Waldorf-Astoria for Sun Myung Moon's Fourth International Congress for Unified Science. Ed Haskell was no longer involved. I had declined the preceding one, in London, as well as the one in Tokyo; but this time I accepted, for my duty was limited to commentary, there were distinquished participants, the trip was easy, and it could be a good show. I was on a panel ably handled by Ernan McMullen, a Jesuit philosopher whom I had known at Notre Dame. The final event was a dry but otherwise elaborate banquet at which we were entertained by a male chorus and a troupe of Korean ballerinas, both excellent. Then Moon spoke, amusingly at first, in somewhat halting English. "You have had the entertainment; now comes that damned commercial"—such was the gist. "Don't think I'm going to sing to you. Or, on second thought, perhaps I will." And he launched into a Korean song. Voices all around the great dining hall took up the chorus. Presently, however, the affair deteriorated. Moon droned on for perhaps an hour in Korean, through an interpreter. It was a sermon, at the intellectual level of a fundamentalist revival meeting. I looked at the dignitaries flanking him at the high table—men who had given the keynote papers and organized the panels. Eugene Wigner, Alvin Weinberg, Sir John Eccles, and other Nobel laureates were among them. As well-behaved guests they listened respectfully to the persistent insult to their intelligence. At last old Wigner got up and hobbled off. Inwardly I applauded this gesture of self-respect, but too soon; through with his private errand, he hobbled back.

Two days later a psychiatrist named Sherry Terkel phoned me from M.I.T. to say that she had Jacques Lacan in tow and he wanted to meet me. She explained that he was a psychiatrist and the new rage of the Paris cafés, superseding Sartre and perhaps Levy-Strauss. She took us to lunch at the Harvard Faculty Club. We talked in French. He would put his face close and ask bewildering, disconnected questions. I remember none; incoherence is fugitive, as in dreams. I was obliged to attend his talk at M.I.T. that afternoon. It was scheduled in a small room, being in French. Roman Jakobson came, and Larry Wylie of *Village in the Vaucluse*, and my old student Sylvain Bromberger of Belgian origin, and the Mexican poet Octavio Paz, and perhaps eight more. At length Lacan entered, with his secretary. "Cher!" he exclaimed, hailing Roman. He talked without notes and to no evident purpose, though his secretary was intently listening and assiduously writing the while. He recounted a little topological curiosity that was engaging in its way, and he remarked on the really amazing magnitude of elephant droppings. Other matters, similarly resistant to integration, followed in train. I was obliged to contribute something by way of discussion, and somehow I succeeded, as did a few others. Paz came through with an extended and well-informed commentary, but got no appreciable response. We then proceeded to a big dinner party for Lacan at the Ritz in Boston. I was seated at another table and so was spared further strain. I had a good talk with Paz, who was at Harvard for the term, and invited him to dine with me at the Society of Fellows. He accepted but did not appear; I never saw him again.

Larry Wylie told me that Lacan made a scene at the Ritz the day after the dinner. He was brought with a party for lunch and was wearing a turtleneck. The head waiter told him they had a rule about neckties, and proffered a tie. Lacan knocked the glassware to the floor and stalked out.

The day after Christmas, Marge and I flew with Doug and Margaret to Caracas; for we had never been in Venezuela, and the trip was one of the cut-rate specials for the alumni of some pertinent college. Bob and Rosalie joined us in Caracas, a long modern city flanked by green mountain ranges. Its center was a clutter of high buildings, but there huddled among them the old cathedral and a few streets of Spanish colonial houses of one story, notable that of Simón Bolívar. A dizzy ride by cable cars took us up and over the jungle-clad northern mountains and down to the port of La Guaira and the beaches, where we witnessed the onset of the last quarter of the century.

Between terms in early February 1976, Marge and I headed again for the tropics on another cut-rate special. This time the goal was the Caribbean beach of Cancún in the Mexican state of Quintana Roo in the peninsula of Yucatán. Preparatory to an early takeoff we slept in the Holiday Inn at the Kennedy Airport.

And then there came both sleet and snow
And it grew wondrous cold.

We were in the lobby at six in the morning, ready to be fed and taken to the plane, when the whistling of the gale culminated in a resounding crash and the tinkling of glass. The glass front wall had blown in and a huge cabinet had crashed, sparing one life by inches. Snow swirled through the lobby. Guests retreated to their rooms until called to breakfast. Presently the tempest invaded the breakfast room and the guests were herded to a dining room. The storm subsided in the afternoon and we flew to a clement clime.

The string of luxury resort hotels on the long offshore beach and the shabby new company town on the mainland were not the Mexico we knew and loved, but we had come for side trips. We visited at last the celebrated Maya ruins at Chichén Itzá and the less celebrated but imposing ones overlooking the Caribbean at Tulum. Maya art and architecture owe their appeal to their strangeness and mystery; the spectator marvels at a mentality so remote. Loveliness is not their forte.

We rode a bus to Chetumal, the Payo Obispo of my map-mad youth, the capital and southern tip of Quintana Roo. From there we went up along the broad Rio Honda by taxi to the little international bridge and walked over into the one Central American country that we had not yet visited, Belize. By then I had been in 103 countries and all the thirty states of Mexico except Campeche, Tabasco, and Colima.

A meeting on American philosophy was arranged in Oklahoma at which Max Fisch would speak on Peirce, and Fred Olafson on Santayana, and others on others. I was flatteringly asked to speak on myself. I wrote "Facts of the matter" for the purpose, and the resulting volume was *American Philosophy from Edwards to Quine*. I spoke twice in New York along the way.

Jerusalem and After 73

By rearranging my lecture schedule at Harvard, I was able to participate in a colloquium at Jerusalem in April 1976. Marge and I met Don Davidson at Kennedy Airport and we flew over Galicia, Catalonia, Sardinia, Calabria, and Crete to Tel Aviv. A shy philosophy student with the Aramaic name of Bar-Eli drove Don, Marge, and me to Jerusalem, over Arab lands of the newly occupied West Bank. The color changed from desert brown to green wherever we crossed to land that had had the benefit of longer Israeli occupation.

The Scottish Presbyterian hospice of St. Andrews, a modestly neo-Gothic pile commanding a panorama of the old walled city, housed us along with the Strawsons, the Dummetts, Jaakko Hintikka, Saul Kripke, Hilary Putnam, and John Searle. The six-day colloquium was on "Meaning and use," and my paper was "Use and its place in meaning." Marge and I were invited to stay a second week, in consideration of a public lecture: "Facts of the matter" again.

Jerusalem's old city is crammed into less than half a square mile. It is ringed by a high crenellated wall that dates partly from Herod but mostly from Suleiman the Magnificent. The southeastern fifth of this holy and hotly contested tract consists of the rectangular Mount, whose high western retaining wall is the Wailing Wall. The exquisite octagonal Dome of the Rock stands on the Mount and shelters a revered rock. Some revere it as the place where Abraham set about to sacrifice Isaac, and others as the place where Mohammed took off for paradise. The rest of the little old city is a mesh of narrow streets, rich in tradition out of all proportion to its cramped dimensions. A church in the center, that of the Holy Sepulchre, purports to harbor the tomb of Jesus. One of the little streets is the Via Dolorosa, punctuated by the twelve Stations of the Cross and ending at Golgotha—all within the walls. It is a picturesque, crowded street of shops and old Middle-Eastern houses, much like any other.

There is a rival sect, though, that locates Golgotha and the tomb some distance beyond the walls. A rocky eminence there, suggestive of a skull, provides the argument; for such is said to be the meaning of 'Golgotha'. The immediate urban vicinity of the walled city boasts such fabled further sites as Mount Zion, the Mount of Olives, Gethsemane, and the Church of St. Peter in Gallicantu (Cockrow), which shelters a Roman structure where Peter denied Jesus.

Some of us symposiasts and our wives were given a short tour to Bethlehem, after a delay due to the Dummetts, who did not think that the pilgrimage would excuse them from mass. The Church of the Nativity, like that of the Holy Sepulchre, was first erected by Constantine, whose inspired mother Helena, here as there, recognized the exact spot.

On another tour we saw where Jesus is said to have raised Lazarus and where the Samaritan did his good deed. We passed Bedouin camps and dropped two thousand feet to the Dead Sea, the lowest place on earth. Driving along its shore, we looked up at the caves of Qumran that yielded the Dead Sea scrolls. The sea water was malodorous and strong; a taste of it irritated my lips for a day. Barren red-brown mountains flanked the water, Israel this side, Jordan that. We were in the Great Rift again, the rift that we had plumbed five years before in Ethiopia, Kenya, and Tanzania.

We came at last to Masada, a mesa of barren rock rising nine hundred precipitous feet above the water. Its fifty-acre summit was where the Jews made their last stand against the Romans. Behind it were the remains of a gigantic ramp by which the Romans stormed the fortress. The community committed mass suicide when it was clear that all was lost.

When we climbed among the ruins of Masada we were in one of the hottest places on earth, but we suffered none, for the moon was just then passing across the face of the sun. It was a miracle in the classic mold, in a land of miracles.

On another day Fred Simons, a kind official of the Van Leer Foundation in Jerusalem, took us and the Strawsons up the Jordan from Jericho. Between our road and the little river there were barbed wire and a military road patrolled by half-tracks. On the farther bank was the hostile Hashemite Kingdom of the Jordan. We looked in on the kibbutz that had harbored my daughter ten years before, and we had lunch in a kibbutz where Simons's daughter was living. In the hills northwest of the Sea of Galilee we visited yet a third, in which the Strawsons' son had lived.

Where the Jordan leaves the Sea of Galilee, some of us changed in the bushes for a swim in the clear water. As I climbed out I met an American and remarked that my plunge probably took care of a fair bit of sinning. I sensed with embarrassment that he took me seriously.

We visited Megiddo, the Armageddon of the Apocalypse. If the predicted unpleasantness comes off, it will be in character; for hostilities have plagued a major portion, it would seem, of Megiddo's six thousand years as a crossroads of trade and culture. Enough remains above and below ground for somber contemplation.

Marge and I flew to the Sinai to see Justinian's monastery of St. Catharine, at the foot of what some take to be the mountain of Moses and the burning bush. Bushes are no longer in evidence. It is desolate desert and a wildly rugged terrain, largely vertical. Happily the little airstrip was a dozen miles away, so that we were in intimate rapport with the unearthly landscape by jeep. Afterward at Elath we descended into an engagingly everted aquarium in which the spectator stood in a submarine glass tower while the varicolored and variformed denizens of the Red Sea, northern branch, swam around the outside peering in. From Elath we looked over at Aqaba in Jordan and we drove down the coast gazing across the water at Saudi Arabia, but never set foot in either.

Bryan Magee was planning a program of interviews, called "Men of Ideas," for British television. It was to include me, and he came to Boston in August 1976 to prepare the content. Between Beacon Hill and Bare Hill we had long talks. Subsequently he compiled tentative questions together with conjectures as to my answers. He sent this material from London, and I responded with preliminary formulations of my real answers. The program was scheduled for a year later.

That summer I turned out four request numbers, one of which was for a *Festschrift* for my Ann Arbor friends Charles Stevenson, Bill Frankena, and Dick Brandt. Føllesdal and others had now and then urged me to broach ethics, and this was the time; for all three honorands were ethicists. The result was "On the nature of moral values." I suspect that the only surprise in it was my choice of the subject.

Marge was attending her aged father in Connecticut when Manolo and Carmen Garrido passed through Boston. I lodged them in the Faculty Club and brought them to Bare Hill. My daughter Margaret was with us and stepped into the gap, producing quiche. Manolo observed me closely as I retrieved a key from a nail on the back of a tree preparatory to unchaining the canoe. He was interested in customs of far places.

I lectured in October at Denton, Texas, and Columbia, Missouri, on "Physical objects." I had an eager and able follower at Missouri in Roger Gibson, who had written his dissertation on my philosophy and was making a book of it. He had come to Harvard for a while the year before to talk with me and attend my lectures.

By this time thirty translations of books of mine had been published and others were under way. I shared in the proceeds but seldom in the process, even when the language was one of the six I was competent to check. I gained entry in just eight cases. In three I was consulted on moot passages, and in five I examined and corrected the whole:

Bunge's translation of *O Sentido* into *El Sentido*, Gochet's of *Word and Object*, Largeault's of *Philosophy of Logic* and *Ontological Relativity*, and Garrido's of *Ontological Relativity*. Of forty-odd translations of articles I checked perhaps six. It was a time-consuming chore and a melancholy one, for I was often miscontrued; but for that very reason it needed urgently to be done. I was busy with some of it in the fall and winter of 1976, and at that time I also read and criticized Gochet's draft of the first half of his commentary, *Quine en perspective*. Feeling at length that his emendations in the light of my clarifications were perfunctory, I stopped; but soon afterward I was similarly engaged with Orenstein's manuscript about my philosophy.

· 1977   The slender *Web of Belief* had proved to serve not so much freshman English as beginning philosophy courses. The publishers urged us to undertake a new edition, slanted more to philosophy. For our possible guidance they engaged two anonymous critics who had been teaching from the book. One of them, who turned out to be Douglas Stalker, provided page-by-page criticism and shrewd advice. It affected me to see our too casual product so thoughtfully treated by so clearly dedicated a teacher of philosophy. I was moved to rewrite the book in large part and to expand it. I passed my effusions to Ullian, and so the revision proceeded in happy alternation.

Late in May I presented a paper at Dartmouth under the Ayer-inspired title "Grammar, truth, and logic," a rehearsal of what I was to present in two weeks in Sweden.

Sweden, Russia, England   74

The semimillennium of the University of Uppsala was celebrated with musical events and symposia on varied subjects throughout 1977. I was invited to a three-day symposium on Philosophy and Grammar in June. Other participants included Roman Jakobson and Einar Haugen of Harvard and my old students David Lewis, Barbara Partee, and Dagfinn Føllesdal. I escaped once into a neighboring colloquium to hear about relations of Arctic languages, and got back to my section just in time to hear something about my views that required an answer; so I saw that I had to keep to my base.

We banqueted in the castle and then some of us repaired to the philosophy building for one of Stig Kanger's wine parties, as we had done four years before. Next day we were given a ten-hour bus tour of iron-age sites and medieval monuments. At the banquet and on the tour we became acquainted with the president of Iceland, Kristján Eldjarn, an archaeologist.

We flew on to Helsinki and boarded the Finnish ship *Ilmatar* for Leningrad. It was a painless way of visiting the world's biggest country and the only country in Europe that I had not yet touched. We would stay on shipboard except for conducted shore excursions, for which we needed no visas.

The Russian island of Kronstadt, with its old hexagonal fort guarding the approach to Leningrad, was built over with heavy industrial or military installations. Continuing, we steamed for some miles along a channel flanked by two filaments of land that had been thrown up by the dredging of the channel and now supported trees and small buildings. Leningrad proved to be restful and nostalgic, thanks to the absence of private motor cars. There were palatial panoramata along the Neva, and long canals reminiscent of Amsterdam were lined with stately but shabby row houses in endless succession. The shrieking slogans in giant standing letters on factory roofs afforded linguistic recreation. In the Hermitage we gravitated to the Impressionists as is our wont; it struck me only too late that we should have used the opportunity to look at Russian work. The Hermitage disappointed Marge, who had some Egyptian objects in mind. I worked out the required Russian words and tracked down the Egyptian section only to find it closed.

Our tour was taken to a restaurant where there were no

other diners, and to a shop that took only foreign money. One guide, Irene, talked of art and culture; another, Natasha, talked of revolution and the peace-loving Soviet. We were taken back to the shore to admire the exterior of the Summer Palace, all gilt and white marble, and the bewildering fountains and monumental vistas. Workers and their families on Sunday outing swarmed in untold thousands.

We were soon in free Finland again and making our way to the big Swedish island of Gotland. Thure Stenström, a professor of English at Uppsala and a native of Gotland, had tried in vain to reserve a hotel room for us there, happily for us; for in the end he got us the trim little guest cottage in the garden of his brother, Gotland's economic minister. We dwelt above a chalk cliff and looked abruptly down on the steeples, chimney pots, medieval roofs, and ruins of Visby and out on the Baltic Sea. Gulls swooped over the town and up the cliff to our windows, turning just in time. High stone walls with crenellation, turrets, and handsome gates enclosed the town. Steep lanes were lined with stone houses whose gables were stepped in the Hanseatic way. Houses were built into the ruins of Gothic churches that had been destroyed in the old wars.

We dined with Thure and his wife Li in a house they had taken for the summer in Kraklingbo, across the island. They gave us a tour of half the island. It is celebrated for its old village churches, and Thure had made a hobby of them. At a roadside we watched a shearing. The wool was thick and the man was deft. When he had done with his snipping, he lifted off the whole matted growth of wool in one piece as if it were a cape.

In Gotland I had a five-day miniature of what I extolled apropos of Bellagio as the productive scholar's ideal vacation, for I did get some work in. Also I sketched the cathedral and lesser buildings from our window.

On June 18 we were met at the Heathrow airport by Bryan Magee and a driver from the British Broadcasting Corporation, for I was to be taped for "Men of Ideas." Bryan and I sat in his flat Sunday morning and rehearsed. I had long since formulated my answers to the questions he had once proposed, but I would not be allowed to read them, however surreptitiously; it would destroy the illusion of spontaneity. My trouble was that I cannot trust myself to speak effectively off the cuff. Anyway the taping took place that evening, amid a tangle of cameras and technicians. Technically it was impressive. Spiritually it was an ordeal.

It had to be done on a weekend because Bryan spent weekdays in the House of Commons, commonly until ten. When he came to America, the summer before, it was a parliamentary recess. Bryan was a marvel at moonlighting.

That trying Sunday had an agreeably discontinuous middle. Bryan took me to lunch at the fabled Garrick Club, whose halls are hung with celebrated portraits of the theatrical great. Freddie Ayer joined us. It was timely; Freddie's publisher had sent me page proofs of Freddie's autobiography, and I had sent Freddie some small factual corrections just before flying to Europe.

He told me that Peter Strawson had been knighted; also that x, years ago, had declined a knighthood. Declining strikes me as ungracious and ungrateful, less modest than arrogant. It is unfair, moreover, to the queen's advisers; people wonder why a knighthood for Peters Medawar and Strawson, Karl Popper, Isaiah, and Freddie, but not for x. The queen's advisers become the butts of snide remarks all undeserved while x basks smugly in the low profile of his sanctimony.

London had changed. Arabs swarmed at our hotel and elsewhere. The orderly queues of yesteryear had given way to mad scrambles. In one such, as we boarded a bus the next morning, my pocket was picked for a hundred dollars. Something loath, I replenished and we persevered in our course to the musea. My daughter Norma showed us the imaginative renovation of her newly acquired little house in Bruton Place, Mayfair, and took us to lunch at her club, the Burke. Bryan took us to Janicek's opera "Janufa" at Covent Garden and clarified it for us, sketching the plot and noting the appropriateness of the music to the evolving theme.

My daughter Elizabeth and her husband Mike drove us to

their vessel. *Hans,* moored in St. Catherine's Docks below the Tower of London. It had been a Dutch eeling boat, sixty-four feet by eleven. They first saw her resting on a tidal flat with a hole in her hull. They bought her as scrap and devoted ingenuity, taste, and a king's ransom to converting her into a dreamboat. The saloon, with its spiral iron ladder and its blond varnished siding, was a triumph of interior decorating. For four nights we were five aboard, the fifth being one of their employees, Paul Christian, who was experienced in boating. We slept well in the galley, the saloon, and an after cabin. In our leisurely way we ascended the Thames to Maidenhead, negotiating ten locks and, descending, ten again. At Twickenham we walked to Hugh Walpole's Strawberry Hill. At Windsor and Eton we prowled the old towns. At Hampton Court we toured the palace and solved the maze. We cased Thameside pubs, and I was taught the difference, both aesthetic and technical, between what connoisseurs call real beer and what they don't. They were good days, soothing to over-televised surfaces.

La Dernière Classe 75

We flew home on my sixty-ninth birthday and repaired to Bare Hill. For the second time ever, I offered to review a book. I did so because I was alarmed by excessive historical claims that I had seen for the newly discovered continuation of Lewis Carroll's *Symbolic Logic,* and I wanted to keep the record straight. Also I wrote requested pieces for Strawson's *Festschrift* and the *Monist.*

I went back to North Carolina for their annual colloquium, to moderate a debate between Goodman and Hellman. Dan Dennett was there. I had first known him when as an undergraduate at Eliot House he won a contest for the best paintings. He became a good philosopher and is a great wit. He is responsible for the *Philosophers' Lexicon,* in which names of philosophers are construed as verbs or common nouns and aptly defined and illustrated. To *quine* is to repudiate a clear distinction. "You think I quine, sir. I assure you I do not." He had been present at the 1976 meeting, and now a year later people were still chuckling over his after-dinner presentation "Where am I?" When he produced a copy, I found it a brilliant spoof and good philosophy withal. I urged publication and was happy to find it later in his *Brainstorms*.

· 1978 In February 1978 a symposium on metaphor was held in Chicago. It was neither my subject nor a proper season for Chicago, but I accepted for three reasons: Marge wanted to see the Oriental Institute, we would be staying with the Davidsons, and I was not required to present a paper. Don and his new wife, Nancy Hirschberg, were happy in an odd and spacious old flat off Jackson Park. Don had accepted a University Professorship there, in a city not of his choosing, because Nancy taught in Chicago; but such was their domestic felicity that they suddenly liked Chicago and were making a hobby of its architecture. A year later Nancy died of cancer.

We escaped Chicago on the last plane before the usual immobilizing blizzard, but four weeks later we were off to the West again. The meeting this time was at Bellingham, in the northwest corner of our forty-eight contiguous states, where I again presented "Physical objects." Marge and I went out among the San Juan Islands to Friday Harbor, a maritime outpost with somewhat the atmosphere of Nantucket and Key West. The nostalgic values keep better on islands. We found on Vancouver Island that even Victoria, despite its size and its status as capital of British Columbia, retained them to a degree. Teatime in the Empress Hotel carried one back.

In another month I was westbound for a third time. A singularly immemorable little colloquium at Columbia, Missouri, featured Wilfrid Sellars and Dick Herrnstein as speakers and me as commentator. Dick's report on experimental results in animal psychology, for all their interest, had no bearing on Wilfrid's review of his familiar views. For my commentary I had received neither paper. I had prepared a commentary on the basis of Wilfrid's earlier papers, and I ad-libbed some comments on Dick.

In the fall term I had given my basic logic course as usual. It was my last year of teaching, and students hoped that in the spring I would again teach *Word and Object;* but I indulged myself by giving instead a specialized course on the philosophy of logic and set theory. To the very end it was the technical side, rather than the speculative, that I found satisfying to teach. My students and auditors in that course were few, lively, and competent. The subject matter did not lend itself to the embarrassing gathering of colleagues that threatens a retiring professor's last class.

My colleagues gave me a resounding dinner in recognition of my retirement. They overwhelmed me with encomia and presented me with Pokorny's monumental Indo-European dictionary. I was deluged with heart-warming letters and telegrams that the chairman had flushed from far and near.

Burt Dreben had become chairman of the Society of Fellows. The annual feast to which all past fellows are invited was a second retirement dinner for me, for my retirement from teaching meant retiring also as Senior Fellow. Again there was an exchange of speeches, and I was presented with a fifth silver candlestick. I was urged to continue to attend the Monday dinners in future years, and I should have been sad not to. They had brightened my life during most of the forty-five years of the Society's history; my attendance record was unrivaled. By way of graceful compromise I have taken to going alternate Mondays.

On May 14 Marge and I took off for four weeks in Europe and Africa. Before a select audience in the Bavarian Academy of Science at Munich I gave the Werner Heisenberg Lecture, "Physische Gegenstände." The president of the Academy took us to a lavish lunch along with Wolfgang Stegmüller, who had become Germany's leading philosopher of science in the twenty-four years since I had known him at Oxford. We were lodged in Academy quarters at the castle Nymphenburg, which is of the time and spirit of Versailles, less vast but vast withal. It faces a semicircular *piazza*, or *Platz*—not to say "square"—rimmed by arcs of matched outbuildings, one of which housed us.

Downtown a clutch of medieval buildings and little streets had survived the *Widerblitz* of 1944. They opened out into the broad *Rathausplatz*, truly a square this time, walled on one side by the long city hall. The basement of this building, *ex vi termini* the *Rathskeller*, housed a vast municipal restaurant, true to form. But this was not to be confused with the *Hofbräuhaus*, a bulky pile on the opposite edge of the medieval quarter. The ground floor of the latter building was furnished with dozens of long bare tables, occupied here and there by a latent worker who was occupied in his turn with a liter mug of beer and perhaps a chunk of bread and a sausage. Amazons purveyed the beer, as many as six of the huge mugs on a single pair of hands and forearms. There were further floors, and, as one mounted, elegance and price mounted *pari passu*. The top was a fashionable restaurant.

We flew to Tunis, the capital of my hundred and sixth country. The Arab quarter was a steep, tight mass of mosques, bazaar, and white plastered houses, threaded by narrow passages and dead ends and topped by the minaret of Jami es Zitouna, twelve centuries old, which had enhanced the romance of stamp collecting in my youth. The European quarter was a conservative southern city, its palm-studded central Avenue Bourguiba only moderately marred thus far by high buildings.

Cato said *"Cartago delenda est"* and lo! in due course *Cartago deleta fuit*, with a vengeance. Its ruins are meagerer than the Roman ones in and about them. The Arab village Sidi Bou Said on a neighboring headland is more immediate in its appeal, with its steep cobbled streets and tight-packed houses. The snowy white of the houses is set off by blue iron balconies, blue shutters, and blue studded doors. The usual knocker is a woman's hand, the *main de Fatima*, clutching a ball. Dougga, an hour's drive west of Tunis through arid scrub, yields truly imposing Roman remains.

A monumental temple, an elaborate theater, baths paved in mosaic, and a street of Roman shops are well preserved.

We traveled south by bus over farming country and desert to Sfax, Sousse, and Gabès. The yellow tan of the desert would give way suddenly to the dense, deep green of an oasis. We drove in a calèche through a big oasis that boasted half a million date palms. Marge's handbag, containing her camera and much else, slipped off the seat into the road. We retraced, searched, and posted a reward, all in vain. This small calamity was symbolic of a great one; for it was just about then that Marge's father died, aged ninety-four. A week later we returned north by train across limitless olive plantations and found the sad news awaiting us in Tunis.

Having thus been away during the shock and the funeral, Marge at length decided to stay with me for our remaining errand in Europe. It was in Cambridge, England, where I was to receive an honorary degree.

At the robing before the ceremony we honorands and our wives sipped wine and met Prince Philip, the Queen's consort, who was to preside as chancellor. The ceremony was much like the one at Oxford eight years before, complete with the light-hearted Latin biographical sketch of each honorand. At the big luncheon in Jesus College afterward the prince made an urbane and thoughtful speech. We were put up by Tony and Miriam Camps at Pembroke College, where he was master. I lectured at Darwin College—"Physical objects" again.

Norma, Elizabeth, and Mike had come up from London for the ceremony, and we followed them back to London. I met my first grandson, Liz and Mike's Benjamin Willard Roberts, four months old.

We spent ten summer weeks at Bare Hill between trips to
Europe. I wrote replies for an issue of an Uruguayan quarterly about my philosophy; the little volume came out years
later in Argentina. Also I wrote an obituary of Gödel. I was
honored by election to his place in the Institut de France.

The quinquennial philosophical congress for 1978 was in
Düsseldorf. We wandered in the city with John Passmore
and Jack Smart, both of Australia, and in misty Neandertal
with Dagfinn. The valley's eponym, Joachim Neander, was a
schoolmaster; can his surname have been his own learned
Hellenization of 'Neumann'? 'Paleander', for 'Altmann',
would have been more prophetic.

The congress was funded by industries—Persil and Sie-
mens—and opened by President Scheel of West Germany.
We were entertained by the Henkels of Persil in their
guarded mansion and by the young Hofgrebes in their modest flat. Guest speakers and spouses were given a cruise on
the Rhine and, as a grand finale, were whisked to Bonn for
Chancellor Schmidt's summer festival. Three thousand
guests from all over the republic were entertained there by
music, acrobatics, mimes, ballet, art exhibits, and slapstick,
and were plied boundlessly with food and drink by butchers,
bakers, brewers, and vintners in booths and cafés. The motif
this time was philosophy.

We left Germany for the Loire and Angers. There the grotesquely carved medieval houses, the Romanesque and
Gothic churches, and the succulent eels, mussels, and onion
tarts sustained a grateful week of browsing and wandering.
The castle is a pentagonal campus strewn with palaces,
chapels, and kindred structures from various centuries, bristling with seventeen towers, and ringed by a mighty thirteenth-century wall, The castle at Saumur, thirty miles
farther up the Loire, conforms better to storybook precon-

ceptions, with its steep roofs, high towers, parapets, and pyramidal pinnacles. Placed high above town and river, it makes for a stiff and rewarding climb.

In Paris we took a cramped room in the contorted Hotel Esmeralda, centuries old, near the ancient church of St.-Julien le Pauvre and across the Petit Pont from Notre Dame. Revisiting my old haunts behind St.-Germain des Prés, we found tiny, tree-shaded Place Furstenberg deserted except for a young couple with a guitar, singing Mexican songs. Mario Laserna, the Colombian ambassador, entertained us in his embassy. I had known him when he was a student of Ernest Nagel's and was helping to plan the University of the Andes.

A logic colloquium was afoot in the Ecole Normale Supérieure. I gave "Clauses and classes," an offshoot of "The variable." Dieudonné was there, a harsh reminder of the smug and uninformed disdain of mathematical logic that once prevailed in the' rank and vile, one was tempted to say, of the mathematical fraternity. His ever hostile interventions were directed at no detail of the discussion, which he scorned, but against the enterprise as such. At length one of the Frenchmen asked why he had come. *"J'étais invité."*

I met Maurice Boffa and Marcel Crabbé, Belgians I had known through their ingenious published results relating to the question of consistency of "New foundations."

We flew to Ponta Delgada. It was dreamlike to revisit familiar spots in this island that I had so often dreamed of in the forty intervening years, but it was not like the best of dreams. Cars infested the little streets, keeping the pedestrian on a cringing *qui vive.* A motor road now rimmed the waterfront. Prosperous shops lined the street of the Pensão Central, and hotels were rising at the shore. Sugar beets were trundled through the cobbled Rua da Misericordia no longer to the clatter and squeak of oxcarts, but in trucks. Prosperity was taking its toll.

The island of Santa Maria consoled us. Its micrometropolis Vila do Porto was still the sequestered fishing village that I remembered from 1960. The green countryside punctuated with white-plastered, red-tiled little houses and the vertiginous east coast were all as before, and oxcarts plied the lanes. It is remarkable that this island, with the only king-size runway in the mid-Atlantic, should have been thus spared. Spaniards would have succumbed to the wiles of the high-rise and *turismo*. I applaud the Portuguese, my sorrows over Ponta Delgada notwithstanding.

In December 1978 I flew to Lincoln, Nebraska, and responded to questions that Edward Becker had sent me from his seminar there on my philosophy, having visited my seminar the preceding spring. I was cheered by the optimism of Nebraskan professors and the pride they took in Nebraska. It is free of corruption, they felt, and it is the only state with a unicameral legislature, which evidently works well. Corrupt Boston and the gloomy, carping liberals of eastern academe were another world. I stood at the top of the skyscraper capitol and looked out over the flat immensity of the prairie with new hope.

· 1979 In February 1979 I flew west again for a week in California. At Berkeley I gave two lectures on "How and why to reify," enlarging on "Clauses and classes." A good walk and talk with my old student Barry Stroud cleared up a point that had puzzled me. Patrick Nowell-Smith had claimed twenty-odd years earlier that what I had disapproved of as Aristotelian essentialism was not Aristotle's. I got the same complaint from others, but was unable to detect my error. I now learned at last that I had had Aristotle right, and they had had him right too, but they had me wrong.

My daughter Margaret was working in advertising in San Francisco. Alfred and Marja Tarski had us to dinner with my old student Bill Craig. Jack and Elizabeth Smart were visiting Stanford and came to my lectures, where they rediscovered Margaret. They and the Tarskis entertained her in subsequent months.

In Los Angeles I presented a one-hour version of "How and why to reify" at U.S.C., establishing my tradition of addressing them on ontology every thirty years. Family again emerged: my nephew William Van Orman Quine was studying there. We had a Mexican lunch and he drove me to the La Brea tar pits where the dinosaur remains had been found.

I flew home for six days and then flew with Marge to Tallahassee and further family: Jack Quine, son of my cousin John, was teaching mathematics at Florida State. I gave the one-hour version of "How and why to reify" and Jack's southern wife, Bettye [sic] Ann, gave a big buffet supper for the philosophers and mathematicians. She is a mathematician and an extraordinary cook and Jack and his brother Jim revealed rare gifts at mandolin, guitar, piano, and country singing. Jack and Bettye Ann took us boating in lush cypress swamps where protected alligators and alligatrices thrive.

I had read in the *World Almanac* and related sources that the highest point in Florida, wryly called Iron Mountain, was only a hundred feet above sea level. I had often mentioned this as an amazing fact, given the size of Florida. In Tallahassee, then, my amazement was compounded; for it is a hilly town, surely topping a hundred feet. I verified later that the editors of the *World Almanac* had meanwhile seen the light and changed their story. Someone evidently had identified Florida with its peninsula and overlooked its capital.

A newspaper had described Tarpon Springs as a village of Greek sponge fishermen—a transplanted bit of Greece. So Marge and I had that as our next objective, to our regret. Our reserved room was in a motel on the bleak highway, and we rashly moved the next day to a room in the village that was assured for only one night. We could find no lodging near or far thereafter, until at last a taxi netted us a dismal motel on the far side of Tampa. We had to stay until our scheduled flight two days later, for all planes were fully booked. So we explored Tampa and I wrote "On the very idea of a third dogma" for a Davidson *Festschrift*. The title was a conflation of two of his.

We flew from Tampa to Akron to see Bob and Rosalie, and thence to Ann Arbor. Dick Brandt had persuaded me to sketch my naturalistic epistemology in a seminar that he was running there for philosophy teachers, so I had prepared and sent such a sketch, entitled "The natural theory of knowledge," for them to study in advance. I discussed it with them for three hours. Also I gave a public lecture: "How and why to reify."

More French Lectures 77

Rudolf Haller of Graz, Austria, ran a symposium each March at Dubrovnik, Yugoslavia. I was invited to kibitz. Our T.W.A. plane reached the Rome airport too late for the connecting flight to Dubrovnik, and there was no T.W.A. agent on the job. Keith Lehrer and his linguist wife, likewise bound for the symposium, were similarly stranded. Shifting for ourselves, the four of us got rooms in Ostia, which is nearer than Rome to the airport. Planes did not fly to Dubrovnik every day, so the next morning we flew to Split and continued by bus. Despite our indignation toward T.W.A., we were content to have walked about Ostia and happy indeed to revisit Split.

David and Renée Kaplan, Pat and Christine Suppes, Ian Hacking, and Karel Lambert converged on Dubrovnik from America, Michael Dummett and Bill Newton-Smith from Oxford, Vuillemin from Paris, Dagfinn from Oslo, several from Germany and Austria, and Marković and Supek from Yugoslavia. We all lodged in the Hotel Excelsior, above the rocky seaside just beyond the south wall of the old city. Our ten three-hour sessions were held just beyond the north wall, so that we walked the length of the splendid old stone-paved midway as we came and went. The nominal theme of the symposium was "Rationality," broad and unindicative, and there was no coordination of papers or sustained struggle with specific issues. Worst, the Yugoslavs talked at great length along lines bearing more on politics than on the semantical and epistemological matters that exercised the rest of us. We had good discussions selectively outside the sessions, however, and it was a joy to settle down for a week in the Dubrovnik that had so delighted us eleven years before.

A vigorous lecture tour in French occupied my next two weeks, April 1979. At the Collège de France I presented the full two hours of "How and why to reify," which I translated as "Les étapes de la réification." Marge, staunch Egyptophile, was offended by the statue in front of the Collège that shows Champollion triumphant with his foot on the head of a pharoah.

I had long admired the mellow domed palace of the Institut de France that looks out on the Seine from the rim of my favorite quarter. Exercising my new prerogative, Marge and I broached it. We sat in a richly appointed little conference room and listened to a round-table colloquium on *grève et chomage*, strikes and unemployment.

At Lille our train was met by Professor Mouloud, accompanied redundantly by an interpreter. Though I had had a Lille degree for fourteen years, it was my first visit. It is a newly old city, largely restored in a Flemish vein after wartime destruction. I lectured to a crowded hall "Sur la théorie naturelle de la connaissance," a development of what I had written for Dick Brandt's group. Lively discussion flared up during the subsequent reception, dinner, and evening. Gochet fetched us early next morning in his snappy red Renault and sped us the length of Belgium to Liège. I learned that the anomalous acute accent on 'Liége', so hard to respect, had now been officially surrendered; we can relax in the *accent grave*.

I had not consented to lecture at Liège; Louvain and Brussels would suffice. But I had consented to join a group for informal discussion. Gochet had publicized the event with posters, packing a big classroom with amiable souls who were expecting more than they were going to get. He discoursed on my philosophy and then put some general questions to me on which I extemporized with little eloquence. Afterward the dean entertained us in a party of twenty at lunch in an old castle. All Belgium lay behind us and it was not yet noon. Then we led a parade of philosophers' cars from Liège to Louvain-la-Neuve for my real lecture of the long day: the first half of my double "Étapes de la réification" from the Collège de France.

The absurd hostility of the Flemings to the Walloons had led to the creation of the French-speaking university and town of Louvain-la-Neuve in what had been farmland. The architecture was harmonious and suggested age and tradition without activating a known style or period. There was a neighborhood of brick houses, another of wooden houses painted in shades of purple, another dominated by row houses with low tan sides and dark mansard roofs. Shops and restaurants showed distinctive personalities within the restraints of harmony. Streets were for feet only, and bore names of classical figures. Parking lots were at the edge of town, landscaped away, and the garages, railway, and station were underground.

In the dark evening of that long day that had begun in Lille, Gochet drove us to Brussels and lodged us in the Fondation Universitaire. There I presented the other half of "Les étapes de la réification" the next day.

Marge flew back to Boston to resume her volunteer work at the Museum of Fine Arts, and I flew to Marseille for Aix-en-Provence. Gilles Granger took me to visit his Alsatian colleague Frey at his luxurious forest lodge. We walked in the woods and saw boars' tracks. Sudden quarries yawned precipitously in the dense growth. We came to a secluded little stone building in which Cézanne had worked. Through a cleft in the forest it commanded a view of Mont Ste.-Victoire. I wandered with both philosophers in the little old streets of Aix, and I lectured again "Sur la théorie naturelle de la connaissance."

I gave the same lecture at Bern. Facilities there are startlingly compact. The railway station houses shops and restaurants at several levels. Henri Lauener walked me across the street from my grand hotel to a low level of the station, and we stepped out of the station elevator onto the university campus on the heights above. That evening he hosted a lavish dinner, at which his colleagues lapsed amusingly from time to time into the opacity of their *schwiezer dütsch*. Bern is rich in the heavily eaved and quaintly carved Swiss brand of picturesqueness, all dramatically set forth on a bold headland in a hairpin turn of the river Aar.

It was still April 1979 when Marge and I attended the meeting of the American Philosophical Society in Philadelphia and went on to Washington for a meeting of the National Academy of Sciences, to which I had been elected two years before. We walked in old Georgetown and elsewhere, refreshing old memories of our Navy years. Einstein's centenary was celebrated at the meeting with speeches by John Wheeler and Gerry Holton and the unveiling of the disturbing seated statue. President Carter gave a restricted group of us a political talk the next day, and I was encouraged by the earnestness, reasonableness, and intelligence that shone through his talk and his manner. I wish subsequent history had borne me out.

Fred Cassidy had instigated a lecture invitation for me in Madison, Wisconsin, by way of implementing an Arthric reunion. I gave "How and why to reify." At "Mendotage," Fred and Hélène's house on the shore of Lake Mendota, we were joined by Harold and Kathryn Cassidy from the Kentucky marches of Indiana and by Ed Haskell and his new wife, Frances, from New York. Hélène was an invalid by then, but brave and active up to her very limits, and Ἄρθρον bloomed. We toured Fred's plant and the ingenious devices by which he and his staff were building the *Dictionary of American Regional English*.

Mathematicians at Madison were honoring Steve Kleene, who was retiring. There was much to honor. Not content with his fundamental contributions as pioneer in recursive number theory and founder of hierarchy theory, Steve had served long and selflessly as editor of the *Journal of Symbolic Logic*. In the disorders of the late sixties, which culminated at Madison in murder, Steve had taken over as dean and seen to the restoration of standards and serenity.

I had first known him and Barkley Rosser in the middle thirties when they were Church's students at Princeton.

Now they were together again; Rosser had joined the faculty at Madison. He and I had a good talk over lunch.

A clutch of honors came my way in that same spring, 1979. I was elected to the Norwegian Academy and chosen for an honorary degree at Harvard and at Uppsala. Only the timing was unfortunate. I could have combined the trip to Uppsala with a formal induction into the Norwegian Academy in the presence of the king; but the Uppsala and Harvard dates conflicted, and I had received and accepted the Harvard invitation first. So I arranged a year's postponement of the Swedish degree, and remained a Norwegian Academician without the flourish of trumpets.

I attended two commencements even so, for the one at Harvard was preceded by one at Cornell at which Doug received his Ph.D. in biology. In July we were back at Cornell again, joined this time by Norma from London, Margaret from San Francisco, Marge's sister Barbara from Hartford, and Bob and Rosalie from Akron, among many others; the occasion was Doug's wedding. He and Maryclaire, née Matthews, proceeded thence to Halifax on a research job at Dalhousie University.

America, Sweden, Iceland   78

Retirement promoted mobility. The second half of 1979, even so, witnessed a lull. The editors in Oklahoma of *Essays on the Philosophy of W. V. Quine* asked me to respond to the essays. I did so for their quarterly. A more eccentric assignment was in religion, at Boston University: Leroy Rouner got me to comment on a paper by Charles Hartshorne, whom I had known since graduate school. A question that had nagged me at the symposium on metaphor at Chicago the year before recurred now with redoubled force: what am I doing here? But I learned things. I came to see why Charles and others insist that sentences about the future are largely neither true nor false. It is in order to reconcile God's omniscience with indeterminism, which in turn is felt to be required for the justification of praise and blame. Also I was reminded of how heavily the theological edifice rests on the purported distinction between metaphycial necessity and contingency. Such are the postulations for safeguarding preconceptions.

Religion resumed, oddly enough, the next morning. My Bare Hill neighbor Holmes Welch, a scholar of Buddhism, got me into a closed meeting conducted by the Dalai Lama. The Lama wore Western clothes and spoke English. After a speech in which he deplored his nation's captivity and favored universal goodwill, he was drawn into learned dialogue by the Mongolian scholars Francis Cleaves and Joe Fletcher and other panelists.

· 1980 My half year of immobility ended with 1979. In January 1980, I braved the blizzard belt and visited the Bertrand Russell archives at Hamilton, Ontario, as one of several consultants on an application for a grant. I was pleased to find six of my books in Russell's personal library, only three of which I had sent him. A pipe cleaner still marked the place in *Mathematical Logic* where I departed from his definition of singular description.

At the archives I observed the miracle of the word processor, my most baffling technological encounter since the holograph—an encounter that took place in the same country a dozen years before. I could have saved much time with a word processor in later years if I had not been a slave to old habits. I still compose with a pen, revise indefatigably with scissors and paste, and turn the eventual collage over to a typist.

Nine days later I was at Stanford to give the Immanuel Kant Lectures, four in number. I called them "Science and Sensibilia" as a takeoff on John Austin's takeoff "Sense and Sensibilia" on Jane Austen's *Sense and Sensibility*. Discussion flourished for two weeks, along with parties and outings. Marge and Margaret were there for part of it, and between the university and the center for Behavioral Sciences we renewed many old friendships. The Moravcsiks threw a party that packed a surprise: Bill Bennett, my fellow student at Oberlin who steered me to Russell in 1927.

At Mt Holyoke in April I gave the first annual lecture in memory of my former student Gail Stine. It was based on two of my Kant Lectures and cleared up the murkiness of "Ontological relativity" by resting that thesis flatly on proxy functions. I called it "What is it all about?".

That same spring I went back to Michigan twice. First it was to comment on Donald Campbell, whose evolutionary epistemology I like. While there I faced a panel of psychologists for a question session. The second trip was for what my former student Brad Angell envisaged as a confrontation of titans. My fellow titans were my veteran confrontees Rod Chisholm and Wilfrid Sellars. My piece was "States of mind." To defray my expenses Brad also got me invited to Oakland University, where I again gave "What is it all about?".

Teachers far and wide who had loyally been using *Methods of Logic* were let down by my publisher, who ran out of copies at the beginning of term. I had ideas that I was eager to use in a revised fourth edition, but I would need another publisher. I saw how to simplify my treatment of the logic of quantification and relate it more neatly to ordinary language by bringing the insights of "The variable" to bear. The shift would make a place even for predicate functors. I began work at it so as to be able to act when I recovered the copyright, which I did a year later. A concurrent project was *Theories and Things*, for which I edited some of my recent pieces and wrote a new one.

We went to Oberlin for my fiftieth reunion, a bright affair further brightened by the presence of fellow Arthrites and by a supplementary reunion in Akron with Bob and Rosalie. Six days later—June 3, 1980—we flew again to Europe. Stig Kanger drove us from the Stockholm airport to Uppsala and took us immediately in our grogginess to the *Hovjuweler*, or court jeweler, for the gold ring that was to mark my honorary degree, and to the clothier for formal attire. We were lodged again in the familiar top floor of the old university guest-house, and after a nap we and the Marc-Wogaus were re-galed in Stig's flat with tumblers of rosé and platters of *smörgåsbord.*

After a lunch the next day with philosophers and wives in an old cellar restaurant below the cathedral close, we all went up the hill to the philosophy house in Villavågan and I presented "What is it all about?". It had not been planned, but I had it with me for Iceland.

The day of the ceremony began at seven with cannon fire from the castle. There were twenty-seven salutes, one for each honorary doctor and two for each *Jubeldoktor,* a recognition of fiftieth anniversaries. In a few hours flags flew, crowds jubilated, and the academic procession in somber tails and white ties, rather than gowns or robes, was led by bright banners into the assembly hall. We honorands were ranged on the daïs. After a welcoming speech by the Rector Magnificus and a lecture in Swedish on biomedical research, the awards began. The "promoter," different for each faculty, stood at a lectern and called forth each honorand. *"Ave,"* he said, shaking one's hand. Then *"Accipe coronam,"* and an assistant placed a laurel wreath, made to measure, on one's head. Simultaneously a cannon detonated outdoors, deviously synchronized. *"Accipe aurum,"* he next said, and pointed to the ring, already on one's finger. Then *"Accipe diploma,"* proferring same. Finally *"Vale,"* another handshake, and one had finished rounding the lectern. One bowed to the king's proxy at the front of the audience and resumed one's seat. The promoters made speeches celebrating the honorands, using either Latin or Swedish or the honorand's native language, at their discretion. Stig appeared after the ceremony with the big brass cannon shell that had been discharged at my crowning. It was smudged; he would get it polished and engraved and send it to me by air. So he did, and it is a tall, cylindrical brass vase that beautifully sets off a few deep red roses.

Some six hundred were banqueted in a hall of the castle, reached by a long curving stone passageway and spiral stone stairs. Sir Denys Wilkinson made a witty speech, and others spoke in other languages. A young chorus sang tricky arrangements of "Alouette" and the like in mock-operatic styles, ending with "Sleepy Time Gal." Tables were removed and we danced and talked until midnight. Thence down the hill in the northern twilight.

Changing planes in the Copenhagen airport, we saw a bouncing teenager in a University-of-Akron sweatshirt. She said in careful English that she was going there to study geography and to get her driver's license.

Our first sign of Iceland was a fixed white disk in the moving white cloud cover. It was a mountaintop crater filled with snow. Our plane was met by my former student Þorsteinn Gylfason and his young American colleague Mike Marlies. They took us immediately on a field trip. It was treeless coutry, some of it bare lava. Smoke and steam rose here and there. Boiling streams flowed into a lake. Boiling mud—plop, plop—smelled of sulphur. Geysers burst skyward, hot and abundant, at appointed times and places.

On my brief visit twenty years before, I had been disappointed to see no medieval traces in Reykjavik of Iceland's thousand-year history. This time we saw a restored old quarter. There were cottages of wooden slats and heavy fieldstone, roofed in thick sod and half buried in it.

My lecture was heralded in the newspaper by a full page, bristling with the edhs and thorns that disappeared from our alphabet seven centuries ago. It was written by Þorsteinn and illustrated by a picture, borrowed from Bryan Magee's *Men of Ideas*, of me in the bonnet and robe of my Cambridge degree. My lecture drew forty-odd auditors, largely townspeople. The next day Mike interviewed me at great length with a tape recorder, and Þorsteinn translated it for another full-page spread. The little nation of a quarter-million, with an archaic language unintelligible even to other Scandanavians, is literate to a man and much concerned with things of the mind. Crime is rare, except for drunken brawls on Saturday nights, and the police are unarmed.

Þorsteinn took us to renew our acquaintance with the

president of Iceland, Kristján Eldjarn. We talked archaeology, and he expressed reservations regarding the Vinland site at the north end of Newfoundland, l'Anse aux Meadows, that had seemed so uncontroversial. He was not one to let national pride prevail over scientific scruples.

He was unusual among Icelanders in having a surname. Ordinarily an Icelander has only a first name and a patronymic that changes with the generations; thus "Gylfason," son of Gylfi. (Note the genitive *a*, as in Slavic.) Listings in the telephone book are alphabetized by first names.

Bob and Rosalie joined us in Iceland. Our new friends took the four of us on a tour of the interior and a picnic at þingvellir, or Thingvalla. It is the site of the ancient outdoor parliament, the slightly elder cousin of the Isle of Man's similarly named Tynwald. It is a lava arena in a rift valley. From it one looks across a lake to a horizon of crags and snowy volcanoes.

The east coast of Greenland, eighteen hundred miles long, boasts the thousand inhabitants of Angmagssalik and few besides. One morning Marge and I flew over. Pack ice, breaking up, littered the blue sea like giant white confetti. We landed on the airstrip of a DEW-line radar station and plodded for ninety minutes over rough terrain and through great expanses of wet snow, much of it a foot deep, to the small Eskimo settlement of Kap Dan. The miserable aboriginal shelters here had given way to wooden Danish cabins, and the kayak to boats with outboard motors. The precarious livelihood of hunting and fishing had given way to the canned goods of Danish welfare, and what was once perhaps a modest litter of shells and bones had given way to an immodest litter of tin cans and plastic. Children peddled beadwork and idols carved of bone. An Eskimo woman in skins and fur performed the drum dance, which involved stamping, strange vocalizing, and the beating of a skin stretched on a hoop.

Before flying back to Reykjavik we were given a breathtaking aerial tour of Greenland's icy mountains, up past the Arctic Circle, in and out of precipitous fjords at low altitudes. It was a land of great granite matterhorns, white with June snow except where too steep to hold it. We were beyond the habitat of living things.

South Africa 79

Our daughter Margaret flew from California on October 3, 1980, met us at Kennedy Airport, and went with us to South Africa. Our flight of seventeen hours and seven thousand miles was broken briefly in the People's Republic of the Cape Verde Islands. South African planes are banned from the African mainland, except for a few countries in the far south. The Cape Verde Islands, anyway, are well placed on the great-circle route. We put down on the flat and barren Ilha do Sal in bright moonlight at two in the morning. A little showcase in the barren terminal offered a bleak display featuring Che Guevara and kindred themes. The airport is said to be a joint facility of Russia and South Africa—strange bedfellows in a strange bed.

We dodged the southwest angle of Angola, flew across the Kalahari Desert of Namibia and Botswana, the German Southwest Africa and Bechuanaland of my youth, and came to rest at Johannesburg. There were few people about, least of all the Zak van Straaten who was to meet us. I was on my way to a police station for advice on my next move when I saw a young man bound for the terminal. I ventured the name, and Zak it was. He took us to supper in a rather elegant restaurant with a surprisingly multiracial clientele, and to our lodgings among the skyscrapers.

The Anglophone university there bears the Afrikaaner or African Dutch name of Witwatersrand and is known as Wits. The Witwatersrand, or White Water Ridge, is the gold-bearing upland that accounts for Johannesburg. Zak taught at Wits.

Jonathan Suzman was the chairman of philosophy. He is

slight, fortyish, with a trim black beard, classical Jewish features, an alert mind, and unflagging ebullience of spirits and good will. His wife, Christine, an attractive young woman taller than he, is a gifted sculptress. His grandfather had come out from Central Europe in the gold rush and made millions in a tobacco monopoly. Jonathan took us to his parents' palatial home amid grand gardens, and then we all proceeded to the Polo Club for a magnificent buffet luncheon. Horses were in the paddocks. Nests of the yellow weaver bird hung from the accacia trees.

At Wits I addressed the social-theory seminar on "Meaning and the alien mind," from notes that I had used on the Harvard anthropologists years before. My public lecture at Wits was lifted from my forthcoming *Theories and Things*, as were my presentations to the philosophy seminar in the next days. My auditors there were faculty, for good students go to Oxford and Cambridge for graduate study, thus keeping abreast of the currents. It became a custom after my seminars to repair to the rotable penthouse of a skyscraper and talk, drink beer, and admire the view. The penthouse had been acquired by the university and ceased to rotate, but circumambulation served nicely.

Zak drove us to the Republic of Botswana. First we entered Bophuthatswana, a semi-autonomous reserve or "homeland" for the Tswana within the Republic of South Africa. After some miles and further formalities, we were in Botswana. Rands had to be changed into pulas, one to one. I speak of money.

Gaborone, the capital, was a sprawling suburb without an urb. The Holiday Inn had ignored our reservations. Ultimately we three Quines were bunked in one room and Zak was put up in the home of a friend of the management. The betrayal proved to be a boon. Zak's host, Sid Youghted, was a university man who served Botswana as a conservation expert and moonlighted as a safari guide. Longing perhaps for intellectual company, and overflowing certainly with the milk of human kindness, he devoted the next day to showing us around in his jeep. After a briefing on beasts and

Bushmen in a little museum. we struck out on a circuit of rough roads. We came to the hilltop site of Livingstone's house, Stanley's colleague the presumptive Dr. Livingstone, and the fallen gravestones of his daughter and her friend. At Manyana the fig tree still lives where Livingstone preached to the heathen. On nearby cliffs there are pale old Bushman paintings of giraffes and an elephant. No Bushmen are about; they are off in the desert, and the local blacks are Tswanas, a Bantu people. Sid communicated with them in Zulu, having grown up in Swaziland. An English-speaking Tswana girl spoke ill to us of his diction. Evidently Tswana and Zulu are distinct dialects of a common language.

The thatched mud houses, round or rectangular, were decorated with three or four horizontal bands of selected mud in different natural tints, the darkest at the bottom. Occasionally there was a smoothly modeled little porch. Big clay pots and urns stood outside. A hollow stump served for churning, as it had served in Fiji for grinding *yaqona*. Usually the houses were grouped in a mud enclosure. In Moshupa an area under a huge old tree was enclosed in palisades of slats for the headman's court. A hoop was set into the ground where the petitioner would stand.

We followed a wagon trail that the English had cut during the Boer war to bypass enemy territory. That meant bumping over bedrock and river bed. Sometimes, in steep places, the English had locked their wagon wheels and slid down. With Sid's able maneuvering, our jeep barely made it.

Next day, crossing Bophuthatswana again on our way back to Johannesburg, we saw zebras of an unfamiliar stripe: diagonal, black and brown on tan, a horse of another color. Continuing through the Transvaal, we found ourselves in trouble over gasoline; for it was Sunday. At Groot Marico a kind Indian illegally siphoned us some gasoline from his car. We joined his big family on their porch for conversation and were served tea. The grandmother, in Indian garb, spoke no English.

David Sapire took us to a gold mine. In helmets, coats, and boots we descended seven hundred feet in a wire cage and walked through long galleries, lighted by our helmets. The pebbly pay dirt was in veins, with gold around the pebbles. Above ground we watched a man open the doors of a furnace with tongs, releasing a hot blast of air. Two men with tongs then lifted out a red-hot beaker and poured molten gold into a mold to make a gold brick. We handled a cool one.

The Blue Train to Cape Town, "best train in the world," was booked up, so we flew. On taking off, we looked down on great golden rectangles, the Johannesburg mine dumps. A trace of gold remains in the slag and may some day be deemed worth extracting.

Cape Town, its precipitous mountains rimmed with green forest and the blue sea, vied in the seaport beauty competition with Rio and Hong Kong. Paul Taylor, Denise Myerson, and David Brooks met our plane and promptly whisked us up Table Mountain in the dizzy cable car. Next day, the same friends drove us to the Cape of Good Hope. It is a high, narrow, rugged mass of fluted rock, looking like a rough paleolithic knife blade on a large scale, pointed at the Antarctic. Cape Agulhas, Africa's southern tip, was visible to the southeast, cleaving the oceans: Atlantic this side, Indian that.

The same friends and others drove us north in a big station wagon to the old Dutch town of Stellenbosch. The traditional Cape farmhouse is low, white-plastered, and gracefully designed with a broad front flanking a scalloped middle façade that suggests the stepped gable of a Hanseatic house softened to the baroque curves of a Portuguese church. We moved on through the wine country, sampling. The "pinotage" grape, a local cross between the *pinot noir* and something called hermitage, is used extensively and well. Then the rolling green countryside broke abruptly into barren mountains of bare rock, a dreamlike scene.

David Brooks lived among steep streets, white houses, and bougainvillea high above Cape Town, with a palm and a fig tree within reach and a grapevine climbing his house. His panorama was dominated by sphingoid Devil Mountain. The philosopher Barney Keaney and his French wife Annette lived high on the cityward slope of Table Mountain, with a brethtaking view steeply down on the city and bay. At a party there I talked with a judge and a member of parliament, both of whom were working optimistically for a better deal for the blacks.

The university campus climbs the beginning of Table Mountain. I gave a public lecture there, "Observation and object," and on our last day I presented something called "Mind and its place in nature, or, the forked animal" to a philosophical audience swollen by non-philosophers. In it I contrasted an archaic intensional orientation to reality with the scientific orientation expressed in extensional terms.

I had meant to use the latter paper again on returning to Johannesburg, but I found that I dilsliked it. Instead I hurriedly worked up something new, "The erosion of the concept of nature." It was based on a typescript on quantum mechanics by the physicist David Mermin that Nobel laureate Ed Purcell had brought to me just before I left America. I had read it on the plane with wild surmise. Reasoning from Bell's Inequality, Mermin describes a constructible apparatus whose observable behavior resists our traditional conceptions of cause and effect. In my talk I speculated on the philosophical implications. Mermin's paper has since appeared in the *Journal of Philosophy* at my urging.

Besides Wits, where the language is English and the architecture is Assorted Traditional, Johannesburg has a great Rand Afrikaaner Universiteit where the language is Afrikaans and the architecture is Magical Modern. The big buildings are ranged on a green campus around an asymmetrical pool and fountain. Some of their walls are movable, for growth. Glass and concrete are combined in startling ways, rich in surprises. Another quad has the dormitories, all brick and glasss with stepped and indented walls, the textures changing from changing standpoints. I had a gala lunch there with the philosophers, linguists, and deans.

Pretoria, one of South Africa's two capitals, has a university that does most of its teaching and examining by mail, spreading culture across Africa. Michael Macnamara of that faculty and a colleague drove us there and showed us the city, purple with blooming jacaranda trees, and the university, imposing for all the strangeness of its ways.

A grand eastward trek with Zak occupied our last five days. Semiarid plains gave way to the wild and wooded Drakensberg with its high waterfalls. We lodged at Pilgrims' Rest, a nostalgic tin-roofed Victorian village in a gold-bearing canyon. The four of us played Scrabble. Zak was bright and congenial company, a chess expert, and a judge of wine. He had been Strawson's pupil, and edited Strawson's *Festschrift*. He was a good driver, and a fast one despite the threat of a thousand-dollar fine.

In Kruger Park we recaptured the excitement of ten years before in the game reserves of East Africa. Baboons swarmed onto the car. Giraffes, zebras, elephants, Cape buffalo and assorted antelopes were in evidence, and we dallied by hippopotamic waters. Pursuant on a report of a kill, we found two glutted, somnolent lions and the sketchy, stinking residue of a giraffe.

On driving south out of the park we looked wistfully across into Mozambique, but it was enemy country. Instead we continued south into Swaziland, the self-styled pearl in the South African oyster. It is a high country of wooded mountains, grassy slopes, and fertile valleys, away from the dust and heat but plagued with forest fires. We saw three. Restaurants and an agricultural mission reflected a Chinese communist presence. Swazies and quasi-Swazies around Pigg's Peak and elsewhere have a jargon called Speak-Speak. Quasi-Swazies of Pigg's Peak speak Speak-Speak.

Approaching Mbabane, the capital, we were suddenly blocked by a murderous swerve of a lumber truck. Zak spun us 180 degrees and saved us by inches. Mbabane had a frontier air and was the capital only in some obscure sense; for it was at Lobamba that we found the broad, white, unapproachable royal palace, the round thatched huts for the king's wives, and the blockhouses of parliament.

We had to hurry back to Johannesburg so as to dress for a

big farewell supper party in Jonathan and Christine Suzman's flat. It was a double farewell; we were off to America the next morning, and Zak was leaving Witwatersrand to chair the department at Cape Town. Our trip home, aggravated by the grim transfers at Kennedy and LaGuardia airports, took nearly twenty-four hours.

Germany and Mexico 80

By November 8, 1980, we were enjoying an Arthric reunion at Harold and Kathryn Cassidy's in Madison, Indiana. They had been hurricaned out of nearby Hanover. I was delighted anew with Madison, an architectural gem out of the old South, huddled at the great Ohio River under the wooded hills.

· 1981   In the next six months I spoke three times at Boston University, ending with the annual affair of Berry's seminar and Joyce Chen's restaurant. It was the last of that; George was retiring. I gave "Observation and object" both at Boston and at Princeton, and worked it over into "Gegenstand und Beobachtung" and "Objecto y observación" in preparation for imminent trips back to Europe and to Mexico.

At Syracuse in May 1981 I received an honorary degree, my twelfth, along with Alexander Haig, who gave the address. Radicals dressed in bloodied nuns' garb protested our alleged aggression in Salvador and tried to silence him, but he coped admirably and I liked his thoughts on public policy. History had another disappointment in store.

We repaired to the sightly village of Canandaigua to walk along the lake with the Jonathan Bennetts and Bill Alston and to dine with Don Campbell and others at the inn. Next day I met the department for discussion, and two weeks later I began this autobiography.

A conference was afoot in celebration of anniversaries of Kant and Hegel in Hegel's native Stuttgart. Dieter Henrich and Dick Rorty had recruited me along with Don Davidson and Hilary Putnam for a panel on our kind of thing, which Rorty might relate to Kant or Hegel as he pleased; hence "Gegenstand und Beobachtung." Lauener persuaded me to present it also at Bern, so on June 23 Marge and I wandered in the old city that I had admired two years before. The square was gay with pennants, flowers, balloons, gilded banners, sidewalk cafés, and street musicians. A mariachi band of Bolivians and Peruvians in ponchos played pipes, guitars, drums, and rhythm sticks and sang beautifully. We had struck a festival. We dined with Lauener and friends on a terrace of the well-named Hotel Bellevue, and between bites and sips we contemplated the jumble of old tile roofs below us and the wooded foothills of the Jura out beyond the Aar.

At Stuttgart we caught up at last with Don Davidson, whom we had narrowly missed three times in the year and a half since Nancy's death. He had been in Stanford just before my two weeks there, in Finland and Sweden just before our days in Uppsala, and in South Africa just before us.

We speakers and wives were received by the mayor of Stuttgart and the governor of Baden-Württemberg in the former palace of the dukes of Württemberg while I quietly turned 73. The mayor was the son of Rommel the Desert Fox. With Hilary, Don, and Sue Larsen we explored what was left of the old quarter and dined in a Greek resteraunt where the retsina flowed.

The gem of the medieval is Schwäbisch Hall, thirty miles northeast. Twelfth-century half-timbered houses sag over steep little streets. Adjacent, below an abrupt line of demarcation, baroque houses flaunt their proud pilasters, balconies, and gilded curlicues. The demarcation is where a great fire was extinguished. The town steepens into a flight of fifty broad steps topped by a church with a Romanesque tower. The river Kocher, which divides the town, is spanned by covered bridges and flanked by segments of city wall. Great communal granaries in stone, with stepped gables in the Hanseatic vein, dominate the heights.

Modern art encroached at one point on the hoary old town, to everyone's delight. Sprawling midway up a high flight of stairs to the tax office are life-size figures in bronze of an old peasant woman and a tax collector struggling to haul a recalcitrant ass up the steps in lieu of taxes.

Don had taken our luggage to Heidelberg in his car, a student had driven us to Schwäbisch Hall, and we closed the triangle by taking a train to Heidelberg. An unexpectedly long walk brought us to our Hotel Garni am Kornmarkt, where we climbed sixty-one steps to a tiny room in the eaves with no bath, no toilet, and no soap in the sink. "*Mi chiamano Mimi*," sang Marge. Our dissatisfaction transpired. A student came in the morning to check on our new and better room and present a propitiatory bouquet.

The session in Heidelberg again comprised Rorty, Putnam, Davidson, and me. We elaborated and debated what we had presented in Stuttgart, but all in English. I was struck once more with the fruitfulness of discussing with Don. We pursue any initial differences with an eye on the problem and an interest in solving it, as scientists might, rather than with the dismal gamesmanship so common in philosophy.

A cog railway ascended the mountain, and Marge and I with it, from the old square where we lodged. We admired the view and descended by sylvan paths to the castle, halfway down. After fifty-two years I remembered only its forty-thousand-gallon wine barrel. The castle is an imposing ruin in red sandstone, its roofless halls and courts ringed with statues and crumbling walls. From its terrace we looked steeply down on the old town and its medieval bridge.

We went on to Berlin so that Marge could study the Egyptian collections, one in West Berlin and one in East. To visit the latter we took a taxi to the Wall, built since our visit of 1954, and walked into East Berlin at Checkpoint Charlie, in a cleared and desolate spot three former blocks from where we had then lodged. The communists imposed vindictive formalities at the crossing; one was the purchase of fifty communist marks, none of which could be exported or redeemed.

Checkpoint Charlie is where Friedrichstrasse, byword of yore, broaches the Wall. We walked north a mile on Friedrichstrasse in East Berlin. There were a few pedestrians and an occasional light truck. As we approached its intersection with Unter den Linden, the crux or crucial crossroads of antebellum Berlin, bleakness gave way to the opera house, the academy, and a government palace or two in rich imperial baroque, restored since the battle of Berlin. A bridge led to an island in the Spree and two museums. Egyptian antiquities were on display, but what were more imposing were reconstructions on a heroic scale of monuments of Babylon, Miletus, and Pergamon.

We spent some of our irredeemable and inextricable Eastmarks in a somber restaurant and then walked Unter den Linden to the nearest permissible vicinity of the international Brandenburg Gate. The forbidden fringe, perhaps a hundred yards across, is demarcated by a low fence and enforced by guards with rifles. We followed the demarcation back to Checkpoint Charlie. The woman in control of freedom's gate invited me to drop my Eastmarks into a one-way receptacle that was ostensibly for the Red Cross, but I preferred to leave them with her in the forlorn hope of doing my bit toward weakening the regime by helping to corrupt one of its minions.

We walked close along freedom's side of the wall, back to the Brandenburg Gate. The smooth surface of the ten-foot concrete wall, pale gray, is rich in wry cartoons and graffiti. High wooden platforms have been erected, where spectators can look across the wall into the patrolled *banlieu* and be grateful for freedom.

Marge devoted the next day to the Egyptian collection in the Charlottenburg, West Berlin, while I walked far and wide. I was drawn again by the grim fascination of the wall. It is a hundred miles long, encircling West Berlin, and is surely the first city wall in history to have been built by outsiders against the welcome within.

I gave three lectures at Göttingen. Marge made her way to Hildesheim for another museum, while Günther Patzig and his wife drove me through the beginnings of the Harz Mountains to Duderstadt, a splendidly picturesque medieval town close under the electrified barrier of Soviet Germany.

After six summer weeks at Bare Hill, we were off for a symposium in Oaxaca, scene of happy memories of thirty-two years before. The symposiasts dwelt, ate, and held forth in the magnigicent sixteenth-century ex-convent of Santa Catalina de Sena, lately converted from a prison to a luxury hotel. It fills a city block and its walls of plastered stone are a yard thick. Archways open into broad patios whose soaring sides are bright with flowering vines. Halls, stairs, arched passages, bedrooms, all are of stone, topped with old beamed ceilings. The charm of the traditional Spanish missions, on a large scale, rewards the eye at every turn.

Don Davidson came. Since leaving us in Germany he had been visiting France and Peru and lecturing in Argentina. My other old students Ronnie Dworkin and Tom Nagel were there with their wives, the latter of whom I had known as Ann Hollander, John's wife. Peter and Diane Hempel came, and Manolo Garrido from Spain. Further participants from northern latitudes were Dudley Shapere, Mark Platts, Bill Wimsatt, Ernest Sosa, David Pears, Joe Sneed, and Simon Blackburn. Add twenty from Mexico, Argentina, and intervening Latin lands.

I presented the first paper, "Objecto y observación," and chaired a session. Having advance copies of some of the papers, I prepared comments, using Spanish for my comments on Spanish papers. To my surprise the authors of these, with one exception, presented them in English. I switched my comments to match.

The symposium was organized by Enrique Villanueva, director of a philosophical institute at the autonomous national university at the edge of Mexico City. The anarchists who plague him there mounted an attack, so he wrote me, in the weeks after the symposium. They protested the participation of foreigners and the use of English.

Women sat on the floor of the Oaxaca market weaving rugs and sarapes and jabbering Zapotec. Up on Monte Albán the visible Mixtec antiquities had burgeoned in the three intervening decades. Excavation had exposed the plaza and adjacent buildings of rough black stone dating back a dozen centuries. Thirty miles southeast at Mitla, Zapotec antiquity had been multiplying *pari passu*. Yagul, another Zapotec site near by, now stands forth as a substantial ancient village; it was still submerged in earth and jungle when we were there before.

Enrique and his wife Julieta took us to their home in Tepoztlán for three days. Their house presents a forbidding stone front to its steep little street, but opens in back to a terrace from which we looked down a grassy slope to a turquoise pool and out over the town. Beyond was the high mountain wall, cloaked with green, flecked with white cascades, and culminating in rugged pinnacles. The highest of these is topped by a *teocalli* to Tepoztécatl, god of agriculture and pulque. Julieta and Enrique's mother plied us with unprecedented delicacies of Mexican cuisine, and Enrique broke out good French wine. They took us to Cuernavaca's cathedral, pride of the Conquistadores, and to the rugged Indian villages of Yautepec, Tlanepantla, and Tlayacapán.

I remembered the Mexico City of 1958 as a coagulated mass of traffic that took hours to cross. Subsequent reports of polluted air and untold crowded millions had given me added cause for dread, but we wanted to see the ethnographic museum, which was built after 1958 and persistently praised. In its imaginative galleries and courtyards it reconstructs dozens of Mexican cultures, ancient and contemporary. Another objective in Mexico City was the new excavation at the Zócalo, beside the cathedral. An entire city block had been razed, exposing the concentric bases of thirteen layers of pyramid. Each monarch had coated his predecessor's pyramid with a new outer shell. Huge stone serpents, plastered and painted, flanked the outermost.

Seen against what I had been dreading, Mexico City stood up well. A subway had cut the old coagulation and perhaps a fair wind was dispersing the smog.

Egypt and Europe   81

· 1982   Marge booked another tour of Egypt for February 1982. To stave off my looming loneliness, I wrote to Ed Haskell proposing that we fly to West Texas and pack into Santa Elena Canyon in the Big Bend of the Rio Grande. Then one morning I awoke resolved to go along to Egypt. I quickly booked, and presently received Ed's favorable answer. If it had come earlier, I would have gone to the Rio Grande instead of the Nile.

Meanwhile I kibitzed in a "workshop," regrettably so called, at Amherst in the philosophy of language under the otherwise able auspices of Barbara Hall Partee and her new husband, Emmon Bach. I stayed two nights with Murray and Jean Kitely, whom I knew from the Hares' in Ewelme in 1970. Dan Dennett and his Swedish protégé Bo Dahlböhm, transported me, and I prized our philosophical discussion out and back.

Marge and I set forth the next day. It was her fourth Egyptian tour and my second. It began in London with the British Museum, so we dined with Norma and had an evening in Kensington with Jonathan and Christine Suzman of Johannesburg. In Cairo we boarded the *Nile Star* for three easy weeks. The ornithologist and painter Steve Quinn and the geologist Norman Newell were sent along by the American Museum of Natural History, and the Egyptologist Barbara Watterson and Egyptian guide Sami were sent by Swan Tours. We would go ashore and visit antiquities on foot or by carriage or bus. In the latter event we would return to shipboard farther along the Nile. Sometimes the party split: bird watchers this way, insatiable antiquarians that.

The Fayum was new to us. It is a thirty-mile westward bulge of the otherwise narrow fertile zone along the Nile, and has been called the breadbasket of Egypt. Its soil does not preserve ancient relics as the desert does, but middle antiquity lives on in the huge and intricate water wheels. They are similar in principle to what I saw in Cambodia, but were invented in Roman times. They are for drainage, not irrigation; they pump water up to the Nile, for the Fayum is below sea level. But for them, the Nile would submerge the breadbasket.

Another site that I had missed before was Abydos. The temple of Seti I, 1300 B.C., lists in bas-relief the Egyptian kings of 1500 years. The ancient Egyptians were kind to our historians, as we with our time capsules in cornerstones try to be to our putative descendants.

Philae, between the old and new Aswan dams, had risen from the depths. In 1964 our Nubian oarsmen had beached us on the top of a drowned temple. It and other, vaster structures, then hidden beneath the waves, had since been reassembled on an island to form an imposing Ptolemaic complex.

I had seen the rest of the sites before, but they wanted revisiting, for the detail is vast and memory fades. Marge had meanwhile learned much and helpfully supplemented what I heard from the guides.

At Aswan we again sailed to Elephantine Island by felucca. While my fellow tourists lingered in the little museum there, I again sought out and prowled the exotic Nubian village, which seemed unchanged. At length I corralled my Hungarian fellow tourist Leslie (for László) Lancy for a quick trajectory of the place, by way of sharing my enthusiasm. Marge, predictably, was irrecoverable from the bowels of the museum.

It was not long after our return to Boston that Larry Kiddle of Oberlin days materialized, to my surprise and delight, in my Cambridge bank. Over lunch we talked long of word origins and college memories. An aftermath was a call from his Ann Arbor colleague, Tom Markey, who moonlights as a publisher and wanted to publish a volume of such of my papers as might interest linguists. I demurred, because the cream had already been skimmed into my books. Tom then sent me a book he had just published, Derek Bickerton's *Roots of Language*. I read it with interest in the mechanics of pidgin and creole languages and excitement over the bold but reasonable speculations on the origin of language. I wrote Tom a long letter of major praise and minor criticism, with a copy to Larry. This precipitated an eleventh-hour invitation to fly to Ann Arbor in mid-April 1982 for a linguistics meeting organized by Tom and including Bickerton. I chaired a dismal session of a somewhat philosophical cast in which the anthropologist Sir Edmund Leach and others were not at their best. Conflicting engagements back home kept me from subsequest sessions in which Bickerton and other linguists were to take up more interesting themes of a factual nature. But I talked long with Larry over dinner and briefly with Bickerton over lunch.

An ex-psychiatrist in Nahant named Carl Smith had conceived an enthusiasm for my naturalized epistemology and interviewed me at length on videotape in 1981. Now in June 1982 he put on a little colloquium in my honor at the Harvard Faculty Club. Speakers included Skinner, Putnam, and the embattled sociobiologist E. O. Wilson. I summarized my ontological position under the title "The ins and outs of existence."

Ron Laura, the young philosopher, weight lifter, and polyglot whom I had known at Oxford in 1974, surprised me in September 1982 by turning up to spend a year at Harvard on leave from teaching in Australia. He had helped me with my Italian lecture in 1974, and I now enlisted his help again; for I was preparing a lecture for an October meeting in Turin.

Margaret's marriage to James McGovern intervened. The scene was a great country mansion in Vermont, 1800 in spirit and 1900 in execution, that had belonged to a son of Abraham Lincoln and is now a museum. Autumn foliage clad the slopes of the surrounding mountains in orange, brown, and yellow, punctuated with patches of snow and the stubborn green of conifers. Relatives gathered for the festivities from as far away as Seattle, in Elizabeth's case, and New Orleans in the case of Doug and Maryclaire. Friends were mostly the young crowd, but Burt and Raya Dreben loyally undertook the long drive. It was a weekend of feasting, dancing, and country walks.

On our way to Turin, Marge and I veered off to Como and cruised up the lake. Towns, dense and picturesque, hugged the shore, and an occasional village at an absurd height clung to the slope. Snowy wastes shone in the Swiss distance. Soon Bellagio emerged, nestling below the magic little mountain of the Villa Serbelloni. We threaded the familiar paths with Ray and Hendrieka Nelson, who were now living the good life of the Villa, and we dined well with the happy complement of incumbents.

The sessions at Turin celebrated Peano and were held in a great book-lined hall of the Accademia delle Scienze that was a match for the Carolina Rediviva at Uppsala. Tullio Viola presided, and I spoke on "Peano come logico." Geymonat, Grattan-Guinness, and Ghizetti also gave papers in Italian, and the Dutch algebraist van der Waerden spoke in French. The palace contains the Egyptian museum, which accounted for Marge's time.

The train from Piedmont into Savoy bore us through bare, towering Alps. Torrents were tinted blue with glacial milk. Chambéry, Savoy's capital, is graced by a monument of four convincing elephants impossibly intersecting in a four-way triumphal arch. The sinuous old quarter of town is dominated abruptly by the medieval tower of a hilltop castle that still houses the government of Savoy. On a slope across town a rugged bronze Jean-Jacques Rousseau surveys his fair city, staff in hand.

We passed a night in Clermont-Ferrand, rubber capital of the Old World as once was Akron of the New. The medieval center of town crowns an extinct volcano and commands a distant view of a higher one, the Puy-de-Dôme. The thousand-year-old Notre Dame du Port is a Romanesque delight, but oddly named, on a dry little old volcano.

We were bound for Conques, intrigued by its pictures. Aurillac, a hillside city dominated by a cliff-hanging castle, had seemed a likely approximation by rail. A bus wound its way from there through the wild mountains of Aveyron to Entreygues, a slate-roofed old village reflected in the river Truyère and backed by high wooded hills in autumn colors. A long bridge of Roman aspect spanned the flood, and as night fell we settled into an inn at the village end of the bridge.

We had to hire a taxi for the eighteen winding miles to Conques. It is an utterly medieval stone and slate village, population 420, nestled in the forested mountains. One inn was open, and our windows commanded the great eleventh-century church of Ste.-Foy at close range.

The canonical Last-Judgment tympanum and the capitals in the little cloister abound in quaintly expressive renderings of saints and sinners, kings and peasants, angels and devils, all short of stature in the southern Romanesque way. Acrobats are shown at their antics, and musicians and artisans with the medieval tools of their trades. From these diversions a zigzag of little streets scales the slope to a modest castle, and the slope continues, as did we. Enticing downward views of church and village opened up at every turn.

In Paris we tramped a dozen miles revisiting chosen scenes and spent hours in the Louvre, where Marge reviewed Egypt. After a four-hour delay at the airport, we sat seven hours cramped and immobile in interior seats of a tight-packed plane and reflected on the days when getting there and back was half the fun.

I promptly learned that I was to fly back to Europe in a few weeks, to be awarded a degree at Bern on December 4, 1982. It was a flying visit in the fullest sense; I was there for just the weekend. Good Henri Lauener made the occasion doubly memorable by handing me a copy of his book about me, just off the press.

George Berry's seminar on my philosophy at Boston University was inherited by my former students Joe Levine and Louise Antony. My annual interrogation, complete with

Chinese dinner, was thus renewed, three days after Bern. Five days later I sat with Fred Skinner in an educational panel at Harvard on how to write. For the third time I asked myself, "What am I doing here?"

India   82

From time to time down the years I had been pressed to visit India. I had been approached by the Fulbright committee, but after my experience of 1950 I would have none of that. Anyway I was not eager to go, nor was Marge. We dreaded the scenes of destitution in Calcutta as well as the risks to our own health, and we had not been fired by thoughts of Indian culture. In the spring of 1982, however, the pressure mounted. I was importuned in letters by Pranab Kumar Sen and Miss R. R. Verma, and in person by Matilal and Chattopadhyaya. I interposed conditions, and they were leveled: there would be no Fulbright involvement, commitment to Air India would be overruled so as to spare us the detour through New York, and we could break our journey. The Indians even volunteered to pay Marge's way.

· 1983   On January 8, 1983, we were off to London in a British plane. We lay over in an airport hotel and then flew by Air India across the Soviet Union. From lamented Latvia onward the world was securely shrouded by overcast or drawn blinds. Night fell long before we could hope to see the mountains of Afghanistan, and it was past midnight when Dr. Sarkar and another young Indian welcomed us to Delhi.

Next morning we were shown New Delhi, a landscaped plain of malls, monumented roundabouts, and lavish government palaces symmetrically deployed over magnificent distances. We were pressed to put in an appearance at a session staged by the Indian Council of Philosophical Research for advanced philosophy students who had been selected competitively. It was meant to end soon, but it went on for a painful further hour. The minister of education, Joshi, then took us to a tent for lunch with the assembled philosophers, among whom were Troy Organ and his wife and Arthur Danto. Afterward Joshi asked the young painter Dhiraj Choudhury to give Marge and me a tour of Old Delhi. Its little streets are shaded by jutting upper stories and jammed with pedicabs, honking cars, jinrikshas, pushcarts, an occasional laden camel or unattended sacred cow, and swarms of barefoot pedestrians in turbans, dhotis, sarees, veils.

The Red Fort, modestly so called, was the royal quarter of Delhi under the Moguls. Instead of walling their city, as in medieval Europe, they walled their palace grounds. The wall of red sandstone, several stories high, gives the impression of an implausibly large building, a half mile long and a quarter wide; but its interior is a spacious campus, rather, of marble palaces. Porches and terraces are screened in an airy latticework of delicate mesh, all carved from solid sheets of marble. At the opposite pole of all Delhi we saw older things. A Moslem tower of about 1200, Qutab Minar, stands eighty yards high, fluted, carved, and ringed at intervals with heavy balconies. Near it stands an iron pillar of 300 A.D., mysteriously free of rust.

Before our first day in India was over, we had flown to Calcutta. The next morning saw the opening, with incense and roses, of an International Conference of Perspectives on Meaning at Jadavpur University. Besides Organ and Danto there were Mark Platts and John McDowell from England and, as the days wore on, Don Davidson, Bob Nozick, and an intermittent Diana Ackerman. Some of the Indians always came in flowing white garb, some in European dress, and some alternated. Bannerjee, eldest of Jadavpur philosophers, told me that a man is said to be a *ful babu*, Bengali for "dandy," if his skirt brushes the grass.

The Indians adhered to English, apart from sacred quotations. Accents ranged from clear to opaque. Interventions in the discussion periods ran to inconscionable lengths. One Kumar, of abundant gray-black hair and beard, Western garb, and distinguished air, could be depended on to intervene copiously in cultivated and disarmingly reasonable north-of-England measures, adding little. There was fierce little Pahi of Jaipur, no less dependable but less readily intelligible, whose harangue would mount in volume and intensity as it approached its termination in a line or two of Sanskrit. Gandhi, grandson of the Mahatma, was a dynamic and clean-cut type in a Nehru jacket who would intervene at length in a fanciful and often strangely poetic style. His enunciation was excellent and his pauses, facial expressions, and gestures bespoke a sincerity, dedication, and inner fire worthy of a historic, nay heroic occasion; but the content was a tissue of philosophical absurdities.

A dead problem that would not lie down was the rivalry between word and sentence as primary vehicle of meaning. In a brief intervention, atypical in that environment, I gave my hackneyed resolution of the dilemma: sentences are the repository of meaning, but, because of their infinite multiplicity, an account of their meaning has to proceed recursively in terms of words and constructions. In due course Kumar repeated, with proper credit and added deliberation, what I had said. But the matter kept recurring in the succeeding days as if nothing had happened. Traditional philosophical problems are not meant to be solved.

I chaired several sessions and presented a paper on "The mentalistic heritage" in which I talked of the antiquity of the mentalistic ideology, its evils, and what we may salvage from it.

Jadavpur University was four miles from our Park Hotel, and we were transferred by car several times daily through the crowded streets. We slithered in among moving cars and pedicabs and fleeing people, and out around stalled objects, honking to induce cooperative evasive action, but never pausing unless in direst straits. The skill and precision of our driver and others were uncanny; margins were fractions of inches and split seconds. There were few scrapes, and only slight ones.

We would assemble in the tropical garden outside the lecture building for box lunches, which came two ways: bland

and tiresome or piquant and agreeable. We were entertained at a succession of dinners: an intimate one for a few of us in Sen's home, a state dinner for dozens in Chattopadhyaya's palatial flat, and sumptuous affairs in the Calcutta Club. Delicacies abounded, and the host or a squad of footmen circulated drinks before dinner, but the drinks were always soda pop. It was customary at the more formal suppers to be summarily dismissed at the appointed terminal hour, which was mercifully early. "I think we have detained you long enough." There was tension on one occasion, when I was talking with Sen on an urgent travel problem, for the throng could not disperse until I as senior guest had taken my leave.

Calcutta's sedate eighteenth-century governor's palace, in Georgian Greek revival, is seen from afar through spacious groves and gardens, at the calm center of one of the world's most appalling concentration of cramped humanity. Serenity prevails again at the palatial marble monument to Victoria, the answer of the British Raj to Shah Jahan's Taj Mahal. Ruined Fort William stands in studied desolation as a grim memento of the Sepoy Mutiny and the Black Hole, an atrocity that the new regime is at some pains to extenuate.

A long bridge thronged with carts and people spans the broad Hooghly River, a lesser mouth of the Ganges. Pilgrims augmented the usual throng and bathed in the foul and sacred stream, for it was a holy weekend. On the farther side, called Howrah, five miles of streets lined with shacks, shops, and markets, and clogged with carts, donkeys, camels, cows, and poor Indians, led us to a zoo where there are white tigers, black on white—living cartoons.

Now and then on a Calcutta sidewalk one comes across the dreaded pile of rags with a pitifully small parcel of humanity inside. Among the beggars in the busy places there may be an alarmingly eroded leper, a living remnant too far gone, almost, for fellow feeling.

We spent long hours in the Mercury Travel Agency with patient Mr. Mukarjee of the Indian Council of Philosophical Research, trying to arrange our travels. On January 17, then, prior to taking off for Nepal, we turned up at Jadavpur again for the inauguration of a new colloquium series, on Sri Aurobindo. Again there were roses and incense. A towering Singh, in Nehru cap and jacket, spoke vigorously and eloquently but implausibly on the power of philosophy to save society. He had been the last maharajah of Kashmir and subsequently a member of parliament. I perceived from his lack of beard and turban that though every Sikh is named Singh (= Lion), the converse does not hold. I can no longer say, "His name is Singh and it makes him Sikh [sic]."

Thereupon we were whisked off to the airport and flown to my 113th country. What to count as a country is indeed arbitrary at points because of colonies and dependencies, but I group these and arrive at 190 as the world total. Of these I have been in 108; my other five—Latvia, Lithuania, Danzig, Newfoundland, and South Vietnam—have been absorbed since my visits. Besides the 113, I have flown through twenty-one without putting down and have looked wistfully across borders into yet another eight.

Katmandu Valley is a broad floor between rugged green ranges terraced for farming. The distant horizon, seen from the airplane, is white Himalaya. Katmandu is noisy, dirty, and colorful. Indian faces alternate with rugged Mongolian ones framed in scarves and soft hats shaped like fezzes. Hindu shrines grade off into Buddhist temples and pagodas. Now and again a little *stupa*, or reliquary, fashioned of masonry in the shape of a fat raindrop, is situated at the side of the road as casually as a watering trough. Half of the city has succumbed to the blight of broad pavements and nondescript Western buildings, but half is still unspoiled. Houses there are mostly of thin bricks like those of ancient Rome, interspersed with dark beams, sometimes elaborately carved, and occasionally a closed balcony. The horizontal timbers above and below a window are usually exposed, extending beyond the sides of the window.

The exotic culminates in the Durbar Square, a bewildering jumble of pagodas and temples, lavishly carved, and grotesque giant statues, comic or fierce, garishly painted. A kaleidoscope of unbridled fantasy. Troops came marching out of a palace close at hand, and kilted bagpipers. Generals stepped into chauffeured limousines. A riderless white horse issued forth, caparisoned in gold and green velvet. Two ornate thrones followed, each carried by two men in uniform.

On foot and by pedicab we made our way south to Patan, an ancient town richer still in golden-roofed temples and pagodas and monumental grotesquerie. In a crowded little bus that offered only standing room, or indeed crouching room for such as I, we traveled nine miles east to Bhagdaon, where all houses are traditional and shrines and temples abound. Potters were busy in an open square, spinning their wheels and deftly turning out black ware like that of Oaxaca.

By motor riksha we went to Swayambhunath, on an abrupt summit west of Katmandu. The assorted temples on this lofty campus are dominated by a giant *stupa* that may date in its essentials from the third century B.C. It is a huge white hemisphere, roughly speaking, surmounted by a gilded cubical tower, which is topped in turn by a tall tapering canopy of gilt rings and a crown. An enormous pair of wavy eyes gazes out from each side of the cube. We plodded back to the hotel through miles of darkening native streets hoping for a taxi.

We tried the "Mountain Flight" for a close look at Everest. The pilot waited two hours for clearer weather and then took off only to despair midway and turn back. Fares were refunded, but there had been rewarding panoramas of the distant jagged peaks and glaciers, a white horizon for hundreds of uninterrupted miles. We had further consolation on another day, flying from Katmandu back to Calcutta. A passenger who proved to be a Nepali pilot identified Everest for us, a little dark triangle beyond a distant wall of white summits. More impressive from our vantage point was Kanchenjanga, a broad and towering white giant among giants at the eastern end of the procession.

There followed a crowded day and a half in Calcutta. We attended a luncheon party and a dinner party and spent hours at the travel agency, besides which I chaired a session at the University of Calcutta and lectured twice to the Jadavpur philosophers. Finally a young woman in philosophy, Dipoli Mukarjee, put us on the evening train for Lucknow.

We had refused to fly, because the declared departure time was five in the morning. We had reserved instead a compartment in first class for what purported to be a fourteen-hour run. Oddly, nobody warned us. Our first inkling of trouble was when Dipoli thought to ask a guard if there was a restaurant car. There was none. She ran off and bought us apples, bananas, cake, and Coca Cola. Our compartment had no beds or bedding; just the upholstered bench and a similar shelf above. There was no semblance of first class apart from the name. The trip, moreover, took twenty-two miserable hours. Occasionally a vendor appeared outside the train, but our steadfast prophylactic regimen kept us aloof except for some more bananas. We were not met at Lucknow, but happily I knew where Professor Verma had reserved our room; so we taxied in the dark to Clark's Hotel, heartily regretting my promise to lecture in Lucknow. The welcoming fruit basket and rose that awaited us in our luxurious quarters elicited a rueful smile or two, and we subsided.

Again in Lucknow the Indian Council of Philosophical Research was launching a conference. At the inauguration I shared the podium with the chancellor, the minister of education, the director of the Indian Council of Philosophical Research, and further dignitaries. The minister and the director were again Joshi and the omnipresent Chattopadhyaya, and the chancellor was another Singh, again no Sikh, but the eighty-two-year-old governor of the state of Uttar Pradesh. All of us spoke; I composed something while awaiting my turn. The governor's speech was intelligent, lively, and philosophically informed; he even knew something of my work. In the afternoon I opened the session with an expanded version of "The ins and outs of existence." We dined in a great tent as guests of the governor's chief of staff and next day in the governor's palace. It contained a theater, and we were regaled with strange music from traditional instruments and a program of solo dance. One musician was reputedly the greatest master of the *tabora*, or drums, and his lightning digital dexterity and stamina were indeed beyond belief. The danseuse was likewise celebrated and very manual in her southeast Asian way, but I was unresponsive.

Miss Verma squandered her time and missed her meetings for a large part of two days in order to confirm our imminent flight to Delhi, for which we were already ticketed. Confirmation in India has to be fought out every inch of the way. Friends of ours were repeatedly bumped from ticketed flights. Marge heard the governor tell his aide to send us by his plane if need be, so perhaps Miss Verma was helped in the end from on high. At any rate she was free to take us picnicking on the third day. I was amazed, on that outing, to see the Indian crocodiles: they have almost needle-like snouts, whereas the African ones are much like alligators.

At Delhi that evening Mr. Mukarjee met our plane and gave us tickets and reservations for eight painstakingly planned days of sightseeing. From Aurangabad, 640 miles to the south, we were motored a hundred miles through a land of buttes and mesas and avenues of monkey-tenanted banyan trees to visit the caves of Ajanta and Ellora. There are dozens, each hewn inside the bedrock to simulate the interior of a built temple. To complete the illusion, a huge one at Ellora has even been cut free of its matrix of bedrock to stand as a monolithic temple inside and out. The ones at Ajanta are Buddhist, dating from the second to seventh centuries; those at Ellora date from the next six centuries and are Buddhist, Hindu, and Jain.

In the taxi to the airport next morning, our local tour representative overheard me telling Marge that I wondered why the hotel bill had been quite so high. At the airport he and a colleague questioned me on the particulars, and at Delhi a week later a refund awaited me. Evidently a clerk in Aurangabad's posh Ajanta Ambassador Hotel had been under suspicion.

John Kenneth Galbraith had told me he liked Udaipur best, and we saw why. Its city palace fronts the shore of a lake for a quarter of a mile, bedecked with marble balconies screened in delicate marble mesh. The interior is a maze of mirrored marble halls and tree-shaded patios. There are two further Mogul palaces on islands in the lake, and the lovelier had become a hotel in which we dwelt. Its marble sides descend sheer into the water, and access is by boat.

At Jaipur the palaces, temples, and city walls are pink. Jai Singh's observatory of 1728 presents a surrealist landscape of high triangular structures in stone, calibrated for measuring altitude, declination, precession, and kindred grist for the astrologers' mill. On a hill at Amber, seven miles away, is the old palace, abandoned when Jai founded Jaipur in 1727. We made the ascent on elephants, as is the custom, and the descent as well, although that part is easier and quicker on foot.

In the road to Agra a big truck lay on its side, and, just beyond, another. After a few miles we encountered a third. Indian drivers, for all their skill at split-inch steering and split-second timing, are not infallible.

Fatehpur Sikri, on the way to Agra, is a ghost town of elegant plazas, palaces, and mosques dating from the sixteenth century when Mogul rule began. Green parrots contrast with the red sandstone walls.

The Taj Mahal, Agra's claim to fame, is indelible in the visual memory of the stubbornest stay-at-home. Even so, in our two days there we were impelled four times to thread the labyrinthine old native quarter and stand again in admiration. One aspect not conveyed in the pictures is the range of scale. The building is big, and yet all the thousands of delicate floral patterns, wrought in semiprecious stones inlaid in the white marble exterior, have the jewel-like precision and intricacy that call for tweezers and magnifying glass.

Back, then, to Delhi for another fort and palace and more tombs, each on the scale and symmetrical plan of the Taj Mahal.

On February 6 we left Delhi for Europe. It was a long and vivid morning—long because we were flying ahead of the sun. Semiarid Rajasthan merged into bare desert, which continued across Pakistan and came to be threaded with a succession of sky-blue streams, mouths of the Indus. Then the yellow sands gave way with a shock to the deep turquoise of the Arabian Sea. We skirted the rugged and unpeopled wastes of coastal Baluchistan and crossed the sharp promontory of eastern Arabia that the United Arab Emirates share with the Sultanate of Oman. Ships speckled the Persian Gulf as we clipped Qatar and Bahrein. In the glare of noon we cut a swathe across Saudi Arabia, devoid of man and vegetation, and grazed Iraq. Then came Jordan, Syria, and a sustained panorama of Cyprus. Europe climaxed the day's drama with breathtaking glimpses down into the Alps in the final hop from Rome to Frankfurt.

The Present Chapter   83

In Frankfurt I kept a rendezvous with Dirk Koppelberg, who came up from Westphalia to interview me on my work. He related it illuminatingly to Neurath's views, which he had been garnering from unpublished letters. I had recognized Neurath as a kindred spirit from his meager philosophical publications, but was impressed now by how much more widely our views agreed.

We flew home, and eleven days later we were off again. Marge set out for her fifth tour of Egypt and I for a two-day colloquium at Barranquilla, Colombia, arranged by a former student of Donald Campbell's named Hernando Gómez. After it I repaired southwestward with Campbell, Gómez, and their wives to Cartagena de Indias, as it was called in the sixteenth century to distinguish it from its eponym in Spain and its grand-eponym in Africa Minor. Its formidable old fort and its little streets tightly lined with balconied colonial houses present an old-world picturesqueness rare in the Americas.

The pace continues. I got back to Boston in March 1983

just in time to address the philosophers of religion on "The ins and outs of existence." In May I received a doctorate at Ripon College, my fifteenth, and presented Fred Cassidy for one at Oberlin. In June, Carl Smith honored me with a second little symposium, which included talks by Skinner and Davidson. I officiated in August at a World Congress of Philosophy in Montreal, and in September at a colloquium on the Vienna Circle in Paris. My homeward flight from Paris was my fifty-sixth crossing of the Atlantic and my tenth in a year and a half. In October I lectured in Maine.

· 1984   In February a happy impulse sped Marge and me to Santo Domingo, *condita* 1494. Restorations are progressing, and my flash impression of forty-two years before underwent grateful revision. The colonial quarter complements elegant Cartagena's, reflecting somewhat the ruggedness of the primeval frontier.

Symposia in honor of David Kaplan and Don Davidson are calling us to Stanford and Rutgers in March and April 1984, and in April and June I am to lecture in Boston, Providence, Ottawa, and Toronto. We are expected in New Orleans in May and in Oxford in September.

My so-called retirement has been blessed with retention of my study in Harvard's Emerson Hall and the help of department secretaries. My trip from home to office takes eight minutes on foot plus six on the subway. I carry cryptograms that Marge's sister clips for me from the Hartford newspaper, and the six-minute ride is par for solving one. Fair weather sometimes tempts me to walk all the way, three miles by the dull route or four and a half along the Charles River.

My spacious paneled study overlooks two quadrangles of Harvard Yard. Squirrels visit my windows. A long wall of the room is filled with shelves filled with books and journals, largely the gifts of generous publishers and authors, and stacked cartons are loaded with more of the same. Incoming books, journals, offprints, and photocopies clutter a window sill, and I get at them as I can. Some I read and file, acknowledging them only if I have something worthwhile to say. Some I sample and file without full reading, or consign to my annual gift to the library, or, in the case of a blank-backed Xerox, add to my store of scratch paper. All my books and articles for decades have been written in ballpoint on backs of Xeroxes and passed to the typist.

My correspondence had been voluminous. I respond to questions in logic and even in philosophy, if they are focused and coherent. My correspondent may then write back without having fully heeded my response, whereupon I drop him; or he may pursue the matter with a reasonable rebuttal or further problem, and our correspondence may continue for a dozen letters. So it was with Howard Burdick, Paul Berent, and others. Many correspondents have sparked welcome corrections in subsequent printings of my books. I also have a thick file of letters from cranks and psychopaths, whom I soon learned not to answer.

My desk is usually neat, with a single job on it; for I abhor loose ends. I pay bills on arrival and I answer a letter on arrival if I already see what to say, for it means one handling instead of two.

Interruptions are few and welcome: Burt Dreben, Nelson Goodman, Is Scheffler, Hilary Putman, or a graduate student with a question or argument about something I have written. Williams, Aiken, Albritton, White, and Owen went their several ways, but Rod Firth is with us, sharing my partition, and Bob Nozick, Jack Rawls, and Stan Cavell are at hand.

At lunches and dinners in Cambridge I have a wealth of bright and varied company. The Society of Fellows is one of five notable resources. Another is Eliot House, whose reservoir of likely company includes professors of politics, mathematics, Islam, and literature in assorted languages. A third resource is the American Academy of Arts and Sciences. Its new Cambridge home, a quasi-Japanese palace in sylvan acres, lends itself to Tuesday lunches, drawing persons of note from Harvard and M.I.T. Fourth, a Shop Club meets monthly in the Faculty Club for a notable dinner and a member's paper on some topic that he is expected to know well enough to be capable of making amusing.

For daily indulgence, finally, there is our Faculty Club table that accreted long ago around the Biblical scholar Harry Wolfson. Jakob Rosenberg, the art historian and son-in-law of Husserl, was a regular. In later years the Squares of the Round Table have comprised Sam Thorne, Morton Keller, Sidney Freedburg, Eduard Sekler, Dante della Terza, and Ihor Ševčenko—thus legal history, painting, architecture, Italian literature, and Byzantium. Three who were snatched from us by untimely deaths were Phoebe Wilson, erudite widow of Tom Wilson of the Harvard Press, and John Parry, debonair Anglo-Welsh globetrotter and professsor of maritime history, and Dick Baxter, a judge on the Hague international court with a quick wit and a gift for mimicry. Sometimes the table fails to materialize, and then I repair to the long table, where the company is random and the conversation often lively and rewarding.

Blest though I am with this bright company, I might have been happier, and Marge as well, if in 1959 we had moved to inner Cambridge instead of Beacon Hill. We have been drawn into a loose circle of casual friendships in our neighborhood, but our relations could have been firmer and richer if the neighborhood circles had appreciably overlapped those lunch and dinner circles. One's capacity for forming close, carefree friendships dwindles after student days, and requires all the encouragement that persistent contact can provide.

This book has been mainly a factual account of external things and events as they have impinged on me and I in my faltering way on them. A perceptive reader may, however, have gained from these indices a clearer picture of my drives and character than I myself enjoy; for I have little bent for soul-searching. This deficiency was evident in the way I bought peace of mind in 1930 and again in 1944 at the price of subsequent misery. My way of coping with spells of nostalgia, loneliness, anxiety, or boredom over the years has been to escape into my projects. Or,

> . . . *when upon my couch I lie*
> *In vacant or in pensive mood,*

I am apt today, as of yore (page 11), idly to compute—determining e.g. that the number of acres that can be circumscribed in a mile is just under fifty-one, or that the distance in statute leagues of the horizon at sea is the square root of the height of the eye in fathoms. (Look, no coefficients.) I have gained facility in mentally manipulating big numbers.

Only rarely do I lapse into a half hour of grief. I did so lately when writing of my fumbling of the project of a jaunt in West Texas with Ed Haskell; the plan can never by renewed, for his health has deteriorated. For the most part my only emotion is impatience. I work impatiently to finish each job, and thus squander the passing moment instead of savoring it.

I am deeply moved by occasional passages of poetry, and so, characteristically, I read little of it. I respond similarly to passages of grand opera, and this is due to the libretto as much as to the music. Otherwise I have a poor memory for fiction, for it resists integration with my system of the world. I appreciate style more than plot. I enjoy the eighteenth-century brand of humor that we get in Fielding's prefaces and belatedly in Dickens; also the humor of W. S. Gilbert and Wodehouse and, in moderation, zany S. J. Perelman.

Encouraged by the indulgent interest of readers who have read all the way to here, I am evidently accomplishing some soul-searching after all. Persisting, I detect two deep traits which the reader will already have divined from my compulsion in childhood to compile, from my preoccupation with political boundaries, from my early collecting of stamps and later collecting of countries, and from my professional concern for mathematical elegance; namely, I am orderly and I am frugal. The one trait was instanced just now in the neatness of my desk and my abhorrence of loose ends, and the other in my use of discarded Xeroxes. Frugality was called for anyway by penury in early decades. It is unrelated to selfishness; I gladly give where love or decency dictates, and I am unhappy with possessions that I see no way of using. Economy of means is the keynote, here as in mathematics. I hate waste. Vandalism is twice the crime that theft is.

My love of earthly boundaries, by the way, stacks up oddly with my disdain of conceptual ones. My challenge of the boundary between analytic and synthetic statements is notorious, and I have been at pains to blur the boundaries between natural science, mathematics, and philosophy. My own philosophical efforts began in mathematical logic and have verged increasingly on linguistics, psychology, anthropology, and physics, in blithe disregard of all barriers but that of ignorance.

A few more reflections now on my habits of work. Early and late I have worked alone. My six short collaborated pieces and my one thin collaborated book are the least of my output. In an earlier chapter I remarked with wonder on my somewhat negative attitude toward schoolwork, toward being instructed, toward working for a boss; this is probably related to my tendency to work alone. It is also probably related to my poor score in professional reading.

Occasionally in my writing I find myself groping unduly for fanciful figures and analogies. I have learned to recognize this as a sign that I am not clear in my mind about the theory I am trying to expound. It is a signal to go walking or canoeing and ponder the ideas without benefit or malefit of pen and paper.

Another occasional stumbling block is boredom, either when writing something that has been imposed as a chore or when writing an uninspired but indispensable segment of some work of my choosing. On some such occasions I took refuge in logic, concocting some unrelated little problem for research. It offers escape and still, being research, it keeps the conscience clear. Once, at least, the ruse issued in a creditable paper, I forget which. Usually not.

I am rather taciturn and seem introverted, which is odd in one professedly not given to soul-searching. I do not easily intervene extempore in public discussion, and when I do intervene I am brief. I like to take time for deliberate formulation. Hence my practice down the decades of preparing copious notes for the classroom and writing my public lectures in full.

I have had neither the aptitude nor the temperament for debate, public or private, when confronted with motives recognizably other than the pursuit of truth. If in discussing with a student I sensed that he was animated rather by some ideological preconception, or by a wish to have been right for the sake of high marks or self-esteem, I made short work of the dialogue. A vast gulf, insufficiently remarked, separates those who are primarily concerned to have been right from those who are primarily concerned to be right. The latter, I like to think. will inherit the earth.

Discussing politics with anyone who deeply disagrees is for me out of the question. Similarly for disputes over religion, telepathy, or occult phenomena, where the purpose is so commonly to sustain a preconception rather than to find and face the facts. Prompt rejoinder on such matters by champions of sound science and sound government is vitally important, but it must be left to persons more gifted in extempore rhetoric and diplomacy than I. I would do more harm than good.

From an advanced point in what I hope may be a long life, I look back incredulously on the recognition I have enjoyed. There are the forty-four translations of books of mine plus fifteen books by others, in five languages, about my work. *The Philosophers' Index* has reported some five hundred publications under the subject heading 'Quine' over the past decade.

Such publications can conceivably take any of four lines: historical integration, fuller explanation, extension, and controversy. The first two lines can lead only so far, and the third, limited as it is by the sporadic character of happy insights, can be taken only so often. Surely, then, the fourth line is the dominant one. In the course of it my doctrines have suffered stubborn misinterpretations which, if I shared them, would impel me to join my critics in lashing out against my doctrines in no uncertain terms.

Publication is stimulated partly by pride in production and by the academic injunction, real or fancied, to publish or perish. There is thus a premium on controversy, fruitful and otherwise, and hence even on misinterpretation, however inadvertent. The effect is most marked in domains such as philosophy, where criteria are less rigid than in the hard sciences.

So I speak of recognition and not of adulation unalloyed; and I am lucky to have had it so abundantly while I am here to marvel at it. In due modesty I am tempted to suggest that it has been excessive, but to suggest this would be to impugn, ungratefully, the judgment of those who have conferred it. Let me just say that I could not have asked better, and then hedge a little, like mother Bonaparte: *"pourvu que ça dure."*

Indexed Autobibliography

Shorter Pieces

1930
Review of Nicod. *Amer. Math. Monthly* 37, pp. 305–307. *71*

1932
"A note on Nicod's postulate." *Mind* 41, pp. 345–350. *87, 243*

1933
"A theorem in the calculus of classes." *Jour. London Math. Soc.* 8, pp. 89–93. *73*

1933–35
Reviews of Peirce. *Isis* 19, pp. 220–229; 22, pp. 285–297, 551–553. *108, 114*

1934
Report on Whitehead. *Amer. Math. Monthly* 41, pp. 129–131. *113*

"A method of generating part of arithmetic without use of intuitive logic." Reprinted in SLP. *14*

1935
Review of Carnap. *Philosophical Review* 44, pp. 394–397. *114*

"Truth by convention." Reprinted in WP. *121–122*

1936
"Toward a calculus of concepts." *Jour. Symb. Logic* 1, pp. 2–25. *117, 301*

"Set-theoretic foundations for logic." Reprinted in SLP. *123*

"Concepts of negative degree." *Proc. Nat. Acad. Sci.* 22, pp. 40–45. *117*

"A theory of classes presupposing no canons of type." Ibid., pp. 320–326. *123*

"New foundations for mathematical logic." Reprinted in FLPV. *126–27, 143, 146, 187, 433*

1937
"On Cantor's theorem." *Jour. Symb. Logic* 2, pp. 120–124. *127, 145*

"Logic based on inclusion and abstraction." Reprinted in SLP. *130–131*

1939
"A logistical approach to the ontological problem." Reprinted in WP. *141*

1940
"Elimination of extra-logical postulates" (with Nelson Goodman). *Jour. Symb. Logic* 5, pp. 104–109. *142*

1941
"Whitehead and the rise of modern logic." Reprinted in SLP. *151*

"Element and number." Reprinted in SLP. *145, 173*

Review of Ferreira da Silva. *Jour. Symb. Logic* 6, pp. 109–110. *172*

1942
"On existence conditions for elements and classes." Ibid. 7, pp. 157–159. *159, 172*

1943
"Notes on existence and necessity." *Jour. of Phil.* 40, pp. 113–127. *173, 181, 193*

1945

"On the logic of quantification." Reprinted in SLP. *186–187*

"On ordered pairs." Reprinted in SLP. *187*

1946

"Concatenation as a basis for arithmetic." Reprinted in SLP. *192*

"Os Estados Unidos e o ressurgimento da lógica." *Vida intelectual nos Estados Unidos* 2 (U.C.B.E.U., São Paulo), pp. 267–286. *172*

Translation of Löwenheim. *Scripta Math.* 12, pp. 125–139. *193*

1947

"The problem of interpreting modal logic." *Jour. Symb. Logic* 12, pp. 43–48. *193*

"On universals." Ibid. pp. 74–84. *148*

"Steps toward a constructive nominalism" (with Goodman). Ibid. pp. 97–122. *198–199*

1948

"On what there is." Reprinted in FLPV. *198, 200, 224, 226*

1950

"On natural deduction." *Jour. Symb. Logic* 15, pp. 93–102. *209*

"Identity, ostension, and hypostasis." Reprinted in FLPV. *218*

"Two dogmas of empiricism." Reprinted in FLPV. *226, 244, 392*

1951

"Semantics and abstract objects." *Proc. Amer. Acad. Arts & Sci.* 80, pp. 90–95. *219*

Reply to Geach. *Aristotelian Soc.* suppl. vol. 25, pp. 149–160. *224*

"It tastes like chicken." *Furioso* 6, pp. 37–39. *225*

"Ontology and ideology." *Phil. Studies* 2, pp. 11–15. *227*

"On Carnap's views on ontology." Reprinted in WP. *227*

"Two theorems about truth functions." Reprinted in SLP. *227*

"A simplification of games in extensive form" (with J. C. C. McKinsey and W. D. Krentel). *Duke Math. Jour.* 18, pp. 885–900. *217*

1952

"The problem of simplifying truth functions." *Amer. Math. Monthly* 59, pp. 521–531. *227*

"On an application of Tarski's theory of truth." Reprinted in SLP. *227*

"On mental entities." Reprinted in WP. *233–234*

"On a supposed antinomy." Reprinted in WP. *234*

1953

"The problem of meaning in linguistics." In FLPV. *227*

"Mr. Strawson on logical theory." Reprinted in WP. *235*

"Three grades of modal involvement." Reprinted in WP. *238*

1954

"Interpretations of sets of conditions." Reprinted in SLP. *232*

"Carnap and logical truth." Reprinted in WP. *244*

"On Frege's way out." Reprinted in SLP. *243–244*

"Logic, symbolic." Reprinted in SLP. *250*

"The scope and language of science." Reprinted in WP. *258–259*

1955

"Posits and reality." Reprinted in WP. *300*

1956

"Unification of universes in set theory." *Jour. Symb. Logic* 21, pp. 267–279. *261*

1957

"Speaking of objects." Reprinted in OR. *271*

1958

"On cores and prime implicants of truth functions." Reprinted in SLP. *279*

1960

"Logic as a source of syntactical insights." Reprinted in WP. *300*

"Variables explained away." Reprinted in SLP. *301*

1961

"The ways of paradox." Reprinted in WP. *304–305*

1962

"Le mythe de la signification." *La philosophie analytique* (Paris: Minuit), pp. 139–169. *272*

1963–65

Reviews of atlases. *N. Y. Rev. of Books* 1, no. 3, p. 8; 2, no. 2, p. 17; 5, no. 4, pp. 18–19. *305–306*

1964

Review of Mencken. Reprinted in TT. *306*

"The foundations of mathematics." Reprinted in WP. *304–305*

"Implicit definition sustained." Reprinted in WP. *142*

"Ontological reduction and the world of numbers." Reprinted in WP. *248, 345*

1966

"Existence and quantification." Reprinted in OR. *340*

1967

"Thoughts on reading Father Owens." *Proc. VII. Inter-Amer. Cong. of Phil.* 11, pp. 60–63. *343*

1968

"Ontological relativity." Reprinted in OR. *342, 345, 442*

"Epistemology naturalized." Reprinted in OR. *345, 350*

"On the limits of decision." Reprinted in TT. *350*

Review of *Times Atlas.* Reprinted in TT. *306*

1969

"Natural kinds." Reprinted in OR. *344*

"Replies." D. Davidson and J. Hintikka, eds., *Words and Objections* (Reidel), pp. 292–352. *346*

1969–70

Review of dictionaries. *N. Y. Rev. of Books* 13, no. 10, pp. 3–4; 14, nos. 1–2, p. 54. *306*

1970

"Philosophical progress in language theory." *Metaphilosophy* 1, pp. 2–19. *344*

"Algebraic logic and predicate functors." Reprinted in WP (1976). *393*

"Truth and disquotation." Reprinted in WP (1976). *393*

1971

"Predicate-functor logic." *Proc. II. Scandinavian Logic Symposium*, pp. 309–315. *366*

1972

"Reflexiones filosóficas sobre el aprendizaje del lenguaje." *Teorema* 6, pp. 6–23. *390*

"Vagaries of definition." Reprinted in WP (1976). *391*

"The variable." Reprinted in WP (1976). *395, 433, 442*

1974

"Paradoxes of plenty." Reprinted in TT. *409–410*

1975

"The nature of natural knowledge." S. Guttenplan, ed., *Mind and Language* (Oxford), pp. 67–81. *405–406*

"Mind and verbal dispositions." Ibid. pp. 83–95. *405*

"On the individuation of attributes." Reprinted in TT. *406*

"Respuestas." M. Garrido, ed., *Aspectos de la filosofía de W. V. Quine* (Valencia: Teorema), pp. 149–168. *410*

"La teoria e l'osservazione." *Rivista de filosofia* 66, pp. 1–19. *407*

"On empirically equivalent systems of the world." *Erkenntnis* 9, pp. 313–328. *411, 416*

1976

"Use and its place in meanings." Reprinted in TT. *419*

1977

"Facts of the matter." R. Shahan, ed., *American Philosophy from Edwards to Quine* (Oklahoma), pp. 176–196. *419*

Review of Lewis Carroll. Reprinted in TT. *427*

1978

"On the nature of moral values." Reprinted in TT. *422*

"Kurt Gödel." Reprinted in TT. *432*

1979

"The ideas of Quine." Bryan Magee, ed., *Men of Ideas* (British Broadcasting Corp.), pp. 168–179. *422, 426*

"Cognitive meaning." *Monist* 62, pp. 129–142. *427*

"Clauses and classes." *Bulletin d'information* 6 (Soc. Fr. de Logique, Math., et Phil. des Sci.), pp. 23–39. *433*

"On the very idea of a third dogma." In TT. *435*

1980
"The variable and its place in reference." Zak van Straaten, ed., *Philosophical Subjects: Essays on the Work of P. F. Strawson* (Oxford), pp. 164–173. *427*

"Sellars on behaviorism, language, and meaning." *Pacific Phil. Qtrly.* 61, pp. 26–30. *428–429*

"What is it all about?" *American Scholar* 50, pp. 43–54. *442, 443*

1981
"The pragmatists' place in empiricism." R. J. Mulvaney and P. J. Zeltner, eds., *Pragmatism* (South Carolina), pp. 21–39. *415*

"Grammar, truth, and Logic." S. Kanger and S. Ohmann, eds., *Philosophy and Logic* (Reidel), pp. 17–28. *423*

"Replies to the eleven essays." *Phil. Topics* 12, pp. 227–243. *440*

1982
"Respuestas." Volumen dedicado a la filosofía de W. V. Quine, *Análisis filosófico* 2 (Buenos Aires), pp. 159–173. *432*

1983
"Gegenstand und Beobachtung." D. Henrich, ed., *Kant oder Hegel?* (Stuttgart: Klett-Cotta), pp. 412–422. *453*

1984
"Sticks and stones; or, the ins and outs of existence." L. S. Rouner, ed., *On Nature* (Notre Dame), pp. 13–26. *460, 469, 473*

1985
"States of mind." *Jour. of Phil.* 82, pp. 5–8. *442*

Index

Davidson (*cont.*)
435, 453–454, 456, 464, 473; travels with 151–158, 233, 368–386
DAVIDSON, Virginia 215, 222, 282, 318, 327, 331, 368, 373, 386
Debts 132, 139, 185
DELLA TERZA, Dante 475
DEMOS, Raphael 111, 126
DENNETT, Daniel 427–428, 458
DEVAUX, Philippe 81, 238
Dewey Lectures 345
Dialects 48, 58, 75, 273–274, 278, 391, 392, 439, 460; German 56–57, 95–96, 438–439; Romance 118, 162, 163, 169, 222, 312, 343
DICK, Marcus W. 241, 309
Dissertation 84–87, 95, 99, 104, 113
Divorce 185, 187, 189–190, 195, 198
DREBEN, Burton S. 192, 200, 224, 232, 300, 303, 339, 388, 429, 461, 474
Dubrovnik 349–350, 436–437
DUMMETT, Michael 242, 253, 261, 309, 398, 402, 405, 419, 436
Dutch 2, 106–107, 111

Eastman Professor 229, 235, 239, 241
Easton 195, 199, 229, 261
Economy 85–86, 476–477
Ecuador 175, 179–180, 263
EDINBURGH, Duke of (Prince Philip) 431
Egypt 321–328, 458–459
EINARSON, Benedict 115–116, 121, 336
EINSTEIN, Albert 97, 99, 125, 200, 395, 439

EISENBUDS 191, 195
ELDJARN, Kristján 424, 445
Eliot House 109, 125, 131, 258, 271, 348, 367, 474
Ellan Vannin 21–25, 32, 108, 259
EMMET, Dorothy 250
England 237, 249–252, 309–310, 400, 409. *See also* Cambridge, Chester, London, Oxford
English ways 236–237, 242, 337–338
EPSTEIN, Hans 348
Essentialism 434
Ethics 422
EVANS, Gareth 394, 402
Extensionality 32, 85

Farm folk 2, 7–11, 22, 23
FEIGL, Herbert 86, 124, 147, 227, 394
FERREIRA DA SILVA, Vicente 172–173, 176
Fiji 284–286
FINE, Jacob 300, 304, 340
Finland 359–360, 397, 424–425
FIRTH, Raymond 282, 284, 288
FIRTH, Roderick 83, 142, 394, 474
Floods 5, 52, 261, 305
Florence 70, 101, 313, 407–408
Florida 158, 161, 386–387, 392, 435
Flying 78, 161–166, 176–181, 184–186, 188–189, 436, 463, 471–472
FOLK, Barbara Boynton 440, 473
FØLLESDAL, Dagfinn 302, 336, 396, 405, 424, 432, 436; travels with 359–366
FORTES, Meyer 282, 286
France 71, 221–223, 310–311, 356, 367, 432–433, 437–438, 461–462. *See also* Paris *and* Royaumont

ROBERTS, Michael 357, 426–427, 431

Rockefeller University 344–345, 388

Rome 69, 100, 101, 314–315, 436

ROSSER, J. Barkley 141, 145–146, 148, 186, 195, 234, 439–440

Royaumont 272–273

RUSSELL, Bertrand 51, 58, 59, 79, 84, 123, 144, 149, 225–226, 441–442. *See also Principia Mathematica*

RYLE, Gilbert 235, 238, 259, 274, 309, 367, 401

SAFIER, Fritz 80, 185

Sailing 1, 147–150, 193–194, 198, 230, 305

St. Pierre 118–119

SAMELSON, Babbie 190

SANDUSKYS 80

San Marino 69, 99–100, 313, 348–349

SAXL, Erwin 394–395

SCHEFFLER, Israel 474

Schemata 142, 186

SCHILPP, Paul Arthur, *see* Library of Living Philosophers

SCHLICK, Moritz 93–94, 96

SCHOLZ, Heinrich 243, 252–253

SCHÖNFINKEL, Moses 113, 117

School 12–13, 31, 36–38, 45–48, 315

Scotland 409

SCOTT, Dana 402, 406–407

SEKLER, Eduard 475

SELL, James Plattenberger 57, 72, 78, 268

SELLARS, Wilfrid 346, 398, 428–429, 442

Set theory 60, 86, 117, 123, 126, 143, 159, 173, 248, 303

ŠEVČCENKO, Ihor 475

SHANNON, Claude 202

SHARFMANS 80

Shearman Lectures 248–249

SHEFFER, Henry M. 81–83, 113–114, 117, 126, 131, 149

Sheldon Fellow 86

Ships 19, 62, 88, 137, 219, 280, 308, 316, 328, 333–335

Sicily 100–101, 334

SIMONS, Fred 421

Sketching 176

SKINNER, B. Frederic 110, 116, 262, 401, 463, 473

SKOLEM, Thoralf 83, 248, 268

SMART, J. J. C. 284, 286, 432, 434

SMITH, Carl 460, 473

SMITH, Cyril and Alice 407

SMITH, Nelson 79–80

Smoking 43, 50 304

SOBOCIŃSKI, Bolesław 104, 243

Social life 43, 53, 57–58; at Harvard 80, 116, 124–125, 138, 147, 160, 191, 475; at Oxford 309, 366, 401–403

Society of Fellows 99, 108–110, 115–116, 120–121, 203, 229, 271, 338–339, 429, 474

Soul-searching 475–478

South Carolina 158, 358, 391, 415

Soviet Union 105, 424–425, 463

Spain 221, 245–246, 390–391, 403–404, 410

Spanish 129, 177–178, 197, 247, 307, 343, 390, 456

Split 349, 436

Sputnik 271

Stamps 26–29, 32